A UNION OF INDIVIDUALS

the formation of the american newspaper guild, 1933–1936

NEW YORK AND LONDON

DANIEL J. LEAB

a union of individuals

the formation of the american

newspaper guild, 1933-1936

COLUMBIA UNIVERSITY PRESS·1970

Copyright © 1970 Columbia University Press
Standard Book Number: 231-03367-2
Library of Congress Catalog Card Number: 75-110603
Printed in the United States of America

acknowledgments

The "gentlemen of the press" formed the American Newspaper Guild in 1933. Three years later it joined the AFL. This work traces the development of the newspapermen's organization from its origin to its emergence as a union affiliated with organized labor.

In chronicling this process of change I benefited greatly from the encouragement and advice of Robert Cross, now President of Swarthmore College. My debt to him is very great. I benefited also from the acute comments of Professors Stuart Bruchey, Sigmund Diamond, John Garraty, John Hohenberg, and William Leuchtenburg of Columbia University, and of Professor David Brody of the University of California at Davis.

I owe special debts to Oliver Pilat, former president of the New York Guild, and James R. Boylan, the editor of the *Columbia Journalism Review*. Both shared freely of their time, knowledge, and research materials; and they gave me the advantage of testing my ideas against those held by men adept in newspaper history and ANG affairs.

To Fred Ross, a former guildsman, I also owe a special obligation, for he shared his notes and his beliefs.

The ANG's history is part of the much vaunted "oral tradition," and more than 50 people have shared their recollections with me. My thanks to each of them not only for talking with a stranger but also for reading and commenting on what he wrote. In this regard, it is necessary to single out Emmet

Crozier for efforts above and beyond what any reasonable man would expect.

In my quest for material I received extraordinary cooperation, and I wish to express my gratitude to those of the Cleveland, New York, Philadelphia, and Twin Cities guilds who aided me. I also want to thank the many librarians and archivists who eased my task; I especially want to thank those at Columbia University, the Franklin D. Roosevelt Memorial Library, the National Archives, the State Historical Society of Wisconsin, and the Wayne State University Labor Archive.

The American Newspaper Guild gave me free rein to go through its past files. Its officers and staff assisted me in every way possible, without making any demands or suggestions.

My friends Michael and Hedva Weinberg did yeoman service for me in Minneapolis with regard to the Twin Cities Guild's records. They saved me time and money when both were in short supply.

Lastly, to my wife, Katharine, I owe a debt beyond expression.

All the people mentioned above have helped give this work whatever merit it may possess. For its defects I alone am responsible.

Daniel J. Leab

contents

Acknowledgments   v

Introduction: Newspapermen
and White Collar Workers   1

1. Before The Blue Eagle   4

2. The Beginnings   33

3. Organization   66

4. From Meeting to Convention:
The First Seven Months   103

5. Toward the Picket Line . . .   134

6. . . . And Away From the Government   176

7. Dissension   205

8. The Guild Becomes a Union   239

Key to Note Abbreviations   285

Notes   289

Bibliography   335

Index   353

A UNION OF INDIVIDUALS

the formation of the american newspaper guild, 1933–1936

introduction: newspapermen and white collar workers

"Show me two white collar workers on a picket line, and I'll organize the entire working class." Samuel Gompers made this comment in criticism of what he considered the failure of these workers as a class to recognize where their real interests lay. Prior to the Great Depression, few white collar workers thought their interests lay with organized labor. Some small white collar unions did exist, mostly in the fields of entertainment (e.g., musicians, actors) and public service (e.g., postal workers, teachers), but in general white collar workers considered themselves superior to other classes of wage earners and above unionization.[1]

At the time of Gompers' remark, white collar workers (even given the varying definitions of the term) comprised but a small percentage of the American labor force. And despite the great expansion of the white collar class in the 1920s, none of the 1930 estimates of its size placed it at much more than a quarter of the total work force. Since then a dramatic change has taken place and the United States has become the first major industrial nation in which manual or blue collar workers have ceased to be the largest single occupational group.[2]

Yet Gompers' remark about white collar workers has retained its pertinence in terms of that group's self-image in the United

1

States. A recent study found that "the degree of unionization among white collar workers continues to be only moderate or slight." Where organized, these workers have proven militant and have not hesitated—especially in recent years—to take to the picket line, but on the whole, little organization of white collar workers has taken place despite their ever-increasing number as well as the tremendous upsurge of unionism in the 1930s and thereafter.[3]

The American Newspaper Guild was part of that upsurge, and commentators during and after the 1930s have referred to its establishment and subsequent career as "an important precedent in white collar unionism."[4] The early history of the ANG differs in important details from that of other white collar unions past and present (especially as regards the charismatic leadership of its first president, Heywood Broun, and the broad range of political and social contacts many of the members had because of their work), but the newspapermen's organization is not atypical of non-blue collar groups. Most of the ANG's founders, like the majority of white collar workers, had a superior if not hostile attitude toward labor unions and had no intention of starting one. Despite the cynicism newspaper work often induced in regard to others, the majority of editorial employees had the usual middle-class aspirations, which were reinforced by the myths associated with journalism. Yet within a relatively short time after its establishment in 1933, the American Newspaper Guild had become a union affiliated with organized labor. This study deals with how and why this change occurred. I am concerned with the processes that by 1936 had transformed the American Newspaper Guild into a militant labor union.

What accounted for these processes? How did the publishers react to them and what influence did this reaction have? Who became a guildsman? Where does the government fit into the relationships between the publishers and their editorial employees? The columnist Heywood Broun is inextricably linked with the establishment of the American Newspaper Guild, but just how much of a role did he play? He made a grand symbol without which the ANG would have collapsed, but who did the necessary day-to-day tasks that ensured its survival? These and other questions about the early history of the American Newspaper Guild are not shrouded in mystery, but they never have been fully answered, certainly not in published accounts.

Although the establishment of the ANG among workers generally hostile to organization demonstrates the possibilities of white collar unionism, little has been written about the ANG's formation. Broun's biographer put together a lackluster work that deals in generalities.[5] A number of labor histories that appeared during the ANG's early years did discuss it but usually superficially and briefly, and sometimes erroneously.[6] Since then, labor historians generally have neglected the foundation of the American Newspaper Guild.[7] Nor has the ANG fared better at the hands of journalism historians. During its early years when the very idea of such an organization caused a stir about possible dangers to freedom of the press, a number of writers dwelt on the ANG, but never at length and certainly without perspective.[8] In more recent years, as the organization has become just another part of the established scene, the tendency has been to ignore it.[9]

The periodical literature of the time which dealt with the ANG failed to treat it impartially, and many of the contemporary articles seem concerned solely with the question of whether the Communists dominated the newspapermen's organization. Today there can be no doubt about the fact that the Communists played a considerable role in the guild movement, although probably a lesser one than both they and their enemies claimed.[10]

The American Newspaper Guild never became a large union, but between 1933 and the end of 1936 it did become a union. The very fact that it did, organizing a quasi-professional group —the cynical, romantic, sophisticated, highly individualistic editorial workers—entitles the ANG to a distinct place in history. This is a study of how it got there. Because it is a study of an uncharted region, I have assumed the cartographer's task —making a detailed map. Or, as the late R. G. Collingwood said about detailing such regions: "if anybody had objected that . . . one couldn't see the wood for the trees I should have answered who wants to? A tree is a thing to look at; but a wood is not a thing to look at; it is a thing to live in."

1·

before the blue eagle

"As a citizen, a workman, a human being, the journalist is . . . nothing but a wage-earning servant, as impotent and unimportant, considered as an individual, as a mill hand. Journalism in America is no longer a profession through which a man can win to a place of real dignity."[1] This statement, made in 1922 by a one-time literary editor of the *Boston Herald*, sums up the situation of the average American newspaperman in the first third of the twentieth century.

Many newspapermen exchanged gripes about low pay, but more often than not, men on the same newspaper did not know how much the fellow a desk away earned. Only this was known for certain: some journalists made a very good living, but, in general, newspapers paid poorly. The available data—presenting a dismal economic picture for the average editorial employee—substantiate the newsmen's belief. A report in *The American Press*, a newspaper industry trade monthly, declared that during the 1920s "the future had not held much in store for most newspapermen: a desk job at the best at $40.00 tops in the tank towns and $60.00 a week in the larger cities." This wage scale gave the journalists, many of whom considered themselves to be professional men, a financial standing (outside the larger cities) little better than that of the average clerk, who earned about $30.00 a week in 1929.[2]

Reporters especially were plagued by low salaries. In Wisconsin during the 1920s some small-town newspapers paid their cub reporters $6.00 a week, and across the country many writers for suburban newspapers earned little more than $1.00 a day. An Atlanta newspaperman recalls that in the South "a reporter who made $50.00 [a week] considered himself in the higher income brackets." Another veteran newspaperman remembered that when he was employed as a cub reporter on the San Antonio *Express*, he was informed that his wages would be $7.00 a week.[3]

The newspaperman's financial situation was only slightly better in the metropolitan areas. There also, publishers attempted to cut costs by keeping editorial payrolls low. Before the First World War, the *St. Louis Post-Dispatch* had set a ceiling of $25.00 a week for reporters. The writer Ferdinand Lundberg recalls that during his Chicago newspaper days in the 1920s, a weekly salary of $40.00 was considered a "princely sum," and that as late as 1926, some newspapers still partially paid their reporters with due-bills received from hotels and restaurants as part payment for advertising. A survey of ten of the more affluent metropolitan newspapers (including *The New York Times*) revealed that just before the Depression set in, their average starting salary for newspapermen, regardless of previous experience, was $44.15 a week; another survey conducted a few years earlier found that three-quarters of the newspapermen on the New York dailies received less than $4,000 a year, with many reporters earning only about $1,000 a year.[4]

Exceptions to this rule of poor pay existed. A number of newspapermen did well financially and a few made very good money, especially those who had the better editorial positions or who had gained recognition as columnists or specialists. Heywood Broun, who sometimes spent as little as an hour producing his syndicated column, for some time averaged $40,000 a year. Arthur Brisbane, an editor and columnist as well as a close associate of William Randolph Hearst, made more than $100,000 a year in the 1920s from his newspaper endeavors alone. A number of other newspapermen enjoyed five-figure incomes, but these exceptions merely proved, as a 1928 International Labour Office (ILO) survey concluded, that "in no country is there such diversity in journalists' salaries as in the United States of America."[5]

From the Armistice to the Depression, spokesmen at newspaper industry meetings and writers in trade journals continually reiterated the need to raise editorial workers' salaries. Typical is the 1927 declaration by Eric Hopwood, president of the American Society of Newspaper Editors, at its annual meeting, that "we have to pay our reporters better." However, such statements by various people in the industry (including some publishers) had little effect. The ILO stated in 1928 that the American editorial worker's economic position had deteriorated since 1914; journalists' salaries had increased by 30 percent but had failed to keep pace with the cost of living, which had risen more than 50 percent. By contrast, the wages of the average American blue collar worker had increased so much since 1914 that his buying power had gone up nearly 30 percent.[6]

Hand in hand with poor pay went onerous working conditions. At the turn of the century Samuel B. Donnelly, president of the International Typographical Union, characterized the conditions under which editorial employees labored as "absolutely revolting to free men." The working conditions are considered to have been a major cause of newspapermen's well-deserved reputation for heavy drinking. Perhaps the most condemning revelation comes from a former city editor of the New York *World*: "Newspapermen give all that is in them to the service of their employers and when they are old and worn out, they are cast adrift like battered wrecks. . . . The luckier ones die young. I myself was a machine and the men I worked with were cogs."[7]

The six-day work week was general newspaper practice, and long hours were the rule. Talcott Williams, the first director of the Columbia University School of Journalism, warned aspiring newsmen that "a day of ten or twelve hours will be no unusual thing. . . ." With reference to editorial workers in the United States, the ILO survey found that "no regulation of the subject" of hours existed, and it estimated that many editorial employees worked ten or more hours a day. The mechanical workers in the newspaper industry fared much better. By 1910 the printers, whom many reporters and deskmen scorned as mere unionized laborers performing dirty and non-creative drudgery, generally had succeeded in obtaining an eight-hour day; and by 1930, despite setbacks, their drive for a five-day, forty-hour week had achieved considerable success.[8]

Reporters especially had to sustain long hours. At a morning daily a reporter would come to work about 11:00 a.m. Once assigned to a story, he would be expected to "stick with it" as long as was necessary, even if this meant a 15-hour day. Rarely did he receive overtime or compensatory time off. Occasionally, the city editor, if very pleased with a story, might arrange for the long-working reporter to receive a small cash bonus or tell him to come in late the next day. A Texas reporter remembers that "from time to time I would get so tired I simply could not tumble down to the office and would spend the day in bed; I was always docked for the lost day." According to a story current in the industry in the 1920s, "the general reporter rarely got home to his family and was not recognized by his children when he did." Some city editors even went so far as to discourage their reporters' marriage ambitions, for family demands on the newsmen's time might interfere with the single-minded pursuit of a story. Walter Howey, the legendary managing editor of the *Chicago Tribune* who was caricatured in the play *The Front Page*, threatened to cut his reporters' salaries or to discharge them if they married.[9]

The newspaper business lacked job stability because of management's periodic shakeups (designed, believed the newsmen, to keep them hustling) and the increasing number of mergers (usually meaning not a transfer but a loss of jobs), as well as the newspapermen's desire to better themselves by moving on to new positions. Rapid turnover in the editorial departments had become so much an established fact by the 1920s that it occasioned little comment. A Columbia University School of Journalism study of graduates from the classes of 1921 to 1925 showed that by 1926 those who had gone directly into newspaper work from the classes of 1923 and 1924 had averaged two positions each; and 1921 and 1922 graduates had averaged three positions each. Hiring and firing were done capriciously.

Summary dismissals, often at the discretion of minor executives, took place frequently. Years later, an *American Press* editorial still called the practice "the curse of newspaper work in America." There was no severance pay except in isolated instances; at best, discharged employees received one or two weeks' notice, although often not even that. Moreover, rarely did the editorial employees receive advance notice of salary cuts—on payday the employee might receive 10 percent less than expected, and he had little recourse.[10]

Unfortunately, the economics of newpapering also had a debilitating effect on the morals and self-respect of many newspapermen. Faced with almost chronic financial embarrassment, many hardworking reporters, deskmen, and editors accepted money and other favors for slanting or suppressing stories. An executive of a Chicago newspaper asserted that "only the dumbwits . . . are without a racket. What's the use of living like a tramp when the filthy lucre is being passed out like rain checks at the ball park." Sports writers probably committed the greatest acts of venality. Onetime heavyweight champion Gene Tunney recalled that in the early days of his fight career he paid sports writers 5 percent of his purses to ensure favorable publicity and that most other fighters in the 1920s did the same. Upton Sinclair, in his bitter 1920 arraignment of the newspaper industry, cried out for the journalists to "respect the integrity" of their calling; all through the 1920s and later, critics of the American press pointed to the continuing "prostitution" of many newpaper employees.[11]

In view of all these difficulties, what prompted men and women to enter newspapering and to endure the irregularities of newspaper life? In part, the answer was to be found in the newspaper worker's desire to achieve fortune, renown, and influence; everybody always knew of someone who had gone on from the ranks of the copy boys to achieve great success. Despite the grim realities of their situation, many newspapermen considered themselves to be middle-class professionals or craftsmen, and it was assumed that with diligence and luck an attractive, high-paying career could be achieved. But the most important factor was the attitude which best can be summed up as "the romance of newspapering."

Based on a series of quixotic ideas, this attitude included acceptance of the myths that the newspaper business was a game, that the newsman (an individualistic go-getter) was the equal of anyone, and that wages, hours, and conditions did not count. What really mattered was high adventure and being "on the inside." Dealing with the famous and the infamous was viewed as compensation in itself. By-line glory and a nodding acquaintance with the near-great had become accepted substitutes for cash. The newspaperman, as Judith Crist points out, "made a virtue of his lack of wordly status, a vice of such personal securities as education or professional training or even domesticity." According to one labor historian, many a journalist viewed himself in composite as "a Richard Harding Davis whose alter ego is Sherlock Holmes while shades of Don Juan and Horace Greeley hover in the background." Not all editorial workers accepted these ideas, but enough did to make any sort of organization among them difficult. In particular, the younger staff members, who formed a majority of the editorial employees on most dailies, burned with the joy of working for a newspaper.[12]

The sources of these romantic notions are evident. As one chronicler of the newspaper industry has pointed out, "more drivel has poured from typewriters regarding the life and times of newspaper editorial employees than of workers for any other commercial organization." These stories did not come from non-newspaper sources only; successful veterans of the business more than added their share. Donald Henderson Clarke, a New York *World* reporter turned novelist, wrote about the business as being "the Land of Our Dreams, a Fairyland of Romance and High Promise." In a manual for young men interested in newspaper careers Chester Lord, the eminent managing editor of the New York *Sun*, in describing the "rewards of journalism" declared that "our young man must look beyond mere pecuniary gains for the rewards of journalism." Though admitting that most newsmen made little money, Lord maintained that "there is more fun in the newspaper business than in any other occupation known to man. . . ." If many newsmen joined the public in accepting these fictions, publishers, more practical, capitalized on them. An old-time reporter commenting on "the romantic blah handed out to all beginners in the newspaper game" affirmed that "without exception they are told the same old story: 'you mustn't consider the economic side if you are going to be a newspaperman.' "[13]

Improvements in the education of the average newspaperman resulted in little modification of these notions. At one time many publishers and editors had believed that a formal education only impeded a journalist in performance of his duties, but in the latter years of the nineteenth century as the American newspaper rapidly expanded in size and function and dealt with a society increasingly complex on all levels, it became clear that the press needed more educated men on its editorial staffs. The newspapers found such men among college graduates, and between 1900 and 1930, as one history of the industry puts it, "the ties between campus and city room were strengthened greatly. . . ." Journalism became an accepted part of the curriculum at an increasing number of colleges during this 30-year period. At the same time, developing interest in specialized training of journalists brought into being a number of university schools of journalism (the most important being the one opened at Columbia University in 1912, which in 1935 became the first graduate school in the field). Because of these schools, whose number increased steadily between 1904, when the first was opened at the University of Missouri, and 1930, the percentage of professionally trained editorial employees rose sharply (though it would be some time before the famous cartoon showing a city editor asking a young hopeful "and what may I ask is a school of journalism?" no longer held true). The proponents of professionalization, dismayed by what they considered the low state of the American press, envisioned that specialized training in professional schools would raise the technical, intellectual, and ethical standards of journalism in the United States. Joseph Pulitzer, the editor-publisher whose bequest helped found the Columbia school, believed it would "make better journalists, who will make better newspapers, which will better serve the public." Journalism certainly benefited from the better-educated editorial worker, but between 1900 and 1930 the "romance of newspapering" continued to be the major lure which brought young men into the business, be they college graduates, journalism school alumni, or high school dropouts.[14]

Editorial workers, despite their belief in the much vaunted code of individuality, promoted as part of the "romance of newspapering," did band together for various reasons into associations (on a group—e.g., editorial writers—basis) and press clubs (usually on a geographical basis). Essentially social and fraternal in nature, these groups were primarily interested in such objectives as professional criticism, burial expense funds, and the "spread of good cheer." Neither type of group attempted to bargain with the newspaper publishers over working conditions or wages and hours. However, the associations and press clubs did serve as useful examples to those newspapermen who later attempted to better their economic lot through organization and collective action. As one chronicler of the American Newspaper Guild's early days stated, these organizations "can be regarded as the embryonic expression of the view that journalists should organize along [professional] lines. . . ."[15]

Typical of the early associations was the Baseball Reporters Association of America (a forerunner of today's Baseball Writers Association), which was organized in 1887. Helped into existence by major league team officials, its main purpose was expressed in the baseball guide statement that "the time has come when the National Game . . . and the baseball reporters of America look to each other for support and assistance." Although the Association did prod club owners to improve press facilities, its principal functions were standardizing the scoring of games and promoting baseball.[16]

The press clubs (some of which still exist in one form or another), while more important because of their larger membership and influence, did little more than the associations to improve the situation of newspapermen. As vehicles for expressing dissatisfaction on the part of editorial workers, the press clubs were hampered by the nature of their membership, which included many non-journalists as well as large numbers of editors and others of management rank.

For a time, the press clubs flourished in many cities (even

though publicity-seeking businessmen rather than the working press often comprised the bulk of the membership); some had elaborate facilities. By 1892, enough clubs had been established to permit formation of the International League of Press Clubs. However, the League, like many of the individual clubs, functioned only briefly, its heyday being the first decade of the twentieth century. By 1918 a notable decline had taken place in the prestige and membership of most of the surviving press clubs. Reasons for this decline include: severe internal political quarrels, often unrelated to the club's stated charter purposes (a situation which alienated many journalist and non-journalist members); a tendency of clubs to finance themselves through admission of members who were not active newspaper workers (a practice that eventually drove away many bona fide editorial employees); and a more stringent policy on the part of publishers regarding the use of their newspapers' columns (a policy that estranged many non-newspaper people who had joined the clubs and had paid fat fees to assure "healthy press relations").[17]

The press clubs, even during the period when they found wide acceptance among newspaper people, experienced the difficulties of other journalist organizations in sustaining cooperative activity among newspapermen. As the president of one of the early press clubs complained at the end of its successful first year, once the organizational meetings had taken place, often he "would call a meeting and himself attend but his fellow members would fail to appear."[18] This type of non-support and indifference to organization, coupled with the attitudes fostered by the "romance of newspapering," explains why the impetus toward unionization of the editorial employees first came, in the 1890s, from the International Typographical Union (ITU), a mechanical workers' union.

Three things apparently stirred ITU interest. First and most important, the ITU believed that its strikes often were hindered by the newsmen. In the 1890s many newspapers still employed as editorial workers a considerable number of men who, if necessary, could set type. The ITU wanted to eliminate this kind of "reporter scabbing." Secondly, the union hoped that organization of the newspapermen would improve its image in the press. The ITU's officers believed, as did most labor leaders at the time, that press coverage of labor news was unfair and untruthful. The union hoped that newspapermen, once organized and active in the labor movement, would stop serving as apologists for the newspaper publishers and for management in general. Finally, the ITU then controlled various specialties within the industry which had developed since the Civil War (e.g., the stereotypers, who had not yet broken away to form their own union), and some of the union's leaders thought of "the newswriters" as one more specialty to organize.[19]

At the June, 1891, convention, the ITU delegates amended its constitution so as to authorize "the issuance of charters to unions of editors and reporters." On October 13, 1891, the first ITU charter for an editorial workers' local was issued to a group of 15 newspapermen in Pittsburgh. Stimulated by the labor agitation preceding the 1892 steel strike, these men had decided to follow the example of the better-paid newspaper mechanical workers and form a union. The journalists did not follow this example for long, however; by May, 1892, the local had died for want of dues-paying members, and its charter had been suspended.[20]

The ITU expended some effort to bring the newspapermen into the union fold. In 1893 it dispensed with the four-year apprenticeship rule in the case of editorial employees, and in 1896, although the newswriters had only two locals in existence, the ITU granted them a vice presidency in order to encourage organizational activity among the editorial employees.[21]

Unhappily, the Pittsburgh experience presaged the fate of almost all the ITU editorial workers' locals. Between 1891 and 1923—when the union in a referendum decided to relinquish jurisdiction over editorial employees—the ITU chartered 59 locals in over 40 cities in the United States and Canada. Of these, only six endured for more than five years, and the great majority folded within eighteen months of their establishment. In general, the locals were very small, sometimes beginning with no more than eight or nine members. The Wheeling, West Virginia, unit had the largest membership—43—of any local in the country. Moreover, although the ITU issued charters for almost 30 years, the editorial employees' interest in organization seems to have been concentrated in two brief periods which account for 75 percent of the 59 locals chartered. Twenty-nine of these were authorized between 1899 and 1904, and fifteen were authorized in 1919.[22]

The failure of the ITU's turn-of-the-century organizing attempts can be traced to several causes. In part, the fault lay with the rank-and-file of the ITU, which did little to assist the national officers' plans to organize the editorial employees. John F. O'Sullivan, a Boston labor news reporter who served (1896-1903) as the first ITU vice president representing the newswriters' locals, found it necessary at one national convention of the typographers to urge that "the local unions take a more active interest. . . ." Two years later, in 1901, he complained that the mechanical workers' locals retained as dues-paying members men now working in the editorial department. This practice, O'Sullivan told the convention, "was not conducive to the growth of the writers' unions and not in harmony with the spirit of the [union] law which provides that men working in any branch of the industry should become members of the union of that particular branch." The editorial locals' growth was stunted further by the ITU refusal, under mechanical locals' pressure, to waive or lower its dues, which were high because of the union's insurance and pension benefits. Many editorial workers could not afford to pay that much to belong to a union. In addition, the mechanical locals generally did not support their editorial brethren. For instance, in New York City a 1912 strike by the newswriters of the important Jewish dailies (then in their heyday with a combined circulation of over 600,000) failed, mainly because the typographers would neither join nor support the editorial employees' walkout.[23]

On the whole, however, the failure of the ITU editorial workers' locals at the turn of the century and later can be traced to the attitude and conduct of the editorial employees. O'Sullivan's successor, E. J. Bracken, admitted that the newspaper writers did not have "a correct knowledge of the aims and objects of organized labor." Q. K. Underwood, who was assistant city editor of the *St. Louis Globe-Democrat* when attempts were made to form a union there, expressed many a newspaperman's point of view when he declared that his experience had been that "newswriters do not want to be unionized." On most newspapers at this time, although the initial response to the formation of an editorial workers' local may have been enthusiastic, very few editorial employees sustained this response for long. After an initial burst of joint activity, most of them preferred to go their own ways in pursuit of their own ambitions—as had been the case with such journalist organizations as the press clubs. Moreover, imbued as they were with the "romance of newspapering," most of them had a white collar spirit. They had little pro-union sentiment and even less liking for trade-union methods. Many of the locals were like ITU Denver Newswriters Union No. 2, which, according to one of its members, "used this alliance—or threat to ally, as it was never more than that in operation—as a bluff that helped Denver reporters get a six-day work week." All too often editorial workers reacted like those in Scranton who, a charter member of the ITU local there recalled, "considered it beneath the dignity of a newspaperman to join a labor union."[24]

In 1900 O'Sullivan had told the ITU convention that he had not found "any hostility to the organization of the writers on the part of the publishers. . . ." With rare exceptions (such as in Butte, Montana, where the newspaper publishers forced the dissolution of a newswriters' local), O'Sullivan's statement continued to prove true for some time. The inability of the ITU editorial workers' locals to establish themselves probably explains why in this period, contrary to the later history of the newspaper industry, the publishers took almost no action to block attempts made to organize their editorial employees.[25]

By 1906 ITU interest in the editorial workers had diminished. At the union's 1906 national convention, the editorial workers' locals, which for the preceding ten years had been represented by a vice president of their own, lost that representation. And the following year all reference to newswriters' locals was struck from the ITU constitution. Behind these actions lay not only the editorial locals' record of failure but also a number of changed circumstances. Rarely now did newspapermen come from the ranks of the printers, and thus a principal reason for ITU interest in the editorial workers was removed. Moreover, the ITU leadership felt that the union's bargaining position had been strengthened greatly by the successful operation of the National Arbitration Agreement, first signed with the American Newspaper Publishers Association in 1901. The ITU, upon the request of interested groups of newspapermen, did continue to charter them as locals, but until after the First World War, only four such locals were chartered, and one of these was the Jewish newspapermen's unit which received so little ITU support during its strike.[26]

The next important wave of organizing activity among editorial employees did not come until 1919. Then postwar conditions caused unionism to be given an unusually friendly reception among a considerable number of newspapermen. They, like white collar workers in general, severely felt the pinch of an inflation which in one year (1919) increased the cost of living nearly 15 percent.[27] Of even more importance to many newsmen was the diminution of their possibilities for promotion as well as for bettering themselves by moving on, for wartime economic pressures had reduced the number of papers being published. Between 1914 and 1918 the consolidation, suspension, or merger of newspapers caused a contraction in the total number of English-language dailies in the United States which one newspaper historian considers "one of the sharpest . . . in American journalism history." The rapid demobilization after the Armistice further aggravated the situation by adding the returning veteran to an already overcrowded labor market, thus giving the publisher more opportunity to depress already inadequate salaries. The leading trade journal, *Editor & Publisher,* commenting editorially on the trend toward organization, pointed out that many newspapermen now seemed to believe that "unions take care of [them] and that individualism does not," and the magazine went on to note unhappily that unionizing, an idea "which seemed to be fantastic, now appears to many [newspapermen] to offer the solution to the question of how to earn a comfortable living in a time when the dollar has lost its buying power."[28]

During the summer and fall of 1919 in a spontaneous movement—very similar to that which in 1933 led to the organization of the American Newspaper Guild—newspapermen across the country banded together into city-wide unions. The events which sparked this movement took place in Boston. There, during the fall and winter of 1918-19, a few newspapermen, paid what they considered "ridiculously low wages" and despairing of obtaining any salary increases through individual negotiation, took over a moribund ITU editorial workers' local and began organizing their fellow reporters and copy editors. By the late spring of 1919, the publishers without formally recognizing the local had granted slight pay raises to all Boston newspapermen, and it had managed to enroll as members 180 of the city's approximately 210 editorial workers. However, the publishers refused to meet with the local's representatives to discuss the editorial workers' demands. In the first week of July, the union, supported by both the mechanical workers' organization and the Boston central labor council, threatened to strike and shut down the city's seven dailies. The publishers reconsidered their position, and on July 22, after more than two weeks of negotiation, they gave in and met the union's salary demands.[29]

Despite this auspicious beginning in Boston, the 1919 movement among newspapermen generally fared poorly and had little lasting result. In less than a year, once the newswriters' initial flush of enthusiasm had passed, a combination of strenuous opposition by the publishers and widespread apathy among the editorial employees had caused the movement to founder. Also, in 1919 no single underlying force or figure came forth to rouse the newsmen in their own behalf, as would Heywood Broun in 1933-34.

The publishers, who had to deal more circumspectly with unionized mechanical workers because of their organizational strength, fought hard against the 1919 flurry of unionizing activity among the editorial employees. In Louisville, a scheduled organization meeting was postponed permanently after a high official of the Courier-Journal and Times Company called a staff meeting the preceding night and served notice that any employee signing an application for a union charter should consider himself automatically discharged. The management of the

New York Telegram not only fired two men who had communicated with ITU representatives about the possibilities of forming a reporters' union but also had the men blacklisted with every other New York newspaper. Publishers did not always resort to such blunt tactics. In San Francisco there was no open opposition to organization, but for a while every two weeks or so one or two people were fired, always for plausible reasons; invariably the fired employees happened to be members of the union. Rarely did the organizational activity of the editorial employees receive publicity, except in the labor press. The publishers denied the editorial unions adequate news coverage. The spokesman for a Bridgeport, Connecticut, local denied that "four men on the *Standard-Telegram* resigned when they joined the union. They did not . . . they were discharged," but his statement received little circulation. At a time when strikes, lockouts, and general industrial unrest had caused almost all labor news to receive prominent display, the Boston newspapers made almost no mention of a possible strike by their editorial employees.[30]

The publishers' actions, however, explain only partially the indifference and reluctance displayed toward organization by the majority of editorial workers. Despite the seriousness of their situation, many journalists preferred to continue following their individual courses, and although a considerable number of newspapermen did evince an interest in unionizing, there remained the problem of sustaining any kind of joint activity among them. For example: at 5 p.m. on August 20, 1919, the bulk of the *Omaha Bee*'s editorial staff, 20 reporters and copy editors, went out on strike after having failed for some time to obtain any satisfaction from the publishers concerning their wage and hour demands. Within 24 hours the strike had ended ingloriously. The morning after the walkout, while their fellow strikers picketed, five of the *Bee* men returned to work, and thereafter throughout the day one after another of the reporters and desk men rushed back to work, hoping that it was not too late to get back their old jobs. Even where the union achieved some success, its members rapidly lost interest in the organization. F. T. Ferguson of *The Missoulian* tersely related the history of the Missoula, Montana, union—which had obtained an ITU charter—as follows: "The union accomplished its purpose —more pay, what other is there?—in the first week of its existence. After that the members couldn't be bothered paying dues. That's the story." The newspapermen's lack of knowledge about organizing and presenting their economic demands in a unified fashion also hampered them, for unlike the mechanical workers they had no tradition of trade unionism upon which to draw. Sometimes they did not even know how to conduct a meeting, and frequently the labor reporter or the former trade unionist, whatever his other qualifications, would be picked to head an editorial workers' group because the newsmen hoped that, at least, he could show them how to organize.[31]

Many of the newly formed editorial workers' groups, believing that affiliation with organized labor would strengthen their bargaining position, had asked for charters from the ITU, and between July 25 and November 8, 1919, the union granted charters to 12 such groups. But by July, 1920, the attitude and behavior of the organized newsmen had caused the ITU executive council to suspend the further chartering of newswriters' groups pending action by the forthcoming national convention. In a statement explaining this action to the convention, Walter Barnett, an ITU vice president, pointed out that many of the newspapermen repeatedly had failed to pay their dues to the International, that they did not fit under the ITU's laws (e.g., those regarding apprenticeship or maximum hours), and that, often eager to strike in pursuit of their demands, they expected the typographers in support to walk out with them. "Luckily," Barnett concluded, "our [union] laws are such that one hundred or one thousand men in the composing room cannot be taken out in support of ten, fifteen, or twenty men." The *New York Times* correspondent who covered the 1920 ITU convention had reported that the delegates "expected [a] contest on the plans to exclude from membership in the International Organization all newswriters . . ." locals. This contest failed to materialize; the delegates quietly referred the matter back to the executive council, where it remained (with the ban on chartering newswriters' groups continuing) until 1923, when the ITU relinquished its jurisdiction over the newswriters. So little did the ITU think of its activity among newspapermen that a 1925 history of the union, sponsored by it, contains no mention of the editorial employees' groups, either those at the turn of the century or those later.[32]

The newswriters movement after the First World War generally failed to achieve its aims. In this it differed very little from the earlier cooperative attempts by newspapermen. But the strong reaction among publishers, engendered by the possibility of an effective editorial employees' union, presaged management's response to organization in the 1930s: the publishers cried "Red" and clamored about threats to freedom of the press. In New Haven, where a newly organized newswriters group, which was anxious to avoid being labeled "class conscious" or "union-dominated," had kept clear of the ITU, the publisher in September, 1919, goaded it into striking and then, taking advantage of the "Red Scare," charged its members with being "Reds." Discussing the situation with a visiting editor he declared: "Watch out for this, Charlie. There's Bolshevism in it and if it ever forces open the sacred portals of journalism the freedom of the press which you and I have defended will be gone forever." Another widespread reaction among publishers was given voice in August, 1919, by W. B. Bryant of the Paterson, New Jersey, *Press-Guardian* after his editorial workers, in a move to strengthen their bargaining position, had begun negotiations with the ITU for a charter: Bryant claimed that he did not object to organized labor, to "the newswriters organized," or to collective bargaining. However, he asked in an angry statement to the trade press, "what I would like to know is whether we are going to sacrifice . . . independence to unionism. Would it be possible for a writer to be independent, to be anything in fact but a union propagandist, after five years of union affiliation?"[33]

Advocates of the opposite point of view ranged from Willard G. Bleyer, dean of the department of journalism of the University of Wisconsin, to Upton Sinclair, both of whom favored organization by the editorial employees, although they differed on what form this organization should take as well as on most other points. Bleyer, who represented the later attitude of many of the founders of the American Newspaper Guild, called for editorial employees to "discard the 'game' idea" and establish a truly professional association which would "advance the newspaper profession in the United States . . . one of the great professions of the world." He believed that creating professional standards in the newspaper industry would lead to better working conditions and higher pay. Sinclair, whose attitude foreshadowed that of leftists in the American Newspaper Guild, urged "one organization of all men and women who write, print, and distribute news to take control and see to it that the newspapers serve public interests." Sinclair thought that such an organization also would ensure that newspaper workers no longer would be treated as "sweated wage slaves" who have to "make their demands . . . as helpless individuals."[34]

Coincident with the expression of Bleyer's views had come an attempt to put such ideas into practice. During the summer of 1919 several St. Louis journalists organized an association which "in a dignified manner" sought to obtain not only higher pay and better working conditions but also "the same distinction which is accorded the associations of physicians, lawyers, or other professional clienteles." The association's president declared that the members recognized "the benefits which union labor has conferred upon the working man" and repudiated "the snobbery which would regard newswriters as being in some mysterious manner too superior to affiliate with union labor," but they believed that newspapermen "should abstain, except as a last resort, from any alliance" with organized labor.[35]

The "St. Louis Plan" enabled some of that city's editorial employees to obtain a sizable retroactive "bonus" which was designed to match the rapidly rising cost of living. Emboldened by this success, the St. Louis organization in October, 1919, established the American Journalists Association (AJA) with itself as the charter chapter. Membership was open to all working newspapermen, including editorial executives. Initial enthusiasm for the AJA ran high; the support it initially received from the newspaper industry establishment foreshadowed the 1933-34 attempts to get the then aborning American Newspaper Guild to model itself on the Institute of Journalists of Great Britain—the less economically minded, more professionally oriented of that country's two editorial employee organizations.[36] However, the AJA soon faded into insignificance. Once the union movement had waned, the publishers became less friendly, for "they did not want any economically minded association among their reporters," as one newspaper historian comments. Moreover, the editorial executives in the AJA found it possible to stifle any effective action planned by employee members. After the effects of the first flurry of publicity wore off and the AJA's character became clear, many of the members lost interest and dropped out. In 1919 the St. Louis chapter alone had about 150 members, but by 1926 the AJA as a whole had dwindled to barely 200 members scattered in most of the states.[37]

The nadir of the movements to organize editorial employees was reached after the ITU relinquished its jurisdiction over the newspapermen. The American Federation of Labor, in the decade (1923-33) before the formation of the American Newspaper Guild, chartered six editorial workers' locals in hopes of forming a national newswriters' union; but three of these locals soon disbanded, and the others had only limited memberships. The Chicago local was composed solely of employees from the city's Jewish newspapers, who had a strong labor orientation. In Kansas City, according to the local's secretary, the unit consisted of "men and women . . . connected with the Labor Movement . . . who contributed to the Labor Press . . . [and who] hope to interest newswriters to the extent of becoming members." In Boston, the local, a carryover from the ITU, drew its membership mostly from the city's labor news reporters, who, having experienced difficulty in gaining admittance to trade union meetings, found that with their own union identification they could gain access more easily to other unions' members and leaders.[38]

Also in the 1920s, some unaffiliated groups of editorial employees, stimulated to action by adverse local conditions, tried to establish independent organizations. Either because of newspapermen's psychological obstacles to working together or because of their fear of publisher reprisals, these efforts failed.

In New York City, for example, during the early 1920s an attempt was made to establish a Presswriters Union by Arthur Warner, a former assistant city editor of the *Evening Post* who in 1919 had been fired after a nighttime search of the staff's desks revealed him to be the author of a round-robin asking for higher pay and maximum hours. Warner failed to arouse any interest among the city's newspapermen except among the staff members of liberal journals such as the *New Republic* and left-wing newspapers such as *The Daily Worker.* The critic Lewis Gannett, who played a small role in this union, recalls that "the only worker on an English-language newspaper who dared let us use his name [was] a lone *Times* man. . . ." Although several meetings took place, attended by a dozen to twenty people, little of a practical nature was accomplished. At one meeting they did elect a slate of officers, and Gannett remembers leaving the room to telephone Heywood Broun and asking him to serve as president. Broun—who "heartily sympathized" with the idea —agreed, with the reservation that he would not strike because he had a contract. Questioned about having held this office some years later when he headed the American Newspaper Guild, Broun remarked, "Oh, yes, I remember! That was the union of which I was president, but I never went to a meeting of it." Ultimately, according to Gannett, the New York Presswriters Union "petered out," although about ten years later its treasury, a few hundred dollars, was turned over to the American Newspaper Guild.[39]

Only one journalists' group in the United States knew long-term success before the establishment of the American Newspaper Guild—the ITU editorial workers' local in Scranton, Pennsylvania.[40] Chartered in 1907, after a false start three years earlier, it prospered over the years and by 1930 not only had obtained for its members the highest wages paid newspapermen in any city Scranton's size but also had assured them of two weeks' paid vacation and protection against abuses of the overtime system. Although a 1930 investigator considered the Scranton Newswriters Union "a successful and unique organization," another observer, while not neglecting the local's achievements, viewed it more critically, declaring that it owed its continued existence to the "benevolent good will" of the publisher of Scranton's largest newspaper. The Scranton group had never been put to the test, nor did this observer believe that if it ever were, the ITU would support the newspapermen. In 1934 the editor of another Pennsylvania newspaper, comparing the ITU unit to some of the newly organized American Newspaper Guild chapters elsewhere in the state, called the Scranton Newswriters Union "nothing more than another name for a social press club." Nevertheless, the union remained the representative of the Scranton newspapermen until 1943, when they chose the American Newspaper Guild as their bargaining agent.[41]

Although the various futile endeavors to organize the editorial employees caused some unrest on individual newspapers, they had little effect on the newspaper industry. Other pressures, including some that directly affected the editorial employees, caused the changes which the industry underwent in the first third of this century. During these years the character of the average newspaper owner changed considerably. He was less and less often a working newspaperman. Personal journalism gave way to corporate ownership. Increasingly, operation of a newspaper became an investment, and the major publishers became, as one critic describes them, "businessmen, employers, and corporation owners indistinguishable from other magnates." Rarely now on the larger newspapers, or even on many of the small ones, did the owner have any direct contact with his editorial employees other than those on the executive level. The holdings of newspaper chains increased rapidly, further depersonalizing the industry. In 1900 eight chains existed, controlling twenty-seven newspapers and about 10 percent of the national daily circulation. During the next decades chain ownership grew enormously and by the beginning of the 1930s, 63 chains, owning over 350 newspapers, controlled about 40 percent of both the daily and the Sunday circulation, with the Scripps, Hearst, Patterson-McCormick, Paul Block, Ridder, and Gannett chains accounting for the bulk of this.[42]

In the years just prior to the outbreak of the First World War many American cities, even smaller ones, had been served by three or four dailies, although the income from newspaper operations alone had not been enough to keep all of these dailies in the black even in the most prosperous years. Usually, one newspaper made handsome profits, a second one provided its owner with a comfortable income, and the others relied on job printing or political patronage to do a little better than just make ends meet. The period 1908-14 marks the high point in the number of English-language daily newspapers published in the United States. Thereafter, the number of dailies published (and consequently the number of newswriting jobs available) declined, although total advertising revenues, in general, rose annually and the newspapers' circulation kept pace with the rapidly growing population and with the constantly rising literacy rate.[43]

During and immediately after the war, the newspaper business was transformed as changes in advertising practices as well as spiraling costs killed off many of the marginal operations. Except for unusual instances, this process left all but the larger cities with only one morning and one evening newspaper. Between 1911 and 1930, 1,391 dailies suspended publication or shifted to a weekly status, and another 362 merged with other newspapers. Although the great majority of these failures came from among the 1,495 newspapers started during these years, the net loss of 258 newspapers (over half of which folded after 1918) included such old and established dailies as the New York *Evening Mail*, which in 1923 ceased publication 56 years after its founding, and the Philadelphia *North American*, which upon its death in 1925 had been published in one form or another for almost a century.[44]

Many of these newspapers died as a result of the changes in advertising practices that took place during and after the war. The key to a daily's existence lay in its advertising revenues (which by the 1930s produced about 70 percent of its income); proceeds from circulation alone could not sustain a newspaper. Local advertisers, anxious to get as much value as possible for their advertising dollar in an increasingly competitive situation, concentrated their advertisements in the local newspaper that seemed most effective in reaching the purchasing public. National advertisers, whose rising expenditures during the 1920s became for many newspapers an ever more important part of their incomes, followed a similar policy, so much so that a newly founded newspaper could not hope for much national advertising until it had demonstrated its vitality for a year or more. Circulation usually determined the advertiser's course, the larger-circulation newspaper being considered the most effective.[45]

During the first third of this century, in city after city mergers of newspapers took place. As a result, the number of one-newspaper towns and cities nearly tripled, increasing from 357 in 1900 to over 900 in 1930. This rise was not caused by the development of a daily press in new areas; a 1933 survey found "no evidence of such an extension of newspapers to new cities." At the same time, publishers in many areas of the country, attempting both to reduce printing costs and to create more attractive rate combinations for advertisers, extended their control over morning or evening rivals—thereby creating numerous local monopolies. By 1933, in over 87 percent of the cities with under 100,000 population, one newspaper or one company (often not of local origin) had a monopoly. Because of the local monopolies created by the time the Depression set in, newspapermen in over 1,000 cities and towns across the country had a choice of accepting their employers' terms or of not practicing journalism there. These conditions contributed to the nomadism of many journalists; they also explain why the American Newspaper Guild in its initial stages found its most vocal and solid support in areas where multiple ownership and more than one daily existed.[46]

For newspapers the 1920s were, as one editorial veteran put it, a "saturnalia of quick mergers, sudden deaths, and phenomenal growth"; many dailies did disappear, but most of the surviving newspapers did a booming business. In 1922, a recession year, Hearst's newspapers were reported to have earned over $100,000,000, and the Brooklyn *Eagle* realized a $400,000 net profit on a gross of nearly $4,000,000. Coincident with the end of the war, total advertising linage rose almost 40 percent in one year, and it continued upward in irregular spurts for the next decade, bringing considerable profits to many dailies. So much did the value of many newspapers increase as a result of their expanded circulation and increased advertising that by the end of the 1920s, dailies in towns of 50,000 or 100,000 population were appraised as being worth one or two million dollars; figures that a decade earlier, according to Henry Luce, "would have appeared fantastic to the papers' owners." *The New York Times* was estimated in 1927 to have an investment in realty and equipment alone of $15,000,000.[47]

Much of the newspaper prosperity of those days, however, rested on relatively weak foundations. Advertising revenues increased enormously as volume went up, but rates did not increase proportionately with circulation. The authors of an industry history estimated that in the late 1920s a reduction as limited as 10 percent in the "swollen advertising revenues" of the dailies would have put most of the profitable ones into the red. A study by the *New York Evening Post* of 56 Sunday newspapers found that advertising gains had been uneven—national advertising linage showed a net gain of 31.7 percent between 1924 and 1929, but local advertising declined 11.9 percent and classified advertising lost 12.5 percent. A survey by another group suggested that by 1930, irrespective of the Depression, newspaper circulation under the conditions then existing had reached its saturation point. Moreover, operating costs rose fantastically, especially between 1927 and 1929, as newspapers —not wanting a strike to interfere with their bonanza operations—granted wage increases to the unionized mechanical workers almost on demand.[48]

The unorganized editorial employees did not fare as well as the mechanical workers. In an industry bedeviled by inflexible costs the items most easily cut were the salaries of newspaper reporters and deskmen. Throughout the mid- and late 1920s, although economic conditions warranted a different practice, most publishers continued to follow a policy of paying most of their editorial employees poorly. Marlen Pew, the conservative editor of *Editor & Publisher,* declared that during the 1920s "too many publishers . . . made editorial workers the butt of their own commercial ineptitude and of . . . senseless dog-eat-dog local rivalry and advertiser greed. . . ." In 1928, a boom year for the business, the New Jersey Press Association, summarizing the budgets that 27 member dailies had submitted for scrutiny, reported the following apportionment of income: 13.3 percent editorial; 13.4 percent net profit. Earlier, an Inland Daily Press Association committee had proposed a model budget for member newspapers which recommended that 15 percent of income be allotted for all editorial department expenses and that at least 12.5 percent be reserved for net profit; by comparison the model budget allocated 23.5 percent for mechanical division expenses, exclusive of paper and ink.[49]

The Great Crash in 1929 affected the newspaper industry almost as adversely as it did other branches of American business. For the next few years many dailies balanced their accounts in red ink, while others operated on the fringes of profit. However, few newspapers folded at this time; they survived even though they suffered economically. A federal government researcher found that over-all newspaper income (i.e., revenue from subscriptions and sales as well as from advertising) dropped almost 40 percent from $1,073,119,652 in 1929 to $667,820,090 in 1933, with the major portion of the drop being in advertising. Dailies in which advertising had occupied 65 percent to 75 percent of the space in 1929, two years later considered themselves fortunate to have 50 percent of the newspaper taken up by advertisers; those in which the earlier proportion had been 50 percent to 55 percent dropped to 30 percent or 35 percent. Total advertising expenditures (i.e., national, local, display, classified, etc.) in daily and Sunday newspapers in Canada and the United States dropped from the 1929 total of $860,000,000 to $470,000,000 in 1933. The *Syracuse Herald* lost over one-third of its daily and Sunday advertising linage between 1929 and 1933, and the *Tulsa World* lost over 45 percent of its daily linage in those years.[50]

At the same time, newspapers suddenly found themselves faced with a major new competitor for the advertiser's dollar. Radio broadcasting between 1930 and 1933 doubled its share of national advertising, going from 5.3 percent to 10.7 percent. Although almost all of this increase had been achieved at the expense of such other advertising media as magazines, bill-boards, and car cards, and even though the dailies while losing volume had continued to maintain the same percentage of na-tional advertising during these years (47.0 percent in 1929, 45.0 percent in 1930, 46.4 percent in 1931, 46.4 percent in 1932, 48.6 percent in 1933), the publishers were upset about broadcasting's increasing share of national advertising. The publishers, whose over-all revenues had dropped drastically and who needed whatever income they could get, according to one industry his-tory "were certain that the advertising budgets allotted to radio each year would have been theirs—and should have been. . . ." Radio, with its free broadcasting of the news, also affected newspaper circulation adversely, especially that of the finan-cially hard-pressed dailies in the smaller cities. One observer of the situation reported that "hundreds of small papers . . . , paying with great difficulty for a 500-word daily news service about events outside their immediate area, found their territory swamped with air news from big centers giving 2,500 words of news free."[51]

Publishers, faced with trade-union restrictions in their me-chanical departments and with fixed costs in many other areas (e.g., the price of newsprint, press association membership dues), had to cut back somewhere and did so among their white collar workers, especially those in the business and editorial departments. The mechanical unions generally managed to maintain their basic pay rate, although occasionally with some severe modification, and they eased the Depression's impact among their laid-off members with "share the work" programs. The unorganized editorial employees, with no such buffer to cushion them, went from already low salaries to lower ones, and everywhere they suffered from large-scale layoffs. In a bitter, satirical fable about the press written by the columnist F.P.A. for the *New Republic*, Blevitch, the apocryphal daily's business manager, says: "We can't cut the compositors, and we have to save somewhere. We have to shave editorial ex-penses."[52]

Newsdom, a New York City trade weekly put out by unem-ployed newspapermen, reported in September, 1931, that several newspapers had "greatly reduced their staffs," with other publishers expected to follow suit. Its "Auction Block," a list of qualified workers available who had registered with the newspaper, grew longer and longer until finally it was discontinued. An industry history reports that Southern newspapers "took great pride" in holding staff reductions to a minimum, but then admits that there had been sizable reductions in the staffs of dailies. A Bureau of Labor Statistics survey of 31 dailies found that the number of editorial workers employed on those newspapers had dropped from 1,506 in April, 1930, to 1,248 in April, 1933.[53]

With regard to pay cuts, the survey found that neither executives and high-priced specialists nor office boys and stenographers suffered so much from reduced pay as did an intermediate earning group which included most reporters, deskmen, and photographers. The Bureau of Labor Statistics estimated that between April, 1930, and April, 1933, this group's earnings declined at least 12 percent and in some cases more than 16 percent. In many areas of the country the cuts were even more extreme. In San Francisco in the early 1930s on most of the city's newspapers three 10 percent pay reductions followed one another in rapid succession. On one of the two dailies in Omaha the publisher reduced the salaries of the editorial staff almost 40 percent. Between 1929 and 1933 most Cleveland reporters and deskmen had their salaries slashed between 30 and 40 percent. By contrast, salaries of Cleveland printers were cut only 6 to 10 percent. In New York City the average weekly salary for reporters dropped $12.00-17.00 between 1928 and 1933. Marlen Pew estimated in February, 1933, that "editorial men have generally been cut . . . an average of 20% to 25%." So prevalent was paring of wages that in March, 1933, when the first cut finally did hit the editorial and business departments of the *Jersey City Journal*, the employees presented sets of expensive golf clubs to the publishers, and according to a trade journal report, "the co-publishers of the paper were told that the employees considered that even with the cut they were being treated much better than most newspaper folks."[54]

The conditions then prevailing accentuated all the evils of

newspaper life. On August 13, 1932, without warning, the *De-troit Mirror*, stating that the city could not support two morning newspapers, suddenly suspended publication—giving all edi-torial employees, veterans and newcomers alike, only one week's pay as severance. Many of the New York City reporters who under extremely adverse weather conditions had been covering the Lindbergh kidnapping story returned to their New Jersey hotels after a hard day's work on March 16, 1932, and learned that most New York dailies as part of a general econ-omy drive had cut editorial workers' already reduced salaries another 10 percent. A sense of job insecurity continually both-ered most San Francisco newspapermen; rumors constantly swept the editorial staffs to the effect that whole departments would be eliminated, leaving entire groups without employ-ment; according to one old-timer, "it was the terrible fear all the while. . . ." Nor was the newsmen's morale helped by news-paper executives like Henry Justin Smith, managing editor of the *Chicago Daily News*. In the course of an interview Smith remarked about the reduced editorial staffs that "obviously it is a process of winnowing out which one would ordinarily describe as survival of the fittest . . . . if we figure that in gen-eral the strongest, most practical, best equipped, and most self-controlled members of the profession are surviving . . . in that case one may view the situation as including the healthy process of weeding out." *The Quill*, a conservative monthly spokesman for the professional journalism fraternity Sigma Delta Chi, in commenting about "the cloud of uncertainty" under which most editorial employees labored, bitterly asked: "Haven't they [the editorial employees] demonstrated themselves worthy . . . never knowing when they might be the next to be fired, not knowing when salaries might be slashed again, forcing them to lower their standard of living even further. . . ."[55]

For most newspapermen the Depression meant fewer oppor-tunities, longer hours, lower salaries. Working conditions, al-ready bad, worsened and job security, already poor, lessened. If the Depression did not make so great a difference in news-papermen's lives as in those of other white collar workers, it was, as one editor said, "because of the fact that they have

never really known any other state in their economic existence."
Most editorial employees had taken an economic beating from
the moment they had obtained employment in the newspaper
industry. Periodic half-hearted attempts since the 1890s—first
by the ITU and then by some of the more concerned editorial
employees—to do something about the newspapermen's economic situation had foundered on the shoals of indifference and
hostility. The majority of editorial employees, caught up in the
"romance of newspapering" with its stress on individual action,
could not function together for any length of time in a social
or fraternal organization. They proved even less able to work
together in an organization dedicated to economic action, especially when its very existence belied their self-asserted stance
as middle-class professionals who could take care of themselves. When in 1919 a sizable number of editorial employees
did band together on the local level (albeit imperfectly), the
publishers reacted quickly and harshly, and made short shrift
of them—being aided in their attack by the employees' failure
to stick together. Thus, during the boom years of the 1920s
newspapermen as a class got less than they should have at a
time when the industry, however weak the foundations its
prosperity was built on, turned over a substantial profit. In the
early 1930s the industry paid the piper and so did the editorial
employee; the mechanical worker with his contract and his
union to back him up escaped the more drastic penalties.

At the end of 1932 *Editor & Publisher* told the industry that
"we hope to see in 1933 an improved condition among newspaper [editorial] employees. . . . They need encouragement."
But the publishers did nothing to provide this encouragement;
rather, they attempted to hamstring the Roosevelt administration's efforts to do anything for the editorial employees. In so
doing they became unwilling midwives to the birth of the
American Newspaper Guild, the first successful long-lived national editorial workers organization.[56]

2 ·

the beginnings

"It would be simple to say that the Depression drew the curtain on irresponsible individualism [in the newspaper business], that the New Deal set the stage for . . . reform, that Heywood Broun stepped from the wings to fill the leading role, and that events wrote the lines." It would be simple, and as Kenneth Stewart, a veteran newspaperman turned journalism teacher, concluded in his memoir, "all true, but too rational."[1]

The organization of newspapermen in 1933 took place in chaotic and confused fashion. Editorial workers across the United States, often quite ignorant of similar activities elsewhere in the country, responded to the exhortations of some of their number. Many local groups were formed as strong feelings of discontent broke through the newsmen's usual inertia. The underlying causes were many, ranging from extreme economic dissatisfaction to professional pride, but the organization movement received most of its initial stimulus from the publishers' unfriendly reactions to the attempts of the National Recovery Administration (NRA) to do something for the editorial employees.

For a time the major vehicle in the New Deal's drive to achieve economic recovery, NRA had been created, in President Franklin D. Roosevelt's words, "to obtain wide re-employment, to shorten the working week, to pay a decent wage for the shorter week, and to prevent unfair competition and disastrous over-production."[2] Under NRA aegis each of the nation's more important industries through its trade associations or similar groups would write for itself a code, subject to federal government approval, that would enable the industry to attain the President's goals. Each of these industries also would organize an "authority" to regulate itself under the code. If self-regulation failed, the President could license business enterprises. Employees were guaranteed "the right to organize and bargain collectively through representatives of their own choosing" by Section 7a of the bill creating NRA.[3] This measure, submitted to Congress on May 17, 1933, had received Congressional approval by June 13. Three days later, the President signed it into law and appointed General Hugh S. Johnson, one of the authors of the legislation, Administrator for National Recovery.[4]

Johnson, a sentimental, tough-talking, former idea man for Bernard Baruch, had helped organize the draft during the First World War and had served as a liaison between the Army and the War Industries Board, a predecessor of NRA in government-business economic cooperation and planning. Even before NRA's official launching, Johnson had begun working on the codes. But their promulgation came slowly; at the end of NRA's second month only eight codes had been approved. Many major industries hesitated. Less important industries sent draft codes to NRA in such numbers (144 in the last half of July alone) that Johnson and his staff were swamped.[5] Desiring to get NRA operative as quickly as possible, Johnson embarked on a sweeping national campaign to get, in his words, "individual employers to make AGREEMENTS WITH THE PRESIDENT HIMSELF to do their part . . ." pending the adoption of codes for their industry. By July 29 employers throughout the United States were receiving in the mail copies of the President's Re-Employment Agreement (PRA), which bound its signers until the end of the year to employ no child labor, to accept Section 7a, and to establish recommended maximum hours and minimum wages (for the editorial employees in the larger circulation areas, the bulk of the editorial workers in the industry, this would mean a five-day, forty-hour week at a weekly salary of at least $14.50). In return, the PRA allowed the employer to display the Blue

Eagle, the NRA emblem. Compliance was voluntary, but in a campaign which one historian has called "unabashed revivalism" Johnson succeeded in so arousing public enthusiasm that initially no employer could avoid at least superficial compliance.[6]

With few exceptions, American newspaper publishers enthusiastically supported the Blue Eagle campaign but proved hesitant about entering into agreements with NRA. As one student of the newspaper code negotiations has pointed out, the publishers "wanted the national economy salvaged, but they doubted that they cared to be rescued themselves" by the Federal government.[7] Their reluctant attitude had already begun to take shape before NRA had been established, first being expressed at a publishers conference which met June 9, the day before the Senate voted on the NRA bill. This meeting had been called by the American Newspaper Publishers Association (ANPA). The 15 men who attended included ANPA officers and directors, presidents of regional publishers associations, representatives from the Hearst chain and from Westchester County Publications, and the president of the National Editorial Association (an organization representing several hundred newspapers, most of which were published in small communities). They unanimously declared themselves "in sympathy" with NRA's proposed objectives, but concluded nevertheless that newspapers should not come under its jurisdiction, stating as their reason the agency's "powers to license [which] gives the power to control and such power potentially completely abridges the freedom of the press."

In the newspaper industry's lengthy, strained negotiations with NRA, the ANPA, asserting itself as never before, took an increasingly prominent role. Its leaders, deciding—in the words of the association's historian—"that there was work to be done to protect newspapers from the NRA legislation . . . ," took the lead in dealing with the government and in drawing up for the daily newspaper business the code that they believed publishers wanted. Although the ANPA—the sole national publishers association—numbered publishers of small dailies among its members, it mainly represented the larger circulation newspapers.

The 431 ANPA members in 1933, though representing only about 20 percent of the English-language dailies published in this country, used about 80 percent of the newsprint newspapers consumed in the United States, employed about the same percentage of newspaper employees, and accounted for more than 75 percent of the total daily circulation.[8]

Initially, the newspaper publishers could not avoid uncertainty about the Roosevelt administration's expectations concerning their industry and NRA. Johnson, at his first press conference, on June 20, said that though he had no knowledge of the position the newspaper industry would take, he did not "know why newspapers would not want to come in. . . ." Three weeks later, *Editor & Publisher*'s Washington correspondent described the Roosevelt administration as being more than anxious that the newspapers come forward with a code. But the ANPA history of the code negotiations declares that during this time, despite extensive speculation in the nation's press, the newspaper publishers had no intimation from official sources about their status under NRA. ANPA leaders on July 13 decided that it would be desirable to obtain direct information and arranged, with the assistance of Bernard Baruch, for a private meeting with Johnson. An ANPA committee—led by Howard Davis, the conservative, forceful business manager of the *New York Herald Tribune* who then was ANPA president—held a dinner conference with Johnson in Washington on July 18. After an extensive discussion about the press and NRA, Johnson cordially bade them goodbye, with the wish that he "might never see them again except socially." Although Johnson added that "certain things are in the fire which if cooked up will bring you back sooner than you expect," the ANPA group left the meeting with what they considered to be a mutual understanding that until the government took further action, newspaper publishers would not undertake to write a code for their business.[9]

Never again would NRA-ANPA relations be so amicable. On July 21, the day the nation's press carried Johnson's announcement of the PRA, the ANPA sent out a special bulletin to its members invoking the issue of freedom of the press and recommending that the newspaper publishers "not at the present time prepare to subscribe to a code. . . ." The bulletin also stated that a survey of wages and hours would be undertaken at once. The vast majority of the nation's press followed the ANPA's recommendations. Many newspaper publishers were troubled by aspects of both the PRA and NRA, including the abolition of child labor (which would eliminate newsboys), the licensing provision (which, it was argued, would end freedom of the press), the necessity to allow unionization under Section 7a, the government demands for reduced hours and increased wages (which, it was believed, would upset existing union contracts and increase costs), and the President's ability to impose new regulations even after agreement upon a code had been reached.[10]

Almost immediately after the issuance of the bulletin, however, the ANPA leadership realized that, given the enthusiastic public support of the Blue Eagle campaign to implement the PRA, newspaper publishers would not be able to remain aloof. Moreover, some important dailies, among them the *Christian Science Monitor*, the *Milwaukee Journal*, and the Philadelphia *Record*, quickly had subscribed to the PRA, including the provision which would give editorial employees a five-day, forty-hour week. Indeed, the *Journal* editorially attacked the ANPA on July 25 for "its self-centered and self-seeking . . . special pleas" in asking the newspapers of the country "to stand aside and apart from a movement for general recovery in the sacred name of freedom of the press." Although the smaller circulation dailies had more to fear economically from the government's attempts to boost wages and cut back hours, among the publishers of these newspapers some dissenters from the ANPA position could be found. Typical was Lee Drake, publisher of the Pendleton, Oregon, *East Oregonian*, who remarked to his business manager that the PRA would bring new advertising and that regulation of hours and wages would not hurt the newspaper.[11]

Anxious to avoid embarrassment, the ANPA moved swiftly to neutralize its critics. On July 24, a day before the *Journal* editorial appeared, Davis had a long telephone conversation with a noncommittal Johnson in an attempt to find out whether newspapers which subscribed to the PRA could be exempted from some of its provisions. Three days later, a joint meeting of ANPA officers and directors, its Committee on Federal Laws, and representatives of various regional and state publishers' associations took place. This group of twenty-five during its five-day session transformed itself into the Daily Newspaper Code Committee and appointed a three-man subcommittee composed of Davis, John Stewart Bryan (a former ANPA president and publisher of the Richmond, Virginia, *News Leader*), and Amon G. Carter (publisher of the Fort Worth *Star-Telegram*) to conduct negotiations with NRA. ANPA counsel Elisha Hanson served as counsel for the subcommittee.[12] Hanson, who, according to a former ANPA general manager, "maybe more than anyone else . . . provided the cogent, forceful, unyielding course that the vast majority of daily newspapers pursued in . . . the NRA code fight," served as a vigorous spokesman for the publishers in their bouts with the government and the American Newspaper Guild throughout the 1930s. A one-time reporter for the *Peoria Journal* and a former Washington correspondent for the Lee Syndicate, Hanson always maintained that editorial employees deserved better treatment, but he bitterly opposed their achieving it through organization—which he considered a threat to freedom of the press—and he proved to be an implacable and hardy foe of the American Newspaper Guild.[13]

By the end of July, Hanson and the subcommittee had begun negotiations with NRA. Johnson, busy with the drafting of more important codes, delegated the handling of the newspaper code to Dudley Cates, an old associate who had left a Chicago insurance company vice presidency to become NRA Assistant Administrator for Industry. Cates held a number of conferences with the publishers' group and, although the talks went on in what *Editor & Publisher* termed "an atmosphere of the greatest secrecy," news of the issues being discussed leaked out, including the problem of exempting editorial staffs from the forty-hour-week provision of the PRA. On this issue, as on most others, Hanson, Davis, Carter, and Bryan refused to compromise. They informally presented their draft proposal on August

7 to Johnson, who said he felt like "a yellow dog" when he read it. Although the publishers' group did concede to call the draft a code rather than merely an agreement, they met none of Johnson's other objections; the next day, August 8, they formally submitted the document to NRA and released it for publication.[14]

An irate Johnson accurately described the draft code when he exclaimed to Hanson and the subcommittee "why this thing is nothing but an exception."[15] It provided for an open shop, exempted newsboys from child labor provision of the PRA, repeated the rights guaranteed the press in the First Amendment to the Constitution, and designated editorial employees as "professionals" so as to take advantage of Section 4 of the PRA, which exempted from the maximum hour regulations "professional persons employed in their profession."[16]

Before the government could take any action whatever on the draft code, publishers began announcing their approval of it. Within two days the Gannett, Hearst, and Scripps-Howard chains, as well as many large metropolitan dailies and small-town newspapers, had indicated their adherence to the draft code. But Johnson balked. Taking personal charge of the negotiations, he held a number of meetings and at one point confronted Hanson and Davis with a draft newspaper code prepared by his office staff. But neither with bluster nor with diplomatic entreaties could the general make very much headway. A new draft code, which the subcommittee presented to Johnson on August 14 and which he approved as the temporary newspaper code the following day, contained few of the modifications he had desired. Johnson, fearful of losing all cooperation from the newspaper publishers, had conceded to the subcommittee a code not much different in principle from their first draft. Moreover, the section devoted to the guarantee of press freedom had become much more intricate. Drafted by someone on the NRA staff and designed to appease the publishers' group, this section of the code stated that the newspaper publishers could not be compelled by the President, regardless of the powers invested in him by the NRA law, "to comply with any other requirements than those herein contained [i.e., within the code] or waive any right to object to the imposition of any further or different requirements, or waive any constitutional rights. . . ." The use to which publishers put these concepts—embodied in somewhat different language in the final newspaper code—would cause considerable difficulties when later (before the demise of NRA), the first National Labor Relations Board attempted to deal with disputes involving the American Newspaper Guild. Nor did the editorial employees fare well in the draft accepted by Johnson. Not only did the temporary newspaper code continue to exempt "professionals" from the maximum-hour regulations, but also it specifically exempted from the forty-hour week and classified as "professional" reporters earning more than $35.00 a week.[17]

The question of whether editorial employees were professionals exempt from maximum hour regulations had been raised even before the newspaper code negotiations started and, naturally, had proved to be a topic of keen interest to many newspapermen. As early as July 28, NRA general counsel Donald Richberg, at a press conference had side-stepped a question about whether NRA considered newspapermen professionals, telling the reporters, "well, I've heard it argued both ways, but I'll leave it to you to decide." A NRA press release on July 31 declared that newspaper reporters, editorial writers, rewrite men, and other members of editorial staffs would be treated as "professional persons" not subject to work-hour limits, but the next day Johnson said that the release had been a "slip" which could be "revised." On August 4, in what appears to have been a publishers' trial balloon, an Associated Press dispatch stated that the administration intended "leaving to each publisher the decision on bringing his news force under a work-week limit." [18]

Editorial employees reacted to these varying statements in several ways. Those few newsmen who had the opportunity attacked the publishers' position in print. Paul Y. Anderson, Pulitzer Prize-winning Washington correspondent for the *St. Louis Post-Dispatch*, in his weekly *Nation* column characterized the publishers' proposals as "dishonest, weasel worded, and treacherous . . . carefully designed to enable the newspapers to escape the obligations which their editorial pages were clamorously urging all other employers to assume." Anderson, considered by Johnson "one of my best friends . . . among the Washington newshawks," also tried to use his personal contacts to offset the publishers' pressure on the administration, as did other newspapermen close to the New Dealers. Heywood Broun in his syndicated daily column asserted that the publishers called for "far too many exceptions" and, commenting specifically on the exemption of professionals from work-hour regulations, said that "the word 'professional' is stretched in this application." Other newspapermen, not so influentially situated and unable to place their objections before the public, wrote to Johnson directly. Richard Cornish, a Philadelphia newspaperman later active in the American Newspaper Guild, wrote to criticize the August 8 proposal of the publishers, concluding his letter with the hope that other newspapermen also wrote Johnson, "for we have no union and this is the only way we may express ourselves." A. F. Finestone, a veteran newsman from Kansas City, Missouri, wrote the general that the newspaper code must protect the editorial employees from exploitation, for "we have no labor organization to protect our interests."[19]

Even before the NRA legislation had been introduced in Congress, the hearings of a House of Representatives committee taking testimony on a bill limiting all industries involved in interstate commerce to a five-day, thirty-hour week in the hope of spreading employment had made clear to a number of newspapermen the necessity of having some kind of organization to protect their interests. On April 28, Congressman William P. Connery, Jr. (D.-Mass.), chairman of the committee, had interrupted the testimony of ITU representative Edward F. Cassidy to declare that "I have taken occasion to say to newspapermen, such as we have here today [reporting the hearings], that if they had the kind of organization among their reporters that you have, the publisher could not fire them and could not cut their wages twenty-five percent without any say on their part. . . ." On May 4, at the conclusion of a forceful presentation by a publishers' spokesman of their views, Connery demonstrated the validity of his statement with respect to yet another area—federal regulation of newspapermen's hours and wages—when he declared that the bill did not apply to reporters and that he accepted the publishers' contention that newspapermen are specialists impossible to include in any general legislation. Only a few newspapermen were aware of these statements, but for them, according to one historian of the ANG's early days, "the unopposed exposition of the publishers' point of view made them [i.e., the editorial employees] acutely aware that their story was not being told at all . . . [and] made the need for editorial employee organization . . . obvious."[20]

The newspaper code negotiations received much more publicity than had the thirty-hour-week bill hearings, and many editorial employees—dissatisfied with their treatment under the temporary code—determined to take action so that the final newspaper code would not neglect them. The more energetic of the newsmen decided to take advantage of the provisions in the NRA code-making process which allowed all interested parties to state their objections or offer their own proposals at the public hearings held before the completion of each final code. The desire to have a say at the hearings and in the negotiations that would follow initially motivated most of the newspapermen who became involved in organizational activities during the late summer and early autumn of 1933, but a goodly number had other aims. Some newspapermen, in addition to establishing a body which would deal with NRA, wanted to create a professional society, similar to the medical and bar associations, which would not only improve conditions economically but also set up professional standards, thereby gaining respect for their craft. Some planned to utilize the general unrest among editorial employees to develop a trade union which, using tactics similar to those of the mechanical workers' unions, would improve hours, wages, and working conditions. Some hoped that the editorial workers, once organized, would free the press from the restricting influences of advertisers and politicians. A few, subservient to Communist discipline, schemed to use the newly formed groups for the party's political ends.

On newspapers across the country, editorial employees banded together. In many localities, editorial departments joined forces on a city-wide or multi-newspaper basis. However, traditional newspaper rivalries persisted in some areas and, despite the shared antagonism to the publishers' actions, the editorial staffs of competing dailies organized independently of each other. The rapid multiplication of these groups made it impossible for all of them to present their views, and representatives from a few of the larger, better organized groups came to be considered spokesmen for all. Until December, 1933, although almost no formal organization existed beyond the local level, some newspapermen, already organized, advised or assisted others nearby, and some of the groups distant from one another exchanged ideas and information through correspondence. In these activities the New York City editorial employees' organization—correctly described by one writer as "the heart of the movement that by the end of 1933 had burgeoned into the American Newspaper Guild"—played an increasingly important role because of its large membership, because of its contacts in the Roosevelt administration, and because of the outspokenness of its leaders, especially Heywood Broun.[21]

By any standard Broun must be considered a most unlikely figure to have become the moving force behind a national editorial employees organization. Described in a *Nation* profile as "a natural and prominent habitue of the theatrical and journalistic Bohemia whose capital was the Algonquin Hotel," Broun was at the time one of the most widely read and highly paid syndicated newspaper columnists in America. Newspapermen generally admired his talents and respected the man despite his idiosyncracies. A hulk of a man, pugnacious and sentimental, lazy, amiable, extremely afraid of death, capable of great compassion and excessive generosity, overly fond of good food and drink, Broun—whose personal sloppiness and sartorial defects once had cause his appearance to be likened by Alexander Woollcott to that of "an unmade bed"—drifted into being a columnist after a short but varied career that had run the gamut of newspaper work. His experience included some straight news reporting, sports writing, drama criticism, book reviewing, and a brief turn overseas in 1918 as a war correspondent with the A.E.F. After his participation in the final attempt to save Sacco and Vanzetti from the electric chair in 1927, Broun, who like most of the Algonquin crowd had been liberal in a generalized sense, moved steadily leftward politically. By 1933 his column, "It Seems to Me," once noted for its bonhomie, increasingly dealt with economic and social issues. This many-faceted, complex man was aptly characterized by one of his contemporaries: "He wasn't a Communist, he wasn't a slob, he wasn't a drunk—he was simply Broun."[22]

In his column of August 7, 1933, Broun, then 44 and at the height of his powers and popularity, called for "A Union of Reporters."[23] He disparaged the newspapermen's traditional individualism as unrewarding and criticized the publishers' code for classifying editorial employees as professionals not subject to maximum-hour regulations. Broun admitted that he had little to fear from his employers in calling for the formation of an editorial workers' union because "fortunately columnists do not get fired very frequently." He also acknowledged that he had no complaints about his working hours, for "no matter how short they make the working day it will still be a good deal longer than the time required to complete this stint." Nor did Broun find it easy to accept in the newspaper business "the conception of the boss and his wage slaves," since among his many bosses there had been "not a Legree in the lot." But, he said, the sight of other newspapermen "working too hard" made him feel "self-conscious" and the thought of the many newspapermen "not working at all" embarrassed him even more. Broun believed that the time had come to organize a newspaper writers' union. And he concluded with the declaration that "beginning at nine o'clock on the morning of October 1, I am going to do the best I can to help in getting one up."

It is difficult to gauge just how much of a change in Broun's thinking this column represented, although there can be no doubt that it reflected a shift from his previous attitudes. Broun had done little more for the New York Presswriters Union of the early 1920s than serve as a name on a letterhead. Only 18 months before the publication of this column, he had ignored an appeal to lead the editorial workers of the country in a fight for their rights. In February, 1932, *Newsdom*—a weekly trade paper which at the time maintained that editorial employees must organize and fight "to protect their jobs" or "be nothing but alot of doormats for publishers to step on"—addressed an editorial open letter to Broun asking him to lead the fight.[24] In what proved to be a very accurate prediction, the open letter declared that Broun "in that city room which stretches from coast to coast . . . [would] find a public that's ready to listen . . . and perhaps to take heed." If Broun knew about the open letter, he did not react to it. Hyman Wishengrad, its author and then the managing editor of *Newsdom*, said that he never got any direct response from Broun.[25]

The immediate inspiration for Broun's column was the anticipated publication of the publishers' code, but what motivated Broun to call for a union remains a subject of some disagreement. Broun's friends and associates agree that he sincerely believed what he wrote in that column, but their interpretations of his motives for writing it vary considerably. Morris Watson, an early ANG "martyr," believes that Broun really wanted to help newspapermen better themselves but did not expect his column to be accepted at face value. Broun's secretary Luella Henkel has no doubts that Broun wanted to organize a union to obtain improved working conditions for the press. Doris Fleeson, a newspaperwoman who later assisted Broun in presenting the editorial employees' proposals to NRA, maintains that he wanted to do something for the newspapermen, whom, he feared, the code would neglect. Broun's attorney, Morris Ernst, questions whether the columnist realized immediately that he had committed himself. George Britt, an experienced reporter who in 1930 had collaborated with Broun on a study of discrimination against Jews in the United States, believes that Broun, becoming more and more committed to working for causes, at this time had assumed an "evangelical attitude" toward helping the editorial employees to improve their lot.[26] It seems to me in light of Broun's later actions in regard to the American Newspaper Guild that he acted on the spur of the moment and probably for a combination of all these reasons. His social awareness had increased greatly over the preceding few years; given his disappointment with the forthcoming code and his enormous emotional capacity, he probably decided that the time had come to do something and used his column, his most immediate avenue of expression.

Broun's column affected newspapermen across the country like a bugle call in the night. By the dozens, from Boston to Honolulu, they wrote to him outlining the newspaperman's depressed economic situation in their areas, stressing its seriousness, expressing agreement with Broun's criticisms of the publishers' code and with his intention to form a union. As knowledge of what Broun had said spread to cities whose newspapers did not subscribe to Broun's column, the number of letters to him increased steadily. Typical of his mail was the letter from H. B. Slocum of the *Schenectady Union-Star,* who wrote "just a word to tell you that your column . . . was a PIP. . . . I have read it several times as well as have the other boys here. . . . I can assure you that they heartily agree with you, in fact are tickled to death to see someone tell the story. . . ."[27]

The strong response to his column forced Broun to take action much earlier than October 1, but although he and other interested New York City newspapermen took a very active part in the negotiations for the final newspaper code, until mid-September, 1933, when a public meeting laid the basis for a Newspaper Guild of New York, the organizational initiative lay elsewhere. In fact, except for his August 7 column, Broun did not write again about NRA and the editorial workers until after the hearings on the final code, held September 22-23. Nevertheless, his August 7 column came to serve as a touchstone for many of the newspapermen's groups then being organized in various parts of the country.

During the week of the August 7 column, several groups of editorial employees in different parts of the country took steps to ensure that NRA would be informed of their point of view. In Rockford, Illinois, newspapermen held meetings to discuss ways of protecting their interests. The *Editor & Publisher* story that reported Broun's call for a union told in its concluding paragraph of newsmen in Texarkana, Arkansas, forming the Texarkana News Craft "as a means of obtaining a voice in the drafting of the NRA code for newspapers." No doubt hopeful that NRA's avowed aim of spreading employment would mean a shorter work day, the Texarkana News Craft sent telegrams to Johnson and other government officials asking that the final newspaper code be worded so as to spread employment among as many newspapermen as possible.[28]

In Philadelphia, and just across the Delaware River in Camden, New Jersey, within a few days after publication of the August 8 publishers' code some editorial employees had drawn up a set of counter-proposals that included a five-day, forty-hour week for almost all newspaper workers, an eight-hour work day except in emergencies, working schedules that banned staggered hours, compensation for overtime either by pay at time-and-a-third or by time off equal to the extra duty, and "restoration of pay cuts" (which on some newspapers in the two cities had reduced salaries almost 25 percent) as soon as possible. These proposals originated with a few staff members of the Philadelphia *Record,* whose owner, J. David Stern, a self-styled "maverick" who within a year would become the first major publisher to sign a contract with a chapter of the American Newspaper Guild, gave tacit approval to his editorial workers' activities. At a meeting on August 13, representatives from the editorial departments of all the Philadelphia and Camden English-language dailies decided to present their proposals formally to NRA with the recommendation that they become "an integral part" of any newspaper code. Before being presented at the NRA hearings on the final code, these proposals, representative of the aspirations of most American editorial workers, had been endorsed by more than 200 Philadelphia and Camden newspapermen (a majority of the editorial employees in the two cities). However, some publishers in the area already had exhibited the intense opposition that most American editorial workers would face in the next few years as they attempted in concert to improve their situation; at some of the Philadelphia and Camden newspapers, management pressure, despite public statements to the contrary, resulted in few or no signatures being collected in the editorial departments of these dailies. For example, according to Andrew M. Parker, a *Record* newsman who had been the driving force behind these proposals and who had been authorized to act as spokesman for the newspapermen supporting them, "at the *Evening Bulletin* . . . orders came from the top 'No Signature' [and] the men in fright destroyed the lists already made. . . ." Although the "Philadelphia code" received considerable support in the two cities, attempts then to organize on any sort of permanent basis had little success. Before the late September NRA hearings on the code took place, two organizational meetings had been called and both times only about a dozen newspapermen attended; no formal organization would be achieved in Philadelphia and Camden until early December.[29]

In Cleveland some newspapermen, believing that publishers' proposals would not extend many benefits to the working press and desiring to back up any protest with the force of numbers, in the first weeks of August undertook to bring together the city's editorial workers for joint action. The resulting Cleveland Editorial Employees Association marks the formal start of the American Newspaper Guild, and after the December 1933 founding convention the officers of the newly established ANG designated the Cleveland group Chapter I.

The organization of the Cleveland newsmen, the beginnings of which antedate Broun's column by a few days, received its impetus from the efforts made by Garland Ashcraft, a well-paid rewrite man and general assignment reporter on the Scripps-Howard *Cleveland Press,* to marshal some kind of protest against a publisher code. Ashcraft, a veteran newsman long since disabused of any notions about the romance of newspapering, had begun agitating among his fellow editorial workers on the *Press,* urging that something be done to protect the newspaperman's economic rights. He found a receptive audience in the *Press* editorial staff, for, as Robert Bordner, then an art editor and copy reader on the *Press,* recalls, "we were good and sore about the possibility of being left out in the cold."[30]

On August 2, some of the *Press* staff, including Ashcraft, Bordner, and labor editor Lloyd White, chipped in a dollar each to send a telegram to Johnson. This wire, apparently signed by Ashcraft alone, though some of the other participants are not sure of this, criticized the publishers for "welching on NRA," said editorial workers should have a five-day, forty-hour work week, and asked that NRA not neglect the working press. The next day, according to Ashcraft, "all the editorial rooms in town were buzzing" about the sending of the wire, and "men discussed the matter on assignment." That night a handful of newsmen from the *Press* and a few from the *Cleveland News* met in the apartment of John Goski, a *Press* photographer. At this meeting, the first of almost nightly discussions for the next two-and-a-half weeks, the newsmen considered ways of drawing NRA's attention to their wants. One of the ideas put forward was unionization. Within a few days, other editorial workers from the *Press* and the *News* as well as some from the *Plain Dealer,* which had the most conservative editorial staff of Cleveland's three English-language dailies, had begun participating in these meetings. At this stage, the organizers of these discussions virtually ignored the editorial workers employed by the foreign-language newspapers and the press associations. When the meetings grew too large for Goski's apartment, the newsmen met elsewhere, often in speakeasies.[31]

Realizing the ineffectiveness of long-distance protest no matter how many newsmen sent or signed telegrams, Ashcraft at these nocturnal meetings urged that Cleveland newspapermen send an attorney to the forthcoming final code hearings who would not only protest the publishers' code but also present the editorial employees' views. Ashcraft would have liked to have gone further and called for immediate formation of a union, but, according to one participant in many of these discussions, Ashcraft "said nothing . . . apparently because he believed that it was premature and that the effort might die aborning."[32]

Petitions authorizing an attorney to speak for the signers had been circulating for a few days when, on August 15 at a small dinner meeting, I. L. Kenen, a political writer for the *News,* declared that no further time should be wasted on petitions. He put forward the idea (which had been proposed and dropped earlier) that on the following Sunday, five days later, a mass meeting of all the interested newspapermen in town be called in order to form a union which would strive to obtain better working conditions for editorial employees as well as serve to protect them from unfair treatment by the NRA code. That afternoon he had outlined his proposal to an old associate, Ralph J. Donaldson, a veteran political writer for the *Plain Dealer* who earlier had discussed with Kenen the possibility of forming a newsmen's organization. Donaldson thought it "probable" that the majority of the *Plain Dealer's* editorial employees would "go along" with the union idea. Kenen got a much warmer response from the dinner group, which included Ashcraft; Goski; Elmer Fehlhaber, another political writer for the *News;* A. L. Roberts, assistant city editor of the *News;* and three or four others. According to Kenen, they all went along with his proposal and "talked about the name and other details . . . [and decided] to call it an association, since the word union might repel some of the more conservative men." Lloyd White recalls some discussion of the word "guild," but that term "was discarded as too fancy." In the next few days this little group (augmented by a few others) personally sounded out enough Cleveland newspapermen to be sure that a mass meeting would have a broad base of attendance; and the meeting was set for Sunday afternoon, August 20, in the auditorium of the Hollenden Hotel. Nine men signed the call for the meeting: John Haas, Frank O'Neil, and Roberts from the *News;* Donaldson, W. G. Lavalle, and Chad Skinner from the *Plain Dealer;* and Ashcraft, Goski, and White from the *Press.*[33]

It took considerable courage for these newsmen to act as they did. In 1933 newspaper jobs were very scarce and the men involved in organizing the Cleveland editorial workers had no job protection whatsoever; as Robert Bordner points out, "nobody knew whether the axe would fall. . . ." The *Press* management, noted for its generally liberal editorial stance, had reacted in ambiguous fashion to so simple an action as the sending of the wire to Johnson. Almost immediately after its dispatch, its contents had become known to Louis Seltzer, the editor of the *Press;* his brother, a news assistant who happened to be in the city room when the message was typed out, brought him a carbon copy. Late that night the editor called Ashcraft, whom he considered the prime instigator, berated him for blackening the good name of the *Press,* and told him to report to the front office first thing in the morning. The next day when Ashcraft went to see Seltzer, rumors of dire consequences for the newsman spread through the *Press* city room, but nothing happened. Ashcraft remembers that he and Seltzer chatted about working conditions and that the editor told him that he had thought the matter over and had decided the whole affair might just as well be forgotten. This incident seems to have had a double effect: encouraging some to act, instilling fear in others. Certainly this fear partially accounts for the fact that only about a third of the editorial workers employed by the city's three dailies attended the August 20 meeting.[34]

Each of the 102 newsmen present at the Hollenden Hotel that afternoon received a copy of the manifesto "For Your Information," which had been mimeographed secretly by the organizers of the meeting on the advertising department machines of the *Press.* This manifesto, after outlining many of the editorial employees' grievances, argued that "it is now time that local room staffs start living and working for something more than the by-line and the pat-on-the-back. NRA holds out . . . [the] first bonafide opportunity to go after realities." The manifesto concluded by enumerating the meeting's aims: (1) a "free and frank discussion" of the general situation of Cleveland newspapermen; (2) a "vote on the question: SHALL WE ORGANIZE?"; (3) should the vote be favorable, the granting of authority to a committee "to study the problem, [and to] draft alternate plans of organization." The meeting's organizers also wanted approval for a plan "to present at the next meeting alternate proposals whereby we should present our side of the code proposition at the final hearings. . . ." In a session that lasted about an hour—including speeches by White (discussing NRA and the newsmen), Ashcraft (outlining what he considered the victimization of newspapermen by publishers), and Kenen (expressing the need for a union)—the assembled newsmen, without so much as a word of dissent, voted unanimously in favor of a motion made by Kenen which embodied the manifesto's proposals and which called for the formation of a Cleveland

Editorial Employees Association. The nine-man committee which had signed the call for the meeting was authorized to present at another mass meeting set for the following Sunday afternoon a constitution and bylaws for such an association.[35]

Heywood Broun's August 7 column urging that reporters form a union had helped mobilize the necessary support for such an organization as the Association. Thomas Q. Lempertz, then on the *Plain Dealer* staff, wrote Broun a few months later that "the bulletin board in the news room was plastered with your . . . wisecracks aimed at the publishers. . . . In the case of the *Plain Dealer* I KNOW that your word carried a great deal of influence." Kenen believes that Broun's column stirred up a great many Cleveland newspapermen and made them suddenly very conscious of their situation. Roberts, immediately after the August 20 meeting at which he presided, sent Broun a telegram that concluded, "UNKNOWN WHAT OTHER CITIES DOING BUT HOPE TO TAKE LEAD AND HOPE YOU WILL TOO STOP THIS WIRE MAKES YOU INTERNATIONAL PRESIDENT PRO TEM. . . ." In an air-mail letter sent that night, Roberts outlined for Broun in greater detail what happened at the meeting, asked him to come to Cleveland (all expenses paid) to address a gathering of newsmen the following Sunday, and told the columnist that "Cleveland editorial men appreciate your efforts and expressions on behalf of the local staffs of the country. You offered us leadership. . . . You called. We're answering 'present'." And after announcing once again to Broun that "so far as we are concerned you are already our international president," Roberts ended with the declaration that "the Cleveland Boys are behind you."[36] The Cleveland newsmen received an encouraging reply from Broun.

The next meeting, held on the afternoon of August 27 at the Hollenden Hotel, drew 112 newspapermen and brought the Cleveland Editorial Employees Association into formal existence. The constitution and bylaws provided for three chapters, one from each daily. All editorial employees of the three dailies were eligible for membership except managing editors, editors in chief, and "those performing the same duties but under other titles."[37] No provision was made for membership of Cleveland editorial workers not employed by the *News,* the *Plain Dealer,* or the *Press.* Every chapter elected three members to the executive committee from which the membership in a general meeting would choose by secret ballot a president, a vice president-treasurer, and a secretary, no more than one officer coming from a single chapter. Each chapter would carry on its own bargaining, although members also could negotiate as individuals if they so desired. As outlined in the constitution, the purposes of the Association were twofold: "to preserve and protect the economic and professional interests of the membership through collective bargaining" and other means, and to "establish and enforce standards of ethics and craftsmanship" among the members. The word "strike" appeared nowhere, but the bylaws did say that no employee could be called upon by the Association "to withhold his services" from his newspaper unless his chapter approved such action by a majority vote. Should such withholding of services become necessary (either because of a strike or a lockout) however, it was stipulated that Association members upon pain of expulsion not give "moral, financial, or professional assistance to the employer in question." To prevent domination of the Association by persons controlling editorial jobs or assignments, any editorial worker "who in his employment has authority over three or more persons" was barred from all executive positions. The constitution did not provide much of an independent financial base for the Association; it set the initiation fee at $.50, called for $.20 monthly dues, and provided that special assessments could be levied only by a two-thirds vote of the whole Association membership.

The cult of the individual, as well as traditional rivalries between editorial staffs, died hard in the newspaper business and the Cleveland Association's constitution and bylaws reflected this, as would the working rules of many of the other editorial workers' groups that sprang up in 1933. Though the Association's constitution and bylaws created neither a powerful nor a militant organization, stormy arguments—both in the committee sessions and at the August 27 mass meeting—marked their drafting and adoption. And within three weeks, except for a few men, the *Plain Dealer* workers had decided to go it alone

as the Plain Dealer Editorial Employee Association. Ideological
and personal differences, exploited to some extent by the *Plain
Dealer* management, had led to the quick destruction of the
unusual, new-found unity of the Cleveland newspapermen. The
differences which plagued the Cleveland Association, centering
on divergences of opinion about the aims, methods, and extent
of organization, also proved to be stumbling blocks for many
other local newsmen's groups, both those which came into being
in 1933 and those established thereafter.[38]

The majority of the *Plain Dealer* editorial staff had shown
only slight interest in the drive for a five-day, forty-hour week
and the proposal for continued agitation against a publishers'
code. As one of their number said, "our chief object was to provide a mechanism for collective action on general wage increases or reductions." During the first week of September the
managements of the *Plain Dealer* and the *News* restored much
of the wage cuts their newspapermen had suffered, and on the
Plain Dealer discontent and unrest decreased greatly. Moreover,
most of the *Plain Dealer* editorial staff considered themselves
professionals and, as self-styled gentlemen of the press, cared
little for the idea of developing a union. On the other hand, the
organizers of the Association from the *Press* and *News* had in
mind more than just a professional society which had no economic purpose beyond a limited interest in wages. Ashcraft
wanted a strong organization which would be "a broad craft
proposition." Bordner hoped to set up "a vertical form of organization for all newspaper workers," including the business,
circulation, and advertising departments. Even White, one of
the least radical of the original organizers and a man interested
only in "obtaining the possible," thought in terms of a union.[39]

The leaders of the *Plain Dealer* chapter, having failed to get
their own way at the sessions of the committee drafting the
constitution and bylaws, tried at the August 27 meeting and at
another one on September 2 to have the Association accept their
ideas. Both times they proposed constitutional amendments
which would have transformed the new organization into three
separate groups, loosely federated and not economically
oriented; at both meetings the assembled membership voted

down the amendments. Realizing the danger to the Association posed by the dissension these *Plain Dealer* proposals represented, Kenen, White, and a few others had attempted to work out some form of compromise. They failed, but they did manage to keep the *Plain Dealer* chapter from withdrawing from the Association until September 10. That afternoon at an acrimonious general membership meeting whatever chance there had been for unity among the Cleveland newsmen was destroyed. The quick-tempered Ashcraft, who resented the attempts to placate the *Plain Dealer* newsmen because he believed that this would undermine the Association, scotched a possible settlement when he accused Donaldson of being a company stooge. Donaldson retorted in equally bitter language. Insults flew back and forth, and more newspapermen became involved in the argument. Finally, most of the *Plain Dealer* newsmen walked out, and at a caucus three days later they determined that their chapter should become an independent organization.[40]

The meeting resumed after the walk-out of the *Plain Dealer* newsmen, and officers were elected. White was chosen president, major factors in his selection being his trade-union experience and his knowledge of NRA's labor policies. Most of the Association membership had at best a rudimentary understanding of the management and functions of a collective bargaining association. Accordingly, they voted for White, a former journeyman printer and ITU member who had worked his way through college in the printing trades and who as labor editor of the *Press* had kept well informed about the relationships between NRA and labor.

The managements of the three Cleveland dailies had not yet taken any strong public stand on the activities of their editorial workers. Seltzer's outburst aside, the only important public reaction by a representative of management was a statement by Paul Bellamy, editor of the *Plain Dealer* and president of the American Society of Newspaper Editors (ASNE). He said that under NRA the newspapermen had a guaranteed right to organization and that he, for one, hoped that some good would come of it. Bellamy's statement notwithstanding, the Association's organizers believed that he and other front-office officials

on the three newspapers worked against them, for instance influencing the *Plain Dealer* editorial workers in their divisive
stand.[41]

Despite the division among the editorial workers on Cleveland's three English-language dailies, the Association grew
rapidly and continued its activities unabated. By mid-October it
had more than 200 members (102 out of 104 *News* and 104 out
of 107 *Press* editorial employees having signed membership
cards) and had begun making arrangements to take in feature
syndicate and press association writers working in Cleveland
as well as the editorial employees staffing the area's foreign-
language and suburban newspapers. As early as August 27, information had been supplied by members of the Association to
a Cincinnati newsman who had written for advice on how to
proceed with organization, and he was but the first of many
who wrote and received assistance; the Association, using
newspaper office supplies and machines, mimeographed its constitution and other materials, which were sent out in reply to
the numerous inquiries it received. In the following two months
the Cleveland newsmen, accurately described by White as
"furious letter writers," contacted friends and acquaintances
across the country in a drive to interest them in organization;
this letter writing campaign received an enormous boost from
the fact that the *Press* served as a training ground for the
Scripps-Howard chain and that former *Press* editorial staffers
could be found in widely scattered newspaper offices. Also, representatives from the Cleveland Association went to Akron,
Columbus, Toledo, and Youngstown, Ohio, and to Rockford,
Illinois, helping newspapermen there to organize. Moreover,
the Association sent two spokesmen to Washington, D.C., to
participate in the September hearings by NRA on the final
newspaper code; the proposals they presented differed little
from the code drawn up by the Philadelphia newsmen.[42]

Although the Cleveland group made very important contributions to the creation of the American Newspaper Guild, the
major effort came from the New York City editorial workers,
then perfecting their own organization. For several reasons the
organizational idea enjoyed greater success in that city than

elsewhere. The goal of most newspapermen, New York attracted a larger proportion of intelligent and energetic newsmen capable of developing an idea into reality. Also the size of the editorial working force necessary to produce the many dailies then published in New York meant that the organizers of the city's newsmen, though faced with some extra organizational problems because of sheer numbers, had a larger core of articulate and militant newspapermen to build on. In addition, this size assured the organizers that, with any success at all, they would have considerable support both in numbers and in funds (from dues). There is some indication, furthermore, that prior to 1933 many New York newsmen had contemplated organization as a solution to their economic woes. An English correspondent who had been stationed in New York for many years—during a talk in 1929 to the American Society of Newspaper Editors on the British Institute of Journalists—told the assembled editors that, based on his New York experiences, if conditions of newspaper employment did not improve, newsmen would organize to help themselves.[43] In early 1932 *Newsdom*'s bitter stories and editorials about the plight of newspapermen (which had concluded with the publication of the open letter to Broun) evoked strong reactions from New York editorial workers. One, who summed up the general tenor of the correspondence *Newsdom* received on this issue, wrote: "Allow me to suggest a constructive measure you could advance . . . unionizing the city rooms and other editorial rooms of newspapers. . . . I am not suggesting anything drastic. The important thing right now is the creation of an organization."[44] Finally, New York City was the home base of Broun, and he gave generously of his time and money, badgered his friends and contacts, and lent his prestige to the cause.

Immediately after publication of his August 7 column calling for a union of reporters, Broun told an interviewer that he was really "very serious" about the matter and was thinking over the best way to proceed. He added that he had chosen October 1 as the target date for the beginning of the organization drive because he wanted to wait until the New York City election had been held so that he would not have to divide his time between politics (he supported La Guardia) and organization work.[45] Seeing that election day in 1933 was November 7 and that La Guardia did not have to run in the September primaries, why Broun chose October 1 remains a mystery that even his closest associates could not explain.[46] In any event, the October date almost immediately became meaningless because Broun began holding at his home informal meetings which had the dual purpose of drawing up some kind of protest to the publishers' code and laying the groundwork for an organization to better newsmen's working conditions. No doubt, one reason for Broun's disregard of the October date he had set was the enthusiastic response his column engendered. Another reason lies in the character of Broun himself. A man of great enthusiasms, he could not wait that long to test his ideas. As Leon Svirsky, at that time a colleague of Broun on the *World-Telegram,* has suggested, the columnist could not resist talking about a union or a protest against the publishers' code, finding out who would support him, how this would be done.[47]

The precise date of the first of these meetings cannot be determined. On September 15, 1933, Broun told *Editor & Publisher* that meetings had been held during the past four or five weeks. George Britt remembers that Broun asked him to the first meeting, which took place a few days after Britt's return to New York on August 10 from a reporting trip abroad. Morris Ernst, who attended a few of the meetings, recalls only that some took place in mid-August. On the reverse side of Roberts' August 20 telegram to Broun informing him about organization in Cleveland, the columnist's secretary Luella Henkel had jotted down in shorthand the basis for the reply Broun wanted sent, which indicated that at a meeting on August 23 an attempt would be made to establish some form of temporary organization in New York City.[48] From these shorthand jottings it can be inferred that some meetings had been held earlier to lay the groundwork for this action.

Confusion also exists about who attended these early meetings in Broun's apartment and how many took place. Any written records that might have existed seem to have disappeared, and memories have faded, often resulting in conflicting recollections of who was there and precisely what was said. Myths have grown up about these meetings and the number of newsmen who claim to have attended has become legion. Wilbur E. Bade, a former ANG official, has commented sarcastically: "There were 5,000 [at those meetings] . . . counting all the guys I've heard say they attended." The composition of the group varied from meeting to meeting. Conflicting assignments, vacations, and occasional trepidation caused a considerable turnover. Altogether, according to Carl Randau, one-time president of the New York Guild, some fifty men and women attended at least one session at Broun's. Among those who are remembered by more than one participant as having taken part in at least one of these meetings were some of the city's most respected editorial workers, including Edward Angly, George Britt, Jonathan Eddy, Doris Fleeson, Lewis Gannett, James Kieran, Joseph Lilly, Carl Randau, Allen Raymond, Leon Svirsky, and Morris Watson. From all available accounts, it seems that four or five meetings were held at Broun's home.[49]

These evening meetings took place in the columnist's cluttered, book-lined study, a not overly large room which could accommodate about 15 to 18 people comfortably. To the first meeting Broun invited not more than ten people, chosen because he knew them well, most of whom were editorial workers of some prominence. Discussion focused less on establishing a union than on obtaining a fair shake from NRA for newspapermen. At the end of the evening, Broun suggested that each of those interested in what had been discussed return a week later with two or three others from his newspaper who might help in the formulation of plans. The tenor of the meetings was very informal; some participants sat on the floor, others sprawled on available furniture. Broun would broach his ideas, asking "will you come along"; others outlined their points of view. Although there was general agreement that action must be taken to protest the inequities of the publishers' code and the general policy of the publishers, even at this embryonic stage there existed among these few newspaper workers a sharp division of opinion about whether any prospective organization should be a union or a more exclusive professional association with limited aims. Doris Fleeson remarked a short time later that "we debated prayerfully whether our pallid infant organization should be named guild, union, or institute." Some suggested that the word union might be too strong, and finally the little group settled on the term guild as a compromise name that would reconcile the differing schools of thought. The full title decided on was Guild of New York Newspaper Men and Women. Precisely who first suggested the use of the word guild is not known. Without presenting any kind of documentation, Broun's biographer claims the honor for him. Lewis Gannett believes that a *New York Times* newsman first proposed using the term, and Lloyd White recalls being told that Edward Angly of the *Herald Tribune* had suggested the name. Others recall various persons introducing the word at several meetings.[50]

There was little of the conspiratorial about these meetings; although fear of the publishers existed, the evening gatherings were by no means a tightly held secret. Knowledge about them spread by word-of-mouth to the offices of all newspapers in the city. According to some reports, more than 200 New York City editorial workers had endorsed the guild's program before its first formal organization session. This program, developed by the guild's organizers, differed from the stated aims of the Cleveland and Philadelphia newsmen only in that it was more ambitious. As outlined in a flier distributed before the first mass meeting, it called for: (1) a five-day, forty-hour week with consecutive days off; (2) paid vacations; (3) a minimum wage of at least $35 a week to newsmen who had one year or more newspaper experience; and (4) dismissal notice on a graduated basis (ranging from one month's notice for newsmen with three years' service on the same newspaper to six months for those with eight or more years' service). The program also took into account a more important future role for the guild in demanding the elimination of Section 14 in the temporary newspaper code, which stated that contract bargaining between newsman and publisher "free from the interference of any third party shall not be affected by this code" and that nothing in the code would necessitate that an employee must "join any organization or refrain from joining . . . in order to secure or obtain employment."[51]

On September 7 NRA had announced that hearings on the final newspaper code probably would begin September 22. Broun and his colleagues decided to call a general meeting of the city's newsmen, believing that the time had come to mass support publicly for their program. On September 14, notices on New York City newspaper bulletin boards announced that on Sunday night, the 17th, at 10 p.m. there would be an open meeting at the City Club to consider a code for newspapers and to select a committee to go to the NRA hearings to oppose certain provisions of the publishers' code.[52]

About 300 attended the meeting, chaired by Joseph Lilly, a respected *World-Telegram* reporter. Lilly defined the objectives of the gathering, adding cautiously that "we are not meeting in any hostility to publishers." The other speakers at the meeting concerned themselves principally with the newspaper code. Broun, introduced as "the only person connected with a New York newspaper who had the courage to start this thing," attacked the publishers' code and urged cooperation with newsmen elsewhere who planned to send representatives to the hearings. Paul Y. Anderson, an outspoken critic of the publishers' code, answered questions about NRA and the newspapermen. He said that newsmen need not be afraid of prosecuting their interests at the hearings because "the law protects you, [and] if anyone attempts to punish you he is going to have a lot of trouble." Anderson's attitude can be summed up by his statement that "the people who holler the loudest are going to get the most." Edward Angly briefly outlined the deliberations that had gone into the drafting of the program. W. Ian Mack, a *World-Telegram* financial writer, concluded the evening's planned oratory with a description of the operations of the Scranton Newswriters Union.[53]

Even though it was a sultry night, discussion in the crowded meeting room lasted well past midnight. Although many spoke, little argument took place. "Few hints were heard that night," recalled Kenneth Stewart, "of the sharp differences that would split us later, the political charges and countercharges, the personal antagonisms." The editorial workers who attended the meeting generally shared the same vague feelings about the announced objectives, and the question of tactics (which soon proved to be an important divisive factor) received very little attention. Unsure of the publishers' reaction to their activity, the newspapermen decided, in order to avoid possible retribution, that, except for the organizers, speakers did not have to state their names or newspaper affiliations. Before the gathering adjourned, Angly, Broun, Fleeson, and Lilly were selected to serve on a committee that would represent the New York newspapermen at the NRA hearings. Disagreement about who should be the fifth member led the assembled newsmen to give the committee the power to decide this; after the meeting the committee enlarged its number by including Morris Watson, an Associated Press correspondent; James Kieran, a *Times* reporter with ties to President Roosevelt; and Francis Emery, a *Brooklyn Eagle* newsman. The meeting also empowered the committee to serve as a steering group in the formation of a permanent organization. Morris Ernst, Broun's friend and attorney and a very active, tough-minded liberal lawyer, was chosen at the meeting to serve as the committee's legal adviser. The assembled newsmen also passed by an overwhelming margin two resolutions. One assessed all present a dollar each to help defray the expenses of the committee's trip to Washington. The other praised the *Daily News* and the *World-Telegram* for going beyond the letter of the temporary newspaper code and extending additional benefits to editorial workers.[54]

This September 17 meeting elicited little overt reaction from publishers. One told Marlen Pew that the organization movement "makes just another publisher problem" and that he had no objection to groups such as the New York Guild if organized newsmen "would remain as free and loyal as they are as individuals."[55] His seeming disinterest and lack of opposition obviously stemmed from the anticipation that the guild and its counterparts in other cities, if they survived, would be little more than social or fraternal organizations. The New York *Daily News* took a different tack. In a lengthy editorial the newspaper admitted that it did not like the prospect of having to deal collectively with its editorial workers. However, the editorial declared, given the publishers' evasions and twisted interpretations of the code, the newspapermen could not be blamed for organizing to protest actions contrary to the spirit of NRA.[56]

In general, from the time of the Cleveland Association's creation until just before the NRA hearings, the publishers—if the
trade press can at all be considered an accurate barometer of
newspaper industry sentiment—had viewed the organization
movement with considerable interest but with only a modicum
of fear. The most important trade publication of the newspaper
industry, *Editor & Publisher,* stressed the editorial employees'
importance and declared that their protests had some justifica-
tion. About the Cleveland Association it said that "the association . . . has served salutary notice and good may come of it."
A month later it made a similar statement about the New York
Guild and the other editorial groups that had sprung up, adding
that while it had heard of no publisher resistance, the publishers
evidently were divided on the question of editorial organization.
The American Press, which addressed itself principally to small-
town and rural newspapers, stressed a different point of view,
one which received considerable emphasis in the following
months. In the magazine's September issue (distributed about
the middle of the month), a statement signed by editor Frank
Parker Stockbridge declared that everyone engaged in the business of journalism, from publisher to copy boy, could "without
compromising a single principle or sacrificing their dignity or
importance subscribe to a program or organization on strictly
professional lines, having for its purpose the elevation of professional standards of competence and ethics." Stockbridge
concluded, however, by declaring that establishing a union
would be a distinct step backwards. *Newsdom,* New York
oriented but nationally distributed, concentrated on explaining
the evils of editorial unions and asserted in its September 9
issue that a good editorial worker did not need a union to
protect him.[57]

An increasing number of editorial workers, however, believed it necessary to organize in some form. In the week just
prior to the NRA hearings Newark newsmen (aided and strongly
influenced by their New York colleagues) established the Guild
for Newark Newspaper Men and Women, Buffalo editorial
workers at a general meeting considered forming an associa-

tion, and a group of Twin Cities reporters and desk men called a meeting for the purpose of organizing. During the first few days of September, the Rockford, Illinois, newspaper staffs (aided by representatives of the Cleveland group) had organized as the Rockford Editorial Employees Association. An *American Press* survey conducted by mail at the beginning of September, although limited in scope, gives some idea of how newsmen across the country at this time felt about organization and what they hoped to achieve. Of 500 replies to a questionnaire (which went to a cross-section varied enough to include a Philadelphia reporter, a Kansas City deskman, an Eastern publisher, and a New Jersey managing editor), 76 percent favored organization; of those opposed, two-thirds were either publishers or editors in chief. Almost every reporter or desk man responding wanted closer ties among editorial workers; 20 percent would have had journalists form a union, 40 percent preferred organization along professional lines, and the rest saw merit in a combination of these two methods. Only 4 percent of all those answering had any interest in an organization of newspaper workers that dealt solely with wages; 20 percent considered the securing of job tenure the most important objective an organization could have; 32 per cent (a figure slightly higher than the percentage of executives in the sample) stressed the elevation of professional standards; the remainder held all three aims as goals of equal importance. Of all the newsmen polled, 60 percent firmly believed that their newspaper bosses would strongly oppose any movement to fix minimum salaries and maximum hours or to secure job tenure. Indications of the accuracy of this belief came almost immediately at the NRA hearings—the first real public confrontation of the publishers and representatives of the editorial workers.[58]

In effect the publishers brought about this open clash. Despite their editorial praise for NRA, many of them resisted its attempts to work out any but the loosest kind of code for the newspaper business. Pleading freedom of the press and tenaciously making use of all the power the industry commanded, the publishers' representatives succeeded in obtaining a temporary code replete with special concessions, a number of which disappointed editorial employees who had hoped it would result in improved working conditions. Although disappointed, the majority of editorial employees retained their faith in NRA, believing that if they presented a forceful enough case something would be done about the concessions before the code became final. Even before the temporary code's provisions had become known, in various areas some newspapermen—disconcerted by the attitude the publishers had displayed—discussed banding together. In advancing this course of action, which rarely envisioned organization on more than the local level, these newspapermen argued that an organized group would have a more powerful voice than a series of individuals. Brouns' column advocating a "union of reporters" accelerated the interest in organization albeit not exactly in the direction he had indicated. Comparatively few newspapermen had any real interest in a union; indeed, most of those who accepted the need for organization did so mainly because they thought it would lead to a code more beneficial to editorial workers. The old rivalries and myths lived on, often hampering organization, but by mid-September (after just a few weeks of organizational effort) editorial workers, most notably in Cleveland, on the local level had joined together as never before. Even if not quite ready, they stood willing to challenge at the NRA hearings on the final code the publishers, whose reluctance to give even a little had resulted in this confrontation.

3 ·

organization

"Knees quaking in fear," a handful of newsmen from New York, Cleveland, and Philadelphia went to Washington in mid-September 1933 to advocate the cause of the editorial department employees at the NRA hearings on the final newspaper code.[1] These hearings took place September 22-23 in the spacious auditorium of the Department of Commerce building. Presiding over them was an NRA Deputy Administrator, Lindsay Rogers, a toughminded Columbia University professor of public law and government. Rogers, after having helped draw up one of the garment industry codes, had been appointed August 24 to handle the drafting of codes for the publishing and allied printing industries (which included the daily newspaper publishing business).[2]

Flanked by seven men from the various NRA advisory boards, Rogers opened the proceedings promptly at 10:00 a.m. on Friday the 22nd, "in the terse impersonal manner of a professor opening a seminar," according to one journalist observer.[3] Despite the dissatisfaction which had been expressed during the preceding five weeks by many editorial employees, government officials, and mechanical union leaders and workers with the temporary newspaper code adopted August 15, the publishers now proposed that, with only insignificant changes, it become the final newspaper code. Elisha Hanson, who presented it, asked for only two minor amendments. He requested that Section 13 be changed so that publishers could seek a stay of the wages and hours provisions of the code not only where a labor shortage existed but also where enforcement of the provisions would cause economic hardship, and he introduced another section that would set up a Code Authority to administer the code. The authority would be composed of three non-voting members appointed by the President of the United States, five ANPA directors, and five representatives from regional trade associations (he named the New England Daily Newspaper Association, the Southern Newspaper Publishers Association, the Del-Mar-Va Association, the Inland Daily Press Association, and the Pacific Northwest Association).[4]

The industry made no move to meet criticisms of its stand on the code. On the contrary, Hanson and the six other spokesmen for the publishers praised the code, justified its more controversial sections (such as that which allowed children under 16 to sell newspapers in the street) and asked for even more preferential treatment. Indeed, the only other amendment offered by the publishers asked that the limitations on maximum weekly working hours be raised to 48 in small towns and 44 in larger communities, saying that the extra working time gained thereby would enable publishers, especially those in small towns, to comply fully rather than just partially with the code.[5] This, said C. R. Butler—president of the Inland Daily Press Association—would relieve them from the ignominy of operating with a "wounded eagle," that is, a blue eagle with a white stripe across its breast, which NRA administrators in many areas granted employers who pleaded inability to meet a code's full terms.

The opponents of the proposed final code had their say after the luncheon recess and on the following day. On the afternoon of the 22nd, sandwiched between the social welfare contingent, who condemned the lenient child labor provisions, and the spokesman who deplored the absence of a fair trade practices clause from the code, were the editorial employees' spokesmen —eleven people, eight of them working journalists, representing fifteen groups of editorial workers in fourteen cities.[6] Edward Angly, Heywood Broun, Doris Fleeson, James Kieran, Alexander Lindey (a member of Ernst's law firm), and Morris

Watson appeared as representatives of the New York Guild. Lindey also had been authorized to speak for the Guild of Newark Newspaper Men and Women, the editorial workers of Buffalo, and the Headline Club of Boston (a year-and-a-half-old group self-described as "a social and benevolent organization"). The Cleveland Editorial Employees Association sent Lloyd White and its able counsel, Ohio State Senator Marvin C. Harrison. White also had been empowered by the newly formed editorial workers groups in Akron and Youngstown, Ohio, and in Rockford, Illinois, to speak for them. Paul Y. Anderson spoke for the Washington correspondents and Andrew M. Parker testified for the editorial employees of Philadelphia and Camden. The veteran Secretary of the AFL, Frank Morrison, represented the two surviving ITU newswriters unions in Scranton and Milwaukee (both had come under AFL jurisdiction) as well as the editorial workers' federal locals in Boston, Chicago, and Kansas City, Kansas—all that remained of the newswriters units the AFL had chartered between 1923 and 1933.[7]

Who in the government arranged for the editorial employees' spokesmen to testify remains unclear. Two days before the hearings began an Associated Press dispatch in *The New York Times*, subheaded "New York, Cleveland, and Philadelphia Newswriters Groups to be Represented at Hearing," reported that on September 19 Broun and Anderson had called on Johnson to outline their position. White recalls that the arrangements for him and Harrison to testify had been made through the latter's Grinnell College schoolmate Harry Hopkins, the Federal Emergency Relief Administrator. Rogers insists that nobody from the government approached him about letting the editorial workers' spokesmen testify. He remembers that Broun called on him in the week before the hearings to talk about the editorial workers and the code, and "against the strong efforts of the publishers I allowed him and a couple of others to make speeches during the hearings."[8]

Even though most of the editorial workers' spokesmen had little experience in presenting an argument publicly or speaking on behalf of others, they set forth the editorial workers' case cogently and vigorously. The six-delegate New York group, the first to testify for the editorial workers, allocated to each of its speakers except Lindey, who made the general introductory remarks, one aspect of the code to discuss. Lindey—who expressed amazement that in the three hours of hearings preceding his testimony no mention had been made of reporters—concluded his statement requesting changes in the proposed code by outlining the New York group's demands. These, which had been modified somewhat since the September 17 City Club meeting, included a five-day, forty-hour week with workdays to be consecutive wherever possible; a minimum wage scale of $20.00 a week for editorial workers with less than a year's experience, $30.00 for all newsmen with between one and two years' experience, and discharge notice, except in cases of gross and flagrant misconduct, ranging from one month for three years' continuous service to six months for eight years' and over.[9] Broun, whom Rogers remembers nipping occasionally at a gin-filled flask during the afternoon, made a colorful but reasoned speech asking for the removal from the code of the section protecting the open shop, which prohibited, as being a violation of the freedom of the press, third party (e.g., union) interference in contract bargaining between a publisher and his employees unless such a party already had played a role in negotiations.[10] Asserting that he knew many newsmen who feared for their jobs if they so much as talked about organization of any kind, Broun said: "you cannot have a free press which rests upon the fears and apprehensions of reporters who are frightened and who feel that they have good reason to be frightened." He added, in a statement which proved prophetic, that "if newswriting guilds cannot obtain those things which seem to us fair then newswriting unions will."[11] Edward Angly summed up the tenor of the remarks by the other New York delegates when he said that newspapermen "would like to be brought in as simple craftsmen and taken up on the heights of the Blue Eagle instead of being left down in the valley of ragged individualism."[12]

The two Cleveland representatives testified next. Harrison spelled out why the Cleveland Association's members believed that the final newspaper code should be much more explicit in regard to newspapermen.[13] Then came White, who presented the longest and most detailed statement of any of the editorial employees' spokesmen.[14] His beat had given him a thorough knowledge of labor affairs and NRA, and he outlined the editorial employees' case in a well-reasoned, thoroughly prepared brief which one chronicler of the hearings has called "the best exposition of the newspapermen's argument presented. . . ."[15] White, whose code proposals amplified the Cleveland Association's program, asked for amendments which differed only slightly from the New York group's requests. He asserted that the newsmen's fundamental objection to the code was that it seemed to place newspapermen "as a class beyond all hope of Roosevelt recovery."[16]

The next witness, Andrew Parker, asked for the adoption of the "Philadelphia code," which, except for being more comprehensive, differed little from the proposals of the New York Guild and the Cleveland Association representatives. The only editorial workers' spokesman to make specific accusations about publisher intimidation of editorial staffs, Parker expounded at length about the situation on the Philadelphia *Evening Bulletin*, where editorial workers had been cautioned not to sign the brief that was to be presented to NRA.[17] He also asserted that *Inquirer* newsmen "were told by an executive of that newspaper that it would be inadvisable for them to have anything to do with the hearing on the newspaper code."[18]

Later in the afternoon Anderson and Morrison concluded the testimony of the editorial workers' spokesmen. Anderson discussed not only what he considered unfair practices used by the wire services covering Washington, D.C., but also said that the proposed code was unjust in classifying as executives (and thus exempt from the NRA labor provisions) the one-man bureaus, that is, the men covering the capital for their home-town newspapers.[19] Morrison dealt with the question of pay and argued that newsmen should get a minimum wage commensurate with the education and enterprise their calling required. To that end he proposed that a minimum weekly wage be established by the final code and that $75.00 a week, rather than $35.00, serve to demarcate the exempt professional.[20]

Even though some of the other editorial workers' spokesmen gave more effective and lengthier presentations than did Broun, his remarks received the bulk of the press coverage. This situation generally prevailed for the next few years in the reporting of the organizational activities of the editorial workers. Deservedly or not, Broun usually received the lion's share of attention.

The appearance of the editorial workers' spokesmen at the code hearings was a turning point in the pre-natal history of the American Newspaper Guild. This was probably the first time editorial employees from different localities came together not for a social event or to cover a story, but as workers consciously concerned with common economic problems and anxious to do something about them. Indeed, the testimony by the editorial employees' spokesmen set the newspapermen's problems and desires on the national stage and raised the possibility of national organization. Years later, Rogers said he believed that the appearance of the editorial workers' spokesmen at the hearings "permitted a good deal of publicity for the proposed Newspaper Guild and enabled it to be organized earlier and with a larger membership than otherwise would have been possible." Broun, writing in mid-November on the effects of the hearings, stated that after he and the other editorial workers' spokesmen had testified, it had become evident that representation before NRA must be regarded as only a first step. Typical of the immediate response of many newsmen to the testimony of the editorial workers' spokesmen is a letter to Broun from Dave Abramson, a Harrisburg, Pennsylvania, reporter. He referred to the columnist's statement about newswriting unions and declared: "just what you have in mind I do not know, but I certainly am ready to do everything I can to make this effort . . . a success."[21]

At the close of the hearings on the 23rd Rogers said that probably it would take at least a week or ten days to formally dispose of the code.[22] However, it took much longer; for almost three months Rogers and other NRA officials negotiated with the publishers to work out the details of the final newspaper code.

The publishers' actions during this time did nothing to allay unrest and dissatisfaction among the editorial workers. A considerable number of newspapers did institute a five-day, forty-hour week for their editorial employees, but many publishers took advantage of the temporary newspaper code provision that exempted from the NRA maximum-hour limitations as professionals all newsmen earning $35.00 or more a week. A Dallas newsman reported that all editorial workers there whose services the publishers "deemed necessary for longer than forty hours, were raised to the $35.00 minimum . . . and . . . worked without regard for the number of hours." The New York Guild received several complaints from outside the city about dailies which had boosted reporters' salaries to $35.00 a week; in some instances the weekly pay raise had been as little as $.50. An *American Press* correspondent claimed that a Midwestern publisher planned to pay all of his reporters $35.20 a week. The analysis of the temporary code prepared by the Pennsylvania Newspaper Publishers Association for its members stated that "if all members of your editorial staff receive more than $35.00 a week there is no limit under NRA to the number of hours they may work in any one week." And in many smaller towns where the publishers of necessity supplemented their incomes by doing commercial printing and thus could choose to be regulated by the catch-all code regulating the printing industries, the exemption unit for weekly wages was $25.00. (The non-metropolitan publishers, a small part of the newspaper business both in terms of personnel and of circulation, had obtained this exemption through the efforts of their trade organization, the National Editorial Association [NEA], which had managed to have it made a substitute provision in the President's Reemployment Agreement.) By and large, the newspaper publishers could and did ignore the editorial workers and their demands. In the last six months of 1933 Elisha Hanson received enough letters and telegrams to fill two large folders asking for interpretations of the temporary code, but only two inquiries concerned editorial workers.[23]

The delay in working out the terms of the final newspaper code as well as the way in which the publishers' representatives presented the industry's case also aroused discontent among editorial workers. Much of the supposedly confidential code negotiations became public. The publishers' generally uncompromising approach to the issues raised at the hearings demonstrated, as a contemporary historian of the newspaper business put it, that the industry desired "the advantages of industrial integration without the responsibilities imposed by regulation." Walter Lippmann believed that the newspapers did not wish to have a code in the true meaning of the term and that it would be better if they said so frankly. Attempts to reach agreement on a code had little success. During October and November, in both Washington and New York, Lindsay Rogers met repeatedly with Hanson, with the publishers on the code committee, and with other publishers. He also held discussions with the heads of the mechanical workers' unions, which spokesmen for the editorial workers (mostly from New York), and with such other interested individuals as those opposing child labor. Despite the innumerable talks, exchanges of correspondence, and formal and informal conferences (including a two-day session in New York which essentially was a re-run of the September hearings), these negotiations failed to resolve many of the issues. The publishers did accept a suggestion, made November 1 by Morris Ernst, that a survey be undertaken within the next 30 days to gather the information necessary for establishing editorial workers' minimum wages. However, the survey, delayed in starting, took much longer than the proposed time limit. Generally, the publishers' position remained unchanged, especially their resistance that any code must include sections guaranteeing the freedom of the press and exempting the newspaper industry from Section 7a. The publishers argued that it was their duty to preserve freedom of the press including maintenance of the open shop where it existed, and their obligation to safeguard newspapers against any restrictive actions which might entail their ability to serve as forceful organs presenting independent opinions and news free from government control.[24] The legal expert Ernest Gross, then a lawyer with NRA, believes that the publishers seriously put forth their First Amendment defense but that few outside of the industry accepted it. It does seem, however, that more than just a few publishers hid behind legalisms to avoid having to pay their employees more and working them less. In any event, the publishers so publicized what they called a major threat to freedom of the press that controversy over it not only obscured the other issues but also created more discussion of that topic than at any time in the 135 years since the violent debates over the Sedition Act of 1798.[25]

Another stumbling block was the bickering between the ANPA, which wanted a single code for all newspapers, and the NEA, which argued that the ANPA-sponsored code ignored the plight of the non-metropolitan newspapers. The NEA said that small-town dailies and weeklies should have a choice between the proposed final newspaper code and the Graphic Arts Code's newspaper section, sponsored by the NEA, which took the non-metropolitan newspapers' interests into account. This competition between the trade associations dismayed many editorial workers because the NEA tried to make its code more attractive by declaring that under it non-metropolitan newspapers would be able to pay lower wages. After considerable negotiation between industry association representatives and government officials, the points of contention were cleared away to the satisfaction of the disputing associations, if not of the editorial workers. NRA finally resolved the problem by permitting two codes with substantially identical labor provisions insofar as they related to newspaper publication; each association dominated the code authority regulating the code it sponsored, and newspapers could choose the code they preferred. However, the commercial printing departments of newspapers were governed by the commercial printing section of the Graphic Arts Code, regardless of the code subscribed to by the publisher.[26]

Ultimately, an acrimonious meeting between Hanson and Donald Richberg, NRA's general counsel, paved the way for agreement on the proposed final newspaper code. At this meeting NRA capitulated to most of the publishers' demands.[27] The publishers' code committee formally presented its final draft, completed December 9, to NRA on December 11. The next day the draft went to the President for his inspection, an unusual step taken because, said Johnson, Roosevelt "wanted to see it." Within a few days it had been transmitted to the various NRA advisory boards, of which only the Labor Advisory Board offered any substantial objections. And these, which included protests about the low minimum wages, the extensive exemptions from the maximum-hour provisions, and the continuation of the newsboy system without greater safeguards for the children involved, were almost wholly ignored. On December 22 the proposed final newspaper code was transmitted officially to President Roosevelt for his approval.[28]

Pending the President's signature, NRA refused to release any information about the code's contents on the grounds that, as with other codes, he might insist on alterations. By this time, however, the code's provisions had leaked out by what *The New York Times* described as "unofficial but reliable sources," and *Editor & Publisher's* first two December issues had described features of the code.[29]

Upon learning of the details of the proposed final code on December 9, Jonathan Eddy, the secretary of the New York Guild, angrily wired Johnson: "UNDER THE CODE AD-VANCED . . . BY THE NEWSPAPER PUBLISHERS THE NEWS-PAPERMEN OF THIS COUNTRY ARE THE ONE GROUP COMPLETELY FROZEN OUT OF ALL IMMEDIATE BENEFITS UNDER THE NRA. . . ." Eddy had good cause for his ire. Although the final draft did not use a dollar figure to classify newsmen as professionals exempt from maximum-hour regulations, it remained vague as to which editorial workers would be considered professionals. Now the provisions of the section regulating hours would not apply to "professional persons employed in their professions, [or] to persons employed in a managerial or personal capacity," but no definition of these terms was given. Also, "news department workers" would continue to work under "present conditions" until such time as the Code Authority could conduct the survey necessary for obtaining the facts about hours and wages that the code "authorized" it to obtain. Further, the code made no provision for editorial employee representation on the Newspaper Industrial Board, the body designed to serve as a board of appeal in labor dis-

putes. (The addition of the NIB was the only major difference
in the code as presented to the NRA in December and as discussed at the public hearings in September.)[30]

What editorial employees thought of the code provisions
concerning them can be gleaned from a six-page memorandum
drawn up by a newspaperman and sent to the President in the
hope that it would influence him to alter some of the provisions.[31] The author deemed it essential that the code contain an
accurate definition of the term "news department worker," if
only to ensure that the proposed wages and hours survey fully
cover the employees who should be included. He doubted the
fairness of any survey conducted by the publishers and recommended that the Bureau of Labor Statistics undertake it.
The writer also suggested that instead of being merely "authorized," the survey be ordered and that a specific time limit for
conducting and concluding it be set, adding that "the publishers
took our suggestion for a survey eagerly only to turn it against
the news department worker in providing for additional delay
by seeking information on hours as well as wages." In objecting
to the vagueness of the terms "professional persons employed
in their profession" and "persons employed in a managerial or
personal capacity," the writer said that unless they were defined precisely, the terms might be stretched "to include anyone from a reporter covering a flea circus to an office boy sent
to the corner haberdashery to buy the publisher a brown shirt."

The publishers had succeeded in obtaining NRA acceptance
of almost everything they wanted. Unlike most other codes,
that for the newspaper industry contained no stipulations about
fair business practices. The code set low minimum wages for
mechanical and business department workers. Although the
publishers failed to obtain exemption from Section 7a and
although the open shop provisions vanished from the final draft
of the code, its Article VII contained a much amplified version
of the temporary code's section on freedom of the press, declaring that a publisher in accepting the final code did not
"consent to any modification thereof, except as each may
thereto subsequently agree, nor . . . [did] he waive any constitutional rights or consent to the imposition of any require-

ments that might interfere with the constitutional guarantee of freedom of the press." The publishers drew up the code in such a way that only those dailies which assented to it were bound by it. In other words, as the NRA historian of the code points out, "it was a purely voluntary code and as such was unique" among the over 540 adopted before the Supreme Court declared NRA unconstitutional on May 27, 1935. Throughout the life of NRA the publishers made use of Article VII and of the voluntary nature of their adherence to the code to cripple the attempts of the American Newspaper Guild to utilize the government agencies which had the duty to protect its rights. As the ANPA history of the code correctly states: "The Daily Newspaper Code became more of a protective and defensive measure for its member than the regulatory controlling system first contemplated by the NRA."[32]

If the final newspaper code had been more responsive to the aspirations of the newsmen than the temporary code had been, their 1933 organization movement might have faded away as ingloriously as had earlier ones. But in the weeks that followed the September NRA hearings, the publishers' public actions as well as what the rank-and-file editorial workers learned about code negotiations served only to spur on the organization movement. Most of the embryonic groups created prior to the hearings increased their membership and strengthened their organization. In other cities, editorial workers formed new local groups. The activity of this period can be summed up by the New York Guild announcement of November 23 that "dues-collecting groups existed in Boston, Buffalo, Cincinnati, Cleveland, Duluth, Minneapolis and St. Paul, New York, Philadelphia, Tulsa, and smaller centers"; that groups were being "formed in Birmingham (Ala.), Chicago, Detroit, Honolulu, Los Angeles, St. Louis, San Francisco, and smaller cities"; and that "state and regional associations were in the process of being created in Ohio, Oklahoma, Westchester County, and northern New Jersey." The New York Guild, which apparently based its announcement on reports (overoptimistic in some instances) from newsmen in these places, presented an inexact picture. The groups in Boston, Buffalo, Honolulu, and Philadelphia had not yet been organized formally; it took several years before permanent groups were formed in Chicago or Los Angeles. But the New York Guild did not exaggerate the scope of the rapidly spreading movement. As *Editor & Publisher* later commented, the mushrooming local newswriters groups were "the most powerful spontaneous organization [movement] ever seen in newspaper circles in this country."[33]

The methods of organization varied in detail from place to place, but usually, as in Cleveland and New York, a few men, sometimes only two or three, provided the impetus. A steering committee that at its largest numbered fewer than ten organized the Newspaper Guild of the Twin Cities of Minneapolis and St. Paul; these few newsmen had learned of Broun's ideas from his column and of the activities of other editorial workers elsewhere, and had posted calls on the editorial room bulletin boards of all newspapers published in the two cities for a meeting to discuss organization. Some Rockford, Illinois, newsmen in an almost superhuman effort drove 900 miles to Cleveland and back in one day to obtain enough firsthand information about the Cleveland Editorial Employees Association to organize their fellow workers. Ralph Holmes, the respected, well-paid theater critic of the *Detroit Times*, served as a prime mover in the organization of the Detroit Newspaper Guild (formally established in January 1934) as well as its first president; "no one surpassed him in his great desire to help alleviate some of the economic injustice . . . fastened on those who worked in the . . . offices of the local newspapers," said two Detroit newsmen, and a former Newspaper Guild official characterized Holmes as "the Broun of Detroit." Russ Wilson, a reporter on the *Des Moines Tribune*, wrote the New York Guild for information about organizing and volunteered to do what he could, even though he believed that the *Tribune*'s executives opposed the idea of an organized newsroom.[34]

Unusual reasons motivated some of the organizers of editorial workers' groups. The most extreme example of this took place in Buffalo, where the men most active in the formation of a guild were the founders of the year-old Buffalo Newspaper Club. They believed that if a guild started in Buffalo the Newspaper Club would die for lack of attention. Therefore, according to Oviatt McConnell, a *Buffalo Times* reporter and later the secretary of the Buffalo Guild, the desire to save the club was "the principal motive" of those who transformed it into a guild. For the majority of American newsmen, however, the compelling force that brought them together was a desire to have a voice in the disposition of the final newspaper code. As one editorial worker put it, the newsmen hoped to ensure that "the code . . . finally adopted contain such provisions as will enable newspaper editorial workers to obtain the full opportunities and advantages being made available to other classes of newspaper workers. . . ."[35]

The strength of the organization movement lay in the medium-sized cities and metropolitan centers of the Northeastern, Middle-Atlantic, and Midwestern states; in those same areas where the American Newspaper Guild had and has many of its chapters and most of its numerical strength. But in the autumn and early winter of 1933 the movement spread well beyond these areas. The seven-man editorial staff of the Columbia, South Carolina, *State* reacted favorably to the idea of organizing and indicated that it planned to win over the reporters on the afternoon newspaper. In Austin, Texas, newspaper workers formed a local group on December 17 after several meetings at which they discussed the pros and cons of organization. The few editorial workers in Sioux Falls, South Dakota, expressed an interest in forming some kind of group, and although nothing came of it, they did begin to organize.

With but few exceptions, successfully organized groups flourished, at least temporarily. On October 31 the two-day-old Cincinnati Newspaper Guild reported that of the city's 130 or so editorial workers, about 75 had signed up. Nathan J. Goldberg, a *Newark Star-Eagle* newsman active in the formation of the Newark group, in mid-November expressed amazement at the growth of its membership, which by then exceeded 125. The temporary executive committee of the Newspaper Guild of Philadelphia and Camden (whose editorial workers finally managed to establish a formal organization at the beginning of December) estimated on December 10 that of the 750 to 800

eligible to join in the two cities, over 350 had done so.[36] *Editor &
Publisher*, a few days earlier, commenting on the organization
movement had estimated that of the 40,000 to 50,000 editorial
workers in the country, at least 10 percent had signed up.[37]

In not a few instances newsmen eager to organize their fellow
newswriters failed in attempts to do so. Factors which had
hindered the earlier ITU and post-Armistice organizing attempts also served as deterrents at this time. Organizational
ferment, although widespread, was not nationwide. The apathy
of many newsmen as well as their dislike of organized labor
was exemplified by what happened when the local AFL branch
called a meeting of Madison, Wisconsin, newspapermen. One
of the three who showed up described the affair as "hardly a
howling success. . . . We sat on the curb in front of the Labor
Temple for an hour waiting for delegates, gave up, and adjourned at 9:02 for 3.2 [beer]." The past failures of other forms
of organization as well as the newsmen's traditional belief in
their superiority over unionized laborers accounted for some
hostility to organization. In Chicago, where some 15 years
earlier a press club had collapsed after the treasurer had ab-
sconded with the funds, a few newsmen tried to evoke interest
in forming a local group, but most of the editorial staffers shied
away from all efforts to organize. In response to an inquiry
from the New York Guild, two Chicago newsmen wired back
that "WE ARE NEWSPAPER WORKERS SATISFIED WITH
JOBS. . . . RECALL CASE MARTY CASEY DECEASED WHO
TRYING TO ORGANIZE GOTHAM REPORTERS OSTRA-
CIZED EIGHT YEARS. . . . CHICAGO NOW BUM PLACE FOR
RACKETEERING ESPECIALLY NEWSPAPERDOM. . . DITCH
DIGGERS HAVE UNIONS WE DONT." Fear of the publishers
also played an important role in dampening organizational enthusiasm in some areas. A Dallas newsman reported that he
had failed to bring his fellow newswriters together even for a
simple discussion of newspaper code proposals, saying that for
the publishers there "any meeting together of newspapermen
and women smacks of unionism . . . so the workers are afraid
even to meet."[38]

What Ashcraft later defined as "job terror" ("the feeling,

given the industry's economic condition, that it was this job or none") affected the organization movement, although not principally because of publishers' actions at this time. In some places lesser editorial executives, acting on the assumption that the publishers would object to organization, told newsmen not to join any group. Past experiences frightened many newsmen, and as a Boston reporter later flippantly remarked about early organization in that city, "if the publishers had said boo during the initial stages . . . every newspaperman in Boston would have quit. . . ." Incidents of intimidation took place, such as those Parker complained of during September NRA hearings or the case of Harry Visel, Sunday editor of a Newark newspaper, fired October 16 with five minutes' notice, who maintained that the discharge (directly ordered by the publisher) came because of his guild activities. Certainly, Broun expected active publisher opposition; Doris Fleeson believes that one reason Broun asked her to help in setting up a guild was that he, being mindful of her publisher's friendly attitude toward newsmen, thought she could speak up safely. Most publishers, however, were preoccupied with the formulation of a newspaper code and its effects on the industry. They paid little attention to the organization movement, remaining either indifferent to or unaware of the editorial workers' fears. *Editor & Publisher* in the first week of November said it could discover "no concerted publisher resistance to the guild idea. . . ."[39]

An interesting indicator of the publishers' unconcern is the trade press, which generally steered a middle course, neither condemning organization nor supporting the local groups. *Editor & Publisher*, while admitting it "spoke with caution" in the issue published just prior to the American Newspaper Guild's founding meeting, solemnly declared: "We have never doubted the right of the reporters to organize for betterment of their conditions . . . but we have had serious doubts about the form the organization should take" and concluded by again speaking out firmly against unionization of newspaper staffs. As the organization movement grew, the magazine (upon which for some time the majority of editorial employees relied for most of their information about the organization movement, there being few other sources of knowledge outside of correspondence about what newsmen across the country were doing until the end of November) emphasized the professionally oriented British Institute of Journalists and virtually ignored that country's larger but more economically minded National Union of Journalists. *The American Press* applauded the coming together of the newsmen in "common cause" and, though expressing antagonism to unionization, welcomed what it considered the organization movement's aims, which, it declared happily, included bringing about not only better working conditions but also elevation of the standards of journalism. Perhaps the strongest statement about the organization movement in the trade press at this time appeared in *Publishers Service Magazine*, which primarily served small-town dailies and weeklies. It published on its front page parts of a letter written by New York *Daily News* rewrite man Nelson Robins, president of the then recently defunct New York Press Club, to *Editor & Publisher*. *Publishers Service* highlighted some of Robins' strong statements against any but a professional association and declared that "amid the recent clamor for organization of editorial department employees it is heartening and encouraging . . . to hear at least one voice crying out for the maintenance of an ideal, which, so we believe, is not only important but vital to those who devote their lives to newspaper careers."[40]

Some among the publishers appreciated the potential consequences of the organization movement. E. H. Harris, the publisher of the Richmond, Indiana, *Palladium-Item*, warned the Inland Daily Press Association convention in mid-October that newspaper managements must be wary; otherwise, their news departments would fall under the control of trade unions. Harvey J. Kelly, chairman of the ANPA's Special Standing Committee, which dealt with labor problems, wrote Hanson in mid-November about his concern in regard to organization, especially as it would affect rates of pay. Kelly, somewhat prophetically, argued that the organizers had made it necessary to consider all employees (not just union members) when any adjustment of pay scales took place; if the publishers failed to do so they would have to give in later anyway and in "some instances under the humiliation of a pistol at the back of the . . . neck in the form of union demands with the alternative of a strike in departments not heretofore organized."[41]

Many newsmen active in the organization movement at this time shared Kelly's concern about the transformation of the local groups into trade-union units. These newsmen accepted the fact that organization might be necessary to share in the benefits NRA accorded salaried employees but had no interest in forming a union, which they believed would put them in the same class as the mechanical workers they scorned. These newsmen supported organization because they hoped to better what they considered their profession as well as their working conditions and they believed that they could use gentlemanly tactics to achieve their ends as did the members of the other professional associations; they had no intention of forcing the publishers to terms through strikes, picket lines, or other trade-union tactics nor did they have any long-range economic goals in mind. Nelson Robins had voiced their ideas when he had written *Editor & Publisher* declaring that "a newspaperman can become a union laborer and demand and get a maximum daily stint, assurance of a minimum wage, and pay for overtime, but if he does he'll sell his birthright for the thinnest mess of pottage ever used in barter."[42]

Yet a third way of thinking existed in many of the local editorial workers' groups, although this view usually was held by only a few newsmen. They expressed agreement with the union idea, but preferred an even more radical step, affiliation with organized labor (i.e., seeking AFL charters). Broun described himself in the fall of 1933 as part of "a very tiny group which believes that the inevitable goal . . . should be affiliation with the American Federation of Labor."[43]

Debate about the direction the editorial groups should take, once organized, took place in many areas; the constitutions drawn up by the newly formed groups reflect the decisions they finally made. Though the union idea never triumphed explicitly at this time, one of two views (professional or economic orientation) usually predominated and determined the group's day-to-day operations. One indication of a group's orientation was its criterion for membership eligibility; a group with economic goals in mind would bar publishers' representatives, or employees with the right to hire and fire, for both might be hindrances or embarrassments. The stated constitutional purpose of the Duluth Newspaper Guild (organized in mid-October) was "to advance the newspaper craft economically and professionally," and it did not accept as eligible managing editors, editors in chief, and those performing like duties although bearing other titles. On the other hand, the leaders of the Oklahoma Newspaper Guild of Tulsa (established in mid-November) asserted that they contemplated a professional organization along the lines of the Institute of Journalists and made eligible for membership any editorial department employee up to publisher.[44]

In New York, despite circumstances which roughly paralleled those of Cleveland, the editorial workers' group avoided splintering.[45] Broun, some of the committee members who had gone to Washington to testify, and a few other newsmen had met informally during the last days of September in Broun's apartment and had drawn up a constitution and bylaws which, while retaining the word guild in the title, would have established an economically oriented organization. The first general public discussion of these drafts took place at an open meeting held at the City Club the evening of October 1, during which the differences of opinion among the supporters of the organization movement in New York became obvious. Instead of considering the constitution and bylaws article by article, as had been planned, the assembled newsmen discussed Article I—renaming the organization the Newspaper Guild of New York—for most of the evening, debating the use of the word guild instead of union or association. So much time was taken up that after finally adopting Article I, the meeting voted to shelve the proposed constitution and bylaws and to have representatives selected by the editorial staffs in the various newspaper and press association offices use the drafts as a basis for working out new proposals to be presented to the membership for their approval. These decisions represented a victory for the conservative group, led by Allen Raymond, a *New York Herald Tribune* re-

porter of unusual prestige. After the meeting, the Guild steering committee added Raymond to its membership. Within ten
days a new constitution, primarily the work of Morris Ernst,
had been written and approved by delegates representing 15
New York dailies and press association offices. On October 18
members of the guild assembled once more at the City Club
to adopt a constitution. Speedy approval was given the proposed framework, which set up the New York Guild as an
organization composed of shop units, or chapters, each of which
would include all of the eligible editorial department workers
employed at a particular newspaper or press association office,
and which provided for a Representative Assembly composed
of elected delegates (one for every twenty-five members in any
office and one for any fraction of ten or more in that office).
The membership would elect by plurality vote guild officers (all
unsalaried) who could be nominated either by the Representative Assembly or by petition among the membership. Dues were
set at $1.00 a month. (However, initial difficulties in collection
meant that the guild continued to be dependent on group collections, individual contributions by Broun and others for a
number of immediate expenses, and the largesse of such bene-
factors as the Eastern Air Transport Company, which had
flown to Washington free of charge the New York newsmen
who had testified at the NRA hearings.)[46]

Controversy throughout the meeting focused primarily on the
article that outlined the guild's purpose, and debate raised
anew the questions of whether the guild would have the power
to carry on collective bargaining either under the NRA or
independently of it. The newsmen finally voted to accept the
proposed text, which defined the guild's purposes as "to improve the conditions under which newspaper men and women
work; to protect their rights of collective action; to raise the
standards of journalism, and for mutual help." Only after much
heated discussion did the newsmen vote editors with the right
to hire and fire eligible for membership and accept that the
executive committee exclusively "shall have the right to act
collectively for the whole membership . . . or for any specific
chapter," albeit the committee could do this only on instruc-

tions from the Representative Assembly, and any negotiations would be subject to ratification by the membership. This meant that although the guild could bargain collectively for its members, it could not do so easily.[47]

The constitution and the bylaws in their entirety satisfied very few New York guildsmen. Many saw what they considered flaws in the compromise provisions adopted. The unionists, who had hoped for a more economically oriented organization, had been forced to scuttle many of their ideas. However, most of the unionists, like Broun, realized the necessity of "hammering out a constitution satisfactory to the majority. . . ." Conversely, Ernst remembers that some disgruntled newsmen told him that the constitution represented a step away from their concept of a middle-class journalists' association. A few guild members, upset by what they considered the non-professional implications of the organization, resigned. Despite disparate opinions about what had been accomplished, a constitution and bylaws had been adopted, and, as a contemporary observer pointed out, "the wonder" was not that they contained faults, "but that out of the welter of conflicting ideas and emotions . . . [was] finally achieved a form acceptable" to all but a few guildsmen.[48]

Compromise also marked the selection of officers. The members, in a mail ballot at the beginning of November, approved the slate drawn up by the Representative Assembly, whose nominations for one-year terms included Raymond for president, Broun for first vice president, and Jonathan Eddy for secretary.[49] These men were installed on November 15. The choice of Raymond, remembered by several early New York Guild members as not being offensive to anyone, represented a concession to those members who considered Broun's ideas on organization too controversial or too radical. Opinion differs as to why Broun chose not to fight for the presidency—he could have won any contest for office handily. Some reasons given include: he was too lazy; he wanted the presidency but did not want to split the guild; he did not want the presidency because he believed his heading the guild would make it seem too much a one-man show; he knew a national organization was in the offing and preferred to head that. Whatever the precise reason, Broun, without any visible indication of disappointment, opted for the first vice presidency.

Jonathan Eddy, the diligent, intelligent newsman who had been elected secretary, later said that he obtained the office because of his availability (his work as a general assignment reporter for the *Times* on the city and suburban beats kept him in New York) and because of his willingness (nobody else had expressed much interest in being secretary). It was not personal dissatisfaction that led to Eddy's activity in the organization movement, although some former colleagues described him as a disgruntled "bar stool Socialist." An employee of *The New York Times* since shortly after his graduation from Cornell in 1924, Eddy (according to *Newsweek*) had "soon become one of the paper's ace reporters," and he earned, even after Depression-inspired pay cuts, more than $95.00 a week in 1933. Moreover, his family was reasonably well off. Yet, despite his financial advantages, Eddy had become fascinated with the idea of helping newspapermen better their situation. Although at first not as openly radical as Broun (Eddy initially spoke out against AFL affiliation), he did assert an insistence upon "our rights" under the NRA provisions for collective bargaining. In pursuit of this goal Eddy said he envisaged an organization "capable of collecting the cold hard facts so necessary for effective negotiations." He attended some of the early meetings in Broun's apartment and took an active part in various organizational activities. By October 10, 1933, he had become secretary *pro tem* of the New York Guild. Previously, Broun's personal secretary Luella Henkel had handled what guild correspondence or other secretarial duties there had been. Eddy had retained his *Times* job when he accepted the unsalaried secretaryship; he assumed that the duties could be handled readily in his spare time. But his guild duties rapidly took up more and more of his time as much of the day-to-day work devolved upon him. Although the guild hired stenographic help and office space for Eddy from its limited funds, his work load remained heavy. He became so overburdened that one former guildsman remembers him at times as "almost literally walking in his sleep." Eddy deserves considerable credit for his endeavors then and later, even though he sometimes acted erroneously or foolishly. In the New York Guild as later in the national organization he labored in Broun's shadow, and, sadly, his unstinting efforts generally were unrecognized. Many people associate Broun with the formation of a national editorial workers' organization, but few remember Eddy, who handled many of the necessary details which led up to the Washington meeting that founded the American Newspaper Guild.[50]

Interest in organization on a national basis had been expressed as early as mid-September, 1933, by some of the organizers of the local editorial workers' groups. Prior to their appearance at the NRA hearings, some of the newsmen who had come to Washington to testify had met together; among the topics they had discussed was, in Bordner's words, "employing an organization secretary to help organize and integrate the incipient newspaper guilds about the country." On September 19, Edward Burks, a *Tulsa Daily World* assistant city editor who had helped establish a group there, wrote Broun inquiring about his intentions and declared that "it is the opinion of the boys on the *World* that the New York newspapermen were too modest, or else lacking the leadership expected of them, in forming the New York Guild. It should have been formed on a national basis."[51]

Little more than expressions of interest could be accomplished at this time. A paucity of information about the various local groups hampered any one from undertaking a concerted national drive. For example, although the New York Guild in the statement it presented to NRA just prior to the September hearings forthrightly declared that its "aims are one with the aims of the organizations of newspaper writers elsewhere," but it introduced this declaration with the lame assertion that "we are informed that newspaper writers in other principal cities have organized . . . or are about to. . . ." An even clearer indication of the ignorance resulting from isolation comes in Eddy's reply to Burks' letter (which, like so many others, had been turned over to him to answer). After describing in detail the methods necessary for organization, Eddy added "of course you already may have done so without our knowing it."[52]

As the local editorial workers' groups which sprouted during the fall began to function more smoothly, correspondence helped to lessen the individual groups' isolation and intensified the desire for a national organization. Although *Editor & Publisher* covered the development of the organization movement, copies were not always readily available everywhere, and the magazine's reports sometimes lacked depth, giving little more than a group's date of organization and the names of its officers. Many newsmen interested in organization wrote to Broun or the New York Guild, which received some publicity outside the trade press, to obtain more detailed information on how to proceed. Eddy in his replies to the many letters of inquiry, besides answering the questions raised, usually made two points. He asked his correspondents to keep the New York Guild informed of their group's activities and he suggested that they call their organization a newspaper guild. He wrote a newsman in Cleveland, "why not Newspaper Guild of Cleveland. This form implies the existence of many organizations of the same structure and suggests the community of purpose shared by us all." Eddy also believed that a uniformity of title would facilitate national organization.[53]

Cleveland was among the first of the local editorial workers' groups to adopt Eddy's suggestion. On October 17 the Cleveland Association's members voted to change its name to the Cleveland Newspaper Guild. The membership also voted that "the executive committee be instructed to proceed with plans for affiliation with newspaper guilds in other cities, to the end that a national association of newspapermen may be formed an a convention held in this city." Three days later the executive committee of the Cleveland Guild voted to invite the New York group to sponsor jointly such an association. These actions marked the first formal steps toward a national organization of editorial workers, but the Cleveland group lacked the wherewithal necessary to implement their plans. It had done much to arouse the interest of newspapermen, especially in the Midwest, and it had made substantial contributions to national organization; but without the activities of the New York group the American Newspaper Guild could not have come into existence. As the secretary of the Duluth Newspaper Guild wrote

Eddy, "we hope that you will tackle the rather big job of getting a national organization started. New York has the prestige with newspapermen throughout the country that is needed to make such a thing go."[54]

Even though in many places editorial workers' groups had barely established themselves or were still little more than committees of organizers transforming interested editorial employees into a formal organization, the New York newsmen pressed forward with the idea of a national organization. On October 25, 1933, the New York Guild invited newspapermen's groups in Buffalo, Cleveland, Newark, Philadelphia, and the Twin Cities to join with it in calling a meeting of representatives of newspaper organizations from all parts of the country to form a national organization with headquarters in Washington. Said Eddy in his letter of invitation: "the proposal is to meet on December 15, 1933 . . . in Washington."[55] The invitations gave few details and made no mention of collective bargaining possibilities. The proposed organization's stated purpose, besides extending what already had taken place on a local level, would be to influence NRA on behalf of newspapermen. The invitation assumed that distinct advantages could be gained for newsmen from NRA by organizing before final approval of the code took place, for Eddy concluded by saying that "if . . . it turns out that Presidential approval will be earlier than we expect, it may be necessary to change the date of the meeting."

Because of developments in the drafting of the code, discussion of the proposed Washington meeting took place among representatives of most of the invited groups much sooner than could have been expected. Although this next step in bringing the local editorial workers' organizations into closer contact was taken by the New York Guild, an outside source supplied the initiative. Lindsay Rogers believed that the editorial workers should have spokesmen at the October 31-November 1 conferences in New York, which would deal with various aspects of the code. On very short notice he asked the New York Guild to coordinate the demands of the various groups and to speak for the newswriters. Thus, on October 26, one day after he had sent out the invitations, Eddy communicated by telegram and air-mail letter with all the editorial groups across the country that the New York Guild knew existed, asking them "to send a delegate to New York to confer with newspaper men from other parts of the country in order to work out a sound line of approach." Eddy also communicated with individuals who had evinced an interest in organization. As he wrote a Birmingham, Alabama, reporter, "an important point is the number of employees for whom we can speak . . . . we realize that you have not a working organization but would it be possible for you to call a meeting of editorial employees there. . . ."[56]

Despite the very limited time available for reply, the New York Guild received enough answers to supply some of the basic hour and wage data needed for arguing the newswriters' case. In addition, delegates came from Boston, Buffalo, Cleveland, Newark, Philadelphia, and Yonkers; on October 31, the evening prior to the newsmen's appearance at the NRA conference, these delegates met with a committee from the New York Guild (Broun, Eddy, Raymond, and Morris Watson). At the Hotel Algonquin the newsmen not only worked out tactics and representation for the next day but also discussed the proposed Washington meeting, and the New York guildsmen received assurances that such a meeting would be well attended. Eddy later declared that "this little meeting on the last day of October marked, in reality, the inception of the American Newspaper Guild."[57]

The New York Guild devoted most of its slender resources to the advancement of national organization, although some of its members began to complain about misappropriation of their dues. Despite criticism, at the beginning of December one newsman estimated that about 80 percent of the work carried on in the New York Guild office was national in character, including publication of a newspaper, *The Guild Reporter.* Press runs of 10,000 at a time when the New York Guild had about 1,100 members indicate a main purpose behind its publication.[58]

The first issue of *The Guild Reporter* (according to its masthead "published temporarily by the Newspaper Guild of New York in the interests of newspaper editorial employees throughout the nation") appeared November 23, 1933. More a broadside appealing for organization than a newspaper, Volume I, Number 1, consisting of two eight-column standard-size pages, described in detail, in articles by Broun, Eddy, and Watson, the genesis of the New York Guild, its NRA activities, and its organization and constitution. The second issue, also only two pages, but in the tabloid size used thereafter, appeared on December 8 and contained as much news of the various local newswriters groups as the editors could squeeze in. Other groups had put out bulletins or news sheets (the Cleveland group issued multipage mimeographed newsletters), but only New York had the resources to undertake such an ambitious and useful project as *The Guild Reporter*. Attaining widespread circulation (Cleveland took 800 copies of the first issue to distribute around Ohio), it helped break down the newsmen's isolation and ignorance about organization; by printing the New York Guild's constitution, it presented a model for editorial employees who were unsure about the drafting of such documents. In response to a request from a Troy newsman for information about the organization movement, Eddy sent 100 copies of *The Guild Reporter* to him, asserting that the newspaper would answer many questions and suggesting that he distribute them to editorial men in newspaper offices not only in Troy but also in Albany. This approach seems to have had some effect. For example, a Rochester, New York, reporter wrote the New York Guild that he and his fellow workers had obtained copies of *The Guild Reporter*, had used it to guide them in cooperative action, and now wanted to know how to proceed further. Both issues of *The Guild Reporter* also played up the forthcoming Washington meeting, making it the lead story.[59]

In November, the New York Guild sent out a formal call for the meeting in Washington and, along with the Cleveland group, strove for large representation. As late as three days before the meeting, Eddy wrote to newsmen who had evinced interest in organization, suggesting (as he did to H. B. Slocum of Schenectady) that "you gather together a number of interested [newsmen], form a committee, take up a collection, and either send a delegate to the meeting or wire us authorization. . . ."[60]

Apparently, 36 delegates representing 20 cities responded to the invitations and exhortations. As Table I shows, a number of delegates served as representatives for groups other than their own. The Monroe, Louisiana, newsworkers, for example, had authorized White by telegram to represent them. In addition, the American Newspaper Guild's records state that newsmen in 22 other localities authorized proxies. The character of these proxies varied greatly. Some were like that which a Yonkers group wired Eddy: "YONKERS GUILD UNABLE TO SEND REPRESENTATIVE TO NATIONAL MEETING STOP PLEASE REPRESENT US BY PROXY AND INCLUDE US AS CHARTER GUILD IN THE NATIONAL BODY." Others were like that received from San Antonio: "AS COMMITTEE REPRESENTING EDITORIAL MEN AND WOMAN ON SAN ANTONIO PAPERS WE EXPRESS SENTIMENTS IN ACCORD WITH NATIONAL GUILD IDEA. . . . ASK INCLUSION AS CHARTER GUILD IN NATIONAL BODY STOP NEED FOR AN ORGANIZATION HERE IS APPARENT. . . ." In a few instances, such as that of Dallas, Newspaper Guild claims to a proxy can be discounted as nothing more than an indication of interest by individuals. The newsmen's organizations had done very well to achieve such representation, but they also exaggerated the numbers and geographical areas they represented. Six months later, Eddy admitted that the Washington meeting had represented only "organized guilds in four cities and interested groups in a score of other cities."[61]

The delegates first met in Broun's suite at the Willard Hotel, where, after having their credentials examined, they got acquainted over coffee and stronger drink. They conducted little business at this morning session beyond voting to advise their constitutional committee that they favored calling the proposed national organization the American Newspaper Guild. The constitutional committee, composed of R. S. Gilfillan; Nathan Goldberg; Luther Huston; I. L. Kenen, the chairman; Andrew Parker; and Don Strouse removed about 10:30 a.m. to a private dining room. There and in separate delegates' rooms the committee put together a constitution and bylaws. The Cleveland, New York, and Philadelphia groups each had prepared drafts. Philadelphia's received short shrift. Cleveland's, prepared

TABLE I: THE WASHINGTON MEETING

Name	Home town	Listed as representing:
A. DELEGATES		
Don Strouse	Akron	Akron
*George W. Combs	Baltimore	Baltimore
Dan Birmingham	Buffalo	Buffalo
J. Winton Leaman	Buffalo	Buffalo
F. W. Morrison	Buffalo	Rochester
Victor Logan	Cincinnati	Cincinnati
Robert Bordner	Cleveland	Cleveland
I. L. Kenen	Cleveland	Columbus; Rockford (Ill.)
Lloyd White	Cleveland	Monroe (La.)
Penrose K. Spohn	Harrisburg	Harrisburg
R. S. Gilfillan	Minneapolis	Minneapolis
Emmet Crozier	Newark	Newark
Nathan Goldberg	Newark	Paterson
Chester Keel	Newark	Hackensack
Heywood Broun	New York	New York
Jonathan Eddy	New York	New York
Doris Fleeson	New York	New York
Luther Huston	New York	New York
Morris Watson	New York	New York
William Edlin	New York	Jewish Writers Club
B. Z. Maiman	New York	Jewish Writers Club
G. Wright Lankford	Norfolk	Norfolk

* Combs wrote *Editor & Publisher* that he was not a delegate to the meeting, had nothing to do with it, and had no connection with the movement. Eddy explained that Combs' name appeared on the list of names of those who had attended the morning session and since the meeting was considered a closed session it had been assumed that all there were delegates (E&P, January 6, 1934, p. 14).

Name	*Home town*	*Listed as representing:*
John Butler	Philadelphia	Philadelphia
Paul C. French	Philadelphia	Philadelphia
John Park Lee	Philadelphia	Philadelphia
Thomas A. Lewis	Philadelphia	Philadelphia
Arch A. MacDonald	Philadelphia	Philadelphia
Joseph F. Palmer	Philadelphia	Philadelphia
Andrew M. Parker	Philadelphia	Philadelphia
Jack Kauffman	Reading	Reading
I. A. Reedy	Reading	Reading
A. Judson Evans	Richmond	Richmond
G. B. Wollan	St. Paul	St. Paul
Edward D. Burks	Tulsa	Tulsa
D. A. de Souza	Washington	Washington
J. B. McDonnell	Washington	Washington
Ned Brooks	Youngstown	Youngstown

B.   PROXIES

Atlantic City	Columbia	Fort Wayne	St. Louis
Austin	Council Bluffs	Gary	San Antonio
Bay City	Dallas	Lansing	Teaneck
Birmingham	Des Moines	New Haven	Troy
Boston	Duluth	Passaic	Yonkers
	El Paso	Saginaw	

Note on Sources: This table is based on "Delegates Who Attended Washington Meeting" and "Proxies at Washington Meeting," lists at ANG headquarters which seem to both have been compiled shortly after the meeting; and "Delegates and Proxies at Founding Convention, December 15, 1933," a list appended to the minutes of this meeting (ANG Proceedings, 1933—these minutes are not to be found among the convention proceedings at ANG headquarters in Washington, D.C., nor among the records the ANG plans to deposit). At the time considerable confusion marked the reporting that dealt with whom the newly formed ANG spoke for. An AP dispatch said 73 cities were represented by delegates or proxies (NYHT, Dec. 16, 1933, p. 8). NYT (Dec. 16, 1933, p. 15) said that delegates from thirty newspapers attended and that "twenty-three other employee associations sent telegraphic authority promising to abide by the action of the delegates." E&P reported delegates from twenty-one cities and proxies for twenty-three others. (R. Mann, "National Guild Asks Five-Day Week," E&P, Dec. 23, 1933, p. 7.)

mostly by Bordner, Kenen, and White, foreshadowed the ANG's ultimate development; it mentioned strikes and lockouts, provided for a somewhat centralized national organization, and called for a membership broad enough to include "anyone in the pay of, or working in, the editorial department of any newspaper or any agency serving or selling to newspaper editorial departments." The Cleveland draft received virtually no consideration, for besides being a complicated document, it went too far for the tastes of most of the committee. Its rejection shows the continuing strength of professionalism. Most of the committee, indeed most of the delegates, had little interest in a labor union and thought, as Luther Huston later said, that "what we were doing was establishing a professional organization, limited to active journalists, which would bargain collectively with employers . . . unrelated to the general labor movement." The New York draft was almost a carbon copy of its own constitution and bylaws. Comparison with the final proposals shows that the committee merely simplified New York's draft and made some additions and amendments decentralizing the national's authority and making clearer provisions for direct national membership. The committee, which operated with virtually no controversy, finished its labors about 12:30 p.m., and its members joined with the rest of the delegates adjourning for lunch to the National Press Club, the site of the afternoon's proceedings.[62]

Broun, White, and James Kieran missed the forenoon proceedings. They, along with Ernest K. Lindley, a reporter close to the President, had been invited to the White House to discuss the proposed newspaper code's treatment of editorial workers. This was the second such visit in four days by newsmen interested in organization. The initiative for these visits seems to have come from Roosevelt. On October 10, Lindley had written Broun that "the President has requested me to corral a small group of newspapermen with whom he can have a private talk, if he so chooses, whenever the newspaper code emerges from the NRA." Lindley, who suggested including somebody from Cleveland, Philadelphia, and Washington, said that the President had specified inclusion in this group of Broun and James

Kieran, a *New York Times* Albany correspondent active in New York Guild affairs who was well known to Roosevelt from his days as governor. However, the delays in finishing the code meant that not until December 11, just after the publishers had submitted their final draft and its terms had become known, did the President talk with a delegation of newsmen.[63] The delegation included Broun, Eddy, Kieran, Lindley, Parker, Allen Raymond, Lloyd White, and Raymond P. Brandt, president of the National Press Club. Gathered around the President, who sat on a couch in his study, they criticized various provisions of the proposed code and suggested a number of revisions that would benefit newspaper workers. Roosevelt responded sympathetically and set another meeting for the morning of the 15th. Only Broun, Kieran, Lindley, and White went to the second meeting because, as White said, the newsmen had found that "efficiency demanded fewer spokesmen." General Johnson and Lindsay Rogers also attended. After both sides had reiterated their arguments, the newsmen were informed that no specific stipulations as to wages or hours could be put into the code at this time because of the absolute lack of reliable statistics. Johnson and the President, however, both gave assurances that provision would be made in the code for a nationwide survey to obtain the necessary information, and the newsmen believed that Roosevelt "virtually promised" appointment of an ANG representative to the fact-finding body which supposedly would analyze the data produced by the survey and draft the code provisions on hours and wages. A few weeks later, White accurately described the tenor of the White House conference when he said that "the NRA had experienced too much trouble with the newspaper code, and that the only thing wanted by General Johnson and Dr. Rogers was to get rid of it regardless of what its provisions were."[64] Although the administration did not want to antagonize the newspapermen who covered its activities, it did want to settle the code. The White House meetings made the editorial workers feel good but resulted in almost no concrete changes in the code.

The newsmen assembled at the National Press Club, however, thought the White House discussions seemed to imply recog-

nition of many of their demands. Robert Bordner remembers
being elated. The Twin Cities Guild delegates reported to their
fellow members that the President's sympathetic attitude would
mean a great deal for the future of the ANG. Moreover, a talk
to the assembled delegates by General Johnson, the main
speaker at lunch, did nothing to dispel this optimistic mood;
indeed, he must have enhanced it by saying that though he could
not urge them to organize, once they had done so NRA would
protect them. He added that while it was impossible to pull
codes off a Christmas tree in the manner of Santa Claus, the
history of the codes "leads up to the purpose for which you
are here."[65]

The luncheon program, which about 200 attended (including
local newsmen, some editors, about 50 Washington correspondents, and a few government officials anxious about the organization movement), proceeded at a fast pace. Johnson spoke for
only 15 minutes before offering to answer questions, which
were few. Broun made the only other speech, and it lasted but
five minutes. Morris Watson concluded the program by presenting Johnson with a code designed to provide for press association employees; they needed a separate code because Lindsay Rogers had ruled that the one prepared by the publishers
would regulate only the editorial employees of newspapers.[66]

Immediately after lunch the delegates assembled in a small
private dining room on the balcony at the Press Club. Broun,
who had been elected chairman, called the meeting to order.
The delegates decided that instead of having voting by groups,
each man should have one vote. An indication of the fears of
at least some delegates came when the assembly voted that
reports of the meeting should not mention names. Adoption of
the constitution and bylaws followed. Luther Huston read aloud
the proposals worked out by the constitutional committee, and
the delegates adopted them with almost no debate. Some argument did develop over the wording in the clause defining purpose, which included the phrase "improve conditions under
which [the members] work by collective bargaining . . . ," but
the delegates who tried to substitute the less trade-union-tinged
words "by collective action," were voted down. By and large,

this portion of the meeting was, as one participant described it, "a routine affair."[67]

Next came the election of officers. The first contest, for the presidency, brought into the open many of the tensions which had and would continue to hamper the organization's progress for some time to come. A New York Guild delegate nominated Broun, who, according to Eddy, "wanted nothing more on God's earth at that time than to be president of the [American Newspaper] Guild." R. S. Gilfillan, who nominated Lloyd White, the only other candidate for the office, has said that he did so not because he wanted to defeat Broun, but because he believed it a public-relations mistake for a fledgling organization such as the ANG to elect a controversial radical its first leader and he hoped that a contested election would lead at least to a debate of this point. After nominations closed, somebody (perhaps Broun) suggested that the two candidates withdraw from the room so that the delegates could discuss their qualifications and suitability for office freely. Broun and White went down to the Press Club bar.[68]

A brief general discussion ensued. Someone spoke about White's experience as a labor reporter and his high standing as a journalist in Cleveland. At this point Eddy drew an envelope from his pocket and said that it contained a copy of a letter from Rogers to Johnson which was pertinent to the matter at hand. He declared it had been given to him in confidence and cautioned the delegates not to disclose its contents to anyone. Kieran, chairing the meeting in Broun's absence, read the letter aloud.[69] It stated that the government, the NRA, and Roosevelt personally had looked with sympathy and interest upon the formation of a national editorial workers organization and indicated that its establishment was desirable. However, "the organization should not take on a form and engage in activities which will make publishers resentful not only of the guilds but also of the National Recovery Administration."[70] Rogers asserted that the election of Broun, with his leanings toward AFL affiliation and his Socialist ties, to·the presidency of the new organization might do just that: "the consequences would be disastrous." Therefore, Rogers, assuming that the President

would appoint an editorial workers' representative to the proposed Newspaper Code Authority, recommended that Roosevelt, before the ANG chose a head, "let it be know [sic] informally, in advance, that he would appoint a certain person.
. . . That person, I am informed would almost assuredly be
elected President of the National Guild Organization."

Behind this attempt to influence the delegates lay the fears
of a number of people, including Eddy, that the ANG under
Broun's leadership would ruin its chances for success by choosing to affiliate with the AFL. Rogers, who liked Broun and
wished the guilds well, thought affiliation would be a grave
mistake.[71] A day or two after the December 11 White House
conference, an overworked and agitated Eddy had communicated his forebodings to Rogers, adding that many others shared
these views. Rogers did not believe it his place to take any
active interest in the newsmen's affairs, but said that if Eddy
"was willing to put . . . [his views] in the form of a memorandum I would consider having Johnson know what he and the
unnamed people who agreed with him thought of the situation."
Rogers almost entirely based his letter to Johnson on the memo,
but made no mention of Eddy, who in a covering note had said:
"it could be used to make me out an S-O-B." Johnson reacted
most unsympathetically to Rogers' suggestions, saying that it
was "none of our business."[72] Johnson apparently said nothing
about the Rogers letter to anyone, and the matter would have
ended there but for an accidental meeting of Eddy with Rogers,
who showed the newsman a copy of the letter to calm any fears
that he might have had about being mentioned in it. This was
the copy Eddy handed to Kieran.

The letter had far from the desired effect. Broun's election,
which had seemed likely, now became inevitable. The New
York delegates, led by Watson, exploded in indignant protest.
The Cleveland delegates denounced the letter as presumptuous.
Many other delegates reacted equally unfavorably. According
to Crozier, Eddy seemed confused and frustrated. Opinions
differ about the vote totals but not about the fact that Broun
won by a large majority. Later, the delegates voted for and
then dropped a plan for a letter of protest to the President

asking that Rogers be removed as Deputy Administrator of the Newspaper Code. Broun, when he discovered what had happened, was "highly indignant" (as he later wrote Johnson). Although Broun recognized Eddy's intention to block his election, the two men, said Crozier, shortly settled their differences and achieved an uneasy truce. Morris Watson does not believe that any sort of lasting animosity existed between Broun and Eddy, but they never became close.[73]

After the delegates had voted to make Broun's election unanimous, he and Lloyd White were summoned from the bar and the meeting proceeded with the election of other officers. The assembly chose White first vice president and Andrew Parker second vice president. Just after their election, the door flew open and Edward Burks burst in announcing that he had come by "train, plane, bus, and oxcart" to speak for Oklahoma newspapermen. He had wanted badly to be on hand for the organization meeting, and, after his car had broken down en route, he had taken a bus to Kansas City, a plane to some place in Pennsylvania, a train from there, and finally a taxicab. Broun said to Burks: "Your arrival is timely; we have just elected a vice president from Cleveland and another from Philadelphia. We need someone from the West. How about Burks of Tulsa for third vice president?" Thus, less than five minutes after his arrival, the young man from Oklahoma found himself a vice president of the American Newspaper Guild. Doris Fleeson considered Burks' enthusiastic arrival "the biggest thrill of that meeting." The delegates elected R. S. Gilfillan and A. Judson Evans of Richmond the fourth and fifth vice presidents; Eddy became secretary, and Emmet Crozier, treasurer. The selections of Doris Fleeson, Ruth McKenney of Akron, and Thomas Brown of Buffalo rounded out the National Executive Committee; the latter two had not attended the meeting but had been very active locally. After voting to make known the results of the meeting, the delegates adjourned the four-hour business session about 5:30 p.m.[74]

The delegates had not known much about each other; most of them had met for the first time on the morning of the 15th of December. Acting in haste, they had relied more on hunch than

on judgment. From these slap-dash beginnings the American
Newspaper Guild grew rapidly if not serenely. Organization did
not mean unionization, however, as events in New York City
demonstrated. The editorial employees concerned with organization certainly hoped to improve their working conditions, but
most of them had no intention of doing so through trade-union
methods such as collective bargaining, striking, and the like.
They believed they could accomplish their ends through NRA
and the exertion of influence. Moreover, they had a sincere interest in improving what they called their "craft." The editorial
workers, representing some of these groups, who formed the
American Newspaper Guild also adhered to these ideas. The
election of Broun, a pronounced unionist, as ANG president
represented no deviation from that adherence. Rather, the election supplied formal recognition of Broun's role within the
organization movement. That someone as important as Broun
should care about their working conditions had impressed many
newspapermen. They looked to him for leadership and he
served as a focal point for their complaints and their organizational plans. His acceptance of this role probably kept the
organization movement from sharing the fate of earlier ones.
Eddy and others like him in New York and elsewhere handled
the day-to-day details and without them the Washington meeting could never have taken place, but without Broun the American Newspaper Guild would never have come into existence.

4 .

from meeting to convention:
the first seven months

The American Newspaper Guild brought into being on December 15, 1933, had only a tenuous hold on life. *Editor & Publisher* might greet it warmly and grant it "a place in the scheme of organized journalism," but the ANG was little more than a hollow shell which took some time to achieve any substance.[1] Its constitutional makeup serves as an excellent illustration of this fragile condition.

The ANG's constitution and bylaws, both of which contained clauses giving them life only until the adoption of a new constitution and bylaws at a convention to be held within the next six months, created an almost completely decentralized national organization—a loose confederation of locals with no formal national program and no rules of procedure.[2] Its framework rested upon local guilds based on municipal or metropolitan areas. These local guilds, which would receive charters from the ANG, served in turn as the parent groups for chapters in the local editorial offices of daily and weekly newspapers, press associations, and feature syndicates. All local guilds, even the ones represented at the founding meeting, had to obtain charters. The constitution opened membership to all persons employed as editorial workers, although it left the final determination to the local guilds, which could bar any person "whose interests, in [their] opinion . . . , as between his employer and fellow employee lie with the employer or conflict with the fellow employee." Where no local group existed, persons eligible for membership could join the ANG directly, pending the chartering of a local guild which, upon establishment, would assume jurisdiction. Elected national officers received no pay and were limited to a reimbursement of $15.00 per day for traveling and other expenses or loss of pay incurred while on ANG business.

The national organization and its officers had virtually no powers. The ANG could take part in local bargaining only at the request of the local group involved. All guild members retained the right to negotiate individually with their employers, but without local guild or ANG support. Though the national organization had the power to bargain with press associations and syndicates of national scope, any agreement achieved was subject to a ratifying vote by two-thirds of the guild members involved. Broun, discussing ANG matters with a reporter, in effect admitted the impotence of the national organization's officers when he declared that "the executive committee cannot bind the Guild." The National Executive Committee had the right to hire an Executive Secretary and such clerical employees as might be necessary, but, because the ANG's only revenue until the next convention would come from two $1.00 assessments of the membership (to be levied in December 1933 and March 1934), this right proved to be of little value.[3]

Behind the creation of such an impotent ANG lay the differences which marked the newsmen's attitudes toward the concept of a national editorial employees organization. Just as had been the case in most of the local groups, essentially only a single negative purpose had united the delegates who formed the ANG. They were against the newspaper code's treatment of editorial employees; and whatever else the various delegates may have had in mind concerning organization, they all wanted something done about the code, although on this matter also their proposed solutions had varied in detail and approach. Just prior to the founding meeting, at least two distinct schools of thought existed on the question of what could be accomplished in the way of national organization. One school held that almost immediately it would be possible to elect national officers who could perform satisfactorily the difficult task of establishing an effective, inclusive, nationwide editorial workers organization. The other favored appointing regional organizers (drawn from newsmen active in local groups), hiring a salaried national organizer, and holding a final national organization meeting about six months later in a city more accessible to the majority of the local groups, at which time a constitution satisfactory to all would be adopted and national officers elected. The constitution and bylaws adopted at the founding meeting as well as most of the actions taken by the newly formed National Executive Committee represented a compromise among these schools of thought. Unfortunately, these compromises did little for the ANG beyond giving it a shaky hold on life. A few months later, Eddy described some of the compromises as "dangerous," tending as they did toward "lack of unity."[4]

The National Executive Committee had met for the first time on the evening of December 15 in the sitting room of Broun's suite at the Willard. Soon after Broun called the meeting to order, two resolutions were introduced which Emmet Crozier, then ANG treasurer, believes had been prepared in advance of the Washington meeting by Broun or some other member of the New York delegation. Broun's support of both resolutions ensured their passage without much comment and without a dissenting vote. One resolution called for the ANG to "establish and maintain cordial and mutually helpful relations with the other organized branches of newspaper work. . . ." When asked the next day to explain what this meant, Broun, aware that most newsmen opposed affiliation with organized labor, said that this resolution referred only to joint protests.[5] Giving as an example a hypothetical NRA decision adversely affecting both the typographers and the editorial workers, he said that a joint protest by the ITU and the ANG would be more effective: "it would be just like a Jewish rabbi and a Methodist minister appearing together before the mayor of some city to make a joint protest on some municipal matter."[6]

The other resolution—which had considerable immediacy

because an Akron Newspaper Circulators Guild planned to apply for admission to the ANG—called upon the new organization "to encourage and aid fellow members in the unorganized departments of newspaper work to organize themselves with the idea of joining this movement toward protecting our mutual interests. . . ." Here too, Broun's comments the next day vitiated the resolution's impact. He declared that the National Executive Committee had not meant that the ANG should set out on its own initiative to organize all unorganized newspaper workers, but only that aid would be given to those editorial department workers who requested it; as for the Akron situation, he said that the definition of news department workers in the ANG's constitution did not cover circulation men.

Broun's true feelings about these resolutions differed greatly from his public statements. Apparently, he had wanted the ANG on record as favoring these actions even though he realized the improbability of their acceptance at that time. He knew that internecine disputes over trade union affiliation and acceptance of such non-news department personnel as the Akron circulation men as guildsmen (not to mention the strongly hostile publisher reaction this move would engender) could result in the death of the ANG while it was aborning. Therefore, despite his probable intimate involvement with the formulation of the resolution, Broun publicly played down their significance. Crozier rightly calls them "empty gestures which accomplished nothing." Nevertheless, their adoption remains important because they indicate the feelings of at least part of the Executive Committee and foreshadow the direction the ANG would take.[7]

Some of the actions of the National Executive Committee, although well intentioned, compounded the ANG's handicaps. After some discussion, the committee's members agreed that though it would be better to meet once every three months, for the present, because of lack of funds, they would rely on the secretary to keep them informed and would use the mails to exchange views and vote on whatever questions might arise. This arrangement lasted much longer than had been anticipated. Not until 1935 did the ANG executive body meet regularly, and the National Executive Committee did not meet again until the end of the June, 1934, convention, by which time its membership had been changed by the adoption of a new constitution and the holding of elections. Few of the committee members serving on December 15, 1933, ever saw each other again on ANG business.[8]

The National Executive Committee also appointed committees on ethics (Broun, Parker, White), finance (Crozier, Eddy, and Parker), and organization (chaired by White and including G. B. Wollan, secretary treasurer of the Twin Cities Guild and its delegate at the founding meeting). Three of the five guildsmen on the organization committee were not in Washington for the founding meeting, and only White also served on the Executive Committee. This situation led to confusion as well as indifferent results. For example, one organization committee member, Curtis R. West of the *Rockford Morning Star*, whose local group did not decide until January 7, 1934, to reorganize and apply for an ANG charter, wrote Eddy on January 8 that until then there had been nothing he could do, and that, anyway, Rockford was a geographically difficult location from which to direct organization for that region.[9]

After the National Executive Committee had adjourned, those members of the finance and organization committees present in Washington held a joint meeting. Wollan proposed the appointment of Eddy to the post of Executive Secretary, but he declined, stating that the nebulous future of the ANG, given the depressed conditions within the newspaper industry, did not justify his resigning from *The New York Times*. The members of the finance and organization committees then decided that the National Executive Committee should immediately solicit applications from guild members for the Executive Secretaryship, with applicants listing the salary they would expect to receive. The bulk of the short meeting dealt with the problem of opening an ANG office. After authorizing a very small staff (the only full-time personnel to be an assistant to the Executive Secretary and a stenographer), the guildsmen decided that headquarters should be established in New York. Because of lack of funds, it was voted that, for the present, the ANG should occupy desk space in the office of the New York Guild, which, it was suggested, "will be kind enough to pay the help" and which also should continue to conduct national organizational work. Upon receipt of funds the ANG should immediately re-imburse the New York Guild, and any funds the New Yorkers had expended "shall be considered first lien against any national income." Broun, who had not attended the joint meeting, concurred with these decisions before leaving December 20 on a two-week cruise.[10]

These arrangements did not work out as planned, for almost immediately it became clear that the ANG would lack the financing to operate in all but the most limited ways for a longer time than had been anticipated. Eddy wrote members of the Executive Committee that selection of an Executive Secretary "is not even to be considered at this time." The only cash the ANG treasury had received by December 27 was $50.00 from the Richmond, Virginia, group. Although more money trickled in during the next weeks, Heywood Broun and others had to provide the cash to get out the mid-January issue of *The Guild Reporter*, whose publication the ANG had assumed. A shortage of funds also restricted the assistance the New York Guild could give. As Emmet Crozier later reported, the New York group "had plunged ahead with so much enthusiasm . . . that after [the December] meeting the New York Guild was tempo-rarily almost broke."[11] It continued to conduct national organi-zational activities, but on a much reduced scale. In its two cramped office rooms the New York Guild in the winter of 1933-34 could afford to maintain only two secretaries (assisted occasionally by part-time help from unemployed newspaper-men, who were paid $4.00 a day). So tight, in fact, did the New York Guild's financial situation become that at one point its treasurer, upon the group's removal to other quarters when it turned over the two-room suite to the ANG in mid-March, insisted that "since the offices are really those of the Newspaper Guild of New York that the ANG pay the expenses of moving the telephone and door name."[12]

For some weeks after the founding meeting, therefore, little could be done beyond attempting to answer the many requests for information about organization that the ANG received from editorial workers across the country. The New York Guild assigned one of its two secretaries to give full time to answering requests, and the guild officers (both those of the New York Guild and those of the ANG in the New York area) helped out. However, newsmen holding down regular jobs just could not devote much time to guild affairs, and this apportionment of the work proved unsatisfactory. The sheer volume of correspondence proved too heavy. A paucity of funds also prevented the ANG from taking advantage of the publicity given the founding meeting. Eddy bore an unusually heavy load, being unable to resign as secretary of the New York Guild until January 5. He wrote a Minneapolis guildsman in mid-January that "you will appreciate that our financial condition makes it impossible to hire sufficient help and that to mimeograph the minutes of [the Washington] meeting as you suggested would necessitate interrupting . . . the general routine." To another correspondent who had outlined various activities that the ANG should undertake, Eddy wrote that the organization had "just barely money enough to struggle along on, without being able to do any . . . work aside from correspondence."[13]

This correspondence, despite the handicaps under which it was carried on, helped considerably to further organization. Newsmen from the same locale, sometimes even from the same newspaper, would write independently to the ANG, asking how to form a guild. In reply, they would receive not only the information they sought but also the names of like-minded newsmen in their area. For instance, Eddy responded to a request for information from two Albany newsmen by suggesting that they get in touch with two Schenectady newsmen who had written him a few days earlier to urge formation of a guild in the Albany-Schenectady-Troy area. When answering other requests for information from this area in the following weeks, Eddy would always include the names of newsmen "particularly intested in helping to form a Troy-Albany-Schenectady unit of the Guild" and add, "it would pay you to get in touch with them." Some of these men eventually got together and at the end of January, 1934, helped form a Tri-City Newspaper Guild with a charter membership of 123 which included about 90 percent of those eligible in Albany and Schenectady.[14]

Occasionally, ANG officers in various areas would supplement the correspondence. Lloyd White (especially active in this regard despite having to spend most of his time covering labor strife) and Garland Ashcraft were driven by Mrs. Ashcraft to a Detroit organizational meeting, where according to Eddy's Detroit correspondent, "White gave a picture of the events in Washington that was so graphic that it won over a skeptical *Detroit News* faction and was a factor in the meeting's success."[15]

By the beginning of February, ANG finances had improved (though its bank balance remained under $500), and the correspondence work became more than just answering requests for information. In the ensuing weeks Eddy, making use of volunteer and part-time workers, followed a plan of obtaining the rosters of editorial employees in a number of unorganized cities and areas and sending the newsmen ANG literature at their homes. He hoped to affiliate them directly with the ANG, after which, if enough of them in an area had enrolled, the machinery of local organization would be set up. Many North Carolina newspapermen received a mimeographed statement, typical of those sent out, which urged the newsmen to improve their working conditions and the standards of their profession by banding together into guilds. The statement claimed that the ANG had been able to enlist the support of Roosevelt and Johnson, but declared in conclusion that "in each community, however, the men employed there must act for themselves . . .; those who wish to take the lead should communicate at once . . ." with the ANG.[16] In many instances, as with St. Joseph, Missouri, editorial writer J. W. Adams, when it was believed that the recipient would respond favorably, a more personal form letter and a current issue of *The Guild Reporter* would be sent along with the mimeographed statement. The results of the campaign remain difficult to gauge. In North Carolina it came to naught, and a mailing to all the alumni officers of Sigma Delta Chi elicited only a moderate response. Eddy's plan played some part in the expansion of the ANG, but certainly a much lesser one than he had anticipated.[17]

Despite the ANG's difficulties, enthusiasm for organization continued to run high during the early months of 1934. *Editor & Publisher* recorded the formal establishment of guilds in such varied places as Jersey City, Omaha, Toledo, Washington, and the Lehigh Valley; Eddy estimated at the end of March that 65 local guilds existed. At the same time, many of the pioneer editorial workers' groups rapidly grew in size as they broadened the base of their membership. Almost immediately after the Washington meeting, the Cleveland Guild began recruiting editorial employees on the city's 25 foreign-language dailies and weeklies. The Newark Guild, like many another group, added to its members by forming new chapters on the newspapers in nearby communities such as Orange. Crozier estimated at the beginning of March that the ANG's membership exceeded 7,000, an increase of about 2,500 since the founding meeting. However, the overoptimistic claims of local groups probably accounted for some of the reported members, for the national organization's finances reflected no such giant upswing.[18]

In some areas the organization movement ran into snags. A considerable number of newsmen remained distrustful of organization and preferred to continue going their own way. A Toledo reporter wrote Broun just before the local group there formally came into being that "among the editorial personnel, some men, who, locally, are big shots . . . seem decidedly cool to the idea of organizing with the common herd." Problems of a similar nature also arose in some of the pioneer guilds. A small group of Harrisburg newsmen had spurred on the organization movement there, providing the money to send a delegate to the Washington meeting and expecting to establish a large guild within a short time. But they ran into what the Harrisburg Guild's secretary called a "stiff situation" because the editorial staffs of two of the city's four dailies showed no interest in organization. Lack of initiative also hampered some groups which already had organized. Moreover, isolated instances of publisher intimidation continued to take place, although, despite the fears expressed by many newsmen, few publishers had openly taken a stand against their editorial employees joining a guild. At this time the most serious draw-

back to organization was the reluctance of many newspapermen to take part.[19]

Meanwhile, the drive to achieve recognition and some gains
from the newspaper code stalled; the President proved to be
in no hurry to approve the code. On December 23, 1933, the
day after Roosevelt formally received it, his press secretary
said that no action would be taken before Christmas. After the
holiday, the code remained unsigned, and, despite statements
by Johnson and the White House that only the pressure of work
held up the President's study and approval of it, reports circulated that White House dissatisfaction with several of its provisions, especially those dealing with child labor, accounted
for the delay. The New York *Daily News* Washington correspondent Doris Fleeson got the Secretary of Labor, Frances
Perkins, to admit this, but only off the record. January passed
into February and still the code lay on the President's desk
awaiting his approval.[20]

During this time a number of guilds initiated a variety of
undertakings. The Cleveland and New York groups managed to
get the local branches of the Civil Works Administration to
hire unemployed newspapermen. Some groups began to collect
data about editorial employees' working conditions in their
area, an activity which the national organization later asked all
guilds to undertake because it hoped to use the information
collected to convince NRA of the need to establish maximum hours and minimum wages for newspapermen. The Newspaper Guild of Philadelphia and Camden investigated the possibilities of cooperative buying. A few guilds even discussed
the possibility of entering into negotiations directly with the
publishers, and at least two took action along this line. The New
York Guild, the most ambitious group, undertook to meet with
the city's publishers in what its president, Allen Raymond, said
should be called "conversations," not negotiations. The New
York Guild invited about 40 publishers and editors to a buffet
dinner at the Hotel Astor so that the organization movement
might be explained to them personally. About 30 representatives from most of the city's dailies attended, although few
were from the top echelons of management; the one publisher

who did appear had drunk too much at an earlier engagement. Despite the amicability of the evening (*Newsweek* described the participants as "lapping up highballs and conversing in tones of brotherly affection"), the dinner accomplished little of a practical nature. The Newark Guild had more success when it negotiated with Paul Block, publisher of the *Star-Eagle*, after its general manager had fired seven men without notice at the end of December, including one desk man over seventy who had been with the newspaper for twenty-two years. A committee headed by Crozier managed to get him reinstated and to obtain satisfactory dismissal bonuses for the others (except for one whose firing the Guild thought warranted). However, despite Block's promises, similar problems arose shortly thereafter.[21]

The majority of the guilds, however, did almost nothing. Indeed, they had no definite ideas about what to do after organizing. A Cincinnati Guild officer writing Eddy for advice on how to proceed reported that his group, having organized, "seems to have come to the end of a blind alley. . . . What to do next?" Newspapermen began to lose interest. The Twin Cities Guild officers wrote Eddy that "so far we have had just words, words, words. Let's do something or [we will] . . . find our membership lagging."[22]

The opportunity to act came on January 17, 1934, when Ralph Pulitzer was appointed to succeed Lindsay Rogers as Deputy Administrator of the Newspaper Code. Pulitzer, one of the former publishers of the New York *World*, had helped to kill that newspaper in 1931. Most guild leaders considered Pulitzer a man whose interests were inimical to editorial workers and opposed his appointment. The New York Guild, many of whose members had lost their jobs when the Pulitzers sold out to the Scripps-Howard chain, spearheaded the protest. On January 22 its Representative Assembly voted by an overwhelming majority to oppose the appointment and drew up a resolution to that effect. Within four days the ANG's Executive Committee, at the instigation of Broun, had decided by telegraphic vote to urge every guild to support the New York protest. Many did, sending wires and letters to Roosevelt and Johnson asking that Pulitzer be ousted. The Oklahoma Newspaper Guild of Tulsa even wired its congressmen and senators.[23] Meanwhile, Broun and Eddy got in touch with the mechanical workers' unions, which, for reasons of their own, disapproved of Pulitzer's appointment. On the morning of February 1, when Broun spoke against the appointment to Johnson in Washington, he did so on behalf of the typographers, stereotypers, and photoengravers as well as the editorial workers (the first instance of that cooperation between the ANG and the mechanical workers' unions which has proved so erratic over the years). That afternoon Pulitzer, who, according to Doris Fleeson, had rented "a swell house" and had been "all set to be a big shot," resigned, citing as a major reason for this action "the opposition to my appointment by the American Newspaper Guild." The newsmen's success surprised them. Eddy said that "perhaps we do not realize the potential . . . of our organization." The guilds created quite a stir with their protest, and the ANG claimed a victory. But the newsmen's success had been obtained at the expense of a man who preferred to avoid controversy and not against the publishers or NRA. In their enthusiasm about Pulitzer's resignation, the newsmen did not realize this, but their inability to do anything about the code soon demonstrated their lack of power.[24]

On February 17 the President finally acted on the newspaper code; he approved it exactly as submitted by the publishers in December, although in his Executive Order promulgating the code and in an accompanying letter to Johnson he added some qualifications and requests. Just as Johnson and NRA had disappointed the editorial workers, so now did the President. He recognized the value of being on the good side of the working press, but he did not want to lose the support the publishers could give to his programs. Roosevelt did not forget the editorial workers, but he did not do much for them. The Executive Order said that a determination of the hours and wages of editorial workers "shall be made not later than 60 days hence," and in his letter to Johnson, the President "requested" that the publishers of newspapers having a circulation of 75,000 or more in cities of 750,000 or more population establish a five-day, forty-hour week for their reporters and newswriters (Johnson did say that, if necessary, the "request" could be changed into an "order"). However, Roosevelt's "request" affected only forty-six papers in nine cities, and despite the survey called for within sixty days, the establishment of maximum hours and minimum wages would be delayed until May 2, 1935, as the various parties involved squabbled and failed to resolve their differing points of view on how long and for how much editorial employees should work. Moreover, press association employees remained completely unprotected, for efforts to have them included in the code had failed.[25]

Roosevelt's limited modifications disappointed the members of the various local guilds, especially after the putative victory in regard to the Pulitzer appointment. In *The Guild Reporter*, the ANG called the President's Executive Order and letter to Johnson "a signal victory . . . for it marks the successful culmination of the first step of . . . [the] fight for a forty-hour, five-day week." Eddy, the probable author of *The Guild Reporter* article, privately admitted his disappointment with the course events had taken. The ANG received many telegrams and letters from cities with less than 750,000 population asking that the organization take some sort of action. The secretary of the Harrisburg Guild summed up the beliefs expressed by the officers of many of these smaller guilds when he said that "the opinion has been expressed here that . . . the guild is a futile gesture against a code that obviously does them no good as it is drawn." A more positive approach came from the Washington Guild, which adopted overwhelmingly a resolution which protested in detail each of the code's provisions relating to editorial workers, suggested alternatives, and requested the ANG to seek "a reopening and general revision of the entire code." The best the ANG could do immediately was to send out a mimeographed letter to all guilds recommending that each, no matter what the population of its community, ask the newspaper publishers there to install at once the five-day, forty-hour week "as current best practice," so recognized by the President in his letter to Johnson. To give uniformity to newsmen's protests, Eddy later arranged for all guilds to receive mimeographed copies of the text of the Washington Guild's resolution.[26]

The ineffectiveness of this response caused a number of guilds to suggest to the ANG's officers that no matter how straitened its finances, it should fill the position of Executive Secretary immediately because the guild movement badly needed a full-time coordinator to promote a national program and to keep in communication with NRA. In the month following the code's promulgation, it became increasingly clear just how little the newsmen had achieved, and the ANG's contacts among the Washington press corps proved unable to do anything for the guild. Washington Guild president D. A. de Souza wrote Eddy that "there is nothing tangible which our fellows who cover NRA can get hold of indicating definitely what is what or . . . who is who. . . . It may be that in New York you know more about it than we do down here." The belief increased that some kind of national guild program was vital, and the number of guilds agitating for the appointment of an Executive Secretary grew accordingly. Eddy admitted to his correspondents that the necessity for the appointment to be made was "becoming increasingly acute" but declared that he could do nothing until Broun returned from a Florida trip. After a conference with Eddy toward the end of March, Broun wrote National Executive Committee members to propose Eddy's appointment as Executive Secretary. No opposition to the appointment was expressed. Eddy became responsible for the national organization's direct contact with the local guilds as well as for the day-to-day operation of the ANG, although newsmen everywhere continued to read about Broun's activities.[27]

Three months earlier Eddy had turned down the position which he now accepted. His interest in the organization of newsmen, which may be said to have become almost obsessive, accounts for this change of mind. Eddy had put a great deal of himself into the ANG. Every morning he would put in a few hours on ANG business before reporting to work at *The New York Times*. Often during the night, he remembers, he would get up to jot down ideas he believed would advance the organization. No one else had indicated any interest in the Executive Secretaryship, and so he took it. At his request, he would receive only $75.00 weekly, a cut of $19.50 from his *Times* salary. On April 7, Eddy left the *Times* and plunged into ANG work full time. His father thought him crazy.[28]

As one of his first official acts Eddy witnessed the contract signing between the Philadelphia Guild and the *Record* on April 8, the first written agreement obtained by any guild. It had been made possible by the benevolent attitude of J. David Stern, the daily's owner, who considered it "impossible to be sure that everybody had fair treatment unless they had some method of representation." The *Record* had already established the five-day, forty-hour week in its news department, but the contract now guaranteed it, the only exceptions being those editorial workers earning $4,500 a year or more and such other specialists that the guild might agree could not be replaced during their time off. The agreement, which in effect granted the newsmen a closed shop, called for all *Record* editorial workers to become guildsmen within 30 days of being employed and exempted only the editor, the managing editor, the assistant managing editor, and the city editor. Other stipulations included severance pay, a $20.00 per week basic minimum wage, compensation for overtime, paid vacations, and a limitation on the use of apprentices.[29] The chapter also received the "checkoff," whereby the newspaper would deduct guild dues from the employees' wages and directly forward them to the chapter's treasurer. Stern had granted the newsmen a contract which many stronger unions in other industries would have had to struggle to obtain.[30]

During the course of these negotiations many of the same feelings which had hurt earlier newsmen's organizations manifested themselves. Guildsmen from other Philadelphia newspapers mistrusted the *Record* chapter and its leaders, considering them to be too much under Stern's influence and less interested in the welfare of the editorial workers than in furthering the *Record* at the expense of the city's other dailies. On the other hand, the *Record* newsmen, fearing that the guild members' insistence upon uniform joint action would ruin their chances for a contract, considered withdrawing from the guild and forming their own organization. Exasperated by what he considered the unfair treatment of the *Record* chapter, its chief spokesman, Andrew Parker, wrote Eddy that "I am burning up, thinking seriously of resigning . . . and letting the whole she-bang go to hell!"[31]

Eddy, at the time of the contract signing, said that "we have reached our first objective . . . and are pressing forward to additional victories." These victories, however, were not achieved for some time; only one other guild managed to obtain a contract in the next six months. Years would pass before any guild in a metropolitan area would obtain a contract comparable to that with the *Record*.[32]

Stern had no desire to support the guildsmen favoring a trade union course for the organization movement. However, his actions helped those newsmen who preferred to direct the guilds away from the professional association idea. Increasing numbers of guildsmen came to advocate a policy of collective bargaining and of using the guilds to attain written contracts granting improved working conditions as NRA continued to demonstrate its inability to do much for editorial workers.

Even in those cities covered by President Roosevelt's "request" to institute a five-day, forty-hour week some newspapers managed to avoid total compliance. A Cleveland newspaper made one-fourth of its 98 editorial employees executives and thus exempt from any maximum-hour limitations. The New York Guild surveyed conditions in the metropolitan area and wrote the President that "most of the newspapers have been strict constructionists when they acceded to your request, and have left large groups of editorial employees unaffected by shorter hours. . . ." Some dailies "chiseled" (to use Johnson's term for undercutting NRA standards) in other ways. In Los Angeles the *Examiner* announced in a city room bulletin-board statement from the managing editor that because of the increased costs due to NRA the newspaper would not hire vacation replacements and that vacations could not be bunched at any time of year. Therefore, staff members had to take the vacation periods assigned them. After reminding the newsmen that "these vacations are gifts pure and simple . . . revocable at any time," the managing editor added that if any member of the staff did not wish to take the vacation time period assigned him, he automatically forfeited his opportunity for a vacation.[33]

In many cases, the situation of newsmen unaffected by the President's "request" deteriorated. An El Paso newsman wrote the President that the publishers there had reduced editorial workers to "a state of virtual peonage" despite the code. In Birmingham, Alabama, the newspaper which as a result of the Blue Eagle campaign had installed a five-day, forty-hour week announced that employees who wished to obtain a vacation had to work an extra day weekly or forego the paid vacation that had been the practice of the dailies for many years.[34] This action was wholly within the rights of the publishers under the code. Nor did NRA respond very encouragingly to the newsmen's complaints, the answer—usually from some assistant— often being, in its entirety: "Your letter addressed to General Johnson is being held for consideration when the entire matter of hours and wages for editorial writers comes up for review."[35]

Review proceeded very slowly. The publishers had reacted with great hostility to the President's Executive Order, written by Johnson, which, among other things, called the code's freedom of the press section "pure surplusage." Johnson tried to mollify the publishers by arranging for the President to issue on February 24 an additional order, one part of which accepted the free press section "without modification, condition, or qualification." The order also postponed the code's effective date from February 26 to March 12 so that, Johnson explained, publishers could consider any questions arising in regard to freedom of the press. George Buckley, the former banker and Chicago newspaper executive handling the code since Pulitzer's resignation, then ruled that the 60 days Roosevelt had prescribed for determining editorial workers' hours and wages commenced not from the date of the President's order (February 17) but from the date the code went into effect. This delayed any necessity for action almost a month, and Ernest Lindley justifiably complained to the President about this decision being "rather legalistic."[36]

Not until April 30 when the Code Authority, which had been authorized to secure the data with which to determine hours and wages, held a hearing on this matter, did the ANPA finally make public its survey of editorial employees' working conditions. The ANG representatives at the hearing declared that this survey, which found editorial workers not underpaid in comparison with other wage earners, was inadequate and obsolete. Eddy and Broun requested that the Authority take cognizance of other surveys being conducted by the guilds and by the Bureau of Labor Statistics.[37]

The day after the newsmen testified, Solomon Barkin, assistant director of the NRA Labor Advisory Board, advised Robert Buck, the Washington Guild vice president who served as the ANG's statistical expert, that "it is most impolitic for your organization to play ball with the Newspaper Code Authority. . . . Despite your efforts they will probably neglect you, and it may be well to play with them the other way round." The wisdom of Barkin's advice became clear some days later when the Authority proposed for NRA approval an amendment to the code whose provisions gave publishers broad discretion to define "editorial executives" exempt from maximum-hour regulation, made no mention of a five-day week, and established minimums that would have helped only a few of the lower paid editorial workers. Even the trade journals found these proposals inadequate. For nearly seven months thereafter, NRA took no action on the amendment, while various groups assembled facts and figures. The guilds and the Bureau of Labor Statistics finished their surveys, and the ANPA conducted another one so that its findings might be as up-to-date as possible.[38] Not until early December, after the completion of all the surveys, did NRA hold a hearing on the Authority's proposed amendment.[39]

Confusion as well as dilatoriness also marked the government's response to the ANG's efforts to be represented on the Newspaper Industrial Board, the body designated by the code to serve as final arbiter in all employer-employee disputes. Even before the board had heard its first case, the publishers' attorneys advised it that, government bodies notwithstanding, any labor dispute involving a publisher assentor to the Code could go nowhere but the Newspaper Industrial Board (NIB). NRA, on the other hand, expected that the board would confine itself generally to cases involving wages, hours, and working conditions. The NIB's eight-man membership was divided equally between labor and management, and they agreed on little. One of the impartial chairmen the NIB appointed said, when a case finally was referred to him: "Well, I am glad you gentlemen at last were able to agree on something." The *New Republic*, noting that an evenly divided board such as the NIB usually benefits the employer in labor disputes because he can gain his ends by producing deadlocks and wearing down his employees' resources, commented that "compelling the ANG or any other union to take its complaint to such an agency . . . is nothing less than delivering it into the hands of the enemy." ANG officials recognized these drawbacks; nevertheless, Eddy believed that "a place on the Board will be of inestimable service to us both in strengthening our organization and in providing a sounding board for our legitimate grievances."[40]

The announcement on April 5 of the NIB's composition had dashed the hopes of the newsmen, for it did not include an ANG representative. Robert Buck reminded Johnson of his and the President's assurances of representation on the NIB to the newspaper workers' delegations that had called at the White House in December. The NRA head replied: "By God, I promised you fellows that . . . and I will keep that promise if I have to split the code wide open to do it." But Johnson could not simply throw a union man off the NIB to make way for a newsman. First, NRA attempted to set up a separate board to deal with editorial workers, claiming that the other NIB labor members objected to the ANG being represented. Heber Blankenhorn, vice chairman of the National Labor Board, pointed out to the newsmen that separation would isolate them, and the union leaders stated that they did not object to ANG participation on the NIB. Johnson finally decided to enlarge the NIB to ten members (one more publisher and one ANG man) even though some of his assistants thought it would lead to trouble. Protracted negotiations between the publishers and NRA ensued while the latter, as one chronicler has said, "held the impatient Guild at arm's length." On May 22 Johnson drew up an order enlarging the NIB, but he did not sign and release it until May 29. Meanwhile, the Code Authority had decided to hold a referendum of assenting publishers to see if they would agree to this change in the code. On June 2 Johnson accepted the necessity for this referendum and in effect nullified his previous order. But two days later he unaccountably appointed Eddy to the enlarged NIB and twice thereafter (June 5 and 6) reassured him about his NIB seat. On June 11, the ANPA's code committee recommended that publishers vote against accepting the enlargement proposal. The Code Authority notified NRA on June 25 that the NIB plan had been voted down 534 to 6. Eddy, lacking Broun's prestige, had found it increasingly difficult to obtain appointments at the White House or with Johnson; he wrote Johnson on July 2, saying that "I hope you will find a moment to tell us *personally* just where the hell we stand now." Johnson finally found a way out of this embarrassing impasse (which, as Hanson said, "the general created through his inability to take a stand"). He spoke to the head of the Pressmen's Union. Its vice president, Shuford B. Marks, who served as secretary of the NIB, resigned from the board July 13 on the understanding that should any matters relating to the pressmen arise, another labor member would appoint Marks his proxy. Eddy was appointed in Marks' place. He received confirmation of his appointment on July 25 and formally took his seat at the August 6 meeting. This appointment gained the newsmen almost nothing. Of the 11 complaints the ANG formally brought before the NIB during its existence, all but one were dismissed, a ruling which in effect meant that the employer won.[41]

From the time of his appointment as Executive Secretary until mid-summer 1934 Eddy had devoted most of his energies and a great deal of the ANG's resources to these campaigns to obtain a place on the NIB and some kind of NRA regulation of hours and wages. In the absence of any clear-cut program he had concentrated the guilds' activities on Washington. He even had convinced Broun, whose health and inclination during the spring of 1934 had led him to pursue a less active role in the organization movement to work for these causes. Eddy labored very hard, writing letters, memoranda, appeals, and manifestoes. He swallowed his pride and made a number of trips to the capital even though he anticipated the run-around he got. He did not totally neglect the other aspects of the ANG, for he advocated the necessity for some kind of collective bargaining and attempted to advise those guilds which considered it. He tried to formulate some kind of master program, and he even found time before the June convention for two organizing trips. However, his principal efforts were directed at the government, and probably the ANG and the newsmen would have been better off had he spent more time in building and forming the organization, visiting the fledgling guilds, and talking to the editorial workers interested in the guilds, who needed the stimulus only an outsider could supply. Given both NRA's and the President's previous disappointments of the newsmen, the ineffective results of Eddy's campaigns could have been foreseen. A strong organization probably would have accomplished more than what Emmet Crozier has termed "futile palaver with government bureaucrats."[42] It certainly would have been more ready to embark on a program of collective bargaining and to defend itself and its members against publisher attacks than the ANG proved to be.

Johnson had regarded many of the items that the editorial workers had submitted for inclusion in the code as being "obviously requests that should be made through collective bargaining."[43] And he told Roosevelt in the letter transmitting the code, made public when the President promulgated it in February, that the guilds doubtless would engage in collective bargaining. As the newsmen became disenchanted with NRA, the guilds began to do just that. Some, such as the Twin Cities group, attempted only to restore the wage cuts instituted after 1929. Other groups, such as the one in Toledo, adopted a complete negotiating program which echoed the *Record*'s contract provisions. By mid-May enough guild chapters had proceeded along these lines for the ANPA's Special Standing Committee (appointed to take up labor questions affecting member publishers) to send out a memorandum warning that guild proposals warranted careful scrutiny by newspaper management. The memorandum added: "do not be misled by the fact that the contract is presented by a 'guild' instead of a union—'a rose by any other name. . . !' " Most guilds undertook no new activity for a time after the June convention, but in the fall their pressure for bargaining talks resumed. Guilds in such diverse places as El Paso, Reading, and Cleveland drew up contracts for submission to publishers.[44]

At the beginning of 1934 the majority of publishers, still concerned with the code, remained indifferent to the guilds. In fact, a few newspaper owners thought that the organized newsmen could be used as a weapon against the mechanical workers unions. John Borg, publisher of the Hackensack-Bergen *Evening Record*, represented this school of thought: he told an assembly of northern New Jersey guildsmen that he understood that they intended to fight the wage monopoly of the unions, and he predicted that if this were the case, the newsmen would find that their "best friend will be the publisher." The guilds' drive against Pulitzer and their continued demands for NRA regulation of hours and wages did cause some newspapers to oppose openly organization of their editorial staffs. *Editor & Publisher* remarked on February 10 that within the last few days it had heard of several publishers who regarded guilds as enemies. However, toward the end of March Eddy still could reassure local guild officials about the publishers' attitude, declaring that in only one or two instances had "the fog of suspected opposition" failed to clear away.[45]

As the guilds' turn toward collective bargaining became clear, however, publisher resistance quickly stiffened. Newsmen received warnings about joining a guild. The head of the Associated Press in New York, for instance, spent some time with one of his leading correspondents seeking to influence him to resign his guild membership. In some areas publishers began to take stronger measures, getting rid of employees they considered leaders of guild activity. The Hearst papers were among those which took strong action. In San Francisco, Louis Burgess, chairman of the *Examiner* chapter and a respected veteran editorial writer, was fired April 4 supposedly for reasons of economy and because of dissatisfaction with his work. Seven weeks later the *Call-Bulletin* forced Dean Jennings, its chief rewrite man and a delegate to the forthcoming ANG convention, to resign.[46]

Jennings, Burgess, and many of the other early "guild martyrs" did not come from the lower paid editorial ranks. They and many other newsmen's leaders came from among the more successful editorial employees. Moreover, despite the guilds' avowed economic aims, these newspapermen also concerned themselves with other issues affecting editorial workers and the industry. They considered adopting ability ratings (the Toledo Guild did adopt standards for apprenticeship), establishing schools for copy boys and junior staff members (the Philadelphia Guild did so), and awarding honors for outstanding reporting (a practice which on the national level resulted in the annual Heywood Broun memorial prizes). Unfortunately, these activities rapidly became sidetracked as circumstances forced the newsmen to concentrate all their energies on the fight for guild survival. The ANG also considered chartering junior guilds in journalism schools and colleges so that the romance of newspapering could be nipped in the bud, but, as one newspaper history points out, "the antagonism of the industry— feared by journalism teachers and university administrators— checked this movement." Guild leaders also found that many of the educators attempted to influence the ANG to become a professional association, and therefore the guildsmen drew away. Some guild leaders expressed interest in rectifying some of the newspaper industry's more flagrant abuses of press freedom and in improving the corporate character of the dailies. The June convention acted to this end when it adopted a code of ethics for newsmen which included a condemnation of some of the more venal practices which marred the American press, such as carrying publicity disguised as news in return for advertising and publishing deliberately misleading stories. The code of ethics exemplified the intellectual ferment that gave the guild movement at this time what one critic called "a refreshingly astringent quality," although it further intensified publisher disapproval of the guilds.[47]

The publishers' opposition hurt organization. Mobile (Ala.)

newsmen cancelled a scheduled get-together after the publisher
fired the most organization-minded reporter; an editorial worker
reported to Eddy that this "action threw the fear of God into a
big percent of the gang and they feel if they start anything
they'll be picked out. . . ." Detroit newsmen began to drop out
of the guild there when the city's newspaper managements
refused to acknowledge their attempts to open negotiations; a
guild leader there later called this period "the most frustrating
time of our lives." Increasingly open publisher hostility notwithstanding, newsmen maintained their interest in organization throughout the spring of 1934. The ANG continued to
receive many letters of inquiry and new guilds continued to
spring up, especially in such non-metropolitan areas as Salt
Lake City, Utah, and Muskegon, Michigan.[48]

In another sense the publishers' actions strengthened the
organization movement by helping to settle the debate going
on among guildsmen between the old concept of newspaper
work as a romantic profession and a new desire to improve
their economic condition by collective action. The intensified
publisher opposition coupled with NRA's failure to do much
for the newsmen led to a perceptible shift away from the professional association concept of the guilds. However, a strong
minority did not care for this move. Thomas Lewis, vice president of the Philadelphia Guild, expressed this sentiment when
he asked *Guild Reporter* readers to practice a little idealism and
not to move to the left. He believed that newsmen should say,
in essence: "Mr. Publisher, your problems are ours and ours are
yours. We've taken the dive and the water's fine. Hop in. Here's
our hand." But too much had happened for guildsmen in large
numbers to accept such a view. The discussions immediately
preceding the convention (which began June 5) concerned themselves not with whether newsmen should bargain collectively
but with what constitutional changes the guilds should make
so that they could bargain more effectively and whether the
ANG should affiliate with organized labor and ask for an AFL
charter.[49]

For most guild members (Eddy estimated 90 percent) affiliation with the AFL, which in effect meant becoming an out-and-

out trade union, represented too radical a move, and they rejected the idea, although many had changed their minds and had come to realize the necessity of effecting changes in the ANG structure which would assist collective bargaining. A Philadelphia Newspaper Guild canvas of guild leaders across the country found 59 out of 60 (one would not commit himself) opposing any move to join the AFL. On other issues the Philadelphia Guild found opposition to any sort of large-scale staff organization and to any national dues higher than $0.50 per month.[50]

The dues problem plagued both the local groups and the national organization. Even those newsmen who avowed great enthusiasm for the guild movement often would fail to pay. Garland Ashcraft found that the Cleveland guildsmen would sit and talk sense in meetings, take care of routine matters, do what else they could, but that "not one damn man jack of them will go up to a fellow member . . . and say, 'Listen, you son of a bitch, get them dues in.' " An audit of the ANG's books found that just before the June convention its cash balance was $47.19. The erratic returns on the two $1.00 assessments (based on each local group's reported membership) had caused this financial straitening. Some guilds virtually ignored the ANG; Buffalo, which claimed a membership of about 200, had sent the ANG only $25.00 by May 24. Many of the smaller groups, although occasionally quite tardy, paid the bulk of their obligations to the ANG. The Monroe, Louisiana, unit had paid in full its $24.00 obligation by March 19 (four days after the second assessment had fallen due); the Fort Worth, Texas, chapter took until July 2, but by then had paid all but $1.00 of the $106.00 it owed. Although the payments from the smaller guilds helped the ANG, it depended for its existence on the income it received from larger ones. These paid several hundred dollars each into the ANG treasury, but often these payments fell short of what the ANG could have expected to receive on the basis of reported membership. The Philadelphia Guild, for example, despite several good-sized payments, on the basis of its self-estimated membership of 600 still owed the ANG about $475.00 on the assessments on May 24.[51]

The national organization's most complicated financial relationship and one that played havoc with its budgetary calculations was that with the New York Guild, which, despite its financial delinquency at this time, still provided about 12 percent of the ANG's income. On the second assessment, as on the first, the New York Guild's overly optimistic estimates of membership and inability to establish an effective dues-collection system resulted in the ANG realizing less revenue than had been anticipated. In April, the New York Guild had claimed 1,500 members. By May 7, having paid the ANG $250.00 on the second assessment, it had revised its reported membership to 1,000. Even on that basis it still owed $750.00. Anxious not to have its vote (based on paid-up membership) reduced at the forthcoming convention, the New York Guild sent the ANG $300.00 on May 7 and gave it a 30-day note for the rest, promising to accept a cut in representation at the convention if it did not pay up.[52]

The ANG met in convention at St. Paul on June 5-8, 1934. The approximately 125 delegates according to ANG spokesmen represented more than 60 guilds claiming a total membership of over 8,000; this was more than just a politic exaggeration: Eddy's figures a year later showed only about 3,700 guildsmen of whom it was estimated that only 1,900 to 2,000 regularly paid dues. A militant tone marked the proceedings, and the decisions of the convention finally turned the guild movement away from the professional association idea and toward a more centralized trade unionism.[53] The delegates voted that guilds could cooperate with other labor organizations if they so wished and overwhelmingly approved a committee report which, on the premise that "it is better to have no contract than a bad one," strongly recommended bargaining goals for the guilds that, as one newspaper industry history has put it, "epitomized the experience of labor unions through decades of industrial strife."[54] The convention's joint committee on collective bargaining and contracts did not submit a model contract because it did not believe that the guilds would accept fixed instructions at this time, but it recommended and the delegates accepted detailed requisites guilds should strive to attain in written agreements, including a minimum wage, maximum hours, compensation for overtime, and similar benefits. The revised constitution adopted by the convention, while still granting the local guilds considerable autonomy, gave the national organization increased authority in matters of collective bargaining.[55] Local groups, though still in control of negotiations, had to submit proposed contracts to the National Executive Committee for recommendations at least 15 days before submitting them to publishers. Individual members remained free to negotiate independently, but the constitution forbade them to accept a wage or other standard of employment inferior to that secured by a guild in any collective action. The ANG received the right to intervene in local bargaining negotiations not only at the request of the guild involved but also at the request of a "substantial fraction of thirty percent or more" of the local membership.

The revised constitution attempted to rectify what Broun in an address opening the four-day meeting called the ANG's lack of unity and cohesiveness. It established a new executive committee structure which, besides the president, secretary, and treasurer, included 14 vice presidents. One served at large, and the other thirteen represented the District of Columbia and regions roughly corresponding to the twelve Federal Reserve Bank districts.[56] The delegates had decided on regional organization rather than state groupings in the belief, as the committee chairman concerned with this matter said, that "this system is wiser, because frequently sections of the same State have closer economic attachments to sections of other States. . . ."[57] High hopes were expressed for the ability of the regional vice president system to provide closer bonds between the guilds and the national organization. *The Guild Reporter* said that delegates believed that each regional vice president would serve as "a sort of super organizer, ambassador, shock absorber, legislator, and traveling magistrate all in one."[58] However, this system functioned little better in knitting the guilds together than had the one adopted in December, 1933. Once again, lack of funds caused the revised Executive Committee for most of its existence to vote by mail and telegram. Because very few guilds existed in New England or in the deep

South, the convention did not select any vice presidents from those regions. Some of the others it chose came to disagree with the ANG's policies and dropped out. Only a few regional groupings were even attempted; only one or two of these can be said to have been successful.

The revised constitution attempted to strengthen the national organization in other respects. Now the constitution of each local guild had to conform to the ANG constitution. A petition by 20 percent or more of a local guild's membership would serve to bring any dispute about conformity before the National Executive Committee, whose decision in the matter would be binding, subject to review by the next national convention. Provision was made for assembling a complete list of members and their addresses. Eddy and Crozier had discussed doing this after the December, 1933, meeting, but had abandoned the project because they had lacked the facilities to set up and maintain a master file.[59] To bolster the ANG's sagging finances, the convention decided, after the longest debate of the meetings, to remove the uncertain and irregular financing provided by periodic assessments and to establish in the revised constitution national dues of $0.50 per member per month to be transmitted to the ANG by the local guilds. These dues would be allocated as follows: $0.35 for national organizational and administrative expenses; $0.05 for a special reserve fund; $0.10 as payment on an annual subscription to *The Guild Reporter*. Local guilds would continue to levy what initiation fees and dues they judged proper. During the debate on dues one delegate had warned that "there is going to be trouble getting this sum. . . ."[60] The events of the next six months proved him right, but it is doubtful that adoption of the alternative figure of $0.25 would have made dues collection any easier. As it was, the convention's actions did little to alleviate the ANG's financial problems.

The delegates also voted to confine exact knowledge of the ANG's financial condition to the National Executive Committee on the grounds that this would deny the publishers precise knowledge of the organization's resources. This action had unfortunate repercussions, for, as Eddy later pointed out, it opened the way for rumors about the stability of the organization and the misuse of ANG funds.[61]

This hardworking convention ran very smoothly, generally unmarred by the bitter factionalism (based on both personal and political differences) which would rend the ANG meetings for the next years. The issue of AFL affiliation, the only one over which feeling might have run high, was neutralized by Broun's actions. The ANG president, as did some of the other delegates, considered affiliation necessary for the ANG to survive and the guilds to gain their economic goals. Much as he wanted affiliation, however, Broun realized that many delegates had come to the convention prepared to vote against it. He also realized that even if he and the other supporters of affiliation could win over a majority of the delegates, the bulk of the guild membership would not accept it. Therefore, not only to avoid a bitter debate but also to keep the ANG from going on record against affiliation and thus closing the question, Broun suggested as almost the first order of business postponing all discussion of affiliation. The delegates accepted the resulting motion unanimously.

The convention reelected Broun, Crozier, and Eddy, who all ran without opposition. The only election contests were for two of the regional vice presidencies, and these contests were brief and reasonably pleasant. Broun—remembered by delegates as being fair, amiable, ready to sit down and talk out any problems—made an excellent chairman. He also used his flair for the dramatic in a manner which bolstered not only the spirits of the delegates but also the morale of guildsmen everywhere. Shortly after a speech by San Francisco newsman Louis Burgess on what organization meant ("there is no neutrality. . . . The issue is whether you be with the men or the managers"), Broun, apparently fighting mad, his hair falling over his eyes, told the visibly moved delegates that "the only tangible reply we can make to the Hearst challenge is to answer 'you fired him, we hired him.' "[62] The delegates unanimously adopted Broun's motion that the ANG hire Burgess, although unsure for just what position. The convention accepted Broun's explanation that "we can take care of the details later."[63]

Aroused by the Burgess speech, the convention adopted as one of its first resolutions a motion condemning Hearst for his opposition to the guilds. For the record he was described as "a son of a bitch," but later in the convention the delegates adopted a less inflammatory substitute measure suggested by Hearst-employed newsmen, which attributed anti-guild activities to the publisher's subordinates and invited him to meet with guild representatives. Other resolutions adopted by the convention called for NRA to oust George Buckley (described as "the tool of the publishers"), for an end to newspaper wage schedules which discriminated against women, and for the immediate imposition of a press association code. The delegates also adopted some resolutions which had nothing to do with the newspaper business, including ones calling for the freeing of Tom Mooney, for Congressional passage of the Lundeen unemployment benefits bill, and for all newsmen to refuse "by distortion and suppression to create political, economic, industrial, and military wars."[64] The sponsors of these resolutions took advantage of the political naivete and idealistic enthusiasm of most of the delegates. Bruce Catton, reporting on the convention to Cleveland newsmen, said that many delegates got so excited that they would have accepted a resolution calling for the complete abolition of capitalism.[65] These resolutions presaged the ANG's future, unhappy forays into political issues, which would cause considerable bitterness and unrest among many guildsmen.

The ANG had begun its life as a weak organization hampered by inadequate financing, a lack of central direction or consistently active national leadership, and (despite some high-sounding phrases) no real purpose beyond influencing the provisions of the newspaper code relating to editorial workers.

By June, 1934, events—especially the failure of NRA or the President to perceptibly improve newspapermen's working conditions—had made it clear that guildsmen could expect to gain little from an organization dedicated to the professional association concept. Increasingly guildsmen accepted the idea that only if the guilds took part in collective bargaining could any improvements be attained. At this point, however, few had decided that the ANG should become a full-fledged trade union affiliated with the AFL.

The June, 1934, convention at St. Paul served to codify many of the changes that had taken place in the young guild movement since its conception and birth. But the process of growth and change had just begun. Although in the next months the guild movement would flounder around, events would soon force the young ANG to evolve at a much faster rate. The St. Paul convention had tabled the question of AFL affiliation. Almost everything that happened to the guild movement during the year before the next convention met served to strengthen the pro-affiliation forces. And as this group gained in power, many of those opposed to them and their ideas dropped out of active participation in the guilds. This in turn further enhanced the position of those who wished to make the guild movement part of organized labor as well as accelerated the process of bringing the guilds into the AFL.

5 ·

toward the picket line . . .

"You don't have to be told," Jonathan Eddy wrote a Cleveland
Guild officer, "that the American Newspaper Guild left St.
Paul broke." To rectify this situation, at treasurer Emmet Crozier's suggestion the National Executive Committee at its initial
meeting in St. Paul on June 8 had adopted unanimously a plan
calling for the new dues schedule to go into effect immediately,
even though the new financial machinery was not designed to
start functioning until July 1. Crozier had estimated, on the
basis of revised local group membership figures calculated for
the convention, that with advance payment of dues this action
would bring $3,823.25 into the ANG treasury. But by the end
of July, despite a strenuous letter-writing campaign by Crozier,
the ANG had received only $1,663.50 from the local groups,
and most of this amount dribbled in toward the end of that
month.[1]

The limited response to Crozier's appeals stemmed from the
same causes as did the difficulties faced by local guild officers in
repairing their financial situations and in maintaining organization. Summer vacation schedules played havoc with their attempts to remain in close contact with the membership. The
expense of sending delegates to the convention had drained a
number of guild treasuries as well as the financial resources of
many of the more active guildsmen. More important, former
attitudes about newspapering reasserted themselves among a
surprisingly large number of editorial workers, and many guilds

across the the country suffered from a general coldness toward organization. Eddy, who continued to believe that "apathy or indifference *can be overcome*," nevertheless expressed amazement at "the indifference or skepticism of editorial workers to the guild movement."[2]

The actions of the convention had turned many editorial workers away from organization. Some of the resolutions passed at St. Paul (e.g., the one calling for the freeing of Tom Mooney) had caused unrest among the less politically oriented guildsmen.[3] The dues schedule seemed too steep to many newsmen, especially those in the rural areas. The secretary of the Grand Forks, North Dakota, Guild wrote Eddy that "our group feels that the dues are too high in proportion to the possible value. . . ." Guild members also objected to the pro-AFL affiliation tendencies of Broun and some other guild leaders, whose comments and agitation at St. Paul as well as the flamboyant manner in which some of the ANG leadership supported the New York Guild in its disputes with the publisher S. I. Newhouse that summer caused a number of defections from the guild ranks. Those newsmen who favored a more professionally minded organization left their guilds or withdrew from active participation in them; as John Prescott put it when he resigned as president of the Reading group: "My sympathy with the movement—particularly the National Guild and its leanings toward the labor union tactics—is insufficient to warrant continuation in a position [of responsibility]."[4]

The growing hostility of newspaper managements to the ANG also contributed to the coolness many editorial workers displayed toward organization. The St. Paul convention had intensified publishers' fears about the ANG's aims. A. L. Miller, publisher of a Battle Creek, Michigan, daily, summed up management's general feelings about the ANG when he declared that, in his opinion, as a result of the convention the organization could neither command respect nor succeed. Across the country during the summer of 1934, as newspaper executives made known their displeasure with the guild movement, many editorial workers, anxious about their jobs in a depression economy, backed away from organization. It took extraordinary bravery for a newsman to join a guild in the face of an editor who made it clear that "no guild member would retain his place on my staff. A guild member always can be fired for incompetence." What often happened was exemplified by the situation in Little Rock, where, according to the NRA Labor Compliance Officer, the great majority of the editorial employees of two dailies would have liked to form a guild but did not do so, probably because of what the officer called management's "personal objection" to the idea.[5]

The trade journals reflected this hardening of publisher opinion. Although *Editor & Publisher* did assert after the convention that "a professional guild is still a possibility," its acerbic comments on the delegates' actions were followed by unremitting criticismn of Broun and the ANG in both the magazine's editorials and the columns of its editor, Marlen Pew. These denunciations, as well as those appearing in the other trade journals, served only to strengthen the pro-union forces as the more hesitant newsmen dropped their guild membership.[6]

For some weeks after the convention this shrinkage was quite precipitant, so much so that by the end of July, total "book" membership in the guilds had declined to less than 6,000—25 percent less than *The Guild Reporter* had claimed but two months earlier—and active paid-up membership had fallen off even more. The ANG seemed to be coming apart. Even in Cleveland, which had led the fight for national organization, the membership began "to get parochial ideas about their own local guilds, their local problems, and their solution," as a guildsman put it. The suspension of *The Guild Reporter* for nearly three months because of financial difficulties contributed to the atomization of the organization. Eddy recognized *The Guild Reporter* as "our one channel of communication, our one means of molding a truly powerful and united, nationwide Guild," but at the time he could do little about its suspension. Lack of funds menaced the existence of Eddy's office, which managed to continue operating only because the tiny staff—one woman for most of the summer—worked overtime and on "days off" without pay. Eddy did what he could, but the national organization suffered because he found it impossible to keep in touch with developments in all the local groups. Moreover, the officers and members of those groups who submitted proposed contracts for review by the National Executive Committee in compliance with the new constitution must have been disappointed when instead of obtaining a broad range of advice from the National Executive Committee, they merely received a letter from Eddy tersely analyzing the contract and sometimes adding that "it is financially impossible for us just now to have a dozen copies of a multi-page document mimeographed and distributed." Certainly many newspapermen must have thought twice about paying dues to an organization which could not live up to its own constitutional requirements. In the years to come the American Newspaper Guild would face more intense publisher opposition and greater internal crises, but as a national organization it reached its nadir in the summer of 1934.[7]

At the very time the ANG appeared to be in the greatest danger of falling apart, however, dedicated militants among its members—usually committed to the idea of the guilds as trade unions, with all that entailed—undertook actions which by helping to coalesce newsmen's sentiments on the local level contributed to the renascence of the ANG. The first of these actions took place in New York, in the borough of Queens. There, on July 11, 1934, in front of the offices of the *Long Island Daily Press*, newsmen established the guilds' first picket line and, as *Editor & Publisher* pointed out, "probably [for] the first time in the history of American journalism . . . editorial workers . . . picketed a newspaper plant."[8]

In November, 1932, Samuel I. Newhouse, then a struggling young publisher with very limited financial resources, had obtained control of the company that published this typical suburban daily, and he had placed Philip Hochstein in charge of editorial operations. Hochstein, later described by the New York Guild newspaper as a man of "liberal if not radical views," ended most of the sweatshop conditions that had prevailed on the *Press*. He gave out pay raises, added staff so that the work load would not fall on a few newsmen, and gradually eliminated space rates (i.e., payment, usually to the younger, newer members of the staff, on the basis of copy published no matter how much work they might have done). Nevertheless, the staff still had to put in very long hours at relatively poor pay. Some of the *Press* newsmen decided to establish a guild chapter, hoping somehow to improve working conditions further, although exactly what they had in mind remains unclear. By June 16, 1934, about six weeks after organization had begun, the chapter included 40 out of about 55 eligible workers.[9]

The management of the *Press* reacted sharply to what it termed "the guild problem," for Newhouse on principle opposed organization of editorial workers. Hochstein said he made no threats to the staff but merely attempted to point out to the chapter's leaders their failure to put forth any sensible plans. The New York Guild charged that attempts had been made to intimidate the chapter's members and that Hochstein had gone along with Newhouse on this policy because he considered the staff "ungrateful and unfair." Clayton Knowles, then the chairman of the *Press* chapter, remembers being called in three times in one week by the front office and each time, during the course of discussion about "outside influences on the staff," being threatened with dismissal for "inefficiency." On July 6, the newspaper's management took action. Claiming that the guild's supposed position on apprentices necessitated reorganization among the younger, newer members of the staff, it threatened to restore space rates within two weeks and fired nine people, eight of them guild members, including Emily Brown, the secretary of the chapter.[10]

Hochstein supposedly told many of the older newsmen to disband the chapter "if they wished to protect the innocent lambs . . . they had led to slaughter." At a special chapter meeting on July 8, the members tabled a resolution to disband because Broun, Eddy, and newly elected New York Guild president Carl Randau had scheduled a conference with Newhouse and Hochstein. This conference, held on July 10, proved inconclusive. That same day, despite the presence of Broun, Eddy, and Randau, at another special gathering many of the *Press* editorial workers accepted the assurances of the city editor (who Hochstein recalls as having no authority to make such statements) that dissolution meant reinstatement of the discharged employees, and voted 18-11 to disband. Broun then asked for a show of hands of whose willing to form a new chapter, and about nine or ten raised their hands but dropped them quickly when several others shouted that such action was dangerous. A few, however, decided to continue in the guild, thus allowing the chapter to remain in existence, at least formally.[11]

A few hours later the New York Guild's Representative Assembly, accepting its executive committee's recommendations, overwhelmingly voted to appeal the case of the *Press* employees in the courts and before NRA, and to picket the newspaper and otherwise publicize the situation. Guild leaders hoped to win the sympathy of *Press* readers and advertisers and thus embarrass Newhouse into some kind of settlement. The leadership believed that the organization movement would lose much if it submitted to Newhouse. As Carl Randau wrote the membership: "This is the fight we all know we might expect. . . . It is directed directly at the life of the Guild in New York." Moreover, the more union-minded of the ANG and New York Guild officers saw an excellent opportunity to win support for their position as well as to rally wavering members and spur organization. At this time New York was one of the few places with sufficient militants for the organization to give a good account of itself, but even there, as Eddy later indicated, "much of the membership back in the offices was disturbed and even contentious."[12]

The picketing that began July 11 lasted only four days, but during that time the New York Guild utilized many of the tactics that other guilds across the country would use again and again in the next years. The majority of the guild forces were volunteers from other chapters: a picket line composed only of *Press* guildsmen would have been an unimpressive sight. Moreover, by virtue of their jobs the editorial employees from various chapters had skills and connections then not usually available to workers in conflict with their employers. The guild made good use of these forces. An automobile procession toured Jamaica, Queens, the home of the *Press*. The cars carried banners attacking the newspaper; the procession included a borrowed sound truck which denounced the *Press* and explained the guild side. A house-to-house canvassing committee distributed copies of a one-sheet newspaper that exhorted "Mr. Reader" not to patronize "a paper that intimidated its writers" and asked "Mr. Advertiser" if he wished to advertise in a "medium that is incurring the enmity of all people working for a living." Another committee sent out news releases to all the mass media and did such a fine job of selective reporting that Hochstein later complained that accounts "published in many of the newspapers of New York and Brooklyn either were distorted or omitted important relevant facts in the case." Several guildsmen made radio appearances, and others asked celebrity acquaintances to join the picket line. *New York Post* newsman Ben Leider had slogans painted in big letters on the side of his biplane and, with Eddy and Emily Brown, flew over the newspaper's offices and other parts of Queens.[13]

The *Press* editorial workers were the first of many guildsmen who looked to Heywood Broun for inspiration during a dispute. Jonathan Eddy, for all his daring and hard work, lacked Broun's charisma. The labor historian B. J. Widick, himself a guildsman in the 1930s, says that "in modern terminology Broun was a father figure." Broun admittedly had no interest in the mechanics of organization and administration. A Cleveland Guild officer complained after the *Press* dispute that Broun never "even sent . . . a message direct through channels to the membership of the organization he officially heads." Although in his later years as ANG president Broun improved somewhat in this regard, he continued to bother very little with the ANG's day-to-day operations. However, he never failed the membership in such crisis situations as the *Press* dispute. Officials could not deal so summarily with Broun as with less noted newspapermen. When, during the *Press* dispute, a policeman halted a leaflet-distributing procession headed by Broun, the columnist consulted with his attorney by phone and then forced a showdown at the local police station which resulted in the guildsmen resuming their activities with the policeman impotently muttering about "those Reds." Broun's presence boosted morale; he added flair and color, and he treated even the lowliest copy boy without condescension. Completely unselfconscious, Broun talked with guild members, marched with them, drank with them. Not only did he pay his own way, something very important to the often poverty-stricken guildsmen, he also contributed funds when necessary. He offered 10 percent of his pay to the *Press* guildsmen in the event of a strike.[14]

But a strike did not take place. The *Press* editorial workers, even those belonging to the New York Guild, did not walk out. Despite the picketing and other demonstrations, the *Press* continued publishing. On July 12, the day after the picketing started, the New York Guild managed to reorganize the *Press* chapter on a reduced scale; but with the exception of Emily Brown, whom Hochstein had discharged, the chapter's members confined their guild activities to non-working hours. William Hofmann, the publisher of the *Press,* ridiculed the guild's tactics in a front-page open letter to Broun and called the picketing "silly." But the guildsmen aroused sufficient stir for Mayor Fiorello La Guardia to intervene. The principals worked out an agreement during a three-hour conference at City Hall the morning of July 14. Newhouse agreed to recognize the employees' right to form a guild chapter, to reinstate for at least three months all discharged employees except those fired for incompetence, to deal with a grievance committee, and to begin negotiations on a detailed contract with the guild and in the event of a deadlock to submit the differences to arbitration. For its part, the guild accepted the arbitration clause and agreed to recognize Long Island (excepting Brooklyn) as a separate territorial division, in effect conceding—given its stated intention in the agreement "to bring about uniform editorial department conditions on daily papers operating in the same field"—that it would not expect New York's suburban newspapers to match the demands made of the larger circulation metropolitan press.[15]

At the conclusion of the City Hall conference, Newhouse, who could not understand why the guildsmen had singled out his newspaper, told Broun: "you've made a guinea pig of the *Press.*" The ANG head replied: "Well, you walked right into our laboratory." Broun and other guild leaders considered the agreement a victory for their side. However, within a week the New York Guild's executive committee complained to the mayor about "deliberate violations" of the peace agreement. Indeed, the chairman of the Press chapter recalls that in the next months the newspaper increasingly harassed its guild employees and attempted to get rid of them. The victory really went not to the Press newsmen but to the more union-minded among the guild leaders, such as Eddy, who now believed that "the important thing . . . [was] that the New York organization is at last an out-and-out labor union." An editorial executive shortly thereafter declared the Press fight significant for the same reasons. The putative victory over the Press garnered far more publicity than did the less happy aftermath, and it helped change the complexion of all the guilds, not just the one in New York.[16] The more professionally minded and the fainthearted among the guildsmen continued to drift away or become passive members; as a result the ANG, though diminished in numbers, became a more purposeful body.

Other guild actions during the summer in New York and elsewhere contributed to this process. The Philadelphia Guild appealed to the Regional Labor Board and forced an election among the Evening Ledger editorial employees as to who should represent them. The guild won, but the publisher, who had not expected his hand-picked anti-guild slate to lose, refused to enter into any serious discussions with the guild's representatives. In Boston the publisher of the Herald and the Traveler refused to negotiate and fired two of the more active guildsmen, but then, after refusing to deal with the news workers' representatives, he increased wages (as much as $9.00 a week in some cases) and established minimum pay scales (Eddy estimated that it cost the publisher more than $10,000 a year). A management spokesman insisted that all this "had no connection whatsoever with the guilds." The Washington Guild convinced the Star's management that it should rescind an economy order that all reporters should carry cameras, a dismaying prospect for the already overworked newsmen. A few guilds, such as the one in Oklahoma City, had general meetings at which members voted on hour and wage demands to present to publishers. In Cleveland negotiations with the News on these issues at one point reached such an impasse that guild leaders there considered calling a strike.[17]

The first vote to strike, however, was taken in New York on August 29 when, following the discharge of three guildsmen, eleven of the fifteen members of the *Jewish Daily Bulletin* chapter voted six to two (with three abstaining) to walk out. The management of the country's only English-language Jewish daily, which also controlled the more prosperous and older news service affiliate—the Jewish Telegraph Agency—claimed that adverse economic conditions had dictated the dismissals, but the New York Guild leaders refused to accept this explanation. Under pressure of the threatened strike, the management agreed to terms which included recognition of the guild, re-employment of the three discharged news workers, establishment of a grievance committee, and reduction of the work week to 40 hours. The *Bulletin* agreement had an unfortunate and portentous aftermath. Jacob Landau, the publisher, who (according to a former employee) needlessly ran the *Bulletin* on a shoestring, quickly violated the agreement. Moreover, pleading financial necessity, he soon stopped paying salaries regularly (they had averaged only $2.85 a day) and began periodically handing out $5.00 and $10.00 to staff members. Because the state Department of Labor had no enforcement machinery, its order to Landau to cease this practice proved useless. By January 1935 he owed the small staff over $1,300 in back wages, and on January 10 the 13 guild members, who included all but two of the editorial staff of the *Bulletin* and the Agency, struck and forced the newspaper to suspend publication. Three days later Landau gave in and agreed not only to pay the employees $1,363 in back wages (at the rate of $200 a week) and to negotiate a new contract but also to observe the old agreement, including the clause calling for a 40-hour week. This swift and apparently successful move strengthened the more union-minded within the guild, but it proved to be a phyrric victory. As long as Landau could exploit his staff the *Bulletin* had survived; the New York Guild put an end to this exploitation but the paper ceased publication in December, 1935, shortly after celebrating its tenth anniversary. Its demise probably resulted from its inherent weaknesses as well as from the additional financial strain caused by the guildsmen. The *Bulletin* situation raised for the first time, however, the yet unresolved problem of what effect guild tactics and demands might have in such a highly competitive industry as newspaper publishing.[18]

Just prior to the initial dispute with the *Bulletin* in August, 1934, the New York Guild had become involved in another altercation with S. I. Newhouse. This conflict—since labeled by the ANG as its "first strike action"—centered on Alexander Crosby, a 28-year-old editorial writer fired from Newhouse's Staten Island *Advance*. Crosby charged that the *Advance* fired him after five years' service because of his guild activities; the managing editor, Newhouse's brother Norman, said that Crosby's dismissal "did not result from his connection with the guild" but from a variety of causes including incompetence, incompatibility with the staff, and disagreement over proper presentation of society news.[19]

Crosby had displayed interest in organization as early as October, 1933, but had curbed his enthusiasm when he had learned of S. I. Newhouse's strong hostility to organization. Eight months later, Crosby's interest had revived sufficiently for him to try to form an *Advance* guild chapter. Both Newhouses made clear their displeasure, but Crosby went ahead with plans for an organizational meeting on July 18. Despite the presence of Broun and other guild leaders, the meeting failed to achieve Crosby's purpose, probably because of the uninvited presence of the city editor. In an open vote from which four *Advance* news workers abstained, fourteen others voted against organization; Crosby alone went on record for forming a chapter, later saying he did so because "I'd decided to quit being yellow." His vote, according to the president of the New York Guild, in effect set up a one-man chapter. Shortly thereafter both S. I. Newhouse and Crosby went on vacation. The publisher cabled an order for Crosby's dismissal, and on July 28 Norman Newhouse fired Crosby, giving him a month's pay as severance.[20]

Guild leaders, still flushed with enthusiasm from the apparently easy victory over Newhouse in the *Press* fight, decided to force Crosby's reinstatement as well as the recognition of the *Advance* news workers' right to organize. On August 13 Mayor La Guardia attempted to mediate, but this time his efforts failed because neither side would give way over the issue of whether Crosby should be reinstated during the arbitration of the dispute. The next night the New York Guild's Representative Assembly, "confident of an easy and speedy victory," according to *The Guild Reporter*, overwhelmingly voted to begin a campaign against the *Advance*. On August 15, picketing began.[21]

The guildsmen hoped to force a settlement by reducing the circulation of the *Advance*. As in the *Press* fight, volunteers paraded and distributed special single-sheet editions of *The Guild Reporter* which gave the guild side and asked readers to shun the *Advance*. Other volunteers picketed at the newspaper's offices and, during rush hours, at both terminals of the Manhattan-Staten Island ferry. On donated radio time Broun, Crosby, and others asked the public to boycott the *Advance*. Guildsmen wrote and then took part in the broadcasting of such propaganda playlets as "The Strange Case of Alexander Crosby," in one scene of which a family discusses the case during dinner and "Dad" convinces "Mother" and "Johnny" that "it's not a private business matter—it's a public issue . . . the publishers of the *Advance* seem to think that they are bigger than the law." A borrowed sound truck toured Staten Island presenting the guild viewpoint. Open-air mass meetings were held at which Broun, Crosby, and others spoke. When S. I. Newhouse returned from his European trip on August 24, the guildsmen assailed him on land and sea and from the air. Broun led a delegation which boarded the liner carrying Newhouse at quarantine and asked him to take Crosby back. While they spoke, an airplane with "Back the Guild" painted on its sides cruised overhead and other guildsmen in a motor boat circled the vessel shouting through megaphones. At the pier 35 more pickets marched, carrying signs charging the publisher with bullying his staff. That night outside Newhouse's Staten Island home guildsmen used a sound truck to hold a street-corner rally while playing a spotlight on his windows.[22]

The guildsmen could annoy Newhouse, but they could not move him. Crosby remained fired. In fact, their campaign boomeranged. The *Advance*'s circulation went up, not down, and the newspaper's attorneys withdrew a petition for a court order to end demonstrations. Newhouse published the only local daily on Staten Island, and the inhabitants had to read the *Advance* if they wanted to find out about such events in their community as the guild activities. The AFL did not respond to Broun's idea that it should publish a competing daily. Because Newhouse ran the only open-shop mechanical department in New York City, the ITU local gave financial support to a publisher who started a competing newspaper on November 13, which, however, failed within a month. The guild's fight continued into the autumn, but more because of its momentum than because of any belief in ultimate victory. About a month after picketing had started, it was limited to Saturdays. Some demonstrations still took place. On November 10 the picketing ended altogether. The Newspaper Industrial Board finally acted on Crosby's appeal on January 15, 1935, but he obtained no relief because the usual deadlock between the publisher members and the labor members took place.[23]

Crosby himself recognized that the "ruckus was in no sense a major event in guild history," but it was not without importance. The Crosby case gave guild leaders bent on a trade-union policy a chance to gain new contacts and strengthen old ones within the established labor movement. Eddy declared: "We now have gone to the unions. We expect and have already received a different kind of cooperation from them." Although they often received little more than token gestures, the news workers made the most of them. The projectionists' union had donated the use of a sound truck and personnel to man it. Some other unions, especially the electrical workers, had sent members to swell guild demonstrations. AFL president William Green, commenting on the guildsmen's activities, wrote the Federation's New York organizer that "I will be glad if you will aid them in every way within your power." The ITU national convention voted its "moral support," and the New York local responded to a guild request for "joint action" against Newhouse.[24]

This cooperation with organized labor, said *Editor & Publisher*, meant that the newspaper industry "need no longer regard the American Newspaper Guild as an independent body of responsible professional newswriters and editors"; the ANG, editorialized the magazine, had become a "radical trades union" and as such "a pitiful wreck." On this last point *Editor & Publisher* erred, for the ANG had begun to revive. The activities of the local groups and especially the New York Guild's aggressive handling of its disputes with Newhouse (which because of Broun's presence received much attention) contributed to the resuscitation of the national organization. Critics attacked not just the local groups but the guild movement as a whole, thereby giving the ANG more substance than it actually had. The continued withdrawal from the guilds of many of the more professionally minded and the timid because of this criticism meant that a smaller but generally much more determined membership remained. The end of the summer vacation period also helped; dues payments received at the national headquarters rose nearly 70 percent between August and November. Although ANG finances remained shaky (especially as the National Executive Committee voted against special assessments to raise a larger defense fund), enough money came in to publish *The Guild Reporter* on a semi-monthly basis, to employ additional office help, and to enable Eddy to visit local groups once again.[25]

With this revival of activity came attempts to make the national organization more meaningful, to formulate guidelines which would serve as over-all ANG policy and would keep the local groups from going off on tangents. The ANG had to function, as Eddy put it, as "a real organization" or the guild movement would result in "nothing but a bunch of confused sheep straggling along." Eddy often acted independently, but he alone did not make policy. He discussed some problems with Broun and Crozier as well as by correspondence with the other national officers; more often he consulted with the leaders of the New York Guild, with whom the ANG once again shared office space. He also would poll the National Executive Committee by mail, although the slowness of this process meant that he periodically undertook actions on the assumption that the committee would ratify them. The policy decisions taken during the fall of 1934 (though some remained operative only until the next convention) formed part of the foundations of the ANG's later operational framework, what unions often refer to as their "international law."[26]

Bargaining with management was the chief concern of guild leaders. Drawing on their limited experience, they framed a negotiating procedure which they hoped would mitigate publisher pressure: editorial workers should never have to deal directly with their own employers; the negotiating committee (as small as possible, preferably two or three men) always should come from guild members not working for the newspaper involved; and a chapter might advise or direct its agents, but during the actual talks it should take no part beyond sending one or two observers to sit in on the negotiations and report on their progress to the membership, which could accept or reject the terms agreed upon. Not all guilds found this procedure satisfactory, and some guildsmen's active dislike of it caused friction between the national organization and the local groups. In lieu of a model contract, Eddy recommended and the National Executive Committee approved a number of features that all guilds should stress in their proposed contracts. These included graduated dismissal notice running up to six months (i.e., so many weeks for so many years worked); a forty-hour week, on a five-day basis if possible; acceptance of arbitration on dismissals only as a concession to the publishers—a guild should never propose it; provisions for overtime either by accumulated time off granted within a limited period or by time-and-a-half in cash; minimum pay scales well above those prescribed by NRA; and signing of the contract directly between the publisher and the guild (rather than the publisher and his employees, which Eddy described as "company unionism").[27]

This last point Eddy and other guild officers deemed particularly important, so much so that an issue of *The Guild Reporter* devoted one-and-one-half out of eight pages to a report on "Company Unionism: A Snare." Both local and national guild leaders believed, and probably rightly, that the newspaper owners hoped to divide and conquer, to split the various guilds into separate units. To prevent this from happening, the leaders considered it imperative that in no case should a chapter sign a contract whose phraseology did not acknowledge the chapter as being part of a local guild.[28]

Its new-found vigor notwithstanding, the ANG had to cope with some familiar, serious problems. Many newspapermen remained poor organizational material. In Reading, Pennsylvania, rivalries between the *Times* and *Eagle* chapters at one point resulted in such bitterness that Eddy received a letter from the president of the latter declaring that "we will not, under any circumstances entertain the idea of associating with *Reading Times* editorial workers in the same guild." Differences also developed along chapter lines in Akron as it became clear that *Beacon Journal* employees would do better in negotiations with their publisher than would the *Times-Press* newsmen. Members of the *Pittsburgh Post-Gazette* chapter complained that its officers used their positions to aid themselves and their friends rather than all the newspaper's editorial workers. A West Coast reporter bitterly recalled "the 'rats' who climbed over guildsmen to monied success," an example being the San Francisco newsman who earned an extra $10.00 a week in exchange for information on guild activities.[29]

Executive responsibility within the ANG remained overly concentrated. The National Executive Committee did not function in the manner envisioned by the creators of the regional vice presidency system. In some cases the region simply covered too much territory. Don Stevens, the vice president for Region XII, took an interest in regional work, but his territory stretched from Arizona to Washington state. Moreover, too many regions had no head or an inactive one; disagreements arose between the regional vice presidents and local guild leaders over the trade-union course or lack of it that many guilds followed; and failure to fill vacancies also hampered the system. Nor did enough of the guilds demonstrate interest in the regional system. By the end of October, only the Philadelphia and Cleveland groups among the larger guilds had undertaken regional organization. Most important, the regional system failed to provide the necessary financing (estimated by Crozier and Eddy at about $1,000) to allow the National Executive Committee to meet periodically. Neither the ANG treasury nor the few extant regional organizations could stand such an outlay. Four times between June, 1934, and May, 1935, Eddy attempted to convene an Executive Committee meeting; he failed each time because not enough members could attend to have a quorum. Thus, decision-making in the ANG continued on a mail-ballot basis, with only those National Executive Committee members in and around New York City taking an in-person role in the organization.[30]

Especially in the Midwest and smaller communities many newspaper workers resented what they considered the ANG's New York orientation, and the national organization did little to assuage this resentment. On September 13, the Madison, Wisconsin, group signed contracts with that city's two dailies—the only guild to obtain a contract with general circulation dailies between April and December, 1934. Although the contracts obtained a closed shop and their 48-hour maximum reduced the work week by 12 hours for some newsmen, they fell considerably short of other guilds' announced goals. A member of the Madison group wrote a story on the agreements for *The Guild Reporter*, but the editors added a "note" half as long which described the dismissal notice granted by the contracts as "strikingly inadequate," called the minimum wages agreed upon too low, and declared the 48-hour maximum work week established longer "than is best practice." The note concluded by pointing out that Daniel Mich, president of the Madison Guild and negotiator of the contracts, was managing editor of one of the two dailies, and though "managing editors are [not] per se scoundrels . . . their interests, no matter what their own most sincere opinion may be, do lie with the publishers," These comments elicited a number of indignant letters to *The Guild Reporter*—which it did not publish—accusing it, as one reporter wrote, of "trying to apply New York standards to Madison." To all who criticized, Eddy replied in the same vein as he did to Mich: "We must not forget that small gains achieved at the sacrifice of basic organizational principles can in the long run do our whole movement irreparable injury." It is doubtful that Eddy's reasoning won over many of the letter-writers; one wrote back that "even a small towner knows better than to cry for the moon—and then raise hell with somebody able enough to get a piece of the cake."[31]

The controversy over *The Guild Reporter*'s comments on the Madison contracts remained limited to correspondence. However, dissatisfaction among many St. Louis guildsmen with what they called "the New York leadership" burst into print when a poll by the organization of its members resulted in overwhelming expressions of discontent with Broun and Eddy, and (by a narrower margin) a call for their resignations. Although the poll also resulted in a 3-1 vote not to secede from the ANG, *Editor & Publisher* overoptimistically claimed that "the national guild is breaking up" and hailed the St. Louis guildsmen for "having awakened to the fact that they have been misled." Special circumstances governed this vote, the bulk of which came from the professionally oriented *Post-Dispatch* chapter, to which more than half the St. Louis guildsmen belonged. The *Post-Dispatch* news workers, much better treated than the staffs of the city's other two dailies, had no real need for organization. Even a sharp critic of that chapter's generally conservative attitude conceded that in January, 1934, "the P.D. men went into the guild . . . largely out of altruism." But as the months passed, they increasingly objected to the pro-union tone the ANG adopted. The poll had been decided on after Eddy in *The Guild Reporter*'s September issue had declared that "we are a labor organization." St. Louis guildsmen favorable to the trade-union position had advised Eddy that the situation called for tact and diplomacy. However, he decided that the time had come to "take up the issues . . . and straighten them out, even though that involved stepping on some people's toes." Although, according to Eddy, "we officers . . . spent long hours in an attempt to handle the matter intelligently in the . . . *Guild Reporter*," its October 15 issue did not reflect this. Almost 15 percent of the eight-page issue attacked the St. Louis Guild's president, ridiculed its efforts, mocked its membership, and belittled the poll.[32]

These invective-laden assaults, however, did not resolve the issue as Eddy had hoped. He had badly misjudged not only the St. Louis situation (especially in accepting *Editor & Publisher*'s evaluation of it as a revolt), but also the general temper of the members of the guilds. While *The Guild Reporter* and Eddy received some letters praising the scabrous attacks and declaring "no apologies are necessary," more mail expressed the opposite point of view, asserting, as Robert Buck put it, that "the whole tone of the October 15th issue is in rotten taste . . . many more such issues will kill the Guild." Eddy realized that he and his colleagues had erred, and the next issues of *The Guild Reporter* carried more amenable statements about the St. Louis group. Several months later, the executive committee of the *Post-Dispatch* chapter asserted that its members were disappointed at being berated in *The Guild Reporter*, but decided to let "it go at that. We bore no ill will."[33]

The St. Louis controversy triggered Broun's short-lived decision—announced October 14—not to seek reelection as ANG president. Referring to "a guild in the middle west" which believed that the New York Guild dominated the national organization, he suggested that the national convention select as ANG head someone not from New York. His other reasons for stepping down included the fact that the ANG's critics used his columns and other expressions of personal opinion to buttress their charges about the organization's supposed radicalism.[34] Within 11 days, however, Broun had reconsidered; on October 25 he told a wildly enthusiastic meeting of the Newark Newspaper Guild that "I decided if there are people who do not like me, then I am not going to retire without a fight." More specifically, Broun told *Editor & Publisher* that he had changed his mind because of its editorial criticism and because of "the censure of his attitude on the part of the St. Louis Newspaper Guild." Morris Ernst believes that the small pro-Communist clique in New York, which later used Broun for its own purposes, had cajoled him into reversing his decision. Exactly why Broun flipflopped remains less important than the fact that for many of the guilds' members, despite his self-acknowledged "loafing . . . on national affairs," he had come to personify the organization. Broun's decision not to stand for reelection had caused them dismay, for, as one of them wrote the columnist: "the [American Newspaper] Guild owes its principles, its power, and its very existence, chiefly to one man, and that is Heywood Broun."[35]

Broun's actions and comments as well as the increasing pro-union tone of other guildsmen did nothing to ease the generally hostile attitude of the newspaper industry, many of whose leaders viewed with suspicion and alarm the direction the guilds had taken. ANPA attorney Elisha Hanson agreed with a publisher's observation that all the editorial workers' leaders "want is to create the worst possible relationship between publishers and their employees so as to build up a large organization." Harvey Kelly, the chairman of the ANPA Special Standing Committee, who considered Eddy an "ass" and Broun "a round and overstuffed gentleman who delights in preening in public," advised editorial executives that the ANG's "radical leadership" and *The Guild Reporter's* "intemperate utterances" justified any management's refusal to sign a contract with a guild.[36]

Lucius T. Russell, the publisher of the *Newark Ledger*, shared these sentiments, a sharing which contributed to a strike vote being taken by that newspaper's guildsmen on November 17. The ensuing strike, the first real showdown between the publisher of a large-circulation daily and his organized editorial employees, ranks as one of the most influential events in ANG history. Since the June convention the guilds had moved toward unionism, but it remained unclear how far this development would go. The *Ledger* strike not only helped to confirm the guild movement's turning away from the professional association idea but also speeded it up. Moreover, at that time many regarded this strike as a test of strength between the publishers and the organized editorial workers. Eddy later estimated that an unfavorable outcome to the strike could have resulted in a 50 percent reduction in the guilds' membership. Probably a clear-cut defeat would have crushed the guild movement.[37]

Russell fancied himself a benevolent aristocrat but, according to *The Guild Reporter*, his editorial staff for many years had worked in a virtual state of terror induced by the publisher's caprices, which included the periodic dismissal or reassignment of staff members without apparent reason.[38] *Ledger* news workers labored long hours for poor pay with little chance for raises.

Russell apparently would put off requests for pay increases by granting interest-free loans which he then got back in weekly installments deducted from the borrower's salary check. Russell, more an entrepreneur than a journalist, managed to get away with all this because, although he engaged and treated well some first-rate newspapermen like Emmet Crozier, he also made extensive use of drifters, alcoholics, and the like, who would accept onerous working conditions because they needed jobs. Among Newark newspapermen the *Ledger* had achieved a reputation as a newspaper where misfits might find employment until they decided to move on or Russell fired them.[39]

Those *Ledger* newsmen who had joined the guild hoped through it to ameliorate these conditions. At the end of October, 1934, the Newark Guild's negotiations committee, headed by Robert Ring, assistant city editor of the *Sunday Call*, drew up a contract for submission to Russell that included provisions for minimum wage scales, a grievance committee, and a dismissal bonus system based on length of service.[40]

The *Ledger* publisher's reaction to the guild's attempts at negotiation precipitated the strike. In effect, he set out to crush the *Ledger* chapter through intimidation. He wanted to continue, in the words of one newspaper industry history, "to run his own shop on a 'rugged individualism basis,' with the individualism on his side." During the first two weeks of November, Ring repeatedly asked Russell to open negotiations; Russell refused even to reply directly, acknowledging Ring's letters only through lengthy statements posted on the bulletin board of the *Ledger* city room. In these statements he questioned the right of the guild to bargain for anyone and asserted that he would deal only with the *Ledger*'s editorial employees and then on an individual basis. Russell characterized the guild's attempts to negotiate as nothing but "the outgrowth of socialistic propaganda that is trying to make everybody class conscious," and declared that "I am not in the slightest concerned about Ring and the [negotiations] committee going before the Regional Labor Board. . . . You [i.e., the staff] can go to all the Regional Boards you damn please but you will get no relief from the *Ledger* until you come to me personally. . . ."[41]

Russell followed this challenge with a more serious one a few days later. Just before noon on November 14 he posted a statement announcing that he intended within two weeks to fire 25 percent of the editorial staff, and that upon returning from his vacation in December he would discharge another 25 percent. He then apparently decided to put this plan into effect immediately. All through the afternoon of the 14th editorial executives summoned members of the staff and fired them on grounds of economy. The *Ledger*, in a single afternoon of confusion and uncertainty, dismissed between 16 and 20 people. But by early evening some semblance of order had returned to the *Ledger* city room, and the number fired had been reduced to eight, a majority of them guild members, including one of the chapter's officers.[42] The dismissal of eight news workers as an isolated incident would not have led to a strike, for Russell had fired larger numbers. This dismissal, however, as one of the strike's leaders later noted, "was an obvious part of a campaign to put the guild out of business. . . . The guild had the choice of striking or surrendering."[43]

Newark Guild and ANG leaders responded promptly if not decisively. Crozier had called a meeting of the Newark Guild's executive committee as soon as he had learned about Russell's statement and had telephoned Eddy at the ANG office in New York. Eddy arrived at the *Ledger* office within an hour, made a copy of Russell's posted statement, and held some hurried conferences. In the meantime, the mass firings had begun. Eddy then returned to New York to inform Broun, the New York Guild leadership, and (by telegram) the ANG's Executive Committee about the events in Newark. At about 4:30 p.m. the Newark Guild's executive committee met and decided to hold a general membership meeting late that night to discuss the situation.[44]

The meeting, which Broun, Eddy, and several New York guild members attended, began shortly before midnight. The majority of the 70-75 persons present recognized that Russell by his actions had threatened the continued existence of a guild chapter at the *Ledger*, and had given ample grounds for a strike. The *Ledger* news workers, however, hesitated to go that far.

Some urged that the guild take the matter to the Regional Labor Board; others suggested that Ring and his committee make another effort to reach some kind of understanding with Russell. One Newark guild officer present that night recalls that several of the *Ledger* workers expressed concern about what might happen to them if they struck. The expressions of militancy included speeches by Broun, the New Yorkers, and other non-*Ledger* employees who feared that a failure to act courageously might lead to unfortunate repercussions for the whole guild movement. Broun summed up the tenor of their remarks in saying that he did not understand the *Ledger* workers' hesitation. Russell had declared war and only one answer was possible: strike. This matter involved the whole guild movement, for if Russell could render the Newark Guild impotent, other publishers soon would adopt similar tactics. Broun went so far as to say that "if you don't strike, we'll come over from New York . . . set up a picket line . . . and carry on the fight without your help," but the meeting adjourned about 3:00 a.m. without making a definite decision to strike.[45]

The Newark Guild's leaders, seeing that many members felt hesitant about a strike, determined to try again to reach some kind of peaceful settlement even though they realized the dangers involved in such action. On the 15th, after a number of telephone calls, Ring and his committee finally did manage to see Russell, but only for about five minutes. The guildsmen proposed a series of talks to try to straighten things out; they asked that Russell in the meantime reinstate the discharged eight, dismiss nobody else for the present, and hire no new reporters for 30 days. Russell merely answered that he would have to consult his attorney.[46]

The next day Ring called Russell again, told him that the *Ledger* chapter planned to hold a meeting late that night, and asked that the publisher make some kind of response to the guild's proposals before 11:00 p.m. Russell did not. That night, just prior to the meeting, Emmet Crozier, who considered himself a moderate and who believed that a strike would play into the hands of those who wished to affiliate the ANG to the AFL, went alone to see Russell and asked him to reconsider his opposition to negotiating with the guild. Russell recounts that he gently told Crozier that he simply could not deal with an irresponsible group like the guild. Crozier recalls that Russell denounced Broun and declared that no "wild-eyed windbag" ever would have anything to say about running the *Ledger*; a guild could do nothing for good reporters so why did Crozier bother with it? The *Ledger* staff must continue to deal personally with the newspaper's publisher. However Russell answered Crozier's proposal, the newsman left firmly convinced that no possibility of compromise existed.[47]

About 40 people, most of them *Ledger* news workers, attended the meeting which began shortly before midnight. Three members of the New York Guild participated, including its executive secretary, Milton Kaufman. Once again those members of the *Ledger* chapter who were opposed to a strike did most of the talking, but they added little to their previous arguments. Kaufman recapitulated Broun's arguments; Crozier described his conference with Russell and asserted that the *Ledger* chapter had no alternative to striking. Debate went on until nearly 4:00 a.m. before a secret ballot resulted in a 24-8 vote by the *Ledger* workers to strike. The Newark Guild's executive committee, telephoned by a member of the strike committee, unanimously approved the vote and accepted the suggestion of scheduling a conference for the next morning to formulate strike plans. Some of the more militant guildsmen spent the rest of the night painting signs, and by 7:00 a.m. on the morning of November 17 a few pickets had begun to parade in front of the *Ledger* building. They carried placards charging the *Ledger* with treating its editorial workers unfairly and urging Newarkers not to buy the newspaper. The Essex County Cigar, Stationery Store, and News Dealers Association, approached by guild leaders who hoped to pressure the publisher, took advantage of the situation and told Russell that its members would continue handling the *Ledger* only if he lowered its wholesale rates.[48]

Whatever hopes the guild may have had that the strike would immediately strengthen its bargaining position proved false. Russell did meet the negotiations committee on the 19th, but in the course of a two-hour conference he again turned down all the guild's proposals. He said, however, that he would negotiate if all the strikers returned to work at once; the committee, placing no faith in his promises, rejected the offer. A week later, on November 26, he met with the committee, this time for only 15 minutes. Russell would not discuss terms beyond stating what he would not accept; this included any contract that raised questions about his "complete authority in the matter of employing and dismissing, and being the sole judge of the qualifications and value of the editorial staff services." The situation remained at this impasse until mid-January despite attempts by the Regional Labor Board and the Essex Trades Council (Newark's central organized labor body) to mediate the controversy.[49]

The Ledger's discharge of the eight news workers had reduced its editorial staff to 47. Of these only 26 struck on November 17, the first day of the strike. Ten more walked out during the next three days. Russell, faced with attacks by both guildsmen and the news dealers association, suspended publication November 21-22. However, he quickly managed to hire some news workers as well as some thugs, whom he thought necessary for protection. Shortly thereafter, he accepted the demands of the news dealers. Throughout the remainder of the strike, the Ledger, although much reduced in content, missed no more editions. The guild leaders, having failed to stop publication of the newspaper, thereupon determined to reduce its advertising and circulation, presuming that if Russell suffered severe enough financial losses he would settle.[50]

Sound trucks roamed the streets explaining the strikers' cause and asking Newarkers not to read the Ledger. Pickets (both guildsmen and volunteers, some of whom received expense money) paraded in front of the Ledger, in downtown Newark, and by newsstands. The strike's backers made use of a Citizen's Committee, which circularized the Ledger's advertisers, asking them not to deal with Russell; on occasion the committee picketed the advertisers in support of this request. The Newark Guild managed to get such dignitaries as the former head of the Essex County Bar Association to address the mass meetings and demonstrations organized at strategic places in the city. Periodically the strikers put out *The Reporter*, a thin tabloid-size newspaper which presented their case and printed statements of support from prominent persons both in and out of the newspaper industry.[51]

Russell countered by placing a series of advertisements in other Newark and metropolitan area newspapers which accused the Newark Guild among other things of bargaining in bad faith, of being Communist-dominated, of attempting to exert editorial control, and of not acting responsibly when given the opportunity. He also asked for arbitration (but not mediation), said no grounds for a strike existed, and reprinted statements (e.g., Pew's comments) unfavorable to the guild. Russell at the same time made use both of the *Ledger*'s editorial and news columns as he tried to discredit the strikers and the whole guild movement.[52]

When the strike began, neither side expected it to last very long, certainly not for 19 weeks. The striking *Ledger* workers, according to *The Guild Reporter*, had hoped for "a swift and triumphant demonstation." Russell, knowing the limited resources of his editorial workers, apparently thought that he could buy off those he needed and starve the others into submission. He did manage to woo the sports editor back to work after five days on the picket line, but the other 43 workers remained impervious to his blandishments and stayed out for the duration of the strike.[53]

Toward the end of January, 1935, the strikers briefly seemed near victory as Russell apparently lost control of the *Ledger*. He and his immediate family owned most of the common stock of the Newark Morning Ledger Company, but it had other shareholders and they worried about what the strike would do to the value of their stock, especially as the company had appraised "good will" as more than 50 percent of its $1,900,000 listed assets. One of these stockholders, William I. Coates of Massachusetts, who worried about his investment of $8,000, came to Newark. Upset by what he learned about the *Ledger*'s financial affairs, he engaged a lawyer, Morris Cohn. The lawyer got in touch with Crozier, explained that he planned shortly to take

Russell to court, and asked the guild leader to help him obtain the names of other stockholders as he believed his client stood a better chance if he filed an action in conjunction with other stockholders. Cohn told Crozier, who worried about the strike being "stalled on dead center," that under a trusteeship a settlement seemed much more likely to come about. "This," recalls Crozier, "was an important break. It seemed to me, as I left Cohn's home . . . that the end was in sight." Some weeks earlier a young former assistant from the New Jersey Attorney General's office had called Crozier offering what he believed important information about the *Ledger*'s financial affairs which he had gathered to support a complaint against Russell, later quashed apparently for political reasons. Crozier now went to see this young lawyer and learned from him the names of the other *Ledger* stockholders and other important information, including that Russell had borrowed large sums from the company and that under his direction it had repurchased stock at a discount. Crozier passed this information on to Cohn, who used much of it as the basis for Coates' petition asking the Chancery Court to remove Russell and appoint trustees to conserve the *Ledger*'s assets. On January 23 Vice Chancellor M. L. Berry acted on this petition and placed the company under the trusteeship of George W. C. McCarter, an attorney, and Henry Puder, Russell's former auditor.[54]

Crozier and the other strikers hoped that with Russell out of the way the *Ledger* would settle. McCarter and Puder did reopen negotiations almost immediately on assuming the trusteeship, but they proved little more amenable than had Russell, who remained very much in the picture. The trustees kept him on as publisher of the *Ledger*, and he continued to agitate against the guild. A series of conferences in February between guild spokesmen and the trustees achieved nothing. The guildsmen considered the concessions offered by the trustees too limited and refused to cease strike activity while negotiating. The trustees considered unreasonable the guild's proposals, which centered on five main points: recognition, a signed contract, a grievance committee, discharge of strike breakers, reinstatement of all strikers including the discharged eight. This round of negotiations ended for all practical purposes on February 20 when, at a brief meeting, the trustees and Russell handed the guild negotiations committee a statement that the strikers' bulletin described as a "pompous, ridiculous memorandum . . . filled with empty phrases and wordy shadow-boxing."[55]

Russell now expressed the fear that he could not "continue to cope . . . single-handed" with the situation, and he told the mechanical workers that the *Ledger* might cease publication unless their unions could bring about a settlement of the strike. After several days of sparring, the Allied Printing Trades Council managed to bring the guild negotiations committee and the trustees together; but long conferences on March 5 and 6 solved nothing—a guild spokesman characterized the trustees' offer as an "assortment of phonus bolonus."[56]

On March 7 the trustees decided to move in a different direction. That morning A. J. Isserman, one of the guild's attorneys, had met with McCarter and had received another proposal for arbitration. Probably the guild would have rejected it; the opportunity to do so, however, never arose. Within three hours of presenting the proposal, McCarter sent word that he assumed the guild would reject the offer and that the trustees had applied for an anti-strike injunction. Russell had readied such a complaint for filing before mid-February and apparently had finally succeeded in convincing the trustees to use it. Later that same day, Berry signed a temporary order (drawn up by the *Ledger* attorneys). Naming a score of strikers, strike sympathizers, and guild members, it restrained them, the ANG, and the Newark Guild from such activities as picketing in front of or near the *Ledger* offices, "molesting" *Ledger* employees in any way, boycotting, and circulating any written or printed material which incited any of the enjoined acts.[57]

The restraining order stunned the members of the Newark Guild; its secretary declared that the "injunction restrains us from everything except breathing and thinking." However, the strike leaders quickly found ways around the hampering provisions of the order. Pickets continued to parade through downtown Newark, but the words on the placards had been changed and many now dealt with the injunction. One placard read:

"An Injunction Has Been Served On The Striking Employees Of The Newark Ledger." The Citizens Committee took over all the picketing of advertisers. Moreover, Russell and the trustees apparently decided to overlook all but the major infractions of the restraining order. Its broad sweep (which included restrictions on the distribution of *The Guild Reporter* as well as the strike paper's publication and distribution) had aroused a generally hostile reaction from the newspaper industry, even from publishers out of sympathy with the strike.[58] At the hearing on March 19 to determine the injunction's permanency, the *Ledger* counsel was unprepared for Isserman's request that the case be transferred to federal court. Accordingly, Berry set another hearing for a week later. The strikers' supporters used this time to good advantage, and the *Ledger*'s financial losses continued to mount. Russell then decided to employ what he called "counter pickets," and these marched through Newark on March 23 and 25 carrying signs attacking the guild and urging support of the *Ledger* and its advertisers. Russell's actions gave the guild cause more publicity and enraged Berry, who at the hearing on March 26 castigated the trustees for permitting the very activity from which they wished the guild enjoined.[59]

The injunction became a dead issue on March 28 when, under the aegis of a federal mediator, the strike ended. Neither side had asked for federal intervention; rather, a Department of Labor conciliator had been sent to Newark on March 13 at President Roosevelt's request. The mediator's first efforts failed, but he ultimately succeeded because Russell, unknown to the guild or the mediator, had decided to sell his *Ledger* holdings to S. I. Newhouse, who made it clear that he would take no action in regard to buying until the strike ended. A series of conferences on March 27-28 resulted in a signed agreement between the trustees and the guild—to remain in force for the duration of the trusteeship—which called for the reinstatement of all the strikers except for the eight discharged prior to November 17, whose cases went to a three-man arbitration committee (an impartial chairman and representatives from both sides) to be established within 15 days. The trustees guaranteed that none of the reinstated news workers would be fired for

30 days and that if any later were dismissed for reasons of economy, they would be given preference when new employees were engaged. The trustees also agreed to discharge immediately all but one of the strike breakers still employed, the exception being the city editor, who had not replaced a striker. All questions of wages, hours, and working conditions not specifically dealt with in the agreement were left to the arbitration committee to decide.[60]

The strikers had hoped to achieve more; their failure to win reinstatement for eight of their number bothered them. But nearly 19 weeks of picketing, often in snowy and bitterly cold weather, had worn them down. They wanted to go back to work, to end the hardship and privation which by March had left one of them in such straitened circumstances that he begged a loan to replace the only suit he had left before it completely fell apart; otherwise, he said, "when it is necessary for me to discard my overcoat, I will either have to stay in bed or join a nudist colony." Toward the end, weekly strike payments, never munificent, had been reduced in many cases to less than half of the low salaries the strikers had received from Russell.[61] The strikers leaped at the chance for settlement; they ratified the agreement within an hour of learning about it. Their last bulletin—issued near midnight on March 28 following ratification—indicated their mixed feelings. It said that the agreement "leaves a few loose ends; it isn't 100% by any means, but we're satisfied it gives us—and the Guild everywhere—a major victory."[62]

However, at best the strikers had won little more than a moral victory. Arbitration did not begin for some months. The *Ledger* management immediately began chipping away at the agreement, and the guildsmen, anxious to avoid another confrontation, responded cautiously. They suffered a major setback on May 20 when the Chancery Court approved the sale of Russell's holdings to S. I. Newhouse and terminated the trusteeship, thus rendering ineffective the strike settlement agreement, which the trustees but no *Ledger* representatives had signed. As a result, the eventual arbitration proved almost meaningless. The arbitrators (in effect, the impartial chairman) granted reinstatement as of the end of the strike to the eight whose cases had remained unsettled, but this decision proved of no consequence because it was limited to the trusteeship period (March 20-May 20). Seven of the newsmen did not even get their back pay for this technical reinstatement. The *Ledger* would not pay and their cases dragged on until March, 1936, when Berry denied a Newark Guild petition; he held that the arbitration agreement expired with the trusteeship and that if the guild wished to collect it "should go to law." On the other issues left to arbitration the guild fared no better. The impartial chairman refused to rule, for instance, on minimum-wage scales. He asserted that to establish these would set retroactive standards that might unduly influence future negotiations. Ultimately, the strike failed even to assure continued life to the *Ledger* chapter. The strikers' very success had resulted in Russell's selling to Newhouse—assuredly no friend of editorial employee organization —and within 15 months after the sale the chapter had ceased to exist as an independent entity. The strike settlement's drawbacks did not become clear until after the trusteeship ended. Many of the strikers and their supporters both in Newark and elsewhere expected that arbitration would bring definite gains, and for some months guildsmen everywhere generally assumed that the *Ledger* workers had won.[63]

In Newark as elsewhere the strike had resulted in an unprecedented display of collective action by the normally individualistic American news workers. Non-striking Newark Guild members took an active part in all aspects of the strike; they even financed and helped prepare a Thanksgiving dinner for the strikers and their families. For a while, guildsmen from New York and other nearby areas considered it their duty to go to Newark whenever possible to assist the strikers. Some guildsmen even further from the scene participated directly. An occasional individual went to Newark to picket; the president of the Washington Guild, D. A. de Souza, died in an automobile crash while on his way to deliver toys that his group had bought as Christmas presents for the strikers' children; a number of St. Louis guildsmen formed a "Correspondence Club for Ledger Scabs" and wrote nasty holiday greetings to those editorial workers who crossed the picket lines. And all across the

country guildsmen who otherwise took no active part contributed to the Newark strike fund.[64]

As the strike dragged on, however, its emotional appeal
lessened and the old indifference and individualism began to
make themselves felt. By mid-December, 1934, Crozier considered it necessary to admonish non-*Ledger* Newark guildsmen for being "slackers." The New York Guild in January, 1935,
hastily formed an emergency committee to encourage participation because, as its chairman said, "there have been days when
only one or two New Yorkers have appeared for picket duty."
A similar drop-off in enthusiasm took place in most guilds.[65]

After this slackening of interest became evident, probably no
single set of actions played a greater role in sustaining the
strikers' morale and thus keeping the strike going than did
Broun's. He picketed often, in both bad weather and good,
bringing along his teenage son and, on one occasion, his new
bride. He confronted Russell in front of the *Ledger* building,
lent the strikers money, touted them on horses, and attempted
to win over strike breakers. Because he feared the injunction
might destroy the strike, he attempted—with great publicity—
to test the validity of the restraining order. Broun expressed
himself as fully prepared to go to jail, but the *Ledger* management, anxious not to add to the commotion the order had stirred
up, made no effort to have him cited for contempt, not even
when he lumbered around the Newark streets distributing
copies of the strike newspaper. A number of participants in the
strike who agree on little else believe that without Broun to
inspire the *Ledger* workers and to jolly them, the strike would
have collapsed.[66]

But the lessening of interest among guildsmen did play havoc
with the strikers' finances, particularly as some of the Newark
leaders refused to countenance the idea of soliciting funds from
organized labor. Local guild contributions to the Newark strike
fund initially had averaged more than $1,000 a week (once go-
ing as high as $1,700), but about mid-December, 1934, a decline
set in. No longer could the strike committee count on a guild
making a weekly contribution. Indeed, even in early December,
when enthusiasm generally still ran high, the Twin Cities Guild

membership had rejected an assessment which would assure a weekly contribution and had reaffirmed the use of voluntary giving. A factor in the dip in contributions may have been the approaching holiday season, but the situation did not improve appreciably even some weeks after Christmas. Jonathan Eddy later said that "for a time we risked the danger of losing the strike for lack of sufficient money to carry on."[67]

The financial problem demonstrated more than just the difficulty of keeping large numbers of editorial workers united in a common cause. It highlighted the inadequacies of the decentralized organizational structure, which had failed to keep pace with the demands caused by the transition from the professional association concept to trade unionism, and it demonstrated the division between guild leaders as to how closely the ANG should cooperate with organized labor. The strikers could have obtained loans from the garment industry unions and possibly others. But just as the Newark leaders had opposed such assistance for fear of creating overly close ties, so did many guild officers elsewhere—one result being that in early February, 1935, the National Executive Committee voted to reject a sizable loan offer made by the ILGWU.[68]

The national organization in February, 1935, took over the handling of the strike's finances in an effort to muster all possible support both within and without the guilds. Because no provision existed for ANG assessment of the membership, Eddy had to forego a plan to raise cash by borrowing against such assessments. Instead, the national organization set up the American Newspaper Guild Emergency Fund, which had to rely—like the strike fund—on voluntary giving. Eddy asked all guilds to vote to contribute weekly $.25 per capita. It was hoped that an appeal by a national fund would rekindle enthusiasm, regularize contributions, and result in more cash, but this did not happen. Drastic economies by the strike committee (mostly at the expense of the *Ledger* workers); a $1,000 contribution in March from the United Mine Workers (solicited by Eddy), which because it went directly to the fund and was not a loan did not need Executive Committee approval; and the Emergency Fund's use of the ANG's limited cash reserves to the extent of

$1,000 allowed for the continued prosecution of the strike when added to what the local guilds managed to contribute. Nevertheless, the Newark Guild and the ANG shared almost $2,000 in debts at the conclusion of the strike. Altogether, including welfare payments made after the settlement, the strike had cost over $26,000.[69] The Newark Guild had managed to raise nearly $3,000 through theater benefits, assessments of working members, and the like; and about $2,000 had come unsolicited from garment-industry unions which had donated it through guild chapters. However, the bulk of the strike's cost was met by the guildsmen everywhere who between November, 1934, and April, 1935, sent nearly $19,000 to Newark, of which about 25 percent came from chapters of the New York Guild.[70]

Probably the most effective non-financial help from a source outside the guilds had come from the Citizens Committee, composed mostly of Newark sympathizers. It had put pressure on Russell in a variety of ways. Other sympathizers with the strike provided help which ran the gamut from good intentions to effective aid. The Newark Guild's supporters in the New Jersey Assembly managed to have passed a resolution which, although not specifically mentioning the strike, endorsed the guild's "efforts to better working conditions for the state's editorial workers." A doctor treated without charge the ailments strikers got from picketing in the nasty weather that plagued Newark during much of the dispute. The American Civil Liberties Union provided the financial base for the short-lived National Anti-Injunction League, a broadly titled organization set up at the instigation of guild sympathizers whose sole purpose was to fight the restraining order handed down by Chancellor Berry.[71]

The strikers also received help from organized labor. More than 100 Newark union locals endorsed the strike and recommended that their members neither buy nor read the *Ledger*; a few locals even went so far as to fine members caught reading the paper. Many of them also circulated "Don't Read the *Ledger*" buttons and sent resolutions to advertisers appealing to them to withdraw from the newspaper. The Essex Trades Council, in addition to attempting to arrange a settlement, offered advice and sponsored a mass meeting in support of the strikers.

AFL president William Green publicly expressed support and advised the state federation "to render . . . such assistance as it is possible to extend." More substantial aid came from the Motion Picture Operators' locals, which lent their sound trucks, and the ILGWU, which lent the strike committee the services of an organizer to advise it on logistics and tactics. In the contest over affiliation that arose within the guild movement during the late spring of 1935 three of the Newark Guild's most ardent advocates of joining the AFL claimed that without organized labor's help some aspects of the strike, such as the boycott of the *Ledger*, would have been much less effective. Crozier summed up the other side's beliefs when he said that while organized labor did "do some very helpful things for us," some of its actions, particularly the attempts at settlement, "were almost fatal for us." From the evidence it seems that Crozier's view was right. Except for the loan offers of some unions and the Mine Workers' contribution, organized labor—both locally and on the national scene—contributed little materially to the strikers' cause. The affiliation controversy obscured the exact value of the aid organized labor provided, but the *Ledger* strike did make clear that a guild would need ANG assistance against any but a financially very weak publisher. The *Ledger* strike also must be considered responsible for the increase in the strength of the Newark pro-affiliation forces. In an election held a few weeks after the settlement (before its drawbacks became known), Crozier lost the local guild presidency to a candidate running on a platform favoring affiliation with the AFL.[72]

Overcoming the guildsmen's initial reluctance to picket-line activity, the militants had carried the day in Newark. But further away from New York City, the militants, although their actions—as in the *Ledger* strike—strengthened the pro-affiliation forces, proved unable to provoke the same kind of action. Lacking the spur provided by the national and New York officers in Newark, local guild officers faced with difficult situations could not overcome the conservatism and the fear of their chapters' members, not even in Cleveland, whose news workers had helped found the ANG.

The Cleveland Guild had strong chapters on two of the city's three dailies (the *Press* and the *News*) and during the winter of 1934 undertook to restore completely the paycuts suffered by editorial employees on both these newspapers. The higher-paying *Press* in a bulletin-board announcement which ignored the guild restored one of the 10 percent paycuts, and the chapter considered that "a fair settlement," according to one local guild official. The publisher of the *News*, Dan R. Hanna, Jr., also paid little attention to the guild. After some delay, he granted limited individual salary increases, but as a Cleveland Guild report points out, "the substantial pay increases inaugurated at the *Press* . . . plus the niggardly response of the *News* publisher plus his irregular manner of answering the Guild with individual increases privately awarded served to intensify the demand of *News* men for a showdown. . . ."[73]

Departing from the mechanical unions' practice of dealing with the Cleveland publishers as a group, the guild—recognizing its inability to support a strike against more than one newspaper and hoping to use a settlement with one publisher to whipsaw the other—decided to concentrate on the financially shaky *News*. Attempts in April and May, 1934, to open negotiations failed, but finally on July 25 talks began between the Hanna forces and a guild committee.[74] At first, between formal negotiation meetings, Hanna tried to bargain with the committee members he employed, but after a few sessions in which the *News* men sat stonily silent, let the publisher or his representative talk, and then walked out, these attempts ceased. The guild negotiating committee "though firm and sometimes indignant" as one of its members put it, carefully avoided saying anything to Hanna which could not be forgotten. The guildsmen, however, showed much less respect for the publisher's attorney, Joseph Hostetler, whose firm represented all three Cleveland dailies and who the committee believed represented "larger interests than those of Mr. Hanna."[75]

Almost immediately, it became apparent that the *News* would make money concessions, but by September the two sides had deadlocked over the guild demands for a preferential shop and dismissal protection. On September 10 the guild committee, which considered Hostetler responsible for the impasse, deliberately staged a stormy scene with him, and, after indulging in some dramatic flourishes—threats to strike and name-calling —walked out and left the attorney and the publisher sitting in astonished silence. The committee members, who represented the more militant among the Cleveland guildsmen, later claimed they never had intended to call a strike but only had hoped to use the threat of one to win acceptance of their demands. However, the committee and its supporters almost certainly believed that (as the local guild constitution required) two-thirds of the chapter would vote the leadership the power to call a strike; Garland Ashcraft, a member of the committee, later told Eddy that "we made a constant poll of the staff [and] we had pledges for the required . . . majority for the strike vote.[76]

To forestall the militants Hanna on September 11 addressed his editorial workers ("a good job . . . full of sob and high pressure appeal," said a committee member). Pleading financial shortcomings, he asked for more time and promised to fire no one and reduce no salaries irrespective of whether the guild and the *News* reached agreement. The publisher found support among the more conservative, who disliked the turn the guild had taken, and the timid, who feared a strike might cause the demise of the *News*. So rapidly did this support mobilize that before the chapter meeting on September 12 the committee, afraid of defeat, decided that in no event should a vote on the issue reach the floor.[77]

That night and at another lengthy meeting of the *News* chapter the following night the guildsmen fought bitterly among themselves. There were, as committee member A. L. Roberts put it, "hot words, accusations of 'selling out,' and what not" but no strike vote. After much debate the chapter finally adopted a resolution, drawn up by one of the more conservative members of the *News* staff and modified by members of the committee, which in effect called for the committee to reopen negotiations and delay settlement of the dismissal protection and preferential shop issues until the *Press* chapter had negotiated a contract, after which the guild should negotiate these issues jointly with the *Press* and the *News*.[78]

The committee members and their supporters believed that

they had suffered a defeat (and Ashcraft so wired Eddy), but the resolution did serve as a compromise which helped heal the splits in the *News* chapter and enabled the negotiations to resume. Even the possibility of a strike seemed to frighten Hanna. To avoid trouble, he replaced Hostetler with another attorney. However, as Roberts put it, the "failure to strike weakened us in negotiations, also. Hard to hammer with a feather." Moreover, as the negotiations dragged on into November, the *News* staff became so impatient that the committee feared the membership would accept anything Hanna offered. Roberts said that "the *News* men might even take it against our arguments—can't say."[79]

Perhaps Hanna did not understand the mood of his men or perhaps, as the Cleveland Guild report on negotiations says, "the publisher developed a bad case of nerves bordering on hysteria"; in any event, by the end of November Hanna and a two-man subcommittee of the original negotiating committee had worked out a contract, which was signed December 20, 1934. Roberts said that "for sentimental reasons" the guildsmen insisted it go into effect on December 15, the anniversary of the ANG's founding. Effective for one year and generally applying to all editorial employees except the editor and the managing editor, the contract's provisions included a minimum wage scale, pay raises for those reporters and desk men earning more than the minimum, a five-day, forty-hour week for much of the staff, and establishment of a grievance committee. The contract even provided that discharged employees receive cash payments based on length of service (a provision that proved its value almost immediately when in a few weeks straitened financial circumstances forced the *News* to pare to all departments—only the editorial workers got dismissal bonuses; the other workers laid off received nothing).[80]

Many Cleveland Guild members as well as the committee recognized the contract's shortcomings such as its failure to provide real protection against arbitrary dismissal and the publisher's refusal to put into writing his pledges about continuing sick leaves and vacations (because he did not want to set a precedent the mechanical unions might use). The Cleveland guildsmen also recognized that J. David Stern, when he signed a contract with the Philadelphia Guild, had granted his *Record* staff more benefits, including the preferential shop. But, as the committee's report on the *News* negotiations concluded: "the contract marks an advance . . . [having been obtained] by bargaining and not by connivance with a friendly publisher. As such it probably represents the best any Guild can negotiate at this time with an unfriendly publisher without taking a successful strike vote."[81]

Hesitation about taking such a course and fear of the consequences had forced the more militant to retreat somewhat from their original positions, but, as Ashcraft later said: "we gained strength while the fire smoldered." When the editorial worker who had led the opposition to the committee ran for *News* chapter chairman in October, he was defeated 70-25. Although at least two-thirds of the *News* chapter in September had opposed a strike, within three weeks the Cleveland Guild's leaders had managed to convince over 50 percent of the staff to walk out if necessary. At the same time, the committee and its supporters quickly had broadened their contacts among the trade unions, and they believed that in the case of a strike (as Ashcraft put it) "we can get volunteer labor pickets for the downtown street corners." The Cleveland Guild's militants had adopted policies too radical for the rank-and-file, but by temporarily backing off they had managed to attain a contract which benefitted the *News* editorial workers.[82]

No such happy ending was written in Oakland, California. There the *Tribune* in the first weeks of November, 1934, discharged three employees, all members of a recently formed chapter of the San Francisco Guild, including the group's chairman and secretary-treasurer. The guild charged that the *Tribune* had fired the men because of guild activities. Joseph R. Knowland, publisher of the *Tribune* and a power in state politics, denied this. He said that the discharge of the three guildsmen as well as of some other non-editorial employees had been made "entirely from the standpoint of efficiency." On November 18, the day after the Newark strike began, the San Francisco Guild decided at a noisy, unruly membership meeting to obtain the reinstatement of the three discharged editorial employees. Knowland expressed his willingness to meet "without prejudice" any group of *Tribune* news workers to discuss the situation, but none would volunteer to do so and most dropped out of the guild. The *Tribune* chapter dissolved; the guild claimed that Knowland's editorial workers feared for their jobs despite his guarantees. The guild then undertook a boycott campaign against the newspaper, hoping to force Knowland to reinstate the fired guildsmen by cutting the *Tribune's* circulation and advertising revenues. The boycott, however, quickly proved a fizzle because the guild was unable to publicize it, supposedly because of pressure exerted by Knowland. Whatever limited effectiveness the guildsmen possessed came from massive distribution of handbills, but this, the only guild action that elicited any response from the *Tribune,* soon ceased because the guildsmen lacked the funds needed to pay the printing costs. *The Guild Reporter* and ANG officers expressed their sympathy, but their attention was focused on Newark, and the San Francisco Guild received little publicity and even less cash (in fact, the only contribution sent West was one for $25.00 from another guild).[83]

A different sort of setback to the San Francisco Guild's campaign of economic warfare came in December, 1934, when the San Francisco *Examiner* demoted to the hotel beat Redfern Mason, for 21 years its music editor, a few days after he had been named chairman of that newspaper's guild chapter and had sent a letter to all its members asking them to join in the fight against the *Tribune*. Mason, noted for the excellence of his criticism, felt humiliated by the demotion and resigned from the *Examiner*. What one observer called "the further example of Mason" served to make San Francisco editorial workers even more cautious in their support of the guild.[84]

The more militant among the Bay Area guildsmen, aware that their geographical isolation and the Newark strike precluded much help from other guilds, decided to seek the aid of organized labor. Some guild members had objected to the aggressive tenor of the campaign planned against the *Tribune;* the appeal to the local AFL body proved too much for them. About 10 percent of the remaining membership resigned; others, including the local guild's president, relinquished their offices and gave up active participation in the organization. The ensuing elections resulted in a much more union-minded group assuming control of the reduced guild, but the appeal to organized labor for help at first produced nothing more tangible than *Guild Reporter* stories announcing "impending backing of the boycott by the unions.[85]

During the spring some union locals in the Bay Area did invite guild speakers to present their case at membership meetings; the local AFL body's secretary did go to Knowland and ask him to reinstate the fired guildsmen; and the Oakland Carmen's Union (appreciative of a guild resolution condemning the installation of one-man street cars in San Francisco) did pass a weak resolution, later adopted by some other union locals in the area, that endorsed the guild and offered it "the wholehearted sympathy of labor." But that was all.[86]

Although the boycott clearly had failed by mid-December, the guild did not formally call it off for some months, and the guildsmen continued through correspondence to make demands of Knowland through April, 1935, when they finally abandoned the case. The San Francisco Guild had taken on an economically entrenched, politically strong publisher without even ensuring the support of his editorial workers. Its belated attempts to obtain organized labor's help had proven futile. The campaign against the *Tribune* not only failed but also resulted in discord among the Bay Area guildsmen. The only ones to gain were the pro-affiliation forces, who won control of the local guild machinery.[87]

What happened in Oakland and Cleveland buoyed the militants and the pro-affiliation guildsmen, but essentially affected only the local guilds. What happened in Newark affected many guilds. The mobilization of support for the *Ledger* strikers compounded the unease many professional association minded guildsmen already had felt because of the militance displayed by the New York Guild. Some of the news workers who did not believe in an out-and-out economically oriented approach had dropped out before the *Ledger* strike; others, like the leader of the St. Louis opposition to Broun, did so during the strike because of it and the measures taken in support of it. A large percentage of guildsmen, aware of what they considered their middle-class status, remained opposed to affiliation with the AFL, but they had come to accept the idea that the guilds at least must cooperate with organized labor if they wished to implement their contract proposals. The more conservative ANG members, many of whom had helped to form the local groups, did not care for this shift in orientation away from a professional association with limited economic overtones. However, unable to stop the change, they gradually dropped out of active participation in organization, many of them even resigning their guild membership. The *Ledger* strike and the reactions to it played an important role in permanently moving the guilds away from the professional association idea but so also did the guildsmen's disenchantment with government agencies and the President as well as the generally disappointing outcome of negotiation attempts with publishers.

6 ·

... and away from the government

"We spent time and money testing to the end every false hope raised by NRA and the government . . . because we . . . had the illusion that beyond the NRA quagmire stood a Great White Father who would see that we got through safely." This bitter comment neatly summarizes guild leaders' feelings about the actions of NRA, the government, and President Roosevelt toward the newspapermen's organization during the last half of 1934 and the first months of 1935.[1]

As early as the summer of 1934, although many guildsmen had retained some faith in the Roosevelt administration, disenchantment with the government's attitude toward the guilds had found expression. "We are telling our men here," reported a Cleveland Guild officer, "that NRA is the bunk, and that if they are expecting to get anywhere . . . , they will have to depend only upon themselves." The president of the Boston Guild went so far as to suggest that the ANG's responsible officers should explore the possibility of a vertical union encompassing all nonmechanical newspaper workers. Even Eddy, very depressed at one point because of his difficulties with Johnson and other government officials, said that "what we get out of Washington will be of benefit to us only for propaganda purposes, mainly among our own membership."[2]

Just prior to the outbreak of the Newark strike, guildsmen—
after five months of trying—held an informal conference with
President Roosevelt. On November 5 Eddy, Broun, James Kieran
(the newsman who served as an intermediary between the
President and the ANG), Carl Randau, and Morris Watson (then
an ANG vice president and head of its press association committee) met for nearly two hours with Roosevelt on the terrace
of his Hyde Park home. Apparently the President—loath to upset anyone personally—did not tell his visitors that the Justice
Department had grave doubts about testing NRA's constitutionality on the basis of a Section 7a case or that the agency's
administrators, dependent on business cooperation, hesitated to
take any action which would estrange employer good will.
Roosevelt and the newspapermen discussed various aspects of
the newspaper industry's labor relations, including the guildsmen's charges of publisher interference with organization, as
well as extension of the five-day, forty-hour week and the drawing up of a code for the press associations. No concrete proposals resulted from this conference. Broun afterward described
the President as being "sympathetic and extremely interested"
even though, according to The Guild Reporter, the delegation
had made no secret of the dissatisfaction of newspapermen with
the slowness of the government to take positive action on the
editorial workers' behalf.[3]

This reluctance on the part of the government allowed the
publishers to thwart any attempt by the guilds to institute
genuine collective bargaining. In so acting, the newspaper
owners relied on Hanson's interpretation of various laws; the
attorney argued that, NRA notwithstanding, collective bargaining did not have to result in a contract—no newspaper could be
forced to sign a contract with a guild. Headlines of Editor &
Publisher and Guild Reporter stories illustrate the widespread
acceptance Hanson's opinion found among publishers in the fall
and winter of 1934 and the spring of 1935: "Guild Contract
Opposed: Rockford Editor Fears 'Regimentation' "; "Contract Is
Refused Phila. Guild Unit: J. C. Martin Prefers to Reach Verbal
Agreements With Staff"; " 'No Contract' N.Y. Herald Tribune
Tells Newspaper Guild"; "Winston-Salem Guild Unit Wins on

5 Points, Withdraws Contract." Editorial executives talked with guild negotiating committees and in many instances improved working conditions, but with rare exceptions they refused to sign contracts, which meant that the guilds remained unrecognized. Probably the guilds' very existence had resulted in managements' making some concessions, but the publishers made these grudgingly and often told their news staffs, as Broun paraphrased it, "you understand, of course, that this has nothing to do with the guild. You would have gotten this much more rapidly if you had not attempted to unionize." Even where strongly organized chapters existed, as on Broun's own newspaper, the *New York World-Telegram*, it proved impossible at this time for guildsmen to obtain a signed contract. Guild proposals during negotiations did lead to a substantial improvement in working conditions. But when the *World-Telegram's* management was asked to sign a contract based on the proposals it already had implemented, it declined and broke off the talks.[4]

J. David Stern, the publisher of the *Record*, had believed that the contract between his newspaper and the Philadelphia Guild would set an example that at least 25 or 30 other publishers would follow, but such did not prove the case. Various guilds obtained, as at the *World-Telegram*, "bulletin board agreements," that is, statements posted in the city room which usually made no mention of guilds or negotiations but did declare what management intended to do for its news staff as regarded hours, wages, and other working conditions, provided that economic conditions did not force a change in policy. Not until the signing of the Madison newspapers in September, 1934, however, did any guild achieve another contract, and not until December, when the *Cleveland News* signed, did a guild manage to obtain a written agreement with another metropolitan daily of large circulation. Moreover, during the first five months of 1935, despite considerable effort on their part, guildsmen managed to sign only three contracts. The Reading, Pennsylvania, *Times* signed with the guild there on February 16 and granted numerous benefits, including a five-day, forty-hour week, a closed shop, paid vacations, and graduated dismissal

notice based on seniority. Although Stern had decided that none
of his other newspapers should sign with guilds until the organization had shown its strength throughout the country (a
position he later modified), he did renew the *Record* contract on
April 8. The new agreement called for overtime to be paid in
cash instead of time off and for reporters on out-of-town assignments to receive time-and-a-third without regard to the actual
time worked. Guild negotiators failed, however, in their attempts to raise the *Record's* relatively low pay-scale, and they
had to settle for a clause stipulating that within 60 days after
the publisher declared a cash dividend or a stock dividend he
would raise wages 10 percent. On April 23 the Philadelphia
Guild also managed to obtain a contract from a publisher of
three weekly newspapers in the labor field: *Labor Record,
Hosiery Worker,* and *Silk and Dye Worker.* The agreement,
covering their combined editorial staff of about 12, included
provisions calling for a five-day, forty-hour week, paid vacations, a closed shop, and time-and-a-half for overtime.[5]

Guild difficulties did not come just in obtaining contracts;
sometimes they lay with the terms some publishers offered for
a written agreement, which presented only limited benefits. Taking advantage of the editorial workers' inexperience and eagerness to obtain a contract, these publishers offered terms that,
although involving some limited improvements in working conditions, would have hurt the guild movement on the whole. In
Akron, for instance, the agreement the publisher worked out
with guildsmen would have raised pay but would have sanc-
tioned wage discrimination based on sex, deprived some members of the benefits from the code's limitation on the maximum
work week, and failed to establish any machinery such as a
grievance committee for the contract's enforcement. Eddy in
his report to the June, 1935, convention summed up this type of
agreement when he declared that "if some of the contracts that
were proposed during the past year actually had been signed,
the chances of subsequently even obtaining satisfactory contracts with other publishers would virtually have been nil."[6]

Newspaper owners responded as they did to guild overtures
for a variety of reasons. Economic conditions within the in-

dustry had improved, but not enough. The press's share of the advertising dollar had increased, but the over-all linage remained far less than it had been in the 1920s. Many publishers sincerely believed that they could not afford to meet guild demands. A Utica executive feared that accepting a 40-hour week in his news department would force the employment of more workers and consequently reduce salaries. His newspaper had neither cut the editorial staff nor reduced pay since 1929; "now it seems a rotten shame," he declared, "that we may be obliged to." Many editorial executives continued to oppose the guilds on principle, as did the Omaha publisher who believed that organization would restrict initiative and place all editorial workers, whatever their merits, on a "deadly parallel." This publisher—his enlightenment evidenced by such benefits to his staff as generous sick pay, group insurance, and paid vacations—thought that a newspaper should share with its employees as it grew. All too many newspaper owners, however, simply opposed organization and tried to fend off the guild so that they would not have to spend more money on their news departments.[7]

The crux of the difficulty rested with those who ran NRA. Johnson and Donald Richberg, the attorney who first assisted and then during 1934 supplanted Johnson, opposed direct government coercion in labor disputes. Aware of the Justice Department's hesitancy in regard to Section 7a and much more interested in economic recovery than in furthering employee organization, they and their supporters within the Roosevelt administration advocated a policy which despite their probably sincere statements in support of labor, in effect would allow each industry to regulate its own labor relations. They cared about the workingman but thought it more important not to jeopardize NRA, which, they believed, could function successfully only if it had the cooperation of business. As one historian has aptly put it, this cooperation "meant that the government should refrain from action business did not approve," such as interfering in the dealings between labor and management. On the other side stood the proponents of direct federal intervention, who asserted that the government should use its power to compel industry to accept collective bargaining. They believed the government should help redress the imbalance of power between the worker and his employer, but this belief had not prevailed.[8]

The editorial workers had not fared well under the National Labor Board (NLB), created almost immediately after the organization of NRA. Intended at first to handle labor disputes arising out of the President's Re-Employment Agreement, the NLB later dealt with those which arose from the codes. The publishers, however, citing the newspaper code, refused to recognize the competence of any body other than the Newspaper Industrial Board (NIB) to deal with cases involving newspaper workers of any sort. Thus, Hearst's attorney wrote the NLB's California regional board, to which at the end of April, 1934, Louis Burgess had appealed his dismissal from the *San Francisco Examiner,* that "regardless of any . . . laws . . . you have not the power to do that which Mr. Burgess requests you to do in his complaint."[9]

This defiant attitude illustrated the impotent state to which the NLB, possessing no independent enforcement powers, had come by the spring of 1934. Legislative attempts to create a stronger labor board failed, although in early June, at the behest of Roosevelt, Congress did pass Public Resolution No. 44, which authorized the President to establish a board to investigate labor disputes. He approved the resolution on June 19, and ten days later he relied on its authority to issue an executive order providing for the replacement of the NLB by the first National Labor Relations Board (NLRB). Although supposedly endowed with more authority, this board also depended for enforcement of its decisions on the Justice Department and NRA.[10]

The NLRB's establishment aroused little interest or enthusiasm among editorial employees. Initially, the new board followed the NLB's policy of avoiding the handling of complaints from all newspaper workers. Chairman Lloyd Garrison told a local guild official that "without a strong showing that the [Newspaper Industrial] Board has broken down or that some particular case of public importance has been mishandled we would not entertain jurisdiction" in newspaper industry labor disputes. The NLRB did take over its predecessor's cases, including Burgess's, which the NLB had assumed because no editorial workers' representative served on the NIB when the case arose. The NLRB finally disposed of the Burgess case, after much bureaucratic shuffling back and forth between San Francisco and Washington, by returning it once again to the California regional board, which ruled on November 8 that Burgess had failed to establish his complaint. He then appealed to the NLRB, even though it had become government policy since Eddy's appointment to the NIB to relegate all newspaper workers' complaints to that code-authorized board.[11]

Guild leaders supported this appeal even though they had expressed doubts about the NLRB. They had no place else to go; the NIB had proven useless to them. All their hard work to obtain representation on it had resulted only in Eddy's gaining firsthand knowledge of its ineffectualness. The board had met five times before Eddy attended his first meeting in August, 1934; of the 21 cases docketed to that date only one had been decided. With an even division between labor and management members, most of the meeting time had been spent wrangling about procedure and jurisdiction. Eddy's substitution for another labor member had done nothing to change the NIB's pattern of internal conflict. Moreover, for most guilds the cost of bringing a case before the NIB was prohibitive. In the late summer and fall of 1934 the ANG began to feel, as one commentator has put it, "publisher resistance like winter's first freeze hardening around it," and the guilds wanted government help more urgently than ever before. But they seemed doomed to the NIB treadmill, until suddenly in November the case of Dean Jennings offered a chance to escape from what *The Guild Reporter* unhappily had dubbed "the Newspaper Run-Around Board."[12]

Jennings, at 28 an energetic guildsman as well as chief rewrite man for the *San Francisco Call-Bulletin*, after more than five years' service on its editorial staff had resigned from the newspaper on May 29, 1934. Two days later he had filed a complaint with the regional labor board claiming that he had resigned under duress in order to collect vacation money due him that he needed to attend the St. Paul ANG convention as a delegate. He later testified that he had arranged his vacation schedule so that he could leave June 1 and drive to St. Paul (an action necessitated by lack of funds) but that on Friday, May 26, he was told that he would have to postpone his departure because the newspaper required his services. Jennings said that he was told the same thing by the publisher, Robert T. Holliday, on Monday, May 28. Holliday asked "which comes first, the Guild or the *Call-Bulletin?*" Jennings, after finding out the vacation schedules of other staff members, decided that the alleged need for his services was a ruse and insisted on his time off coming as arranged. Holliday offered to let Jennings go at the end of the work week on June 2, but this would have left insufficient time to drive to St. Paul. The publisher then suggested flying there, but made no response to the query: "who is going to pay for it?" According to Jennings, Holliday warned him that his job might no longer exist upon his return but did agree late in the afternoon of May 28 to pay out the vacation money. But when the guildsman went to pick it up the next day, the cashier told him that Holliday had the check. Jennings went to see the publisher, who once again tried without success to dissuade him from going. Holliday then told him that "the only way that you can have this check is to resign." Jennings did so, took the check, walked out of the publisher's office with "tears streaming down my face," and went to the convention. The circumstances of his resignation greatly affected other *Call-Bulletin* editorial workers, many of whom expressed fear for their jobs. On June 15, after two lengthy meetings in as many days to discuss the situation, a spate of resignations reduced the guild chapter on the newspaper from more than 40 to less than 6.[13]

Meanwhile, the local guild's attorney filed a complaint against the *Call-Bulletin* with the Regional Labor Board because he believed that Jennings had little chance before the NIB, which as yet had no ANG representative. The regional board, unsure how to proceed with the complaint, referred it to the NLB, which on June 9, ruled that the case should be turned over to the NIB. Nine days later, however, the NLB reversed itself and referred the complaint back to San Francisco—ostensibly because the NIB had not yet set up the necessary machinery to hear such complaints but more probably because of the bitter row at this time over Eddy's appointment to the NIB. Thereafter, the case languished despite local guild efforts to revive it, while the regional board dealt with the many more serious problems raised by the West Coast longshoremen's walkout.[14]

On October 5, 1934, after four postponements, the regional board—in this instance the chairman alone—finally held a hearing on the case. Jennings, his attorney, a local and a national guild officer, and three *Call-Bulletin* staffers presented one side. Despite repeated invitations, the newspaper was represented only by a letter read into the record by the chairman. A member of the law firm of John F. Neylan in challenging the board's jurisdiction in another newspaper labor case had added that this challenge also applied to the Jennings case; only the NIB had the right to adjudicate newspaper labor disputes. After the hearing, the regional board, without taking further action or making any recommendation, sent the records of the case to Washington.[15]

What would the NLRB do? None of the parties to the dispute knew for sure. Various alternatives existed: the NLRB could send the case to the NIB, return it to the regional board, or decide to deal with it. The labor board chose to do the last, and toward the end of October it wired Jennings' attorney that it had scheduled a hearing on the complaint and "WILL PROCEED TO RENDER ITS DECISION ON THE ALLEGED VIOLATION OF SECTION SEVEN A STOP IF SUCH VIOLATION IS PROVEN. . . ." Immediately the character of the controversy changed, and it became a national issue. Both sides made extensive preparations. The ANG, sensing its first real opportunity to score a victory over a major newspaper owner, scheduled Alexander Lindey (who had represented several guilds at the first code hearing) and Eddy to speak for Jennings. The publishers, afraid they would lose their independence from government regulation, an independence they claimed the code guaranteed them, turned once more to Elisha Hanson.[16]

The hearing took place on November 13 before NLRB members Harry Millis, a noted University of Chicago economist, and Edwin Smith, a former commissioner of labor and industries in

Massachusetts, with Smith acting as chairman. Garrison had resigned some weeks earlier and had returned to the deanship of the University of Wisconsin Law School. Hanson, the first speaker, completely ignored the merits of the case and presented a complex theoretical argument punctuated by many case citations. He maintained that only the NIB could rule on the Jennings complaint and that any other ruling would violate the freedom of the press.[17] Hanson did not deny the validity of the executive order establishing the NLRB but said that applying this order to the newspaper industry modified the newspaper code without its assentors' consent; and this, he declared, violated Article VII of the code, which guaranteed against modifications or changes unless the assenting newspapers agreed.[18] Neither the *Call-Bulletin* nor other newspapers, said Hanson, had consented to creating the NLRB; nor had they agreed to give it superior jurisdiction over newspaper labor disputes. "Therefore," he told Millis and Smith, "you must dismiss this complaint for lack of jurisdiction.[19] In his presentation Hanson had made no threats, but under questioning by Smith, he made it clear that he believed alternatives existed for the publishers if "one party to the code" attempted to change it without the other's consent.[20] On emerging from the closed hearing, he amplified this theme for waiting reporters: if the NLRB asserted jurisdiction and the newspaper industry asked his advice, he would tell the publishers to "liquidate" the code immediately.[21]

The spokesmen for Jennings put forth neither so complex nor so lengthy a presentation as had Hanson. Lindey declared that the NLRB did have the authority to judge whether any Section 7a violations had been committed and said that the case did not revolve around constitutional guarantees of free speech and press. His comments to the waiting reporters summed up his argument: "To say that the *Call-Bulletin* is not subject to the jurisdiction of the NLRB simply because the newspaper chooses not to submit is equivalent to saying the *Call-Bulletin* is not subject to any law that Congress passes unless the *Call-Bulletin* accepts that law." Eddy traced what he called the history of *Call-Bulletin* coercion against the guild and said that "the request that [Jennings] . . . resign was an effort to conceal the fact that he was under coercion . . . to keep him from attending the convention.[22]

Francis Biddle, the prominent Philadelphia attorney who became NLRB chairman less than a week after the hearing, rejected all attempts to shunt the case to the NIB despite the qualms of Professor Millis, who saw a row coming and would have preferred, if possible, to avoid a decision. Biddle thought "a showdown would clear the air," and his views prevailed.[23]

On December 3, 1934, the NLRB ruled that the *Call-Bulletin*, in violation of Section 7a, had interfered with the organization of its employees when it had tried to make it impossible for Jennings to attend the ANG convention. The decision dealt at length with Hanson's argument and concluded that "no genuine issue of freedom of the press can be fabricated out of the Executive Order giving the . . . [NLRB] authority to hold hearings and make findings of fact regarding complaints . . . [of] violations of Section 7a by newspaper publishers." The *Call-Bulletin* was given ten days to reinstate Jennings; because the newspaper had relied solely on the argument of proper jurisdiction, it could submit evidence during this grace period on the merits of the case and if it wished to contest these, the NLRB would arrange "the necessary further hearing."[24]

This ruling incensed newspaper industry executives. Neylan, the Hearst attorney who earlier had snubbed the case, expressed the view of many in the industry when he declared: "Legally, the decision represented pettifogging at its worst. Morally, . . . [it was] a betrayal of trust. . . . The so-called decision . . . was designed to seize the overlordship of the press . . . for three obscure appointed politicians." ANPA President Howard Davis used gentler language but came to the same conclusion. Even *The New York Times*, which had avoided the controversies between the industry and the government over the code, now editorialized about the threat to a free press. Biddle recalls feeling as if almost the entire press of the United States echoed the line that "unhallowed hands had been laid on the ark of the covenant."[25]

Of course, the NLRB ruling cheered guildsmen, who believed

that they had escaped from the NIB morass and that hereafter the government would enforce editorial workers' rights under Section 7a. "To us," wrote Broun, "the decision marked almost a Magna Carta victory." Moreover, this decision especially pleased those guildsmen who wished to avoid turning the organization into a thoroughgoing trade union, for government action offered an appealing alternative to strikes and picket lines.[26]

The decision had appeared in the morning newspapers of December 4. With Broun and other ANG officials in Washington to attend an NRA hearing on wage and hour amendments to the newspaper code, the local guild had scheduled a party for that night at the National Press Club to mark the ANG's first anniversary; this party now became a victory celebration. But the merriment ended early when a reporter read to the assemblage, amidst hisses and boos, an NLRB press release stating that at the request of NRA Acting General Counsel Blackwell Smith the NLRB had consented to reopen the Jennings case in order to allow NRA to present further evidence about the adoption of the newspaper code.[27]

The next morning, just before the hearing on the code amendments began, Broun secured permission from the NRA administrator chairing it to read a prepared statement. Charging that "NRA allowed itself to be terrorized by the publishers," Broun announced the guildsmen's withdrawal from the hearing. Singling out Donald Richberg, who because of his increasing importance in coordinating various aspects of the New Deal recovery program newsmen had dubbed "Assistant President," Broun said that as long as "the corridors of Mr. Richberg are filled with mysterious, high-pressure representatives of the publishers, we belong elsewhere. . . . We are going back to the picket lines in Newark, the air is cleaner there." And then Broun, in a maneuver which *Editor & Publisher*'s Washington correspondent described as being "executed with the finesse of a well-rehearsed play," led most of his colleagues out of the room; two stayed behind to make further statements of protest and then they also stalked out.[28]

On December 7 the NLRB, as requested by Blackwell Smith,

held another hearing on the Jennings case. Smith represented NRA but, according to Biddle, added nothing except for a long memorandum from Richberg, who suggested that the words "may decline" in the Executive Order establishing the labor board should be interpreted to mean "shall decline" when it came to dealing with a labor dispute in any industry where a code provided the means of settlement, such as the newspaper code did with the NIB. Five days later, on December 12, the NLRB reaffirmed its order to reinstate Jennings, saying of Richberg's argument that "it is unnecessary to torture the meaning of plain language. The word 'may' permits but does not compel us to decline jurisdiction." Once again the *Call-Bulletin* was allowed ten days to comply with the decision, this time until December 22.[29]

The guildsmen had looked to the government, and, after some hesitation, it seemed to have justified their confidence. But the division over labor policy within the Roosevelt administration (already very sharp because of conflicts over how to handle the labor situation in such other areas as the auto industry) coupled with intense publisher resistance led to a quick erosion of this apparent victory. The Jennings case had brought to a head the antagonism between the two schools of thought within the administration that had contended indecisively since the establishment of the NLB over what role the government should play in labor relations.[30] On one side stood the advocates of direct federal intervention through agencies like the NLRB; on the other stood the advocates of industrial self-government (Richberg foremost among them), who would have had the NIB handle the Jennings complaint. The proponents of direct federal intervention seemed to have won, but the other side worked hard to reverse the situation. Having failed on the question of jurisdiction, Richberg, who had accused the guildsmen of not acting in good faith and of malicious trouble-making, now attempted to vitiate the enforcement of the NLRB's reinstatement order. Among other things, he suggested that if the labor board sent the case to NRA for enforcement, the whole matter be turned over to the NIB for another hearing.[31]

Although much of this backstairs activity was unknown at

the time, enough information about it leaked out for guildsmen to become concerned and for the mass media to speculate about, as *Time* put it, "whether the NRA Compliance Division would take away Mr. Hearst's Blue Eagle . . . on the Labor Board's say-so."[32] Broun thought not, and where he had alluded to Biddle's Harvard training in an earlier column on the case and had ended with a goodnatured "Hold 'em Harvard," he now bitterly accused Richberg of acting as if "he wanted to win his 'J' from dear old Judas College."[33] An attempt by Broun and other ANG leaders to bring pressure to bear on Richberg through an open letter to him resulted only in an exchange of insults in additional letters released to the press. Richberg did not slacken his exertions to reverse the NLRB ruling.[34]

The newspaper industry also exerted great pressure. Almost immediately after the reaffirmation of the order reinstating Jennings, Howard Davis had called for an "emergency meeting" of the publishers' code committee. As long as some doubt had remained about the NLRB's intentions, Davis, who was chairman both of this committee and of the code authority, had considered it "most important we build up our case [by] showing attempts at sabotage by the Newspaper Guild. . . ." But he now believed the industry must take stronger action. Moreover, as one journalist observer pointed out, the very fact that the ANG had shown some signs of strength would lead normally hostile publishers to draw together to smash it if they could.[35]

Sixteen of the original twenty-six committee members as well as eighteen other interested and important publishers participated in the conference which took place in New York on December 17-18. Exactly what transpired at this conference remained secret, but *Editor & Publisher* did find out that all the participants considered the situation grave and that considerable disagreement existed about how to counter the NLRB ruling. After much discussion, they decided to send a long letter of protest to NRA in the name of "the six associations of daily newspaper publishers, representing more than 1200 newspapers which have assented to the Code." This letter, sent December 19, recapitulated the earlier arguments which said that only the NIB could adjudicate newspaper labor disputes and that for any other agency to do so violated the freedom of the press as well as the integrity of the code. A day earlier the code authority had sent a similar protest.[36]

The administration took these protests seriously, fearing that the publishers might simply withdraw *en masse* from NRA. This action seemed imminent when on December 27 the NLRB announced that the Jennings case had been turned over to NRA for enforcement because the *Call-Bulletin* had refused to reinstate Jennings when he appeared at the newspaper's offices on December 22. Upon learning of this transfer, Davis made public the December 19 letter to NRA, issued a strong statement to the press, and made use of the Associated Press wire facilities to tell publishers of assenting newspapers to expect an immediate call for a convention to consider continuance of the code. No one doubted that such a convention would lead to the dumping of the code.[37] Louis Howe, the President's secretary and troubleshooter, managed on December 28 to appease Davis and the other newspaper industry representatives sufficiently for them to consent to defer the convention call. The NRA decision, announced that same day, to turn over the records of the Jennings case to the NIB and to seek its recommendation before acting on the NLRB request to remove the *Call-Bulletin*'s Blue Eagle obviously played a part in the deferring of the convention call.[38]

The threatened convention, in addition to worrying government bureaucrats and guild officers anxious about the Jennings case, aroused the heads of the mechanical workers' unions and other organized labor officials, who feared that a victory for the publishers gained under such circumstances would lead to a change in government labor policies. This fear presented an unusual opportunity to those guild leaders who believed their organization's only chance for successful survival lay in close ties, if not affiliation, with the trade-union movement. Eddy, whose experiences had soured him on NRA, expressed the sentiment of those guildsmen and their supporters when he declared at the beginning of January, 1935, that "the publisher-directed maneuvers of NRA and other branches of the government have driven home to us . . . that our interests must be with those of other wage-earners and that standing alone we should quickly be crushed." The ANG, once shy of organized labor, now openly courted its support and during the second week of January joined with the other labor groups represented on the NIB to issue a statement which expressed grave concern over the publisher pressure on the government and called for a conference of representatives of newspaper employees and other interested parties to take place at AFL headquarters in Washington on January 18. The ANG worked hard to make this conference a success. Its small overburdened office staff sent out numerous invitations and followup letters, all within the space of a few days.[39]

Meanwhile, the Jennings case remained unresolved. Francis Biddle has described the NRA request for an NIB recommendation as "a good way of marking time," and so it proved. The NIB received the records of the case at the end of December, 1934, even though not scheduled to hold another meeting until mid-January, 1935.[40]

The sidetracking of the Jennings case to the NIB notwithstanding, publisher representatives continued pressuring various administration officials. Howe succeeded in obtaining further postponement of the convention call, but became so exasperated by what he considered the industry's inflexible attitude that he threatened to have the President broadcast an attack on the publishers unless they moderated their position. On January 11, 1935, Hanson met with Richberg, and these two foes of the NLRB worked out a settlement which would squelch the labor board. But other administration officials still had to be won over, including Secretary of Labor Frances Perkins, whose department had vague supervisory ties to the NLRB.[41]

While the Hanson-Richberg proposals circulated in Washington, the NIB met in New York for four days beginning January 14. Besides the Jennings case, it dealt with a number of other labor disputes, some of which involved guild members. Acrimonious exchanges between publisher and labor members took place with greater regularity than usual. Most of the guild complaints resulted in the usual deadlock, but at this session of the NIB the publisher members for the first and only time voted in favor of a guildsman. A publisher of Italian newspapers, Generoso Pope, had fired from one of his New York papers (*Il Progresso*) Alphonse Toinetti, a veteran employee and active guildsman. The guild complaint asked for Toinetti's reinstatement as well as recognition of the *Progresso* chapter for bargaining purposes and an end to Pope's threats against guildsmen. The usual deadlock denied the guild satisfaction on the issues of collective bargaining and discrimination, but the NIB, on a publisher-member's motion, did vote that Pope should "reinstate Toinetti immediately . . . on *Il Progresso* and/or affiliated newspapers." This victory, however, as *The Guild Reporter* put it, "carried a joker." Pope took advantage of the "and/or" clause and assigned Toinetti to *L'Opinione*, published in Philadelphia. Before the twist to the reinstatement became known, the decision buoyed many guildsmen; Eddy later said that it confused guildsmen by raising false hopes. It seemed that the furor aroused by the Jennings case had forced the publishers to reassess their policies on less controversial disputes. Actually, as Eddy later recognized: "the publishers were . . . under public pressure to demonstrate that the [NIB] was effective and this . . . influenced [them] in going as far as they did."[42]

On the afternoon of January 16 the NIB dealt with the Jennings case. So bitterly did the two sides divide over what to do that after two hours or so of sharp argument they could not even agree on how to indicate that they had discussed the case. Finally, they voted simply to send a transcript of their discussion to the NLRB and let that speak for itself.[43]

The NIB's failure did not help matters the next morning when Secretary Perkins met with Hanson to talk over the situation. Their meeting proved fruitless. According to Hanson, "she was adamant that the . . . [NLRB] should have appellate jurisdiction. . . . I was equally adamant . . . that the publishers . . . [would] call a convention unless the . . . [NLRB] were divested of all claims of jurisdiction over the newspaper code." She asked for more time to study the case. Hanson passed this request on, but Davis and the other newspaper industry representatives, impatient to resolve the situation, would wait no longer. On January 18 Davis fired what *Time* called the newspaper industry's "big gun" and issued a call for a convention to meet January 28 in New York.[44]

Also on the 18th, the guildsmen unleashed what one commentator has called their "ultimate weapon." In the council
room of the AFL's Washington headquarters there took place
the conference called by the labor members of the NIB, a meeting in which the ANG had invested much energy and hope.
Broun, Eddy, and Robert Buck of the Washington Guild represented the ANG. Claude Baker, first vice president of the
ITU, presided. A number of other union leaders attended, including John Frey, head of the AFL Metal Trades Department,
and Francis Gorman, vice president of the United Textile
Workers. Discussion centered on the possibility of cooperation
between the ANG and organized labor to exercise pressure in
government quarters for the enforcement of the NLRB decision
reinstating Jennings. For obvious reasons the labor officials
present unanimously agreed with the guild speakers' opinion
that all questions of compliance with Section 7a should go to
the NLRB and nowhere else, but Buck failed in an attempt to
translate this agreement into positive action by obtaining endorsement of a resolution upholding freedom of the press and
condemning the publishers. Beyond an invitation to Broun to
address the AFL executive council at the end of January so that
it might consider action on the Jennings case, nothing tangible
for the ANG materialized from this conference. Yet, despite the
absence of concrete results, the meeting had, as *The Guild Reporter* pointed out, "laid the groundwork for future cooperation." The ANG had taken steps, unsteady as they seemed at
the time, toward closer association with organized labor.[45]

Before the publishers convention could meet, the President
acted to resolve the situation. On January 22 he sent a letter of
"request," in effect a demand, to Biddle which Richberg and
Howe had drafted and which, with but slight modifications,
embodied the settlement that the NRA official and Hanson had
worked out. The President's request did not mention the Jennings case specifically, but his intention to bring the controversy
to a close was clear. In his letter the President, after noting that
only "a very small number of codes contained provisions for
handling labor disputes," stated that as a rule of procedure the
NLRB in future would refuse to hear any cases that code-
authorized boards could handle. Roosevelt also indicated that

while the NLRB could hear complaints that such boards had failed to act properly or had violated Section 7a, reports to this effect henceforth should go directly to the President, who would decide what action to take. The President's request circumscribed and diminished the NLRB's powers and, temporarily at least, allowed Richberg and the other members of the administration who opposed federal regulation of labor relations to have their way; industry should have the opportunity to regulate itself under the codes wherever labor-relations machinery already existed.[46]

The reasons for Roosevelt's decision remain unclear. However, Biddle believes, and probably correctly, that "more fundamental considerations" motivated the President than just "a desire to conciliate the newspaper publishers." Before he acted, his aides certainly must have brought many related items to his attention: the possibility of gaining Hearst backing in 1936; the damage to the New Deal recovery program that might ensue from the collapse of the newspaper code; the proposed legislation for extending NRA; and, perhaps most important, the impending decision about the code-authorized labor board in the automotive industry, where a similarly unsettled situation existed.[47]

All the parties involved in the Jennings case recognized that the President's request had ended the matter. A very pleased Hanson told reporters that "we have no statement to make. The President's letter speaks for itself." Davis immediately cancelled the convention, informing publishers that a satisfactory adjustment of the differences which necessitated the call had been made.[48] Shortly thereafter, Biddle wrote the lawyers of other editorial workers who had appealed to the NLRB (including Burgess, whose appeal a board attorney recommended be allowed) that under the circumstances the NLRB must advise them to present their complaints directly to the Newspaper Industrial Board.[49] Jennings remembers Roosevelt's letter as a cruel blow, and to him all seemed lost. In April, 1935, he resigned as the San Francisco Guild's executive secretary, its only paid office, a position which he had held for four months. Soon thereafter, at double his newspaper salary, he became a Resettlement Administration information officer in the Mountain States. He went on to become a prolific and financially success-ful writer of magazine articles and books.[50]

Guild leaders recognized that the publishers had won, that, as Broun said, the Jennings case and all that it stood for had be-come "no more than a pressed flower for our memory book." The columnist, incensed and frustrated about a turn of events which had resulted in defeat being snatched from the jaws of victory, accused the President of surrendering "at the point of a wooden gun" and charged that no one "could dodge the fact that the newspaper publishers had cracked down on the Presi-dent of the United States . . . and Franklin D. Roosevelt has cracked up." Eddy asked the ANG's Executive Committee mem-bers for permission to resign from the NIB as a protest against the President's action, and they consented quickly and unan-imously. A St. Louis reporter's comments epitomize many guildsmen's reactions; he called Roosevelt's letter "a crowning betrayal" and said that Broun's statement seemed too mild, for the ANG president "speaking for publication . . . could not ex-press the rage and the sense of being gypped. . . ."[51]

Roosevelt quickly sought to dispel the impression that his administration had surrendered to the publishers. On January 23, less than 24 hours after the request to Biddle, the President said at a press conference that "now it's very important that the Code Authority carry through its part of the agreement. . . ." That same day W. Averill Harriman, then NRA Administrative Officer, told reporters that "NRA definitely is on the spot now. It's our duty to see that the code board functions properly and provides justice in the Jennings and all other cases." In pursuit of this duty and apparently at the instigation of the President, Harriman arranged for and took part in a conference between NRA officials and the NIB to see what could be done about ending the continual bitter deadlocks as well as expediting the handling of the cases. This conference, held in Washington January 28-29 and attended by all the NIB except for one pub-lisher whose business forced his absence, produced meager results. Although an NRA spokesman summing up the meetings said that "the sharp cleavage of opinion and lack of cooperation between the labor and publisher members showed signs of dissolving somewhat," bitterness marked the entire proceedings. Harriman did secure, however, assurances that the NIB would deal more quickly with cases; and Harvey Kelly, its chairman, scheduled a meeting for February to enact this change in procedure as well as to deal with other NRA suggestions.[52]

Eddy believed that NRA only "went through the motions of putting it up to the publishers to provide some machinery that will actually assure the right to collective bargaining," but he believed that these motions mollified some of the guildsmen who, though upset about the outcome of the Jennings case, still hoped to gain some benefits through NRA, especially in the area of hours and wages. Although only a relatively small minority of the membership, these guildsmen still totalled enough of the membership that Eddy considered it unwise to take any drastic action that would appear as a slap at NRA. He explained to a Cleveland Guild officer who urged the ANG to dump the NIB that "you can't just pick up your marbles and go home. You have got to remember the membership. As soon as you start doing the things that you know to be right, without convincing most of the membership first, you bust the ranks."[53]

However, even the most die-hard advocates of working through NRA soon recognized the futility of bringing cases before the NIB, later judged by one study as "perhaps the most ineffective of all active industrial relations tribunals inside or outside the NRA." At the NIB's February meeting it did simplify the procedure for handling complaints, but this proved not to expedite their adjudication. Delay and deadlock remained hallmarks of the NIB. The government proved slow in doing anything about this. On March 6, in a letter later released to the press, Harriman asked Kelly why the NIB had failed to adopt the suggestions put forth by NRA officials in January. Harriman had a number of criticisms, but he concentrated on the NIB's failure to complete its proposed panel of five impartial chairmen, saying that he found it difficult to understand why the panel remained incomplete for almost a year after the board's organization. Kelly waited three weeks to reply; he then blamed the delay on "sabotage" by the employee members and denied the validity of Harriman's criticisms. Not until mid-May did the NIB complete the empaneling of the impartial chairmen.[54]

Long before then, the ANG, like most of the mechanical workers' unions, had decided to bring no new cases before the board. In the few months that the NIB continued to exist after the Jennings case terminated, only the New York Guild filed a complaint with it; other guilds heeded Eddy's advice to avoid the NIB. The ANG did not withdraw from the board, although Eddy missed its last meetings, giving his proxy to the printers' representative. The ANG remained, not because the leadership feared withdrawal would cause unrest among guildsmen, but because the other employee members had asked the ANG to stay on, afraid that the government would fill the seat left vacant with someone who might side with the publishers.[55]

At the time of the President's action on the Jennings case, *The Guild Reporter* said that Roosevelt had ushered the guilds to the portals of the AFL: "we are on our own . . . and we shall not have reached our full strength until we have made common cause with the organized labor movement in the United States." In the heat of the moment the ANG newspaper somewhat overstated the situation, but the continued ineffectiveness of the NIB further strengthened the sentiment that *The Guild Reporter* had expressed. On the whole, the Roosevelt administration's failure to deal successfully with the problem of labor relations between the publishers and their organized editorial employees strengthened the pro-affiliation forces within the ANG.[56]

These forces also gained from the government's failure to expedite the adoption of an amendment modifying the code's regulation of hours and wages.[57] In May, 1934, the newspaper industry had presented such an amendment to NRA. Carl Johnson had summed up his fellow guildsmen's feelings about the proposal's hours and wage provisions when he described them as "so objectionable" as to be "almost inconceivable." NRA officials, who lacked hard data about editorial department employment conditions and who were not quite sure how to proceed, had decided to postpone taking any action on the industry's proposals until the ANPA, the guilds, and the Bureau of Labor Statistics had finished their surveys of the newspaper workers' hours and wages. Publishers had no reason to contest this delay, and the ANG officers had favored it initially because they assumed that the surveys would show the justice of their cause. Eddy and Buck especially had faith in the BLS survey, believing that "the opportunity to obtain this sort of study and present it effectively outweighs the desirability of hastening the hearing." The surveys continued through the summer of 1934. Toward the end of October, as NRA statisticians began collating the results, the ANG asked the agency to hold a hearing on the amendment. Because Hanson's obligations to his other clients prevented him from appearing in November, NRA finally scheduled the hearing for December 5, which coincided with the initial brouhaha over the Jennings case.[58]

Despite the NRA's disappointing performance in other areas affecting them, many guildsmen still remained hopeful that the Roosevelt administration would take action to shorten editorial workers' hours and increase their wages; and, in guilds as disparate as the ones in St. Louis and the Twin Cities, committees worked out demands that the ANG should make at the hearing. The reaction to the stalking out of Broun and the other ANG spokesmen on December 5 as a protest against NRA's intervention in the Jennings case also indicates the hopes of many guildsmen that at least on the question of the code amendment the government would side with them. These guildsmen understood the need for the ANG to do something dramatic in regard to the Jennings case but questioned the wisdom of withdrawing from the hearing, a maneuver they considered an unjustified as well as a wild and foolish gesture. Feeling ran so strong that in some guilds the membership acted formally; the Rockford, Illinois, Guild, for instance, passed a resolution demanding an explanation, "for at our distance the action of the national Guild officers appeared very indiscreet and uncalled for." But events in relation to the amendment also eroded faith in NRA and the government in the area of regulating hours and wages.[59]

Taking advantage of the interest of NRA's Labor Advisory Board in the situation, Robert Buck by December 14 had managed to arrange for another hearing at which Gustav Peck, deputy NRA administrator and Harriman's assistant, would preside jointly with Jack Tate, the young lawyer who during the fall had become the NRA acting divisional administrator in charge of the newspaper code and whom guild officials thought inclined to favor the publishers. However, the invitation extended to the ANG on December 20 made no mention of a public hearing or of Peck; it only specified a "conference in order that the [American Newspaper] Guild . . . [might] be afforded a further opportunity for the presentation of its proposals and evidence in their support." It took another week of active negotiating by Buck and other ANG representatives before NRA issued a formal notice for a hearing in which Peck would take part.[60]

The ANG utilized this hearing, held January 17, 1935, to introduce a substitute amendment which called for a five-day, forty-hour week (with exceptions for emergencies; "extra hours compensated for by 1½ hours off for each hour of overtime work") as well as a weekly minimum wage of $45.00. The ANG amendment also provided for a conditional weekly minimum of $25.00 for editorial workers on newspapers able to prove inability to pay the higher scale. "Learners," to be limited to 3 percent of the editorial staff of any newspaper, would receive 70 percent of the basic minimum. Spokesmen for the journalism schools and a newspapermen's national fraternity as well as Eddy attacked the amendment the industry had proposed, but Morris Ernst presented the bulk of the ANG case. As *The Guild Reporter* described it, he "spoke for six hours uninterruptedly, except for a luncheon period, without any attempt at oratory—a steady stream of analysis of the contentions of the publishers and a description of the plight and counter proposals of the news writers." During the course of the hearing it came out, to the shock of many guildsmen, that the government had accepted the refusal of the Hearst and Scripps-Howard chains as well as other newspapers to supply payroll data to the Bureau of Labor Statistics for its survey of the hours and wages of news staffs. Of 47 newspapers contacted, 16 had refused to cooperate.[61] Both individual publishers and the chain business offices had referred the BLS to the ANPA surveys.[62]

The ANG wage proposals had just about doubled the scales proposed by the newspaper industry. NRA officials squabbled among themselves from January to April in attempting to reconcile these differences and draw up some kind of amendment to the code. Tate and other NRA administrators—having learned, as one history puts it, "the weary art of the possible with the publishers"—supported the industry proposals as a good start. The Labor Advisory Board and other NRA policy makers fought against the adoption of the proposals. Clyde Mills, the ITU officer who served as labor adviser on the newspaper code, argued that the industry amendment would help only two percent of the editorial employees. The Research and Planning Division, although it considered the ANG's wage proposals "far in excess of anything the publishers would agree to, if not in excess of a fair proposal," called the pay rates established by the industry amendment "too low," and recommended a substitute whose weekly minimum wage scale ranged from $16.00 to $27.00 (these minimums, said Spencer Reed of Research and Planning, would cost each newspaper very little). Tate, faced with strong and vocal opposition to the publishers' proposals, sent them back to the code authority, which made some slight adjustments in the wage provisions before returning the proposals to NRA in mid-April. However, maximum-hour provisions remained those the code earlier had set up for other newspaper workers, without any mention of a five-day week. The minimum weekly wage rate for small towns went up only $.50 to $12.50, although pay scales in intermediate population areas improved by a few dollars; in the larger cities the minimum remained $25.00. Cub reporters got 70 percent of whatever minimums prevailed in their population area. Mills and others objected to these proposals (presented as amendments to various sections of the code rather than as a single amendment), but on April 27, 1935, Tate recommended they be accepted, and on May 2 NRA formally made them part of the code.[63]

The Guild Reporter called these additions to the code "a sop." Their inadequacy in the view of most guildsmen as well as the long delay in their formulation strengthened the hand of those within the guilds who argued, as did Morris Watson, that "no law, be it Section 7a or any other, is going to reach a publisher or press association unless its prospective beneficiaries—which means us—force its enforcement with something more than a polite 'pretty please.' " NRA's failure stood in high relief at this time when it seemed that the Newark strike had resulted in victory, that guildsmen had defeated management and gained improvements in the working conditions of the *Ledger* editorial employees.[64]

The hour and wage amendments completed the code, doing so just before it ceased to function. The newspaper code was scheduled to expire on June 16, 1935 (Article VIII stipulated that the code's duration was co-terminous with the National Industrial Recovery Act, which ran for only two years). Whether the industry would have renewed the code remains problematical, as well as academic, for on May 27, but 25 days after NRA had promulgated the hour and wage provisions and just over a week before the ANG's annual convention would open, the Supreme Court declared a portion of the National Industrial Recovery Act unconstitutional and, as Arthur Schlesinger, Jr., put it, "knocked down with a series of blunt strokes the entire edifice of NRA." A revamped publisher code committee had just begun discussions about the future relations of the newspaper industry and NRA in view of the code's forthcoming termination when it learned of the Court's decision and recessed. The next day the committee met again and, in what one historian has called "a final show of literalmindedness," decided that since the code had been scheduled to run until June 16, publishers should observe it until then, for, said Davis, "the newspapers, in assenting to the code, had entered into a contract with the President . . . for the period ending June 16. . . ." For all practical purposes, despite such formalities as a final NIB meeting in June, the code structure in the newspaper industry, as elsewhere, crumbled with the Court decision.[65]

Very few guildsmen expressed sorrow over the passing of NRA. A few weeks earlier, in testifying before a Senate committee, Buck had expressed the feelings of most guildsmen about the code and NRA when he declared that "we do not need a code, and God knows we do not want one; it has bothered us long enough." Commenting on the Supreme Court decision, *The Guild Reporter*, speaking for the leadership, said that "the destroying . . . of NRA . . . is a great opportunity for the Guild. . . . [It] should bring home to newspapermen and women the need for organization. We must capitalize that awakening speedily and to the limit of our power."[66]

Even before NRA's demise, ANG leaders had begun attempts to build up such power. Toward the end of April, 1935, the ANG's Executive Committee voted to hire William Davy as an organizer. A knowledgeable radical who had led a variegated career as a worker and small businessman before he became executive secretary of the Cleveland Guild, Davy, remembered by a former guildsman as "an electric type of fellow," had done a first-rate job in that position. The Cleveland Guild's leaders had proposed that the ANG appoint Davy an organizer some months earlier and had received a favorable response from Eddy and Broun, but the Newark strike's drain on all available funds had resulted in the postponement of formal action until April.[67]

Eddy and other ANG officers recognized that they needed an organizer and that they could use more than one. By the end of 1934 it had become clear that Eddy alone could not cope with both the day-to-day administrative chores and the task of organizing guild chapters everywhere across the country that editorial workers evinced interest in the ANG. Eddy had taken various trips to see interested news workers, but he just did not have the time available to spend more than a few days anywhere and often he could not fit a locality into his itinerary. Moreover, given the increasing impotence of NRA and the government in the labor field as well as the rising hostility of publishers, quick visits by nearby guildsmen (even when such was possible or practicable) no longer sufficed. As Milton Kaufman, the New York Guild's executive secretary, noted in his April, 1935, report: "the novelty has worn off"; spontaneous organization, he believed, had come to an end. Pleas for assistance in forming guilds still came to Broun and the ANG, but these now represented one or two individuals, not groups. A typical letter concluded: "This is what I want to ask you—with what information I've given you, are you in a position to say if it's advisable to start a guild . . . ? Would it be good tactics for me to start it? How many good prospects does one need before asking for recognition? Is there any printed information on how best to proceed . . . ?"[68]

The appointment of Davy (who began his work in Chicago in May) did not solve the ANG's organizational problems, but it did indicate the course ANG leaders intended to pursue, a course they expected guildsmen would probably accept because of disappointment with NRA and the Roosevelt administration. Buck summed it up at the June, 1935, convention when he declared that "the last year's experience has carried the lesson . . . that guild members must expect nothing from the government. They must expect benefits only from the exercise of strength which they create for themselves by organization."[69]

Most guildsmen recognized, as Eddy pointed out, "that despite its palpable inadequacies and faults, NRA lent an aura of government sanction to the simple right of self organization." But as the newspaper industry in the months between the conventions proved increasingly hostile, more and more guildsmen came to resent what they considered the inadequacies of the Roosevelt administration in protecting that right, and they came to believe, as Broun put it: "there is no Santa Claus; not even in the White House." Since the June, 1934, convention the ANG had won representation on the NIB, but only after considerable governmental shillyshallying. Moreover, the victory had proved useless. When the guildsmen, attempting to escape the endless deadlocks and sharp bickering that rendered the NIB impotent, seemingly had found a way out through the NLRB, Roosevelt by his decision on the Jennings case had blocked that route and the administration's promised attempts to improve the functioning of the NIB had not resulted in very worthwhile consequences. Even on the question of hours and wages, the one area in which NRA had shown the most promise initially as far as the guildsmen were concerned, it had failed to do much for the editorial workers.[70]

By the beginning of June, 1935, there still existed a diversity of ideas about the future of the guilds among the membership. But because of the events that had led to a continuing withdrawal of the more conservative, professional-association-minded guildsmen, only two points of view had considerable rank-and-file support. Both of these views accepted the need for an economically oriented organization, but one argued for operating within the framework of the AFL and the other maintained that, given the character of the AFL as well as other circumstances, cooperation was preferable to affiliation. Guildsmen anticipated that the question would be dealt with at the ANG convention scheduled to begin on June 3.

7.

dissension

"I am aware of the fact that this is going to be a contentious convention," said Broun in his opening address to the guildsmen assembled in Cleveland at the Hollenden Hotel. And events bore him out; between the opening session on June 3 and adjournment on June 7, despite his efforts to squelch unnecessary bickering, the more than 90 delegates and alternates representing 37 guilds fought long and bitterly over everything from major issues like affiliation to minor points of grammar.[1]

The exact number of delegates present varied from day to day as job schedules and limited finances, among other factors, forced some guildsmen to come to Cleveland late and others to leave before the convention adjourned. The ANG constitution gave each guild at least three votes (often cast by only one or two delegates—all that some local groups could afford to send); the constitution also provided that guilds be allotted an additional vote for each 200 members in good standing on the basis of dues paid to the national organization. Only five guilds proved able to take advantage of this provision: Cleveland, Twin Cities, and St. Louis each had four votes; Philadelphia had five; and New York had eight.[2]

A substantial number of delegates—although they realized that New York's membership provided about 15 percent of the ANG's income—considered that guild's convention vote exaggerated and part of a scheme to change the ANG. These delegates strongly objected to what a former guildsman has called "the New York point of view," which, in addition to calling for the more widely accepted policy of affiliation, emphasized such controversial goals as centralization of authority in the national organization, support of various left-wing political causes, and transformation of the ANG into an industrial union by including business department and other unorganized non-mechanical newspaper workers. These delegates also believed that the ANG officials in New York were interested only in furthering such aims and charged these officials with being generally unresponsive to guildsmen who did not agree with them. Broun, whom almost everybody liked and respected, generally was exempt from the criticism leveled at such officials as Eddy, Watson, and Clyde Beals, the volunteer editor of The Guild Reporter.[3]

Most of the delegates recognized that to a large extent the convention would shape the future course of the guild movement, and as the fight over ANG policies grew more intense so also did the emotions of the delegates: ideological and political differences soon turned into personal hostility. The equal strength of the forces facing each other probably contributed to the personalization of this hostility. Two of the Twin Cities Guild delegates estimated that except on the question of affiliation, over two-thirds of the convention was committed on most of the important issues either to "the New York bloc" or "the National bloc" with but a thin margin separating them.[4] As a result of the necessity to woo the unaligned delegates, continued canvassing took place (of the larger delegations, of all Hearst employees, of all delegates who belonged to guilds with less than 50 members, and so on).

A year earlier, the St. Paul convention had voted to table the question of affiliation because of the limited sentiment among the membership for such a move. Events since then had considerably strengthened the pro-affiliation forces. What Eddy called "the first real inquiry" from any local group about affiliation had come at the end of November, 1934, when guildsmen in St. Paul—upset by the intransigence of the publisher of the Daily News there and outraged at NRA's ineptitude in dealing with the situation—had raised the possibility of their guild becoming part of the AFL as a means of pressuring the publisher. Some other guilds later raised questions about affiliation, but not until the spring of 1935 did it become clear that the annual convention could not avoid dealing with the issue.[5]

As the convention had drawn closer, discussion within the guilds about affiliation had increased. Those in favor of affiliation usually cited the advantages which would accrue; the report of the pro-AFL committee in the New York Guild declared that "if we were part of the American Federation of Labor we could ask and get cooperation as fellow members . . . , but as an isolated group our appeals for assistance take the nature of a plea for charitable aid." Those opposed to joining the AFL divided into two camps: conservatives and ultra-radicals. The more serious conservatives argued (as did Detroit Guild president Ralph Holmes, who believed in "cooperation" with organized labor) that given the character and quality of the AFL, the ANG while still in the formative stages should not determine so definite a future policy as affiliation. Some in the conservative camp had more selfish reasons: they feared that entrance into the AFL would lead guildsmen to the "brick-layer level of the social stratum" or, as a New York reporter said: "affiliation means security for the incompetent at the expense of the competent." The ultra-radicals, influenced by the then-current Communist party line that declared the AFL an agency of capitalism as evil as the "bosses," held that as a New York Guild chapter paper put it: "Green's organization was led by a lot of grasping reactionaries with whom no class conscious worker would be found on the same roster."[6]

In the weeks immediately preceding the convention, many guilds conducted polls of their membership to ascertain what views were held about affiliation. Despite *Guild Reporter* attempts to make the results seem like a groundswell in favor of joining the AFL, they proved inconclusive. The majority of delegates came to Cleveland uninstructed, free to vote as they thought best on the issue.[7]

Three possible ways of effecting affiliation existed: the ANG could give up its independence and become a federal union under the direct jurisdiction of the AFL executive council; the guildsmen could become part of the ITU (if it would agree to reassume jurisdiction over editorial workers) with guild chapters incorporated into the typographers union as locals; or the newsmen's organization could obtain a charter from the AFL as a separate autonomous union. "Affiliation either as a federal union or as subsidiaries of the ITU," said Eddy, "had insuperable disadvantages," and some months before the convention the pro-affiliationists had decided to work for approval by the guilds of obtaining an AFL charter.[8]

The convention took its first steps toward dealing with the problem of affiliation at its opening session on Monday morning, June 3, when the delegates acted favorably on a proposal put forth by the National Executive Committee (which until that weekend had not met since the last convention). In an attempt to get the arguments on joining the AFL presented quickly and fully to the delegates, the Executive Committee, which named the members of the various convention bodies but which, in Broun's words, "felt it had no right to appoint a committee that might bring in a majority and minority report," had proposed forming a special labor-relations committee (made up of three delegates for affiliation and three against presided over by an impartial non-voting chairman) to present the case for each side.[9]

On Thursday morning, June 6, the divided committee made its dual report to the convention. Robert Buck presented the pro-affiliation side. He enumerated 12 reasons for joining the AFL, chief among them being: the ANG had become a labor union and thus belonged in the labor movement; the AFL would give the guilds much-needed support in strikes and organizing campaigns; although some guildsmen might resign because of affiliation, the over-all membership should increase materially because the greater feeling of security resulting from joining the AFL would encourage the more timid to join guilds. Harold T. Meek, a *St. Louis Post-Dispatch* reporter and president of that newspaper's guild chapter, spoke for the anti-affiliation group. He argued that the AFL had a record of oppressing smaller unions like the ANG, that affiliation would bring jurisdictional strife, that editorial workers could not be classified with other labor, that in case of a walkout at a factory the demand for its product usually remained after the end of a strike but a newspaper might suffer permanent damage to the detriment of its workers and affiliation increased the likelihood of strikes.[10]

In the interim before the two sides had reported back to the convention, it had become clear in caucuses and other meetings of delegates that an attempt to force through the convention a motion instructing the ANG's officers to apply for a charter from the AFL would invite defeat for the project. Although the motion would carry, the probably slight margin of victory would cause a serious schism. The pro-affiliation forces discovered, however, that many of those who had doubts about voting for a tie with the AFL would accept a plan which would allow the convention to recommend a course of action but would leave the final decision up to a poll of the ANG's membership with joining the AFL dependent on affiliation obtaining at least a two-thirds majority. A sizable number of delegates continued to fight strongly against affiliation, but believing that over one-third of the guildsmen voting in a referendum would oppose ties with the AFL, these delegates indicated that they would accept such a plan.[11]

Late in the afternoon of June 6, after much acrimonious debate and a confusing series of parliamentary maneuvers by partisans of both sides, the report recommending affiliation carried by a roll-call vote of 76½ to 47½. Buck then moved to submit the convention's recommendation to the guilds for their consideration. His motion made it mandatory for ANG officers to take steps immediately to join the AFL if two-thirds of the entire paid-up membership as of August 31, 1935, voted for affiliation.[12]

Some delegates, led by New York guildsmen, made a determined attempt to amend Buck's motion and called for a majority vote with merely an "instruction" to affiliate, not a mandate. These amendments—reflecting the attempt at this convention by the New Yorkers and their allies to transform the ANG into a highly centralized, more radical trade union—had the dual purpose of making it easier to achieve affiliation and increasing the national officers' authority, which a grant of discretionary power on such an important issue obviously would do. But this and other attempts at amendment failed, and the delegates finally agreed to instruct "the secretary to cast a unanimous ballot" for Buck's motion.[13]

The fight over affiliation had cut across many ideological lines at the convention. The Twin Cities delegates, for instance, supported the pro-AFL report even though they considered "extremist" most other aspects of the program put forth by the New York group and its allies, especially those proposals which dealt with revising the ANG's organizational structure. As the Twin Cities delegates later reported to their guild's members, "it was on the revision of the constitution that the issue was joined between the New York and National blocs."[14]

The leaders of the New York bloc had come to the convention ready to present for adoption by the delegates a finished constitution that invested a much smaller executive body with very broad powers, stripped the guilds of most of their autonomy, and transformed the ANG into an out-and-out union incorporating non-mechanical newspaper workers. Although the vast majority of the delegates recognized the need to revise the ANG's constitution, many of them objected to these proposals. Some of the delegates, including Crozier, Meek, and Paul French of the Philadelphia Guild, had learned about the plans of what they dubbed "the New York crowd" prior to the convention. They had communicated with each other, and once in Cleveland had organized to fight proposals which they believed would "remodel the ANG into nothing more than a small, mobile fighting unit for wars of the Newark type." They succeeded in having some representatives of their side (including French) appointed to the convention's constitution committee, where they strenuously objected to the New Yorkers' proposals, arguing that conditions throughout the country varied widely from those in the New York area and that many of the proposed changes seemed "impractical" as well as "revolutionary." So embattled did the committee become that word spread through the convention that any changes in the constitution would not take place until the following year. I. L. Kenen, the committee's chairman, recalls that in marathon meetings the members fought over every word and comma. The committee met almost continuously between Tuesday morning (when it convened) and Thursday night (when the convention debated the draft constitution the committee finally had pieced together), the only break coming during the day on Wednesday, June 5, when in a preliminary report it submitted the major questions in dispute to the convention.[15]

Despite the endeavors of the more conservative delegates, on June 5 the convention voted for the proposals to reallocate the voting apportionment in future national conventions so as to favor larger guilds, to provide for the removal of national officers between conventions, to amend the constitution in future by majority rather than two-thirds vote, and to replace the regional system with district councils wherever circumstances called for two or more guilds to function together. After extended debate, the convention also accepted the idea of a reduced national executive body, albeit with the proviso that the constitution committee provide for adequate geographical representation. The opponents of this "small board plan," as Kenen termed it, raised the cry of "New York domination" but could not overcome the sort of argument which, after descrying the failure of the ANG's Executive Committee to meet even once between conventions, declared "the plan set up last year is utterly impractical, physically impossible, and should be changed to one, whether representative or not, that can function efficiently."[16]

Although the convention did adopt a resolution favoring an industrial union in the newspaper industry and did instruct the constitution committee to embody that sentiment in some portion of the constitution, the delegates, at Broun's suggestion, voted to delay at least for a year a proposal that would have extended the ANG's jurisdiction (at the discretion of each guild) to the business, clerical, circulation, and promotion departments. Broun said that although he had favored such an extension for some time, to do so now would complicate plans for affiliation as well as most assuredly arouse an unfavorable reaction from many guildsmen.[17]

Those opposed to "the New York crowd" won a clear-cut

victory only in defeating the proposal that all funds and properties of the guilds should belong to the ANG, although each guild would continue to administer them as long as it remained in good standing with the national organization. The advocates of this proposal argued that it would put the ANG on a stronger financial basis. Newark Guild counsel A. J. Isserman—who had helped draw up the document the New Yorkers brought to Cleveland and who had gone there at the invitation of some New York area guildsmen—had worked closely with the constitution committee. At the request of one of its members and with the consent of the delegates, Isserman appeared on the convention floor to argue for this proposal. He cited the many financial problems raised by the *Ledger* strike, explained the financial policies of other unions, and declared "centralization of funds" necessary for the future successful functioning of the ANG. Heated debate punctuated by shouts and exchanges of personal insults followed his appearance. Finally, the proposal lost 77 to 44 on a roll-call vote.[18]

Having, as Kenen put it, "assayed the mood of the convention," the constitution committee returned to its labors. During the wrangling over its preliminary report Broun repeatedly had told the delegates that "we are not taking final action, we are merely making a recommendation . . . ," but the majority of the committee's members proved perfectly willing to accept these expressions of opinion as instructions. The committee—styling itself "in substantial accord" although not in complete agreement on any point—presented its draft constitution to the convention Thursday night; the fight over the provisions went on into the early hours of Friday morning as the conservatives tried to rewrite the constitution from the floor. They managed to defeat a proposal for higher dues as well as to rescind such provisions as those which would have given national officers the power to call a strike where a local unit had not voted one, to discipline a member writing anything detrimental to the ANG, and to adopt a policy of collective bargaining enforceable in the guilds. On the whole, however, the conservatives failed; the 62 to 50 vote against them on the attempt to move ANG headquarters from New York indicates their margin of defeat.[19]

The new constitution generally embodied "the New York point of view," especially with regard to ANG officers. A compact, more powerful National Executive Board (NEB) replaced the ineffective National Executive Committee. The NEB could call a strike, despite the refusal of local guild officials to do so, at the behest of the majority of a unit (which to exist had to have seven members); it could suspend local guilds for causes outlined in the constitution (ranging from refusal to collect or remit dues to taking court actions against the ANG) and recommend revocation of these guilds' charters to the national convention; it could disapprove of any agreement which it found violated ANG collective bargaining principles; and it could levy "in an emergency" weekly assessments of not more than $.50 for not more than 16 weeks for the purpose of assisting strike activities or bolstering the defense fund. (The constitution now allowed the NEB to declare an emergency at any time that the defense fund fell below $20,000; on May 31, 1935, the ANG Reserve Fund totaled $1,079.27.)[20] In what many delegates considered a sop to the more conservative group, the constitution provided for a National Council, composed of the presidents of all guilds, which would review all NEB decisions dealing with charter suspensions and which would serve "as the agency for removal or suspension of the National Executive Board." The Council never functioned, and the next convention ended even its paper existence.

The ANG's new executive body consisted of a president, a treasurer, a vice president for wire service employees, four vice presidents at large, and a non-voting executive secretary. Eddy's opponents, who anticipated his reelection to that post, believed they had "disciplined" him by taking away his vote.[21] To assure geographical distribution of national officers the constitution provided that at least one of the NEB's seven voting members come from each of the six regions that replaced the 13 established a year earlier. To ensure no repetition of the National Executive Committee's year-long failure to meet, the constitution made it mandatory that the NEB hold sessions between conventions.

On Friday, June 7, at its last session, the convention elected the NEB. For regional vice president, Buck and Don Stevens of the *San Francisco Examiner* ran without opposition; Thomas Sherman of the *St. Louis Post-Dispatch* trounced his opponents; and Carl Johnson of the *Duluth Herald* won a close race. In the contest for wire service employees vice president, Morris Watson won decisively. The convention chose Garland Ashcraft treasurer by four votes. Broun was elected president by acclamation. Two delegates who were on opposite sides at the Cleveland meeting recall that although Broun had favored or even advocated many of the proposals put forth by "the New York crowd," he had done nothing to damage the respect, if not veneration, that many guildsmen had for him.[22]

Eddy inspired no such affection or loyalty. For many at the convention he stood as a symbol of all the evils they believed were inherent in "the New York point of view," and they determined to oppose his reelection. They did not expect to win, but only to put Eddy "on notice"; R. S. Gilfillan, one of their leaders, recalls that he did not know "what we'd have done if Eddy really had been beaten."[23]

The national organizer, Bill Davy (a member of "the New York crowd," though not recognized as such by many delegates), declined to stand against Eddy, as did Crozier, who said that he had had "a bellyful of the whole thing" (he also had refused to run again for treasurer). The nominating committee submitted Eddy's name without opposition, and he left the convention to wait out his reelection in the hotel bar. Before the voting began, a group of delegates nominated Davy (ill upstairs in his room) without asking his permission, and he ran ahead of Eddy on the first count of the roll-call vote. But the rules of the convention specified that both tellers had to report before the chair could announce the result. One of the tellers, a New York delegate, disappeared when it became evident that Eddy had lost. Meanwhile, Eddy, having learned of the vote, rushed back to the convention and appealed to the delegates "to give me a chance to defend myself." Cries of "out of order" shouted him down. Confusion ensued as "the New York crowd" made a series of what Harold Meek, sitting in for the absent Broun as chairman, later called "nutty motions." The confusion as well as the contest for Executive Secretary ended only when Herman Nelson, the young reporter who cast the Rockford Guild's three votes at the convention, switched to Eddy, thus ensuring his reelection by 1½ votes. The conservatives charged that Eddy's supporters had worked on Nelson during the confusion, but he does not recall any real pressure being exerted on him and claims that, given the closeness of the vote, he deemed it wrong to "dump" Eddy, who, he believed, "had done so much" for the ANG. Davy, who feels that if he had chosen to run he would have won, almost immediately after the balloting (though still quite ill) spoke to the delegates at the behest of Eddy's supporters and announced that "John has done certain things I don't approve of . . . [but] now get this and get it right. I am for John first, last, and all."[24]

The delegates during this convention had laid bare the divisions within the ANG at the same time that they had transformed it. The fight over Eddy's reelection only highlighted this division, evident also in the other hotly contested issues at the convention. Events in Cleveland had clearly demonstrated the power of a small group of guildsmen from New York and their allies. Although not yet strong enough to get what they wanted organizationally without a fight, they had pushed through the convention most of their program and thus had paved the way not only for institutionalizing their power but also for reorganizing the guild movement so that it would be better prepared to meet the challenges it would face.

Before the ANG's revised organizational structure could begin regular operations, the guildsmen found themselves in contention with a publisher, this time in Lorain, Ohio, a small town about 30 miles west of Cleveland. Since December, 1934, Samuel A. Horvitz, publisher of the *Journal*, Lorain's only daily newspaper, had discriminated against guild members on the editorial staff of 14. He had succeeded through intimidation and cajolery in convincing three of the *Journal* news workers to resign their guild memberships, but eight continued to hold out. Leaders of the Cleveland Guild (to which, despite the geographical separation, the Lorain editorial employees belonged) as well as Eddy and other ANG leaders had been aware of the *Journal* situation, but, because of the unfavorable aspects of carrying on a strike in an open-shop steel town like Lorain and because of the depletion of funds resulting from the *Ledger* fight, they adopted the mildest attitude possible toward Horvitz. In early June, the situation came to a head. On June 8 Horvitz fired Evelyn Bailing Kieffer, a leader of the Lorain guildsmen's negotiating committee and for ten years the paper's society editor. When the next day the other Lorain guildsmen protested this dismissal, Horvitz told them they must either immediately sign individual agreements not to strike without a week's notice or consider themselves discharged. Correctly believing that Horvitz meant to use such agreements to obtain a breathing space in which to hire scabs to replace them, the unit voted against signing the no-strike pledges. On June 11 four or five (the number varies in different accounts) of the remaining guildsmen found themselves barred from the newspaper office, in effect locked out. Seven of the guildsmen, including Mrs. Kieffer, promptly set up a picket line, and the Cleveland Guild's executive committee decided to back them in a fight against Horvitz.[25]

In the next days the Cleveland Guild sent some carloads of members to Lorain, but these proved of little help. It also appealed to Cleveland's central AFL body and with the volunteers that group supplied established on June 21 at 6 a.m. a mass picket line (c.100) before the *Journal* plant. Until then the seven Lorain guildsmen had marched alone; the Cleveland guildsmen who came there usually concerned themselves with other tasks. When the newspaper's printers—all ITU members—reported for work and saw the mass picket line, they refused to cross it, even with police protection. Frank Maloy, the *Journal's* managing editor, had no such compunctions. In crossing the line, however, he indulged in a verbal exchange with one of the volunteer pickets that ended with Maloy's glasses broken, either by a slap or a punch, before he continued on to work. Shortly thereafter, the mayor, asserting that he acted under the general code of Ohio, issued a proclamation declaring the vicinity of the *Journal* a riot area and forbidding more than four pickets there. Lorain's acting police chief then ordered the area barricaded, brought in a number of policemen and deputy sheriffs armed

with sawed-off shotguns and rifles, and read the mayor's proclamation to the by now more than 125 chanting pickets. They
dispersed and the printers went to work some five hours late.[26]
That afternoon Horvitz's attorneys obtained a temporary injunction which limited the pickets allowed before the *Journal*
office to two. Thereafter the guildsmen proved unable to re-
establish any effective or meaningful activity against Horvitz,
despite a quick visit by Broun during which, on the evening of
July 12, he addressed probably the largest gathering till then in
Lorain's history, tore up the injunction before the audience, and
along with other speakers, including Davy, led about 300 of the
assemblage on a march before the *Journal* office in defiance of
the court order.[27]

The Lorain guildsmen's failure to make any progress notwithstanding, the fight against the lockout in terms of benefits to the
workers, printing bills, and the like cost the ANG money it
could ill afford to spend. The Cleveland Guild, which had nearly
bankrupted itself in hosting the convention, could contribute
little despite its large membership, although it did advance some
money against repayment by the ANG. By June 17, the NEB had
voted by mail to levy a $.50 assessment of the ANG member-
ship. Although collection of this assessment should have taken
place during the last week in June, the money came in very
slowly; and to pay for operations in Lorain, it became necessary
to make use of what remained of the ANG Reserve Fund. The
national organization constantly had to scramble to find the
funds to maintain the fight in Lorain, especially in the first
weeks, when the outgo ran over $200 weekly. This lack of cash
made it difficult not only to carry on daily activities there but
also to provide competent leadership to do so. The little group
comprising the Lorain unit, according to Eddy, did not contain
anyone sufficiently experienced to assume effective control of
operations there. Ashcraft had sacrificed his vacation to get
things started, but a full-time newspaper job and duties as ANG
treasurer made it impossible for him to continue to oversee
guild activity in Lorain. Bill Davy replaced him, but the NEB
members believed that the Lorain situation should not hold up
the ANG's expansion program, and in mid-July he returned to

his work as national organizer. With no funds available to send someone else to Lorain, leadership of the fight there devolved upon a series of Cleveland guildsmen who grabbed what time they could to handle the situation. But their efforts lacked continuity of responsibility and action. Consequently, other guilds remained uninformed about the Lorain fight, picketing became unsystematic, and the guildsmen's strike paper appeared very irregularly. Broun's visit, for instance, had served to inspire the setting up of a citizens committee to aid the Lorain guildsmen, but because they lacked direction, three weeks elapsed without a meeting.[28]

Formally, the fight continued until the end of October, but in reality it had petered out long before then. Eddy, after a visit to Lorain in early August, noted that the community, which at first had favored the guildsmen because of the general dislike of Horvitz, had lost interest. The fact that Horvitz published the town's only newspaper severely hampered the ANG, and it failed in efforts to get another newspaper established. Federal mediation attempts in September proved worthless because of Horvitz's intransigence. In mid-October ANG leaders advised those Lorain guildsmen who had not already done so to obtain jobs elsewhere. The Cleveland Guild helped some of them find employment, the the ANG continued benefits for two of the locked-out workers for ten weeks.[29]

The ANG lost badly in Lorain. The chances for success, negligible from the start, quickly became nil because of the maladroitness of the guildsmen in dealing with the lockout. The NEB later defended its policies rather lamely by saying that Horvitz had to lay out large sums to defeat the guildsmen (which seems an exaggeration) and that therefore "we had at least demonstrated that an open attack is costly to the publishers even when we are extremely weak."[30] The ANG had kept faith with its members in Lorain, but in such an irresolute and unimpressive manner that it lost face with many editorial workers. Well before the Lorain fight ended, it exposed the ANG anew as a weak organization, unsure of itself and unable to protect its units.

The ANG's shortage of funds continued to be the bane of its

existence, and the problem was rooted in inconstant membership and irregular dues payment. Eddy had reported to the Cleveland meeting that as of the end of May, 1935, the guilds had total book membership of 5,415, but Ashcraft later estimated that "the dependable revenue membership" then averaged less than 3,500.[31] Moreover, what this membership paid to the ANG varied from month to month. For instance, revenues during the first four months of 1935 totaled about $6,000, but in May the guilds, attempting to ensure their right of representation at the forthcoming convention, paid $2,828.50 to the national organization.[32]

In an attempt to deal with the ANG's financial difficulties as well as some of its other problems, the NEB had met in Cleveland after the convention adjourned. The board, judging that the complexity and variety of the questions facing it precluded any hasty action, decided in a brief meeting that a finance committee composed of Ashcraft (the new treasurer), Eddy, and Watson should meet within a month and establish some kind of guidelines for future ANG fiscal policy as well as draw up a budget. Then this committee, joined by Broun, should reconstitute itself as a subcommittee of the NEB and outline specific proposals for the approval of the entire executive board. Before the finance committee could meet, the struggle with Horvitz began.[33]

The $.50 assessment for financing the Lorain fight had aroused little opposition among guildsmen. Although they proved slow in paying the assessment, the vast majority accepted the need for it. However, when at the same time Eddy suggested to the NEB that the ANG impose monthly assessments in order to produce more working capital than the convention had provided with its continuance of national dues at $.50 a month, he encountered opposition, especially from Buck. The Washington guildsman argued that the convention—which he said had the final say according to the constitution—had acted wisely to keep dues low. Buck believed that to double national dues (which imposition of a monthly assessment meant) would result in less money and fewer members. He opposed levying any additional assessments except for such unavoidable emergencies as the Lorain situation until the membership paid the nearly $10,000 owed in back dues. This action, he said, would help the ANG financially as much as any assessments. Although the argument ostensibly centered on finances, it actually involved conflicting notions about the future direction, character, and philosophy of the guild movement.[34]

After the finance committee's deliberations on June 29 and 30, Ashcraft, Eddy, and Watson, in two day-long sessions that stretched well into the evening, talked over the ANG's problems and drew up a set of 20 resolutions which, in addition to setting forth a most ambitious program, furthered the centralization of authority advocated by "the New York crowd" at the convention. These resolutions (some of which, for practical reasons, later underwent modification) included decisions to close the columns of The Guild Reporter to any NEB members who wished to criticize a policy after the board had adopted it, to hire Clyde Beals at $75.00 a week as The Guild Reporter's full-time editor (despite the questions raised at the convention about his policies while he served as volunteer editor during the spring), to instruct Beals that its editorial policy must follow the mandates of the convention, to outlaw contracts either negotiated or signed by units rather than guilds, to take steps to suspend two guilds very delinquent in dues, and to retain Davy and hire an additional organizer—each at $50.00 a week and expenses. Ashcraft's proposed budget envisaged a large deficit, but Eddy and Watson apparently shared his belief that spontaneous organization at an end, new guilds, as Ashcraft put it, "would be *acquired only with an outlay of money for organizational work. We are no longer homesteading. . . . If we increase the acreage we must buy the land.*"[35]

On July 1 Ashcraft, Eddy, and Watson, joined by Broun, met as an NEB subcommittee and unanimously recommended that the other executive board members accept all 20 resolutions. Eddy no longer had a vote on the ANG's executive body, but the endorsement of the other three meant that the proposals needed only the support of one additional NEB member to become effective. Board members debated these resolutions (as they would other ANG business) by mail. Each member who believed he had something to say sent carbons to all the others, some of whom then responded in like manner. Only *St. Louis Post-Dispatch* newsman Julius Klyman, serving as proxy for the vacationing Sherman during July, expressed no opinion; he voted but felt it improper as a substitute to take part in the discussion. Buck and Carl Johnson expressed disappointment at what the former termed "the railroading of measures" through the NEB. Buck especially objected to those resolutions which he considered attempts at regimenting the guilds. Although some resolutions met more opposition than others, within three weeks they all had gained approval.[36]

Their acceptance did not resolve the discord among NEB members. Buck continually inveighed against what he considered attempts to centralize the guild movement "contrary to the view expressed by the majority at the convention." He believed, as he put it, that "the, shall we call them intellectuals, intended to impose the goosestep on locals and mere members." Although a stickler for due procedure, Buck became so upset at one point in August that he threatened to appeal to the rank-and-file over the head of the NEB. The precise nature of his ideas about the guild movement's future at this time remains unclear, but he apparently assumed that affiliation would give the ANG enough muscle vis-à-vis the publishers to continue as a loose association of guilds, which would pursue definite economic aims. Although broadening its geographic base, the ANG would remain primarily an organization for editorial workers. On the other side, Eddy, who had gained articulate allies with the election of Ashcraft and Stevens to the NEB, continued to press for the complete implementation of the program that "the New York crowd" had presented to the convention. They declared its adoption necessary for the survival of the ANG as a viable organization which would obtain economic gains for all sorts of newspaper workers from publishers.[37]

However, more than just an interest in furthering the ANG moved some of the NEB to support "the New York point of view." As over the months the guild movement had fallen on difficult times, the eagerness to work for it had fallen off among the membership. But among the more zealous remained the small number of guildsmen who belonged to the Communist party, and they continued if not increased their energetic efforts to do what they could for the ANG. This they did not only to further the guild movement but also to promote their party's interests (and temporarily during the heyday of the Popular Front when the party abandoned its sectarianism, the Communists achieved control of the national organization and a number of local guilds). These guildsmen, without whom the ANG probably would have fallen on even harder times, soon had much more influence than their very limited numbers warranted. Moreover, the Communist guildsmen's strenuous activity won over to their cause other guildsmen who were eager for the success of the ANG; not all joined the party, but many did. Ashcraft, for instance, at this time "was one of those who," as a former Ohio Communist party organizer puts it, "first became party sympathizers because of the help they received from us . . . and who later joined the party when they saw how effective a party cell could be in promoting the growth of a union." In the fall of 1935 those on the NEB who, whether party members or not, accepted the then-current Communist line about the AFL as "a tool of the bosses," believed that even though affiliation might be a good thing, the ANG must guard itself against that "union-busting, horse-trading, political, corrupt, reactionary organization," to use Eddy's words. These NEB members saw Buck, with his ties to the AFL, as an agent of an organization which opposed industrial unionism and what they called "significant progressive political action." They also believed that the "reactionary, obstructive, and destructive" Buck stood in their way and that he could draw on his considerable experience in the labor movement to mobilize sentiment against them if he were not neutralized.[38]

Ideology played its part in the infighting among NEB members but so did the ANG's continuing financial difficulties. Although dues receipts did not fall off so drastically in the summer of 1935 as after the 1934 convention, they did go down; and this reduction in income coupled with the slow response to the assessment meant that, given the money allocated to the Lorain fight and the ANG's weekly expenses, the national organization operated at a bigger deficit than anticipated.

Thus, a serious financial problem arose when Harvey Kelly, winding up the NIB's affairs, asked the ANG to make good some $550.00 for guilds that had failed to pay their bills to the board for transcripts and the like. The matter came to a head in mid-July after Kelly wrote the NIB's other employee members asking them "to take such steps as necessary to bring about settlement by the ANG of its obligations, or else a clear repudiation of that obligation." The president of the photoengravers union said that if the ANG could not pay, the NIB's other employee members should settle the debt. Ashcraft, declaring that he felt "rather Sovietish about it" at first urged that the ANG repudiate the debt because paying it would "clean out our treasury." He changed his stand after receiving a long-distance call from Broun, who expressed fear that some in the AFL would use a repudiation to oppose the ANG's admission on the grounds of financial irresponsibility. Ashcraft then proposed that the ANG pay the NIB bill, and the NEB (with Klyman and Stevens dissenting) promptly voted by mail to do so. At the same time, Ashcraft had moved that the national organization levy another $.50 assessment, but this motion had hard going. Buck restated his belief that assessments, except in emergencies, violated the convention's mandate to keep dues low and said that given Ashcraft's original budget he had made no case for another assessment. Other NEB members questioned whether the guilds involved would reimburse the national organization when their finances improved and said that the membership would not accept another levy so soon. After three weeks of debate by mail, the NEB in mid-August (over the objections of Buck, Broun, and Johnson) voted the assessment.[39]

In the interim the ANG nearly went bankrupt. Even after cutting back on the ambitious program voted in early July, expenses far outstripped income, and the payment to the NIB just about wiped out the ANG's bank account. Lack of funds made it necessary for the NEB to accept Ashcraft's motion that all ANG activity temporarily cease. Publication of *The Guild Reporter* was held up. Volunteer help kept Davy's Chicago office open, but he had to suspend his organizing work. He, as well as Beals and Eddy, went without pay for two weeks. And the NEB's forthcoming meeting (which would have cost over $700.00 in travel expenses) was postponed from the beginning of September to mid-October. By the end of August, however, the ANG had renewed its activities thanks to the rise in receipts from dues as guildsmen anxious to vote in the referendum on affiliation paid arrears. The two assessments also brought in some cash.[40]

Ashcraft, to outline what he considered a serious situation as well as to explain the need for the second assessment, drafted a statement for the September *Guild Reporter*. Buck, Sherman, and Watson objected to its peevish tone. As it then seemed that *The Guild Reporter* would carry no statement whatsoever, Eddy drafted one in the name of the finance committee, to which he also signed the names of Watson and Ashcraft. The latter approved of the statement when it appeared, for it generally echoed his ideas on the direction and financing of the guild movement. The statement drew Buck's ire, however, as did Eddy's argument in the same issue that assessments might serve to pay for operating expenses. On September 9 Buck wrote a letter for publication in *The Guild Reporter* in which he reiterated his stand on assessments and questioned the legality of applying funds received from them to purposes other than those for which they specifically had been levied. When Beals and Watson saw this letter on September 11, they immediately called Washington and asked Buck to add something about the need to pay assessments once the NEB voted them, and he dictated some such statement over the phone. The additional paragraphs notwithstanding, Beals, Eddy, and Watson decided that the letter violated the rule (passed in July) about individual NEB members opposing the board's decisions in *The Guild Reporter*. The next day Beals wired Buck that he had asked for an NEB vote on withholding from publication the letter. The vote resulted in a tie (Buck refused to take part; Sherman and Broun supported publication; Stevens and Ashcraft opposed it; Watson and Johnson expressed no opinion). Eddy, anxious to forestall interference with his plans, interpreted this vote to mean that the letter should not be printed. Buck later charged that "a reason for the incomplete vote might be found in Eddy's letter [of] September 16 to [NEB members] in which he says that 'due to an oversight no place was included on the ballot sent out . . . on Buck's letter . . . please write your judgment on this matter on the ballot'."[41]

Meanwhile, Buck, who had anticipated that *The Guild Reporter's* columns would be closed to him, had inspired the Washington Guild to send a statement to all other guilds declaring that "we face a choice between a large [organization] . . . paying small dues in sufficient numbers to finance ordinary expenditures or a small union of trained seals paying high dues. . . ." In this statement, sent out by coincidence on September 12, the very day Buck learned that publication of his letter depended on an NEB vote, the Washington Guild reported its payment of the first assessment, indicated its willingness to pay the second, expressed its members' opposition to any others until the dues situation cleared up, and invited other guilds "to consider this question and communicate to us their opinion." Despite the favorable response the Washington Guild elicited from other guilds and despite the obvious unwillingness of guildsmen to pay the second assessment (by the end of September it had produced only $229.50), Eddy pressed for the adoption of a third assessment. By the end of the month, the NEB had approved it five to two (Buck and Johnson dissenting).[42]

Against this background of increasing internecine conflict the referendum on affiliation took place between September 15 and 30. Each guild made provision for its members to vote by secret ballot at a designated place. Guildsmen cast special ballots provided by the national organization on the basis of having paid dues through July as well as the first assessment. Altogether, guilds certified 3,526 voters eligible on or before September 5 (the cutoff date for so doing) and 607 thereafter.[43]

Neither side found much new to add to its arguments after the convention or proved very vociferous.[44] The only notable action came from the pro-affiliation side, which sent out a statement to the entire ANG membership in mid-August. Sponsored by an informal committee of 37 guildsmen (mostly industrial-union-minded) from 25 guilds, this statement acknowledged that the AFL leadership might have faults but argued that "we are not advocating affiliation with a few individuals who hold office in the Federation; we are proposing that we join the great mass of organized workers and march with them to a common goal." This statement had its origin in discussions at the beginning of July between Newark Guild officer Victor Pasche and Cleveland Guild president Elmer Fehlhaber, both congenial to Ashcraft's view of the ANG. Despite Buck's previous strong pro-affiliation stance, he was not asked to join in sponsoring the statement. Eddy, when apprised of the planned committee and statement, termed the project a sound idea, but suggested that since "it would probably incite the antis to a similar move . . . it might . . . be better to let the antis start shooting first." But the disorganized and dispirited antis never did.[45]

As the returns came in at the beginning of October, affiliation seemed certain of the necessary two-thirds majority, but it fell just short, getting 65.4 percent of the ballots cast. The six tellers (including Broun as a representative of the pro-affiliation side) decided unanimously to interpret rigidly the rules governing the referendum and disqualified the votes of 11 guilds because of various technicalities, the most common infraction being certification after September 5. Their votes would not have changed the outcome. The final and official tally made at ANG headquarters in New York on October 16 was 1,841 for affiliation and 973 against.[46]

Three days later, on October 19, the delayed NEB meeting began there with Buck's announcement that he intended to resign as an ANG officer as soon as the board adjourned. In his letter of resignation he declared that Eddy and Ashcraft were "temperamentally unsuited to the offices they held," charged them with impeding the proper functioning of the board, and said he considered it his duty "to take such steps as he could to prevent their reelection. . . ." Because he judged it "improper" to campaign against them while a member of the NEB, he resigned. The campaign against Buck had had its desired effect. One can easily sympathize with him. He had worked hard to further the ANG's interests with the AFL and NRA as well as other government agencies, and felt outraged at what had happened to him. But it is questionable whether Buck's various beliefs if implemented would have benefited the guild movement, which needed more cohesion and substance than low dues, guild autonomy, and the like would provide.[47]

Despite Buck's impending withdrawal, bitter wrangling marked most of the NEB's two-day meeting. The arguments that had split the NEB since the Cleveland convention came up repeatedly. Ashcraft talked of the need to levy assessments and to impose tighter controls so that the ANG could grow; Buck denounced "these dictatorial things, these absolutes." The personal antipathies that some members of the NEB had come to feel toward each other heightened the pitch of the arguments. Broun had a hard time keeping the sessions orderly, and they produced few concrete results. In the area of finance Buck had his way as the board narrowly voted that "routine expenses should be met from ordinary revenues" and that the NEB's power "to levy assessments will be exercised only in extreme emergencies to support necessary special campaigns." To raise the extra funds that the ANG needed, the NEB after much discussion voted to sell guildsmen $25,000 worth of non-interest-bearing "defense certificates" in amounts from $2.00 to $100.00. Stevens and Buck had made similar proposals during the summer, and board members had exchanged considerable correspondence on this idea. Broun summed up the rationale behind accepting this plan when he said that he hoped it would raise a lot of money, but if not "it will then be out of the picture as a substitute for raising dues."[48]

Only on the question of affiliation did the NEB act with dispatch and near unanimity. Because it fought so over other issues, the board did not deal with affiliation until the afternoon of October 20, shortly before it adjourned. To mitigate the possibility of the ANG being isolated from organized labor, the NEB voted six to one (Sherman dissenting) that Broun write AFL president William Green that the ANG had not turned its back on organized labor, that, as Watson put it, "we almost voted to go in. . . ." Then, as Sherman put it, "to end agitation on a sore spot," the NEB decided against pressing affiliation for the time being. With debate centered more on *The Guild Reporter*'s editorial practices than on the issue at hand, the board voted six to one (Broun dissenting) that the "*Reporter* refrain from editorial partisanship in the question of . . . affiliation until further direction" came from the NEB. (It voted in February to lift this ban.)[49]

Broun and Eddy had managed to work together during the NEB meeting, but their relationship remained uneasy. Eddy, who had to deal with the ANG's day-to-day problems and who believed he did all the work, resented the fact that Broun got most of the credit. It also galled him that the ANG so obviously needed Broun more than it did him. The coolness between the two men remained an impediment to the smooth working of the NEB.[50]

An even greater obstacle resulted from the impasse that arose over choosing Buck's replacement, who, according to the ANG constitution, had to come from the same region. Four guilds presented candidates and after much politicking by letter and telephone, a mail ballot at the beginning of December resulted in a tie. Johnson, Sherman, and Watson supported Louis Heath, a wire service staff man nominated by Buck's guild; Ashcraft, Broun, and Stevens voted for H. Bowen Smith, the energetic president of the Baltimore Guild, which despite the NEB decision to defer action on affiliation had been one of the two guilds (Newark was the other) to urge that as soon as possible another referendum be taken on joining the AFL. William D. Wolfe, a Philadelphia guildsmen, and W. Earle Homan, president of the Reading Guild, received no votes. Because it seemed that a second ballot would not break the deadlock, Broun suggested Homan as a compromise candidate. Ashcraft, Broun, Sherman, and Stevens voted for Homan; Johnson stayed with Heath; Watson did not vote. The addition of Homan (much to his surprise) to the NEB toward the end of January dissipated the surface tension among board members.[51]

On another level, however, conflict increased as the proponents of "the New York point of view" began to fight among themselves. Much of this had to do with their relationship to the Communist party. Ashcraft, a cantankerous individualist as well as a dedicated guildsman, found it difficult to submit to any discipline, let alone that of the Communist party. He found party discipline especially distasteful at times because he believed that the guildsmen in the Communist fraction in New York used their proximity to the party's national leadership to further personal ambitions. Eddy, who declares that he never joined the party, and Ashcraft had worked closely together on many issues, including the hamstringing of Buck. But they had also clashed fiercely at times, and both men had abrasive personalities. Stevens, a one-time Wobbly and a revolutionary at heart who had considered the October NEB meeting so important that he had given up his newspaper job so that he could come East, recalls that the areas in which Ashcraft and his allies disagreed with others of the Communist fraction and their supporters included the question of how to handle finances and how to employ Davy. The New York Communist fraction, managing to obtain support for its views among the party leadership, kept rejecting Ashcraft's ideas, telling him he did not know nor understand the party line; he, in turn, believed that with reference to the ANG they kept switching the line on him. No real resolution of these difficulties—which aroused intense emotion even though involving only a few persons both on and off the NEB—took place until the 1936 convention.[52]

This friction within the ANG leadership exacerbated the organization's already shaky situation, especially as regarded finances. A lack of cash forced cancellation of the NEB's December meeting. Davy, forced once again by lack of funds to suspend his activities, complained of being "eternally hogtied financially." The straightening out of technicalities in the wording of the defense certificates, which one NEB member believed took "an unconscionably long time," delayed their sale. Installation at national headquarters of an involved system for recording individually the dues payments of the entire membership cost the ANG several hundred dollars it could ill afford and initially resulted only in a more complete tabulation of what guildsmen owed. "The outstanding thing about dues collections so far," said *The Guild Reporter* at the end of 1935, "is that with the exception of about 15 guilds of various sizes, locals have been constantly slumping and . . . [having to be] rejuvenated." Ashcraft's somewhat trimmed-down budget for the last quarter of 1935, approved by the NEB at its October meeting, had envisaged little or no increase in the organization's deficit. But the ANG, which at the end of September already had lost $1,054.87 on its operations for the year, went $895.88 further into the red during the last three months of 1935.[53]

Faced with the ANG's imminent financial collapse, Broun and Eddy, appealed for cash to David Dubinsky, Sidney Hillman, and John L. Lewis, all of whom had proved helpful during the Ledger strike. Circumstances favored the guildsmen's plea. The showdown over industrial versus craft unionism, which also involved considerable personal rivalry for power within the AFL, had come at its annual convention in October, 1935. The proponents of industrial unionism lost but decided to go ahead on their own and form the Committee for Industrial Organization (CIO). On November 9, the CIO elected Lewis its president, and under his and Hillman's guidance it quickly became a going concern. Willing to use whatever platform he could to make known the CIO's plans and ideals, Lewis accepted an invitation to address on December 18 a general membership meeting of the New York Guild. He spoke about "effectuating a larger and more ambitious form of organization among the workers of this country." Just before the meeting he talked with Broun, Eddy, Randau, and Watson and agreed to help the ANG financially. Shortly thereafter the United Mine Workers contributed $2,000 to the ANG. This money enabled it to meet its more pressing debts and stave off bankruptcy, but myriad financial problems remained.[54]

Given these continuing financial difficulties as well as the divisions among the leadership, it is no wonder that the guild movement had made little progress in the months after the 1935 convention. In Cleveland, Louis Seltzer, the editor of the Scripps-Howard daily, the Press, told a committee of guildsmen on July 6 that Roy Howard, the head of the chain, had decided he would deal no further with any guild until after the completion of the referendum on affiliation. The Press negotiations, which had dragged on since mid-1934, finally resumed in November, 1935, but without immediate results. In December the Cleveland News used the delay in negotiating an agreement with the Press as an excuse to hold off renewing its contract.

Philadelphia guildsmen, making use of the recently passed Wagner Act, had appealed in October to the reconstituted NLRB, charging the publisher of the *Inquirer* with unfair labor practices. But the guildsmen proved unable to follow through on their charge. The matter dragged on until March, 1936, when the NLRB's regional director in Philadelphia dismissed the charge, declaring the guild had not presented a convincing case.[55]

In some ways, in fact, the guilds retrogressed. During the fall and early winter it became clear that S. I. Newhouse had managed to undercut the position of the guild on the *Ledger*; in December, that newspaper's unit, to the consternation of Newark Guild officials, voted to terminate until January 1, 1937, the negotiations which had been going on for the last months to resolve the many issues left in abeyance by the strike settlement. In many places across the country during the summer and fall of 1935, despite the protests of guilds in these localities, publishers ended the five-day week which the ANG had called "its first major gain." Except in the case of the wire services, where the six-day week soon became standard, reinstitution of the longer work schedule followed no consistent pattern. In some cities only one or two newspapers extended the work week; in others the extension affected only parts of the editorial departments; and in still others nothing at all happened. The reinstatement of the six-day week in the New York office of the Associated Press caused the guild unit there to request the ANG to seek a conference with management to negotiate about the longer hours. The NEB sent a registered letter to the AP asking for talks. On October 18, a few hours after delivery of the letter, the AP fired Morris Watson. The ANG immediately appealed to the NLRB, and a long fight ensued from which the guildsmen emerged victorious 18 months later. But in the fall of 1935 it seemed that the newsmen's organization could not even protect its national officers.[56]

Publishers by and large ignored the requests of guildsmen; only a few guilds managed to obtain written agreements. On July 26 the Reading Guild signed a contract with the *Labor Advocate,* a weekly, but the agreement only formalized benefits

that the tiny editorial staff already enjoyed. New York guildsmen did obtain two signed agreements through negotiation, but
both proved wanting. The *Daily News* unit's leaders and its
publisher, Captain Patterson, judged, according to the statement
heading their agreement, that "the collapse of NRA created a
unique situation." Therefore they concluded at the beginning
of June, 1935, what they termed an "emergency agreement."
Scheduled to run for a year unless superseded by some other
pact between the *News* and the New York Guild, this agreement
called only for continuing the five-day week for *News* editorial
employees and for maintaining the $15.00 weekly minimum
wage for copy boys. The Representative Assembly refused to
ratify the agreement because it violated the ANG constitution's
prohibition of direct negotiations between a publisher and his
employees. Patterson said he could deal only with the unit because as a member of the New York Publishers Association he
felt obliged to abide by its stand of refusing to formally recognize the New York Guild. A general membership meeting of
that group on June 19 reaffirmed the Representative Assembly's
action, but in the interests of harmony it voted to approve the
News agreement if the words "by permission" of the New York
Guild were added. Ashcraft correctly labeled this solution "a
snide proposition" for, as a newspaper industry history points
out, the accord certainly verged on being a company union
agreement and as such contrary to everything the guilds stood
for.[57]

Guildsmen negotiated a more substantial contract with the
New York Post, but it also had considerable drawbacks. J. David
Stern, who had bought the *Post* in 1933, had made it plain during the negotiations that since he "was building it up from
zero," he would concede nothing that might cost him even one
cent, and he would not discuss establishment of minimum wage
schedules for editorial employees. Stern admitted that he paid
the organized mechanical workers better than the editorial staff,
but—according to Milton Kaufman, the chief guild negotiator
—he then "with a shrug of his shoulders said that that was the
status quo." The *Post* unit, moreover, desperate to get some
kind of benefits, in a close vote had decided to forego the

minimums in order not to antagonize Stern, who, they feared, might just close down the newspaper for good if pressed too far. The guild negotiators, recognizing their lack of bargaining power, acceded to Stern's conditions. On the whole, the contract (signed July 25 and at the request of the guildsmen to run only nine months) followed the terms of the second *Record* agreement and did bring the *Post* staff some benefits. But the provision for a five-day, forty-hour week allowed many exceptions, and in other ways, as with sick leave, Stern lagged behind the prevailing practices on other New York dailies.[58]

From the Cleveland convention until the end of 1935 only in the contract obtained with the *New York Amsterdam News,* a Harlem weekly, did guildsmen achieve substantial gains in a written agreement, and it took an 11-week struggle to get them. The *Amsterdam News,* like all American Negro newspapers at the time, suffered from a paucity of advertising. As Gunnar Myrdal points out, "the main observation about the advertising in the Negro press is that there is so little of it." Many potential advertisers, when approached, said they could reach the Negro market as effectively in the daily white press as in a black newspaper, which thus had to depend on circulation for its revenue. Being then what one sociologist has termed "an additional newspaper," the Negro newspaper operated within very narrow financial boundaries which left little money available for editorial expenses. In general, the black journalist working for a Negro newspaper (and *de facto* segregation confined him to the black press except in the rarest of instances) received only a fraction of what his white counterpart earned. In fact, many black newspapermen often worked for years without regular salaries (receiving $5.00 or $10.00 now and then) while sustaining themselves with menial jobs. The *Amsterdam News,* one of the more prestigious of the Negro newspapers, did pay its editorial employees, but they worked for so little and under such poor conditions that they snapped at the chance to organize a guild unit. By mid-1934, most of the newspaper's editorial staff had become guildsmen.[59]

The newspaper, because of a change in editoral executives, recently had adopted a strong, liberal, pro-union stance, but the owner, Mrs. Sadie Warren Davis, who treated her employees in a very feudal manner, frowned on organization. In December, 1934, she had threatened to fire anyone who did not resign from the guild. She soon relented, but the unit by then had voted secretly and unanimously to strike if necessary. No further trouble occurred until July, when, pleading financial necessity, she arbitrarily cancelled all vacations. The unit then asked the New York Guild to undertake negotiations with Mrs. Davis. Recognizing the economic difficulties faced by a Negro newspaper, the guild representatives did not ask for a wage increase or make any other demand that might cost much money; they simply sought to obtain a contract so that the *Amsterdam News* editorial staff could have greater job security. However, a conference proved fruitless, as did an attempt by a committee of distinguished Negroes to intercede on behalf of the guildsmen. Mrs. Davis refused to recognize the right of the guild to carry on negotiations for her staff. The continued attempts to do so angered her, and on Monday, October 7, she discharged seven of the editorial workers (giving them a few days' notice); the next day she fired two more (also giving them some notice); and finally on the morning of October 9, two days before the newspaper went to press, she locked out all the guildsmen or almost the entire staff. Two news workers resigned from the guild and continued with the *Amsterdam News*, but 15 others, including the city editor and the acting editor, stayed with the guild. The leaders of the New York Guild, anticipating the possibility of a lockout, had prepared picket signs, rented a headquarters around the corner from the newspaper's offices, and made arrangements for financing a campaign in support of the staff.[60]

Racial prejudice existed among New York guildsmen (some had complained loudly and angrily about "niggers" attending meetings) but in general the membership, like the leadership—which strongly had pressed the case of the *Amsterdam News* unit during the negotiation attempts—showed no hesitation in supporting the 15 locked-out news workers, even though they and the other Negro guildsmen altogether represented less than two percent of the New York group. At a time when Jim Crow held sway almost as strongly in the North as in the South, the New York Guild wholeheartedly entered into the fray to win reinstatement for the Negro guildsmen. Theodore Poston, one of the leaders of the unit, believes that in good part the willingness to support the *Amsterdam News* workers arose because Communists active in both the national and New York organizations hoped to win recruits for the party from among the locked-out Negroes as well as others who might become involved, but he also believes that in general the membership, whatever their politics, responded splendidly to the need to help fellow guildsmen in distress.[61]

The Guild Reporter later summed up the struggle: "the whole lock-out fight was characterized by a smooth efficiency gained from . . . previous experience in struggles with publishers." Negro organized labor as well as New York's central AFL body endorsed the guild's fight against the lock-out. At first, the newspaper's close ties with the local police precinct resulted in the pickets being limited to two (usually a white and a black), but a concerted effort on October 18 by guildsmen, including attempts by Broun to have himself arrested, succeeded in ending this limitation. Despite boldface editorial admonitions by the *Amsterdam News* urging "us Negroes [to] remember that the Guild is an organization of white newspapermen," both prominent and ordinary members of the Harlem community in large numbers joined the white guildsmen and sympathizers in manning the picket lines established not only in front of the newspaper's office but also before newsstands, its print shop, and those businesses which continued to advertise in it. A concentrated attack by guildsmen and sympathizers caused the *Amsterdam News* to lose both display and classified advertising, and linage fell from 1,250 inches on October 10 to 764 on December 14. The guild-inspired boycott also affected the newspaper's circulation, which dropped precipitously (despite a 50 percent slash in price to five cents) as a massive postcard campaign resulted in hundreds of readers sending signed notices to Mrs. Davis pledging not to read the *Amsterdam News* until it reinstated the guildsmen.[62]

Attempts at negotiating a peaceful solution proved unsuccessful. Immediately after the lock-out began, Mayor La Guardia tried to bring both sides together. Mrs. Davis and her daughter, Mrs. Odessa Morse, the nominal president of the company putting out the *Amsterdam News*, accepted the mayor's invitation for a conference October 14 with New York Guild representatives. However, neither of the two women nor any other management spokesman appeared; two days later La Guardia released a report by Mrs. Elinore Herrick, NLRB regional director for the New York area, which completely contravened the *Amsterdam News*'s claims that no lock-out existed and that financial conditions had made necessary the discharge merely of some part-time employees. Mrs. Herrick said that the failure of the two women to attend the conference "shows clearly the real issue in this case was a determination on the part of the employer to defeat unionization." Repeated attempts thereafter by the guildsmen to obtain a conference with representatives of the newspaper resulted only in one abortive meeting on November 7. Aiken Pope, Mrs. Davis's counsel, who all along advised her to take a hard line, told the guildsmen at this conference that the newspaper had agreed to a meeting only because so many persons had urged one. He did admit that the guildsmen had hurt the *Amsterdam News* economically, but said that it would not reinstate any of the discharged workers. Mrs. Davis indicated that she would cease publication rather than negotiate, and her daughter emphasized this when she told the employees' representatives at the meeting that "we'll all go down together."[63]

The end of the struggle came suddenly. In the face of the guildsmen's attacks on the newspaper's sources of revenue, its debts mounted steadily. Mrs. Davis tried to sell the paper, but the problem of what to do about the locked-out employees stalled talks with prospective buyers. Finally, on December 20, the newspaper's three largest creditors (Pentagon Printing Company, Powers Engraving Company, International News Photos), without whom the *Amsterdam News* could not publish, instituted bankruptcy proceedings, forcing the establishment of a receivership. That same day the court-appointed receiver consulted with the New York Guild. So also did Doctors C. B.

Powell and P. M. H. Savory, two prominent Negro physician-businessmen who had bid on the newspaper. On Christmas Eve, after four days and nights of nearly continuous negotiations, the doctors and the guildsmen reached an agreement; it would go into effect when the prospective buyers took over the newspaper (which they did the second week of January, 1936). In the interim the receiver agreed to run the newspaper under the same terms.[64] The settlement called for a two-year contract whose provisions included the firing of all scabs; a five-day, forty-hour week; time off for overtime; a guild shop; graduated dismissal notice; an adjustment committee (headed by an impartial chairman with representatives from labor and management); and reinstatement of the nine locked-out full-time employees with a ninety-day moratorium on their replacement.[65]

Nation, which strongly supported the guild movement, although admitting the *Amsterdam News* fight had been "in no sense a major battle" called its successful conclusion "a heartening event." Certainly it brightened the ANG's otherwise lackluster record since the 1935 convention. Altogether only 426 newspapermen had joined guilds during that time (which did not even begin to make up for those who dropped out). Moreover, between July 1 and December 31, 1935, only two new guilds (Cincinnati and Tacoma) had been chartered. By contrast, at least five guilds had become comatose.[66]

Once again the ANG had survived, albeit barely and as a poverty-stricken organization with a limited, fluctuating membership. The guilds' generally poor record since the Cleveland convention had failed to vouchsafe the confidence which despite the strife there many guildsmen had expressed in the future of the ANG. The bitter discord that had wrecked the NEB in the months following the convention had weakened the organization seriously, and this weakness coupled with the increasing disregard or hostility most publishers displayed toward the guilds had resulted in wide-ranging questions being asked both inside and outside the guild movement about what would happen to it. A small group, mostly centered in New York City, had fought hard to capture absolute control of the organization. Before falling into fighting among themselves, the members of this group had eliminated or neutralized most of the group's opponents on the national level. That portion of the leadership which had survived the internecine struggle and had obtained control of the organization by the beginning of 1936 still intended to put across affiliation with organized labor as well as a program of industrial unionism. But these leaders recognized that unless some guild could make a good showing against a major publisher (and for all their enthusiastic rhetoric about the *Amsterdam News* victory, they considered that struggle as little more than a sideshow), they would fail to attain their aims and, more importantly, the ANG would wither away as had other newspapermen's organizations in the past.

8 ·

the guild becomes a union

"We knew we had to put up or shut up in order to succeed," recalls Don Stevens. "We recognized that the feeling was we were done if we did not fight and win." In line with this estimation of the situation, the ANG leaders by the beginning of 1936 had determined to confront an urban newspaper operated by a chain publisher. They had decided that such a confrontation (which they rightly considered easy to effect given the general attitude of the newspaper industry toward the guilds), if successfully concluded, definitely would prove the viability of the ANG and the worth of their policies. Therefore, the ANG's leaders moved to forestall any possible strikes by guilds which would not fit into this plan of action.[1]

Although, according to the national organization's constitution, the initiative and final decision about striking rested with the guild and unit involved, the local guildsmen looked to the national leadership for guidance—partly because they needed advice on how to proceed in the unfamiliar area of collective bargaining and partly because they expected the ANG to provide the financial support necessary to sustain a strike. In effect this dependence of the local guildsmen upon the national organization gave the ANG leaders a veto power, and they used it to decide when and with whom the showdown they had determined upon would take place.[2]

This confrontation did not come with any of the newspapers published by the smaller chains (e.g., those of Frank Gannett

239

or Paul Block). On these dailies guilds generally did not have very strong units. Moreover, in most of the localities serviced by these chains the ANG leadership believed a strike would garner little support. Nor did the showdown come with any of the Scripps-Howard newspapers; it might well have, though, for members of various guilds had become exercised by their failure to obtain a written agreement from any of the dailies published by that chain. Despite the Scripps-Howard newspapers' generally strong editorial support of labor and despite the willingness of the newspapers' executives to negotiate, no written agreement had resulted. Disgruntled guildsmen who had expected quick action on contracts accused the chain's chairman, Roy Howard, of "shadow boxing, stalling, and straddling." A few guildsmen even charged the ANG leadership with refraining from attacking any Scripps-Howard newspaper because Broun had a contract with the chain and because the columnist during the late 1920s and early 1930s had been close to Howard (so much so that during one of their many tours of New York night life a quipster had said: "Here comes Roy Howard with his tame bear").[3]

The erstwhile social relationship between Broun and Howard, which by 1936 had long since become more formal, and the columnist's legal ties with the chain had little if anything to do with the ANG leadership's decision to avoid a confrontation with Scripps-Howard. Certainly, Broun had no compunctions about challenging the chain which syndicated his column. As early as the summer of 1934, when negotiations bogged down with the *World-Telegram*, Broun's home newspaper, he declared—in sharp contrast to his stand many years earlier—that "contract or no contract I would go out on strike with the guild if it ever came to that. I know of no higher loyalty."[4]

The other ANG leaders may have wished to prevent Broun from suffering the public embarrassment that would result from a strike at any Scripps-Howard newspaper, but much more compelling reasons caused the avoidance of open conflict with the chain at this time. Its generally liberal pro-labor editorial stance made it doubtful that a guild conducting a strike against a Scripps-Howard daily would receive much assistance from the community elements that had supported past ANG action. Furthermore, it still seemed possible that some guild might succeed in obtaining a contract from one of the chain's dailies. Unlike the vast majority of the American press, these dailies had negotiated with guild representatives. Even though the chain's executives did not like the idea of their editorial workers organizing (Howard later described the ANG as "a pistol against [the] belly") in a number of instances talks had led to Scripps-Howard dailies instituting improvements in working conditions. The announcements of these improvements had ignored the very existence of the guildsmen and at best had granted only a portion of their demands, but the newspapers never completely shut out the possibility of a contract. Indeed, at the beginning of January, 1936, the Washington Guild and the chain's capital outlet, the *Daily News*, concluded a verbal agreement which guaranteed that the guild could act as bargaining agent for the *News* and negotiate on its behalf for a signed agreement. The *News*, till then the only one of Washington's five dailies which had bargained collectively with its editorial workers, also agreed to certain changes in working conditions, including the institution of a minimum wage scale and graduated dismissal notice or severance pay.[5]

On February 24, 1936, the chain's prestigious Cleveland daily, the *Press* (known as "the mother paper of the Scripps-Howard organization") announced that it had signed a contract with the guild there. After nearly 16 months of intermittent negotiations, the *Press* and the Cleveland Guild had worked out an agreement by January, 1936, but the final decision on the publisher side rested with the chain's top executives. And they did not decide that the *Press* should sign until after holding a series of special conferences among themselves which resulted in some modifications and additions in the proposed agreement. The guildsmen accepted these. Bruce Catton, then president of the Cleveland Guild and one of the negotiators, believes that the Scripps-Howard management gave in because it took at face value the guild's bluff that the *Press* editorial staff would strike if the chain refused to sign, and it did not wish to tarnish its liberal pro-labor image.[6]

Made retroactive to February 10 and scheduled to last for one year (with automatic renewals unless either party gave 90-day notice in writing), the contract included provisions for overtime compensation either by equal time off or payment at regular rates, institution of a minimum wage schedule for editorial workers which resulted in immediate pay hikes for about 20 percent of the staff, and establishment of a liberal system of dismissal pay ranging up to 20 weeks' salary after 15 years' service (the *Press* agreed separately to take into account time worked on other Scripps-Howard newspapers in determining dismissal pay). The contract also maintained the forty-hour work week, but continuance of the five-day week was relegated to a supplementary written agreement. Scripps-Howard officials—recognizing that the contract would serve as a pattern in guildsmen's negotiations with other of the chain's newspapers and anxious to avoid setting a precedent on the length of the work week—had insisted that because local managements determined the number of working days, this important issue would have to be dealt with separately. A ten-point preamble dealing with publisher-editorial worker relationships made up more than half the contract, and Scripps-Howard utilized this preamble to further hedge its acceptance: for instance, item 4 stated that "both parties recognize that the Guild occupies a position unique in American industry because editorial work is individualistic and creative and thus . . . probably different from that performed by other types of organized crafts . . . ," and item 5 said that "this accord is not in fact a so-called 'trades union contract' but a friendly reciprocal agreement. . . ."[7]

Fifteen days later, in mid-March, the NEB warmly congratulated "our Cleveland brothers . . . [on their] splendid achievements" but warned other guilds against signing similar contracts. Besides suggesting the "need for a most careful inspection of the supplementary work agreement," the NEB took strong exception to the preamble, which it characterized as "a superfluity, dangerous . . . , and in part stating palpable untruths." These comments (a product of collaboration by Ashcraft, Eddy, and Stevens and approved by almost all the NEB) had some validity but betrayed shortsightedness. Whatever the *Press* contract's drawbacks, the immediate advantages outweighed them. Besides establishing more satisfactory working conditions for *Press* editorial workers, the contract gave the floundering guild movement a tremendous boost by demonstrating the willingness of one of the country's largest newspaper organizations to negotiate a written agreement with the ANG. Moreover, as a newspaper industry history points out, the contract "set up precedents and machinery useful in future negotiations and making collective bargaining part of the editorial workers' economic mores."[8]

Fortunately for the ANG, already plagued by strained relationships, the NEB statement received scant attention. Bruce Catton recalls that it had little impact on the Cleveland guildsmen, who were still jubilant about obtaining the contract; and it seems to have made an equally weak impression on guildsmen elsewhere, probably because their attention had turned to the strike the Milwaukee Guild had called against Hearst's *Wisconsin News*. The ANG leaders also might have avoided or at least deferred the Wisconsin confrontation, but they believed it the showdown they had been looking for and they accepted battle with Hearst, then America's largest and most unpopular newspaper magnate.[9]

By 1936 Hearst's once-vigorous publishing empire had fallen on hard times, in large part because of his extravagance and mismanagement; within months it would face complete collapse. But at the beginning of 1936 to most observers Hearst still seemed the press lord of the United States. The largest single employer of editorial workers, the Hearst press, once noted for its relative generosity toward them, had become known for shabby treatment of its news staffs. The Hearst newspapers in the mid-1930s commanded approximately 13 percent of the total daily circulation in this country and about 24 percent of the Sunday circulation. Although read by many, they came under sharp attack because of their aggressive patriotism, rabid anti-Communism, demagogic attacks on the New Deal, indiscriminate use of the word "un-American," and outspoken admiration for the various brands of European fascism. Indeed, the publisher became so unpopular at one point that in some areas the Hearst-Metrotone newsreel found it expedient to remove his name.[10]

Hearst never had masked his hostility to the guild movement. By the end of 1935, however, his executives moved more circumspectly against the guilds than they had when dealing with newsmen like Burgess. Attempts by guildsmen during the latter part of 1935 to open talks on improving working conditions, restoring pay cuts, or forestalling the reinstatement of the six-day week invariably led nowhere. Individual guilds found it impossible to discover what Hearst executives had the authority to negotiate and make a firm commitment. All efforts at this time to contact Hearst personally failed. He ignored letters, telegrams, and telephone calls. In addition, the chain did more than just avoid negotiations. Even though the chain's executives now did so more gingerly, they continued their efforts to stop the organization of Hearst editorial staffs and used tactics ranging from cajolery to intimidation. On many Hearst newspapers, after years when usually the only salary revision had been downwards, individuals suddenly received raises, but this select few rarely included active guildsmen. "At every Hearst office I know anything about," said Eddy, "the rumor mill is turning out whizbangs by the . . . bushel . . . most calculated to scare members."[11]

The chain's tactics agitated Hearst-employed guildsmen everywhere, but because of a combination of circumstances a strike first resulted in Milwaukee, which did not have a particularly strong guild. The Milwaukee Guild had not been established formally until the spring of 1935, and by the end of that year it had a membership which hovered at around 100. The unit at the *Wisconsin News*, the Hearst daily there, numbered 35 and ranked as the most thoroughly organized, for it included about 90 percent of those eligible for membership. The other units lagged far behind; on the *Sentinel* (another Hearst newspaper, produced in the same building as the *News*, but operated under a lease arrangement by Paul Block) the guild had enrolled only about half of those eligible, and on the *Journal* not even that many. The editorial employees on Milwaukee's other daily, the Socialist *Leader,* comprised one of the few remaining locals of the ITU Newswriters Union.[12]

The train of events that culminated in the strike against the *News* began on October 31, 1935, when John H. Black, Hearst's resident publisher, announced in a city room bulletin-board statement that as of November 4 the newspaper's editorial employees would return to a six-day work week without any salary increase. Gunnar Mickelsen, a *Journal* newsman and the spark-plug of the Milwaukee Guild, urged the *News* unit to strike and queried ANG headquarters about the possibilities of support. When Carl Johnson (NEB member for the region which included the Milwaukee Guild) learned about Mickelsen's actions, he urged "extreme caution" in selecting the *News* as "the place for a test fight." Johnson warned that the *News* staff lacked militancy and that the Milwaukee Guild as a whole did not have "the local unity which would get behind such a fight." This assessment quickly proved correct. The *News* guildsmen, although bitter about their low wages (a few earned less than $20.00 a week after long service) and quite vociferous about the reinstitution of the six-day week, recoiled from Mickelsen's plea for drastic action. They did so, he thought, in good part because they received no firm assurances of help from the *Sentinel* or *Journal* units. But apparently most of the *News* workers could not even conceive of striking. Mary Van Vuren— then, like Mickelsen, a member of the Milwaukee Guild's executive board and a strong supporter of militant action—believes that to many of the *News* unit "a strike was like the coming of an explosive millennium."[13]

After much discussion among themselves the Milwaukee guildsmen finally resolved to meet the situation by including a demand for a five-day week in the contract being drawn up for presentation to the publishers of the *Journal, News,* and *Sentinel.* Formulated in November-December with the assistance of friendly attorneys and union officials, the final draft of this contract—to which each unit added minor particulars dealing with specific conditions at its newspaper—also included provisions for a closed shop, time-and-a-half for overtime, dismissal bonuses based on length of service, a vacation schedule, a

grievance committee, and a weekly minimum wage scale ranging a contract with its editorial workers would be "unwise."
years' experience.[14]

During January, 1936, the guild presented its demands to all
three dailies. The *Journal* and the *Sentinel* managed to put off
the negotiating committee, but at the *News* a series of conferences ensued. Black, whom even the more militant among the
guildsmen characterized as a "decent trustworthy guy" and a
"fine man," at the first conferences in mid-January indicated
that he would negotiate toward a signed agreement despite his
objections to many of the contract demands. However, apparently as a result of orders received from Hearst higherups, he
then retreated from this position. At the third conference in late
January Black announced that the *News* had decided that signing a contract with its editorial workers would be "unwise."
Black said he did not understand why the guildsmen believed
a contract was necessary. If when they came to him with worthwhile suggestions he adopted them as "the policy of the company," would not that constitute sufficient agreement? The
guild representatives said no, and in explaining why they spoke
not just for the Milwaukee Guild in 1936 but for all guildsmen
then and now: the guild representatives said they wanted not
only improved working conditions but also the surety that the
company could not change them at will.[15]

A fourth conference took place at the beginning of February,
and again the guild failed to make any headway. Just a few
hours before this conference, the *News* had announced raises
of from $1.65 to $10.00 a week for much of its editorial staff.
When queried about the timing of this action, *News* executives
said that it was "purely a coincidence." Mickelsen called that
explanation "hogwash" and correctly interpreted the raises as
a "sellout bid." A fifth meeting on Monday, February 10, proved
equally futile and ended after a few minutes when Black flatly
refused to do more than listen to suggestions and promise "to
try to do everything I can for the staff." The guild committee—
some of whose members had anticipated a more ameliorative
position on management's part because of the raises—accused
him of failing to bargain in good faith and stalked out. The *News*

unit then empowered the guild's executive board to call a strike at its discretion. The board decided to wait and see what would happen before informing Black about this strike vote. During the next few days Black called *News* guildsmen into his office individually and in small groups to discuss the situation and pledged "to fight with New York to get what I can for you."[16]

On Thursday the board, through a committee of two, told Black about the strike vote. He agreed with them that the situation had taken a serious turn but said that the guild would never gain recognition in Milwaukee without a fight. He indicated that he would expect a strike the next day, for "then you would at least have a week's pay in your pocket." That night the board did decide to call a strike on Friday, but the following morning it had to reverse itself when it became clear that a sizable minority of *News* guildsmen opposed the idea of striking. The raises as well as Black's talks had had a telling effect on these workers, an effect heightened by an eloquent hour-long appeal that Black delivered to much of the staff that morning. On Friday night the *News* unit failed by three votes to reaffirm the previous strike motion, and it instructed the executive board to continue negotiations. On Sunday morning the guild held its annual meeting, elected a new president (illness had sent the old one to the Mayo Clinic), and reshuffled the executive board. About noon the board met and decided that the guild must act against the *News* or else face destruction, an opinion shared by Bill Davy, who had arrived in Milwaukee on Friday to offer what assistance he could.[17]

During Sunday afternoon and evening, board members telephoned *News* guildsmen, sounded them out, and invited those who indicated interest in a strike to a meeting that evening at Mary Van Vuren's apartment. The board did not call those it considered informers for Black; it could not reach some members of the unit; and a number of *News* guildsmen expressed opposition to a walkout, but 22 of the *News* staff came. They all accepted the need for an immediate strike to force recognition of the guild and consideration of its demands, and agreed to participate. Ostensibly because the meeting ended at a very late hour but actually in order to catch the publisher unaware as well as to prevent a repetition of Friday's fiasco, all 22 spent the rest of the night at the Van Vuren apartment. Early in the morning of February 17 they took taxis to the *News* offices, where at seven a.m. in below-zero weather they established a picket line and announced their strike.[18]

The more militant Milwaukee guildsmen, in anticipation of a strike, had begun in January to solicit support from organized labor. The executive board of the Federated Trades Council of Milwaukee (the city's central AFL body) voted to give "full moral support" to the guildsmen's "endeavors to have contracts signed with the newspapers in this city." Henry Ohl, Jr., president of the Wisconsin Federation of Labor (the state AFL body) several times declared the state labor movement's "sympathy with the guild cause." And other prominent Milwaukee and state union officials said that in a fight with a Hearst newspaper the guildsmen would most certainly get "tremendous popular support."[19]

Given these rather lame assurances and the lukewarm stance of a sizable portion of the Milwaukee Guild (at one point even the unflagging Mickelsen burst out "Christ, if we could only inject a nickel's worth of class consciousness into a half-dozen of these guys, we'd have less trouble"), what determined the ANG leaders' decision to accept Milwaukee as the strategic spot for their planned showdown? Certainly, thanks to Carl Johnson's comments as well as the later reports of others, the ANG leaders in New York must have known of Mickelsen's zealous over-optimism (as late as February 8 he wrote Eddy that the *News* would give in "short of a strike"). Nonetheless, the ANG leadership accepted the challenge in Milwaukee. Over four months before the strike Don Stevens summed up the major reasons why: "we . . . rather jumped at the Milwaukee idea because of the local political complexion there, the organized labor strength, and ordinance on picketing, and the support that could be got nationally for a fight on Hearst. . . ."[20]

Guild leaders banked on the benevolent neutrality if not the support of the Milwaukee city government, headed by the labor-minded Socialist mayor, Dan Hoan. During most of his 24-year tenure, which began in 1916, Hoan, who gained an excellent reputation for municipal administration, dealt with a Common Council controlled by non-Socialists. But in 1932 under the impact of the Depression the Socialists made great gains in the municipal elections, and with the aid of some independents Hoan's forces obtained a majority on the Council. In September, 1935, they pushed through an ordinance to deal with the increasing labor unrest faced by the city. Many guildsmen, in Milwaukee and elsewhere, believed that this ordinance, although it never had been applied, would help the *News* unit. The Boncel Ordinance—named after its sponsor, the Socialist alderman Frank Boncel—provided that if an employer refused to bargain collectively and if this refusal resulted in a crowd of more than 200 outside the struck premises on two successive days, the mayor or chief of police upon the recommendation of a committee of employers, labor officials, and clergy could order the closing of the business involved within 24 hours. Guild officers in Milwaukee and at New York headquarters recognized that the failure of affiliation limited the help the *News* unit could get from the AFL, but they believed that because of Hearst's unpopularity and the large percentage of organization among the Milwaukee labor force, a strike by editorial employees would get a friendly reception, and the city's workers would rally to the guild as a fellow union on the picket line. Moreover, some of the ANG's leaders who had an inkling of Hearst's financial difficulties believed that a nationwide "hate Hearst" campaign in support of the *News* workers might squeeze the publisher economically and force him to deal with the ANG in Milwaukee and elsewhere.[21]

Unfortunately for the *News* strikers, events did not follow the charted course. Eddy, who arrived in Milwaukee on February 19 and who spent days at a time there during the next months overseeing strike operations, met with Hoan on February 20 and exchanged pleasantries. Eddy quickly realized, however, that the mayor, fighting hard to avoid defeat in the April municipal elections, could offer the strikers nothing concrete. Certainly he could not invoke the Boncel Ordinance, for to do so would lead to cries of suppression of the press and play right into the hands of his opponents. Nor could Hoan do much after the election; he won, but almost all his supporters lost. On February 24 William Green wired the guildsmen that the AFL "is deeply interested in the strike" and informed them that he had called upon members of the AFL bodies in Milwaukee and Wisconsin "to accord all support and sustenance possible." Green's appeal, however, had only a limited response. The five printing trades unions offered the guild their "moral support," $210 in contributions during the course of the long strike, and not much else. Indeed, in July, with the strike nowhere near settlement, the printing trades union took advertisements in the "Centennial Edition" of the *News*. The Federated Trades Council did appoint a three-man committee—J. F. Frederick, its organizer; Herman Seide, its executive secretary; Otto Jirikowic, the business agent of the machinists union—to see what it could do about bringing the *News* and the strikers together. After a meeting with Black on February 21 proved completely fruitless, the committee lapsed into quiescence. Davy later complained that union leader after union leader "promised to do this and that and almost every damned one of them pizz [sic] out." And in general most of the more than 60,000 union members in Milwaukee proved as reluctant as their leaders to assist the guild. Its so-called mass demonstrations against the *News*, few of which drew 1,000 or more and many of which had less than 250 participants, received much of their support from such non-AFL groups as the Workers Alliance (an organization of unemployed, relief clients, and WPA workers). Moreover, Hearst, despite his increasing financial problems, proved ready to spend whatever sums seemed necessary to defeat the guildsmen in Milwaukee.[22]

"The Hearst management will not enter into any agreement written or verbal that recognizes the guild," H. L. Bitner, general manager of the chain's newspapers, told the Milwaukee Guild executive board on March 8. A few days earlier he had vetoed over the telephone a tentative arrangement between Black and the guild which, in return for recognition of it as bargaining agent for the *News* editorial workers, would have ended the strike. At the meeting on March 8 Bitner merely stated that the *News* would stipulate what it would do for its editorial employees. When the guildsmen asked what recourse they would have if management went back on its word, Black said such an act would subject the *News* to unfavorable public opinion and "preclude the newspaper from going into court with clean hands." Given the general press blackout that took place whenever a newspaper had labor troubles, the guildsmen rejected Bitner's offer, deciding that the public never would get a chance to form an opinion.

On March 12 the Allied Printing Trades Council decided to see what it could do. Shortly thereafter a committee composed of the council's head as well as Ohl and Seide (representing the state and local AFL bodies) brought the guildsmen and the *News* together. Beginning March 27 in nearly three days of continuous meetings, the two sides (with Black and Harvey Kelly, now general counsel on labor for the Hearst chain, acting for the *News*) hammered out a settlement. The guild and the newspaper would exchange letters, one of which would state that as a result of negotiations between the *News* and the guild a statement of policy had been achieved. This statement, which the committee of three union men would witness, called for a five-day, forty-hour week, with a $45 minimum for employees with three years' experience and $25 for beginners; sick pay for a limited period; and up to three months' severance pay. One of the guild negotiators informed Eddy that "there is an even chance that Bitner will reject the letter idea," and he did. The talks had ended about 1:30 a.m. on March 30. Less than 48 hours later, on April 1, with the guildsmen waiting to receive word of final details, the *News* posted an "employment policy." Announced as "not a contract but a policy which will be in effect for at least a year and as long thereafter as economic conditions warrant," it called for a five-day week with beginners to get $25 and veterans of three years to get $40 minimum, sick pay (duration at the discretion of management), overtime in pay or compensatory time off, vacations, and up to five weeks' severance pay. The *News* declared the strike over, informed all strikers of this policy by registered mail, and gave them a week to return to work. Some accepted the offer, and Black then announced that the *News* would fill staff vacancies since those out had been given an opportunity to return. *The Guild Re-porter* called the time limit for returning to work "a lockout." For the next months all attempts by guildsmen to open talks with the *News* failed. Hearst refused to see Broun, and when guild representatives approached Black that summer he told them the Hearst management considered the strike "a closed incident."[23]

Neither the *News* workers who walked out nor most other Milwaukee guildsmen had anticipated a long strike. Their initial optimism seemed vindicated when on the morning of February 17 three more *News* editorial workers joined the strike. But within a week defections reduced the strikers' ranks once more to 22, and as the fight wore on others dropped by the wayside. At the beginning of April there were only 16 active strikers—"a pretty small number," as one of them, Herbert Langendorff, told the delegates at the ANG's annual convention. Only 14 held out until September 1, when the strike ended. Not all the dropouts returned to the *News*: some took non-newspaper jobs in Mil-waukee, and others left the city.

At the start of the strike a serious problem was the blustery winter weather. The first week the temperature rarely rose above 0° F, and the pickets could only walk 15 or 20 minutes before requiring replacements. This necessity to have at least two sets of pickets stretched the guild's already thin forces. Despite the cold, the guild, under the direction of Davy and then, after he took ill, of Eddy, quickly had established opera-tions against the *News*. A strike committee which included *Journal* and *Sentinel* unit members was set up with J. Nash McCrea, a 16-year *News* veteran, as chairman. Because the *Leader* thoroughly covered the guild's activities, it was decided to save money and to defer publication of a strike paper, but otherwise the tactics employed by the committee generally followed those utilized by other guilds in their strikes. A cam-paign to cut *News* circulation and advertising started almost immediately.[24] Even on the first day a borrowed sound truck was cruising the streets telling the guild side of the story and asking the public not to buy the *News*. Soon thereafter the strikers and their supporters began distributing leaflets all over the city. Then, in March, they started to call their way through the Milwaukee phone book. With these methods the strike committee claimed to be making large dents in the *News*'s circulation (20 percent the first month), but the guildsmen really did not know. Milton Kaufman, the New York Guild's executive secretary, who was sent to Milwaukee for a time by ANG headquarters to advise the strikers, reported to the NEB that "we have no friends in the plant to give us an idea of the press run." In May the strikers embarked on a house-to-house canvass to obtain cancellations of *News* subscriptions. The drive continued to the end of the strike and made splendid headway. At the end of June the *News* found it necessary to agree to compensate the carriers for lost customers on some home delivery routes because so many subscribers had cancelled that some newsboys found themselves working for almost nothing and threatened to strike. The guildsmen only obtained a real idea of how much damage they had done altogether to the newspaper's circulation when after the end of the strike the returning strikers tried to help regain lost readers.[25]

Guildsmen wrote to and visited *News* advertisers, asking them to stop, or at least cut down, their use of the newspaper. To reinforce these requests pickets appeared at the end of February in front of the premises of several of the more important *News* advertisers such as department stores. On March 7 the *News* obtained an injunction restraining the pickets from carrying signs directed specifically against its advertisers, but the judge ruled that the strikers could picket anywhere they wanted provided the signs referred only to "the facts of the strike." At the end of March, strikers survived an attempt by the *News* to have them found in contempt of the injunction. The strikers rightly considered the outcome of these court battles "a practical victory," but they proved unable to make use of it, for as the strike wore on and enthusiasm for it waned, they lacked the volunteer manpower to maintain the picketing except on a scattered basis. Nonetheless, they continued their efforts to cut down the *News*'s advertising. *The Guild Striker*—launched in mid-March after the guildsmen decided that the *Leader* alone did not affect the press blackout on their activities that seemed broken only by prejudicial coverage—attacked those businesses which continued to buy space in the *News* (e.g., "Rat Peril at Gimbels") and ran an "unfair list," asking the public to remember that these businesses hampered the guildsmen "fighting Hearst for the right to bargain collectively." Only the *News* management knew exactly how much linage the newspaper lost, but in its contempt action it claimed that five weeks of guild activity had cost it $8,000 in advertising (which, as McCrea boasted: "to a paper that isn't the big paper of the city . . . is some loss"). And at the end of June guildsmen announced that so many local businesses had dropped away that national advertising now constituted more than 50 percent of the *News's* advertising linage.[26]

To herald its cause the guild in the first months of the strike held weekly "mass demonstrations," the largest being the second, on February 29. Broun, during one of his brief jaunts to Milwaukee, led a group estimated at over 1,500 around the *News* offices and through the city's downtown shopping area. Accompanied by a brass band, the crowd marched to the Milwaukee Auditorium, outside of which Broun and others addressed the marchers for over an hour. Some later demonstrations proved less peaceful. On March 14 considerable jostling took place between pickets and police as the demonstrators vented their verbal ire on scabs and others who passed their lines; a police captain had the buttons ripped from his uniform. A week later, on the 21st, pushing and shoving between police and demonstrators resulted in three arrests. Broun, in Milwaukee for this demonstration, protested, saying: "if you're going to arrest these men for what they did you'll have to arrest me too." The police, who had a reputation as one of the finest law enforcement bodies in America, obliged him. After being released on bail, he returned to Milwaukee in mid-April, stood trial, was found guilty, and paid a small fine.[27] Broun's instinctive action in joining the arrested men once again demonstrated his worth to the ANG. His marching buoyed the strikers and his presence made their cause newsworthy. When, in Broun's absence, some 100 plainclothesmen on the evening of April 17 charged the demonstrators, forcibly dispersed them, and injured a number in the process, few newspapers picked up the story. This melee cost Mickelsen, one of the five arrested that night, his job. Upon learning of the "inciting to riot" charge placed against him, the *Journal* suspended Mickelsen. After he pleaded guilty to "failure to obey the lawful order of a traffic officer," the newspaper discharged him. This April 17 fracas marked the culmination of the rough encounters between the guild and the police, who for some time also had irritated the strikers by their reluctance to deal with those who tried to provoke the pickets. Through the intervention of Mayor Hoan, a guild delegation managed to see the chief of police. According to McCrea, after presenting all its other arguments, the delegation suggested that the power of the press had built up the department's reputation and could also do the reverse. Whatever was said, no more clashes occurred; and as the next demonstrations failed to attract crowds the guild in mid-May decided to call them off, and they did not resume until August.[28]

The day the strike started Eddy, acting for the NEB (which later by telegraphic ballot confirmed his actions), advanced the Milwaukee Guild $600 from the ANG's limited cash reserves. He also established a strike fund and set up a committee composed of Ashcraft, Beals (chairman), Broun, Watson, and himself to handle it. The committee immediately appealed by telegram to all guilds to make weekly contributions to the fund for the duration of the strike of $1.00 per member or as near that as possible. More than just a recognition of the futility of assessments governed the decision to rely upon voluntary contributions to finance the strike; those responsible for this decision apparently hoped to avoid the wrangling which had accompanied the levying of assessments in the past and thus to forestall any embarrassing questions that guilds might raise about the whys and wherefores of this strike. But the leadership's action failed to salve the initial unease felt by members of a number of guilds. At first some of these guildsmen even considered deferring their group's support for the strike pending an investigation of the situation in Milwaukee. This attitude reflected not only the divisions within the ANG but also a feeling that "the New York crowd" might have provoked the

News strike to serve its own purposes. The Twin Cities Guild, which knew of Johnson's reservations, wired several people in Milwaukee for information, and the St. Louis Guild sent a representative there for the same reason. The members of the Lansing Guild went so far as to characterize the strike as "ill advised" and resolved that "any donations . . . to the strike fund be made by individuals and not by the [Lansing] guild." The ANG leadership considered the situation serious enough to allow it to become public so that *The Guild Reporter* might refute what it called "scab rumors." Meanwhile, statements by Broun as well as Eddy and others in Milwaukee had laid to rest many of the doubts raised, and most guilds responded magnificently. Between February 17 and September 1 they gave more than 90 percent of the nearly $26,000 spent to maintain the strike, although contributions lagged as it dragged on. Despite the generosity of guilds like that in Detroit, which donated half its treasury, the strike committee by the summer was encountering serious financial problems. The ANG managed to continue providing the strikers with enough cash to carry on, but they had to trim and then trim again their budget and curtail their activities.[29]

The ANG did more than just collect money for the strikers and send Broun, Eddy, and others to Milwaukee. It also attempted to bring national pressure to bear against Hearst. At the end of April it arranged for the formation of a two-part citizens committee (a general committee and a writers committee) with each division made up of such prominent individuals such as John Dewey and Dorothy Thompson. Committee members appealed for funds (some donated money as well) and other aid for the strikers. Attempting to make use of Hearst's unpopularity, the committee worked to organize a national boycott of all Hearst publications. *The Guild Reporter* for a while published an "unfair list" of national advertisers who continued to buy space in the *News*. Eddy and other ANG officials solicited support from labor leaders on every level and tried to get the heads of the printing trades unions to intercede in Milwaukee. None of the actions promoted by the ANG had any real effect on the *News*, but they did help to sustain the strikers, who became increasingly hungry for affirmation of any kind as the strike wore on.[30]

The spirit as well as the interest of other Milwaukee guildsmen had dulled as an apparently endless fight continued. The *News* seemed able to block all the guild's maneuvers. In mid-April Kaufman reported to Eddy that he felt a sense of desperation growing among the strikers. Some of them suggested hiring thugs experienced in industrial warfare "to set the town on its ear," but the strike committee voted down this suggestion. Other plans caused increased wrangling among its members, especially between McCrea and Mickelsen, whose personal antipathy reinforced deep divisions over how to proceed. In June, partly because of this dissension, Davy became chairman of a restructured committee which included Mickelsen as well as McCrea, who now became treasurer. Davy found it increasingly difficult to persuade strikers to picket or take part in the circulation cutting campaign. He had to hire help, an expense the strike's sagging finances could ill afford. Richard Bellamy, then a young newsman on the *Journal*, recalls that by the summer many Milwaukee newspapermen, even those sympathetic to the strike, had begun to question the value of continuing it; there no longer seemed anything special about it. This attitude obviously hurt the strikers, and their morale must have declined even further in mid-July when they managed to avoid a deficit at a fund-raising picnic only because the winner of the grand prize (a new car) generously agreed to donate it to the guild. Despite all the obstacles, the fight went on, even though to many of the strikers it seemed to have evolved into an endurance contest, with all the advantages held by one side.[31]

Two events which intrinsically had nothing to do with the *News* strike ultimately resulted in its termination. At the beginning of June the ANG convention voted for affiliation with the AFL, an action formally consummated the next month. In mid-August the Seattle Guild struck Hearst's daily there and immediately forced the newspaper's suspension by obtaining so much support that the mechanical workers had to respect the picket lines. The *News* strikers took heart from the guild success in Seattle and their attempt to emulate it gave new life to the

258 a union of individuals

strike in Milwaukee. On August 19, with the help of about 50 sympathizers, the guildsmen picketed every entrance of the building where the *News* was published, including a back door left unattended in the past so that the members of the printing trades unions could go to work without crossing a picket line. The mechanical workers hesitated for about 90 minutes but finally went into the plant through the coffee shop. To the consternation of the pickets, whose numbers had increased to about 100 by the 22nd, the mechanical workers followed the police through the lines established by the guildsmen for the next three days. The Milwaukee strikers, unlike those in Seattle, could not muster sufficient numbers to block entry or even to make access difficult. The members of the printing trades unions, whatever their feelings about the strike, really had no alternative; if they stayed away from their jobs without sufficient cause, they would have trouble with their international officers, who considered it necessary to fulfill contractual obligations. Meanwhile, on August 12, the Federated Trades Council, having received formal notification of the AFL's acceptance of the ANG, had decided to seat guild delegates. These, a week later, asked the council to place the *News* on its "we do not patronize" list. Earlier, the council, citing the guild's lack of AFL ties, had refused a similar request. Affiliation made denial more difficult. The council, apparently anxious to avoid serious involvement in the *News* strike, appointed a committee (Ohl, Seide, Frederick, and Benjamin Dolnick—an ILGWU organizer) to see Hearst officials, which it did on August 24. Faced with another financial drain in Seattle as well as renewed agitation in Milwaukee, the chain proposed an end to the *News* strike: the newspaper would reinstate six of the strikers on the basis of its April 1 employment policy. The guildsmen rejected this offer, insisting that at a minimum the *News* must take back all the remaining strikers. Further conferences took place between the *News* and the labor committee, and finally, on September 1, they worked out a settlement acceptable to the strike committee. Guild leaders in Milwaukee and elsewhere later said they believed that the Seattle strike influenced the chain to settle in Milwaukee. And despite the chain's denials, the Seattle strike probably did that, but it also resulted in the Milwaukee guildsmen toning down their demands, for the ANG just did not have the wherewithal to battle Hearst for any length of time in two cities at once.[32]

According to *The Guild Reporter*, Hearst cabled from Germany his personal acceptance of the Milwaukee settlement. Scheduled to run for a year, it generally followed the lines of the employment policy announced by the *News* in April. The *News* did agree, however, that for editorial employees with three or more years' experience the work week would consist of "five days of eight hours each" and that the labor committee could witness and sign the statement of company policy (also signed by Black) which embodied these terms. The committee, on behalf of the strikers, also made a verbal agreement with Black that the *News* would not discriminate in any way against the returning employees and that the time spent out on strike would not count as a lapse of service in figuring continuous years of employment for benefits such as vacations. The strikers in turn (through the committee) said that they would assist the *News* in regaining lost circulation and advertising. The 14 remaining strikers returned to work in a body at 9 a.m. on September 2. Black greeted them in a warm, friendly manner. One immediately retired to become a housewife, having returned only to demonstrate her loyalty to the guild. The other 13 encountered almost no trouble. The *News* discharged a number of staff it had taken on during the strike. Black, in order to create amity among his newly reunited staff, slightly raised the pay of those who had not profited directly from the settlement. Five weeks after he returned to work, McCrea reported to Eddy that "everything's going to turn out O.K."[33]

Both sides claimed victory. Black, who said the *News* had made no concessions, indicated his certainty that the council had intervened only because it wanted to save the AFL's newest affiliate from certain defeat. Bitner denied that the guildsmen had won anything: "the *Wisconsin News* has accorded no recognition—made no settlement . . ."; the guildsmen "simply called off the strike," and those who returned to the *News* did so "purely as individuals . . . under standard practices . . . an-

nounced and put in force . . . about six months ago." George
Mann, the Milwaukee Guild's president, declared that the strikers had won "what newspapermen have demanded ever since
they banded together—recognition of the right to bargain collectively," and that the guildsmen had returned to work under
conditions "considered highly acceptable." The Guild Reporter
spoke of "significant gains." Broun described the settlement as
"a compromise with a considerable tinge of victory." Certainly
neither side could claim a clear-cut success. The Milwaukee
Guild had called the strike in order to obtain recognition as
bargaining agent for the News editorial workers; it failed to
achieve this (and the unit split because of the walkout) but the
newspaper's publisher did jointly sign with a committee representing the guildsmen a statement embodying the terms of settlement. The employment policy announced April 1 by the News
did not satisfy the strikers, but its provisions represented an
improvement on the working conditions they had walked out
on; in the end the newspaper even agreed to some modifications
of this policy. In addition, the general adherence of the Journal
and the Sentinel to the News's April 1 employment policy meant
that the strike also benefited those dailies' editorial employees
whose working conditions were not up to the standards set
forth in the policy. Time summed up the immediate results of
the strike when it said that although the guild "had scored no
knockout in Milwaukee, it certainly had won a victory of a sort
on points." In a larger sense, however, those in the ANG who
had wanted a showdown to demonstrate the organization's
viability had won the real victory. Despite the partial blurring
of the Milwaukee outcome by the Seattle situation, the fight
against the News demonstrated that the guild movement could
hold its own, even against a Hearst; the chain tried but could
not break the strike. Even if the general public did not understand this, many newspaper workers did. Moreover, the response of the membership to the crusade against Hearst helped
to heal much of the dissension which had wracked the guild
movement in the months after the 1935 convention as well as
to consolidate the position of the ANG leadership in New York.
Except for some initial hesitancy, the membership across the

country had rallied in support of the Milwaukee strikers and for some time thereafter it more readily than ever before accepted the decisions made by the leadership—not only in regard to the strike but also in other ANG matters. In fine, the strike against the *Wisconsin News* probably did more to strengthen the ANG at a time when it badly needed strengthening than any other action of importance it had thus far undertaken.[34]

Certainly the idea of advancing the guild movement through district organization had failed. The 1935 convention had voted that guilds should league into districts and should set up a district council to govern joint activities wherever geography or community of interest indicated that guildsmen should function together. Eddy—who had championed the district idea and who had believed it would bring about greater unity within the guild movement and speed up ANG expansion—recognized immediately that "the most troublesome problem will undoubtedly be in connection with financing . . .," and so it turned out. The hesitancy of most guildsmen to pay more dues resulted in some areas never organizing district setups, and even where they were constituted, they generally remained paper organizations because they lacked funds. Only one bright spot sparkled in an otherwise bleak record: the joint financing during the spring of 1936 of Morgan Hull as West Coast organizer by the ANG and a number of guilds (the ANG and the Northern California Newspaper Guild each put up $25 weekly; several smaller guilds contributed what they could when they could).[35]

The Guild Reporter termed the joint financing, undertaken at Don Stevens' suggestion and scheduled to last for only two months (April-May), an "experimental arrangement." Hull, a hard worker even though a pedestrian newspaperman (he finished his journalistic career in the 1940s as a public relations man for the Communist party, which he had joined in 1934), quickly justified this experiment. Besides helping to organize the Seattle Guild, he did splendid missionary work for the guild movement among the editorial workers of the Pacific Northwest. In addition, he managed, without even having to call for a strike vote from the unit involved, to save the job of a militant Tacoma guildsman, Rex Kelley, whose guild activity had resulted in his discharge on May 2 from the *Times*, ostensibly for incompetence. Hull arrived in Tacoma a few days later, arranged for testimonials by public officials for the discharged newsman, whipped up support from local radicals and the city's labor unions, and by May 20 had achieved Kelley's reinstatement as well as the editor's agreement to recognize the guild as bargaining agent for the *Times*'s editorial workers if the organization could demonstrate that it represented a majority of them.[36] Hull had the good fortune to tackle a weak link in a weak chain, the Scripps League, which besides everything else did not wish then to hazard its pro-labor reputation, but he had made the most of his opportunities and at almost no cost had achieved a victory which at least temporarily enhanced the guild movement's reputation in the area.[37]

An equally bloodless victory had been achieved in the Philadelphia suburb of Ardmore at the end of February. Guildsmen forced the *Main Line Daily Times* to reinstate three of four members fired after a dispute with the publisher over irregular pay days. When Eddy learned of a possible strike there, he asked Homan to settle the dispute as gracefully as possible but to settle it, for nothing should distract from the nascent *Wisconsin News* campaign. The publisher of the financially weak *Times*, aware of the Philadelphia Guild's willingness to picket and believing that a strike would kill the newspaper, quickly came to terms, although the guildsmen won little but reinstatement.[38]

During the first five months of 1936 few guilds achieved more than had been accomplished in Tacoma and Ardmore. Outside of the agreements obtained from the Scripps-Howard newspapers in Washington and Cleveland, the only agreements of any kind that the guilds won were renewals of contracts with the *Cleveland News* and the *Philadelphia Record*. Negotiations with the *News* went on for so long (partly because of the publisher's illness and partly because of his hesitancy) that the old contract ran four months past its expiration date. Finally, in April, 1936, the guild and the *News* signed a new contract which, to the dissatisfaction of many *News* guildsmen, differed not a whit from the old one. The *Record* agreed to institute some small pay raises but otherwise made no changes. And in New York talks with Stern's newspaper there nearly broke off after his representatives made it clear that the *Post* would negotiate a minimum wage schedule only if the guild would waive all other requests (e.g., sick leave, extension of vacation) that in the editor's words would "place an impossible financial burden upon this newspaper."[39]

Most other guilds which attempted negotiations at this time failed even to get meaningful responses from publishers, although a few newspapers made some improvements in their editorial employees' working conditions. In New Jersey during the spring the *Hudson Dispatch* and the *Jersey Journal* restored pay cuts made three years earlier. The *St. Louis Post-Dispatch* deferred a request to institute a five-day, forty-hour week but acted on a variety of other complaints ranging from poor lighting in the city room to inequitable vacations. The *Brooklyn Eagle* agreed to maintain a five-day week. And in Minneapolis the management of the *Tribune* announced wage increases, the institution of sick pay, and the establishment of an eight-hour work day with cash compensation for overtime. If other guilds achieved such minor improvements, they remained unknown, for as a committee reported to the 1936 convention, the national organization had "no complete record of these matters."[40]

In an attempt to achieve some kind of uniformity in these matters, the previous convention had required the NEB to prepare a model contract. After long delay it finally had been drawn up by Victor Pasche, secretary treasurer of the Newark Guild, and A. J. Isserman in consultation with Eddy during the winter. The model contract's provisions included a broad-based definition of editorial workers (e.g., news department telephone operators), a work week of five eight-hour days, establishment of a grievance committee, graduated dismissal bonuses, paid vacations and sick leave, and the preferential shop (i.e., an employer could hire non-guildsmen provided they joined a guild within a limited time). Approved by the NEB at its spring meeting, March 6-7 in New York City, the model contract for some time served as the general basis for guildsmen's demands.[41]

Unlike the NEB's fall meeting, this one exuded harmony. The

resignation of Buck and the absence of Johnson (Eddy later acidly called him "our intellectual giant from Duluth") as well as the willingness of Ashcraft to subordinate his misgivings meant that the ANG's New York leaders generally had things their own way. Much of the meeting dealt with the *News* strike, but the board also handled other matters. Fearful that the sale (finally begun in late December) of the defense certificates might cut contributions for the strike, the NEB voted to remove the limitations on selling them outside the guilds and decided to stop their sale within the ANG except in cases where the membership already had made commitments in regard to the certificates. (Originally suggested as an alternative to raising dues, the certificates garnered the ANG less than $1,700, most of which came from guildsmen in the first months of 1936.) The board also agreed to set up five small annual cash awards for excellence in newspaper work in honor of D. A. de Souza, the Washington guildsman killed enroute to Newark with Christmas presents for the Newark strikers' families. The NEB further called upon all guilds to instruct their delegates to the 1936 convention on the issue of affiliation so as to "decide the question with a minimum of delay."[42]

Eddy reiterated this plea in his annual report, presented to the membership in the mid-May edition of *The Guild Reporter*. The report's other recommendations included proposals for an increase in ANG dues to $.75 a month, establishment of an "American Newspaper Guild Dismissal Bonus Rate," greater uniformity in guild "law" throughout the country, closer coordination between the ANG and local guilds in collective bargaining situations, and "some positive action looking to relief from attacks from within the ranks of labor when we are engaged in strikes." NEB members voted acceptance of all the report's 12 recommendations, although in a few instances by only the narrowest of margins. Johnson voiced the most disagreement, but Homan also had considerable reservations. For him, some of Eddy's proposals seemed too contentious even if correct; on the questions of guild "law" for instance, Homan could "see no point in making an issue over the charge that the national is striving to control every local." A separate report drafted by Don Stevens said in effect that the ANG could not maintain even its then hand-to-mouth existence unless the convention voted to raise dues. Although treasurer and in the past an active supporter of higher dues, Ashcraft—apparently still smarting over what he considered cavalier treatment by the New York Communists—refused to vote on the Stevens report; "we have tried by telephone, telegraph, and personal visits to straighten Ash out," said Eddy, but to no avail.[43]

Just prior to the convention, which met at the Hotel Astor in New York City May 29-June 2, the NEB held another meeting. By this time, board members knew that a majority of the delegates would come instructed by their guilds to vote for affiliation. In some guilds, as in Detroit, the executive committee had decided the issue; in others, as in Philadelphia, the membership had voted on the matter. In anticipation of affiliation, the NEB recommended that the convention extend the ANG's jurisdiction to those areas that other AFL unions embraced, such as Canada. At this meeting the NEB also adopted "subject to the delegates' wishes," the makeup of the convention committees as well as the order of business.[44]

More than 100 delegates and alternates registered at the convention. They represented 37 guilds; altogether the ANG now had more than 55, for even though some had collapsed, others had revived and nine new ones—Bridgeport, Champaign-Urbana, Chicago, Denver, Great Falls (Montana), Indianapolis, Knoxville, Santa Monica, and Seattle—had been chartered between January and June, 1936. This convention had its share of wrangling and intense debate, but nothing like what had taken place at Cleveland in 1935, despite the fact that once again tremendous activity took place behind the scenes. By contrast with the previous convention, the opponents of "the New York point of view" put up a very poor fight in 1936. They had tried, mostly by letter, to drum up some kind of unified front, but had failed. They lacked the discipline and know-how of "the New York crowd," and the New Yorkers maintained as firm a grip on this convention as on the NEB. Although Broun presided in his usual impartial fashion, he just about gave the show away when at one point in the debate over dues he said: "New York has—I mean the majority report has 15 minutes left." The opponents of "the New York crowd" bitterly recognized the hopelessness of their position; Buck, as he told the delegates, refused to debate in a convention "that has already made up its mind upon all points." On all roll-call votes but one, "the New York crowd" won by better than 3 to 1; on the exception it won by over 2 to 1.[45]

The sheer size of the New York delegation's vote partially accounted for these sweeping triumphs. The host guild had 18 votes, or nearly 20 percent of the total and more than three times that of any other guild—thanks to the constitution adopted in 1935, which besides giving each guild a vote, allocated additional ones for the first 50 members, the next 50, and thereafter for every 100 or fraction thereof. The New York Guild claimed nearly 1,100 members, a sizable portion of the guild movement whether one reckoned ANG membership as those enrolled on the books (more than 5,500 according to a press release issued at the convention) or as dependable dues payers (who, according to the treasurer's report to the delegates had increased since June, 1935, by some 700 to about 4,200). Nor, despite the fact that the New Yorkers ranked among the ANG's greatest debtors because of dues delinquencies, could anyone gainsay *Time*'s judgment that "New York was . . . the national tower . . . of financial strength." For four of the first five months of 1936, the New York Guild, in addition to its heavy Milwaukee strike contributions, remitted at least three times as much as any other guild to the national organization and for the whole period accounted for over 20 percent of the ANG's income. Therefore, even though some guildsmen privately expressed doubts about the New York Guild's membership figures, none publicly challenged its claims.[46]

More than just the mere numbers of the host guild helped "the New York crowd" achieve its overwhelming majorities. The convention reflected the changes that had taken place in the guildsmen's leadership on the local level. The "gentlemen of the press" idea had died, killed by the events of the preceding three years. By mid-1936 few guild leaders retained any illusions about the direction the ANG must take to obtain even its minimum goals. As usually happens in developing organizations, those guild leaders who advocated a militant ANG—one which would force the publishers to make concessions—took a more forward position than much of the membership. Of course, these leaders differed as to how to achieve what they envisaged, but the majority of those who came to the convention as delegates proved ready to vote not only for affiliation but also for those changes in the ANG which they believed would make it a stronger organization.

The Communists helped give this majority direction and in so doing played a most significant role in establishing the one-sidedness of the convention. The Communists, who operated as a disciplined organized fraction within the caucus that endeavored to put across "the New York point of view," had much greater influence than numbers. Although only a small minority of "the New York crowd," party members in effect had captured it, and they now had a great deal to say about its actions. Ever since the ANG began, the Communists had worked hard to ensure at least its survival, if not success, albeit along a course consistent with the current party line. Earl Browder, then chief Communist spokesman in the United States, recalls that he had urged party members to throw their full energies into support of the guilds. The party members ("busy little beavers," one of their guild opponents later dubbed them) had done so, and in willingly accepting many onerous duties, the Communists had done more than just help the guild movement. They had made their way into its hierarchy both on the local and national levels, and they had won some recruits (e.g., Ashcraft) for the party. The advent of the Popular Front in the months after the 1935 convention had greatly accelerated the processes of infiltration and recruitment (which reached its peak in 1937-39). Some guildsmen suspected the motives of the party members, but in 1936 Communism had not yet become a dread word, and as one dedicated guildsman told a Senate investigating committee years later: "I was sincerely interested in organizing the Newspaper Guild. . . . I was willing to get any help I could." Broun had much the same attitude, though on a broader basis, and in the context of the times it must have

seemed logical; at the beginning of 1936 in answer to a guildsman's letter pointing out the Communist record of divisiveness
and insincerity, Broun wrote: "I prefer to be naive and help in
the fight against fascism rather than be cut down by storm
troopers while coldly twiddling a pair of logical thumbs." A few
years later, Norman Thomas in looking back on this period
commented that "it is the tendency of the Communist party to
seek to control or destroy the things it gets into." The 1936
convention made clear that the Communists had just about
achieved the former (and it would take years of struggle on the
part of the guildsmen to break fully the hold of the party).
During the convention some delegates like Bruce Catton, then
a strong proponent of making the ANG an integral part of the
labor movement, recognized that "something was going on,"
but their eagerness to put their ideas across, to build up an
organization which would counter the publishers who exploited
them, blotted out everything else.[47]

The NEB, assuming correctly that affiliation would have a
bearing on the other issues brought before the convention,
scheduled debate on the matter for May 30, the second day of
the meetings, probably the earliest possible time given the
necessary opening-day rigamarole. On the morning of the 30th
the labor relations committee brought in a majority report endorsed by five of the committee's members (Edward Levinson
of New York, George Mann of Milwaukee, Nathan Goldberg of
Newark, Robert Fitzsimmons of St. Paul, and Homan) and two
individual minority reports. One minority report, by Julius
Klyman of St. Louis, declared that the rift in organized labor
over industrial unionism showed the AFL to be "a crumbling
institution which in its present setup may not survive another
six months and that it would be ridiculous for this organization
to move into a house which might collapse before the moving
is complete." The other minority report, presented by Alfred
Larke of Buffalo, called for another referendum if only to delay
action until a final showdown had taken place within the AFL
on the industrial union question. The majority report, read by
Levinson, asked that the convention instruct the ANG's officers
to apply immediately for admission to the AFL. Except for Kly-

man's verbal attack on a delegate from the Washington Guild, which had more to do with the ANG's internal politics than the issue at hand, the exchanges over the reports generated little heat. Indeed, a general air of lassitude seems to have marked the short debate, probably because of affiliation's assured victory. Levinson summed up the arguments for the majority report when he said: "since we have become through necessity and . . . choice a labor union, it would be logical that we seek to join hands with other trade unions in this country, and . . . join the AFL." He added that a referendum would cater to the wishes of a minority of the membership and "it is now time for the majority and a very substantial one to take the advantage of the rights which naturally belong to it. . . ." Broun, who during the convention made no secret of his support for industrial unionism, said that guildsmen's expressions of opinion on the issue "could be a damned sight more important" inside the AFL than out; "the labor map is going through quick changes," he declared, "and we want to be, however small our part, with the map makers, and not peering in through the school window from the outside." On a roll-call vote the majority report won 83 to 5, with only St. Louis—instructed to vote against affiliation for the reasons Klyman expounded—and Lansing in the negative. Buffalo's delegates, ordered by their guild to abstain on this issue, did so. The Baltimore delegate, instructed against affiliation, missed the vote; after the lunch break he sought to have his guild's two votes recorded but failed as the convention, expressing concern about the future results of late recording of absent votes (especially in close decisions), decided against establishing such a precedent.[48]

Revision of the constitution took up much more time than any other issue at the convention. Buck, who considered the document adopted in 1935 at Cleveland "too long, poorly written, not well arranged," introduced a new constitution and set of bylaws which he had drafted and had distributed to the guilds as a printed pamphlet some weeks prior to the convention. Based on his study of the rules of 75 of the 109 unions affiliated with the AFL, Buck's constitution and bylaws had a dual purpose: to make the ANG operate like the labor union he believed it had become (and his work assumed that the convention would vote for affiliation) and to break what he considered the strangle hold of "the New York crowd" on the guild movement. Buck's proposals included election of a paid, full-time president who would replace the secretary as chief organizer and executive, combining of the offices of secretary and treasurer so as to centralize administrative responsibility, limiting guilds to a maximum of 10 votes at a convention, moving ANG headquarters from New York, making strikes dependent upon a two-thirds vote by secret ballot of all members of the guild involved, and retention of the low $.50 monthly national dues.[49]

Buck's constitution contained many good features, some of which the ANG adopted the following year—including the combining of the offices of secretary and treasurer and the creation of a paid, full-time administrative post in the form of an elected executive vice president. But whether enactment of all or even the majority of Buck's proposals would have benefited the guild movement remains open to conjecture, for many of them, such as the retention of low national dues and the necessity for a two-thirds majority to call a strike, would have hampered the ANG's development. Even Paul French, the lone dissenter on the 1935 constitution committee, believed that although some of "Buck's points are improvements . . . others seem to have . . . little worth." In any event, the whole question of adopting Buck's constitution at the convention quickly became academic. He had tried to strike out at the power of "the New York crowd," and it treated his work with what he later called "cold scorn."[50]

Probably to the surprise of few at the convention the constitution committee when it first reported back to the delegates on the afternoon of Sunday, May 31, announced that it had decided to make any revisions on the basis of the old constitution. Buck, a member of the committee, acquiesced in this decision, recognizing that he had little choice. Some of his proposals did reach the convention floor, but they went no further. On the 31st, following presentation of a preliminary report by the committee, debate ensued on some of the points at issue among its members. The minority broached the matter of changing the existing set-up of officers. Recognizing the value of Broun, as one delegate put it, "as president unpaid [for] reasons of ballyhoo, prestige, advice," but still asserting the ANG's need for a paid full-time administrator, the minority proposed that an executive vice president assume over-all responsibility for day-to-day matters. Milton Kaufman summed up the other side's arguments when he said "better to have another organizer in the field at this time than to have another paid officer. . . ." On a roll-call vote the minority lost 68 to 16. Its attempt to combine the office of secretary and treasurer received equally short shrift. Ashcraft admitted that having the officers in separate cities did not work well, but he undercut attempts to make use of this admission by declaring: "put them both in the same city." On Monday, at the convention's only evening session, the delegates voted overwhelmingly to accept the finance committee's recommendations to raise dues to $.75 (effective August 1), and an attempt to move ANG headquarters from New York to Washington lost badly. Discussion and voting on suggested constitutional revisions proceeded so laboriously that at midnight one of the delegates moved for adjournment, saying "we are all punch drunk." Shortly thereafter, the delegates, having earlier in the convention decided to elect the ANG's officers at the end of Monday's session, turned to that business and put off final action on the constitution until Tuesday morning. At this, the last session of the convention, the opponents of "the New York crowd" fared no better than the night before. They continued to lose on almost all issues that came to a vote and suffered a crushing defeat 61 to 12 in a roll-call vote on the question of how much of a guild's membership had to endorse a strike call; the convention voted that such a call need only obtain a majority.[51]

All this deliberation produced a little-revised constitution with few structural changes in the ANG beyond those necessary for it to become an AFL international union. Thus, the convention did broaden the ANG's geographical jurisdiction to include Canada and the United States overseas territories, made provision for adding a vice president for Canada when at least 50 members had enrolled there, and transformed all the national functions into international ones so that, for example, the National Executive Board became the International Executive Board (IEB). The delegates also slightly extended the ANG's eligibility provisions by voting that editorial employees of news ticker agencies, radio news services, and newsreel companies could become guild members. Most of the other modifications in the constitution tended to increase centralization of the guild movement. Local guilds now had to inform the IEB of all collective bargaining developments and to modify them if the board found they conflicted with ANG policies as outlined by the constitution or the recommendations of the annual convention. In 1936 these recommendations, as voted by the delegates, included the following: that all guilds use the model contract as a guide for collective bargaining, that all guilds file complaints with the NLRB only with the advice and consent of the IEB, and that all guild contracts wherever possible contain a clause providing that "no editorial employee shall be dismissed except for gross incompetence as decided by the guild grievance committee or except for proof satisfactory to the . . . committee of need for retrenchment." The constitution now also stipulated (what heretofore had been only suggested policy) that "every effort shall be made that negotiators are not members of the unit involved" and where a guild had members on only one newspaper or working for only one employer the district council "shall conduct negotiations"; in each case members of the unit involved could sit in as "observers." All guilds now had to submit local constitutions and bylaws to the IEB for a ruling as to whether they conformed with ANG policies. To meet the threat some publishers posed by signing their editorial workers to so-called individual contracts (Newhouse had further undermined the Newark Guild by signing such agreements with most of his news staff although they really only bound the workers), the constitution now forbade guildsmen to enter into written agreements with their employers except where the local guild granted permission or the person involved earned $200 a week or more; for the first time the ANG impinged directly on the relationship a guildsman might wish to have with his employer, and a disgruntled member of the New

York Guild said the exceptions exempted only Broun. Other matters with which constitutional revisions dealt included disciplinary action of guildsmen and IEB processes.[52]

The convention took another step in the direction of centralization by authorizing the creation of nine councils to coordinate collective bargaining activities with the more important chains. Each council would consist of a representative from every guild unit in the chain; in its report to the convention the chain papers committee named the chairmen of these councils and recommended that the Executive Secretary oversee their operations with the power to recommend the removal of any council member or chairman who failed, in his opinion, to carry out his duties. Despite some talk about "a dictatorial set-up," the delegates approved this arrangement. Although the convention did not specifically authorize the councils to negotiate on a chain-wide basis, "it was the obvious expectation," as one labor history points out, "that they would ultimately evolve into bargaining units." They did not, but they did help to expand organization on some chains.[53]

The convention also voted that the incoming treasurer would have no vote on the IEB. The decision stemmed not from an attempt to punish anyone as had been the case with Eddy the previous year, but rather grew out of the fact that the old constitution had provided that no more than two voting members of the Executive Board should come from any one of the ANG's regional divisions. The events of the past 12 months had illustrated the need for the secretary and the treasurer to be in geographical proximity but, with Eddy as well as New Yorkers Broun and Watson assured of reelection, something had to be done about the constitution to enable someone else from that region to take the office of treasurer. The leaders of "the New York crowd" apparently assumed that dropping the limiting proviso would give the ANG too much of a New York air. Accordingly, they decided on the plan of doing away with the treasurer's IEB vote. The election of ANG officers, held between 12:30 and 1:00 a.m. on the 2nd of June, went very quickly. Broun, Homan, and Watson achieved reelection unanimously. Ashcraft, who became a regional vice president, also received a unanimous vote, as did Betty Ballantine, a young but experienced San Francisco journalist who became the first female regional vice president. Eddy also ran unopposed, but the Twin Cities and Washington guilds cast their votes against him. Don Stevens won easily over his rival (58-19) for the position of treasurer, and Gunnar Mickelsen obtained election as a regional vice president by a similar margin (56-19). Julius Klyman defeated Thomas Sherman (elected in 1935) and Alton Jackson, a Winston-Salem newspaperman; the vote: Klyman, 58; Jackson, 10; Sherman, 5.[54]

Generally speaking, few of the debates at this convention produced heated argument; the fights over the resolutions proposed for the delegates' affirmation probably engendered the most controversy. In the past the ANG both at its annual meeting and through the NEB had passed judgment or announced its support on a variety of matters, many of which had nothing to do with the newspaper industry. But in 1936 there began what one observer later called the ANG's "virtual mania" to pass resolutions. At every session of this convention but the opening one the delegates passed resolutions of some kind. These ranged from urging guildsmen's wives to form auxiliary units to reaffirming the ANG's stand in favor of industrial unionism in the newspaper industry, from thanking those radio stations which extended guilds air time to protesting the deportation proceedings against the Communist Emil Gardos, a Hungarian-born Cleveland guildsman and editor of a radical newspaper. At one point after the passage of a series of resolutions, including ones which expressed opposition to war and called on Kentucky's governor to pardon some imprisoned Harlan County coalminers, Broun considered it necessary to point out that he considered it "unfair" to criticize the ANG "for going out of its field" as it seemed to him that any resolution which "directly concerns organized labor . . . very properly falls into our field."[55]

Just before the convention adjourned, Buck declared bitterly that the ANG "now more firmly than ever [had] adhered itself to the City of New York." And so it had. In retrospect it is possible to see that if nothing else the 1936 convention demonstrated the power of "the New York crowd" and of the small clique that dominated it, and that would control the destiny of the ANG for the next few years. Although important for the future, the manifestation of a small group's control over the ANG should not overshadow the significance of affiliation.

The American Newspaper Guild became a labor union at the 1936 convention in fact if not altogether in theory. This change scared some guildsmen: Herman Dinsmore, later chairman of the *New York Times* unit, recalls worriedly wondering about being on the same level as the mechanical workers. This change disturbed others—a member of the Philadelphia Guild executive council declared he felt that the ANG "has ceased to be a newspaper organization. . . . I no longer intend to be active." In terms of the general response of the membership Broun summed up the situation quite nicely right after the convention vote on affiliation when he said that a few would drop out, that the lukewarm had already done so, and that the bulk of the membership had earnestly committed itself to the trade-union idea.[56]

The ANG's commitment stiffened the resolve of those publishers who had expressed opposition to organization of their editorial employees and resulted in others on the management side refusing to deal with the guilds. Arthur Hays Sulzberger, according to a bulletin issued by the *New York Times* unit, told the guildsmen negotiating for it that "I believe it . . . contrary to the best interests of objective newspaper reporting to have an editorial staff composed exclusively of members of a labor union. For that reason . . . we will not recognize the guild until we have to." Roy Howard took an even stronger position. On July 30 the management of the *New York World-Telegram* in a 3,000-word printed statement, to which he formally called the attention of the New York Guild, broke off all negotiations and said that the "recent developments and policies of the American Newspaper Guild . . . have made any contract impossible . . . [for] any newspaper that insists on intellectual freedom . . . and an independent press." Many of the Hearst newspapers treated the statement—which most contemporary observers believed Howard had helped draft—as important news, supposedly (according to an industry history) "as a lesson to W.R.'s men from a 'liberal' publisher." Apparently in a similar vein, the ANPA sent a precis of the statement to all its members. *Editor & Publisher* summed up the industry's general attitude toward affiliation (and the other actions of the convention) in saying that the ANG "as an American Federation of Labor member . . . represents a philosophy we cannot accept. . . ."[57]

Given the industry's attitude, guilds, as might be expected, achieved few gains in the weeks after the New York meeting. Renewals of contracts took place with the Madison, Wisconsin, newspapers and with Stern's *New York Post*, but these pacts won little for the guildsmen involved. The Madison contracts contained almost nothing new beyond extending the previous ones for two years and giving the guild the opportunity during that time to negotiate raises and other improvements for its members. The *New York Post* finally agreed to a limited minimum wage schedule, resulting in raises for the news staff, but the newspaper refused to liberalize almost all the other provisions of the old contract. In Minneapolis the *Journal* flatly refused either to sign a contract or to designate the guild as bargaining agent but the newspaper after negotiations that had gone on since the spring did post in August a bulletin board statement of policy which included establishment of a minimum wage schedule and institution of graduated dismissal notice. At this time, the most significant step forward for the guilds in the area of collective bargaining involved only one man: Morris Watson. After his discharge by the Associated Press in October, 1935, the ANG had filed a complaint with the NLRB. This action began a lengthy legal process which included a series of hearings and an attempt by the AP to enjoin the NLRB from holding a hearing. In May, after the AP twice had refused to comply with orders reinstating Watson, the NLRB filed a petition for enforcement in the Second Circuit Court of Appeals. The court heard arguments on the case in June and on July 13 handed down a decision sustaining the NLRB's order as well as the constitutionality of the Wagner Act. The AP decided to appeal to the Supreme Court; the justices moved very slowly but in April, 1937, as one of a clutch of cases upholding the Wagner

Act they denied the AP's appeal. Given the complexion of the
Court in 1936 and its past record on New Deal measures, the
decision by the appeals court did not have to foreshadow the
victory that the ANG loudly proclaimed, but Watson did win,
and, as the historian of the ANPA points out, this "victory . . .
assured the American Newspaper Guild a permanent place in
newspaper life."[58]

Both during and after the convention, despite Green's statements to the contrary, some guildsmen expressed fears that the
AFL would stall until its fall convention on the ANG's request
for a charter and that this would leave the guild movement in
a kind of limbo.[59] In mid-June, as soon after the convention as
circumstances allowed, Eddy went to Washington to see Green,
who reassured him by saying that the AFL Executive Council
would act on the ANG's charter at its forthcoming July meeting. Eddy also inquired about the possibilities of the ANG
getting financial help. As usual, its treasury was nearly empty;
the Amalgamated Clothing Workers had donated $400 to the
guildsmen during the convention, but that had gone immediately to pay pressing bills in Milwaukee. Much as Eddy and
other guild leaders did not want to beg more money from organized labor, they realized that no real alternative existed
given the anticipated post-convention dues lapse and the continuing need for cash not only to maintain the *News* strike but
also to keep the national organization running. AFL officials
made no definite commitments but indicated that various unions
would lend the ANG about $2,000 and arrange for some kind of
organizational assistance. While in Washington Eddy also saw
John L. Lewis, and when the mine workers' leader learned of
the AFL response to the ANG's pleas he offered the guildsmen
a $4,000 loan from the UMW.[60]

Eddy hesitated to accept the proffered loan. He realized that
many of the guildsmen, with the vote on affiliation just having
been taken, would deem it strange that the ANG should com-
mence a flirtation with the more radical CIO. "The New York
crowd," with its hold on the convention, could have rammed
through a vote along the lines Klyman had suggested, which
would have brought the ANG closer to the CIO, but decided

against such action. Eddy, having been involved in this decision, understood the need for circumspection in regard to the CIO. He also feared that acceptance of the Lewis loan might damage the ANG's chances for quick action on its application for an AFL charter. This fear stemmed from the knowledge that the AFL Executive Council had grown ever more hostile to Lewis as controversy over the CIO increasingly factionalized organized labor. Lewis, the guiding spirit of the CIO, no doubt had a genuine interest in the guildsmen, but probably he also could not resist undercutting Green by doubling the AFL's offer to the ANG. Moreover, he must have calculated that it would not hurt the CIO's public relations to help the newspapermen's organization.[61]

The ANG's financial situation overcame whatever misgivings its leadership had about accepting a loan from Lewis. By the end of June the situation had become critical; the ANG lacked the funds needed to reimburse Eddy and others for their expenses. He had to borrow money to meet his hotel bills. "Godamity," he wrote Davy and Hull, "we can't hold off much longer from asking the UMW to Daddy please give us a lift." And on June 30, after a meeting of the IEB finance committee, the ANG formally advised Lewis that "our circumstances remain such as to make it incumbent upon us . . . to welcome with gratitude your offer of financial assistance from the United Mine Workers of America." In order to avoid embarrassment during the AFL charter application process the ANG leadership decided not to make public immediately its acceptance of Lewis's offer, and it did not do so until the end of July.[62]

On July 8 the AFL Executive Council began a week-long series of meetings which dealt primarily with the split in organized labor, but which also took up the matter of the ANG. At these meetings the Council also dealt with the guildsmen. At its first session on July 8 it voted to grant the ANG a charter as an AFL international union, and a week later it authorized Green to loan the guildsmen $2,000 for organizational purposes. Before the AFL would actually grant the charter, however, a conference would have to take place between the ANG and the printing trades unions to discuss and define areas of jurisdiction.[63]

The conference took place July 22 at the AFL's Washington headquarters. Beals, Eddy, and Stevens represented the ANG. The ITU sent no one but set forth its position in a letter which declared that it had relinquished jurisdiction over editorial employees in 1923. Besides the other printing trades unions, representatives from the commercial telegraphers' union and the International Alliance of Theatre and Stage Employees attended. No conflicts arose during the talks and the guildsmen found it necessary to make only one concession. IATSE contracts covered newsreel photographers, even those doing editorial work, and so the ANG agreed to the deletion of "newsreel companies" from the charter. Eddy and the IATSE representatives also agreed to exchange letters in which the ANG would undertake not to claim jurisdiction over newsreel photographers who did editorial work while IATSE would promise to help the ANG enroll regular editorial employees of the newsreel companies. After the conference, Green announced that as no obstacles existed to granting a charter, the ANG had become an affiliate of the AFL, and on July 24 he confirmed this statement in a letter to Eddy.[64]

Besides extending a $2,000 loan, the AFL alleviated another of the ANG's financial burdens by agreeing to bear the cost of a full-time organizer. Although on the AFL payroll and ultimately liable to its executives, he would work for the ANG under the general direction of the IEB. For this job Eddy proposed first Davy and then Hull, both of whom already had proven their worth as organizers. Green would accept neither, partly because he considered them too radical and partly because he did not want anybody on the AFL payroll near the *News* strike. The AFL head also took the position (and correctly so) that the man engaged as organizer could do a better job if he had a metropolitan newspaper background that clearly gave him professional standing. Green preferred that if possible an ANG officer take the job. Don Stevens, who fit Green's specifications, had come to Washington for the July 22 conference and had favorably impressed the AFL head (who apparently had no inkling of the guildsman's political leanings); and Stevens received the appointment.[65]

On August 7, 1936—three years to the day after Broun's column calling for a union of reporters had appeared—the IEB held an open meeting at the Hotel Biltmore in New York to mark the formal presentation by Green to the ANG of its AFL charter. About 250 people attended, mostly guildsmen from the metropolitan area. They heard Green, in the course of a lengthy talk, take some sharp digs at the CIO unions, which a few days earlier the AFL Executive Council had tried, found guilty of dual unionism and violating their charters, and ordered to withdraw from the CIO by September 5 upon pain of suspension. These and other remarks about the "family dispute in the house of labor" nettled Broun, an ardent proponent of industrial unionism, and to the surprise of all present, at the conclusion of the ceremonies Broun announced that he intended to resign as ANG president the next day and requested that acceptance or rejection of this action be made the issue of a referendum on affiliation with the CIO. Just before the meeting Broun had apprised Lewis of his intentions by telephone and had been told to "keep your shirt on." Broun's indignation apparently got the better of him. After the meeting, other guild leaders, recognizing the dangers in his impulsive action, succeeded in convincing him to delay doing anything for the moment. However, he attended the August 10 meeting of the CIO, which decided to proceed with its plans despite the suspension threat, and he joined that body as an individual although he expressed the hope that this would result in a referendum in which the ANG membership "will support me in declaring adherence" to the principles and leadership of the CIO. The leaders of "the New York crowd" recognized that the ANG could not just "walk into the AFL and then walk right out again," as one of them said. Broun later recalled that they "lashed into me . . . accused me of infantile conduct." Despite his statements about a referendum, they won him over to their point of view and managed to squelch any action on this issue until the next convention.[66]

Broun's pro-CIO statements notwithstanding, the 1936 convention's immediate aftermath has the air of anticlimax about it. The publishers generally reacted to affiliation as expected;

it confirmed their anti-ANG stance and gave them yet another excuse to avoid dealings with the guilds. The exigencies of the ANG's financial situation as well as the predilections of those in control of the national organization led them to deal with the CIO, but circumstances forced them to move cautiously. The AFL, unwilling to make an extensive commitment in such an apparently fruitless field as editorial employee organization, reacted favorably but gingerly to the ANG's request for affiliation. By the fall of 1936 the American Newspaper Guild formally had become part of organized labor. Since the summer of 1933 the guild movement had come a long way.

The American Newspaper Guild began in 1933 not as a union but as a loose association of local groups, most of which had come into being spontaneously. Many of the leaders and members of these groups had thought of them and the ANG as the editorial employees' counterpart of the sort of professional societies that lawyers, engineers, and doctors had established. Many newspaper workers said one way or another: "what we need is something like the American Medical Association."

Within three years, however, of the ANG's founding, although its *raison d'etre* had remained the improvement of newspapermen's working conditions, it had changed radically as had the avowed means of achieving this goal. Instead of relying on the federal government to obtain benefits for the editorial worker, the ANG had decided to wrest these directly from the publishers. No longer a loose association, it had become a relatively centralized union, had adopted a rudimentary but broad collective-bargaining program, and had become part of organized labor through affiliation with the AFL. The American Newspaper Guild would change still more before it reached its present form (less than a year after going into the AFL it left that body to join the CIO and did so as an industrial union, having extended its jurisdiction to a broad range of non-editorial employees stretching from the business office to the maintenance department). But the most important changes, the vital ones that transformed the ANG, took place between 1933 and 1936; if not for these it would have been stillborn.

The hostility of the publishers, the inability of the various federal labor boards at this time to protect guildsmen, the failure of NRA perceptibly to improve working conditions for editorial employees, all made it quite clear that the ANG could not achieve its stated ends as a newspapermen's version of the AMA. Among the more dedicated guildsmen some believed that the ANG could achieve positive results only as a union, and still others believed that such a union must belong to organized labor. Certainly, events in Newark, Oakland, even in New York, had demonstrated that if the guilds adopted a union stance, they lacked the wherewithal to maintain it by themselves. Other equally dedicated guildsmen fought the union idea as well as affiliation, but circumstances mitigated their opposition. Their charges that a small group (which at times they labelled as Communist) captured the guild movement and transformed it constitute an oversimplification. The guildsmen who changed the ANG into a union affiliated with the AFL did scheme toward accomplishing that end, but they did not so much capture the guild movement as inherit it, for those opposed to their ideas dropped out of the guilds, which, under the pressure of events, had already begun to change.

As for the Communists, their role during these years should neither be over- nor underestimated. On the one hand, as ardent workers within the guild movement the Communists provided much of the energy which sustained it and carried the ANG through the early battles with the publishers. On the other hand, the Communists generated a great deal of dissension among the guildsmen which probably helped the publishers and for a time prior to the Second World War did lead to the ANG's falling under the control of a mediocre, small-minded Stalinist leadership.

Without Heywood Broun, there probably would have been an American Newspaper Guild; certainly he did not start the guild movement. The newspapermen's agitation about NRA would have taken place even if he had not written his column. But what would have happened to the ANG in the three years after its founding if he had not been president and fitfully active? Those who handled the organization's day-to-day activities probably would have done so anyway. But did they possess the necessary respect to head a national organization? Could they have attracted the attention (much less held it) of Roosevelt or other government officials? Did they have the outlets or contacts necessary to publicize or otherwise push the guild movement? Would striking guildsmen have been as cheered by anyone else as they were by the lumbering presence of Broun? Would the industry despite many publishers' dislike for the columnist have the same regard for some other newspaperman who became an ANG spokesman or officer? In all instances the record shows that the answer must be "no." The American Newspaper Guild might have gone on without Broun, but his participation (erratic as it was) assured its survival during these early troubled years.

In the fall of 1936 but for the ANG's existence the newspaper industry had changed little since the guild movement had begun three years earlier. The American Newspaper Guild had not yet accomplished much for the editorial employee, but it had demonstrated that it was possible, even among such white collar workers uncongenial to organization as newspapermen, to create a union of individuals.

KEY TO NOTE ABBREVIATIONS

Sources which have been assigned abbreviations in the notes to the text are listed below in alphabetical order.

ACLU
American Civil Liberties Union papers. Microfilm copy at the New York Public Library. New York, New York.

ANG
American Newspaper Guild papers. At the time I used them, the ANG's records for its early years, with few exceptions, were scattered about its Washington, D.C., offices and storerooms. Since then, the ANG has made plans to deposit its papers with a library. Where possible with ANG material, full citations are given, but for most of its records it is possible only to indicate that they are at the ANG's offices.

ANG Proceedings
American Newspaper Guild. Proceedings of the founding meeting and of the annual conventions. Microfilm copy. The Bancroft Library, University of California. Berkeley, California.

ANPA Bulletin
Bulletin of the American Newspaper Publishers Association.

CNG
Cleveland Newspaper Guild papers. Cleveland, Ohio.

COHC
Oral History Collection, Columbia University. New York, New York.

DNG
Detroit Newspaper Guild Collection. Labor History Archives of Wayne State University. Detroit, Michigan.

FDRL	Franklin D. Roosevelt Library. Hyde Park, New York.
E&P	*Editor & Publisher.*
GR	*The Guild Reporter.*
JCU	Journalism Library, Columbia University. New York, New York.
NLB-NRC	National Labor Board case files. Washington National Records Center. Washington, D.C.
NLRB-NRC	National Labor Relations Board (1934-35) case files. Washington National Records Center. Washington, D.C.
NRA	Files on the Daily Newspaper Publishing Business. Consolidated files on industries governed by Approved Codes. National Recovery Administration. Record Group 9. National Archives. Washington, D.C. Unless otherwise indicated, the file referred to is 288-16.
NRA Document Series	U.S. National Archives and Record Service. *Document Series of the National Recovery Administration 1933-36.* National Archives Microfilm Publication: Microcopy No. 213, Roll 44. Washington, D.C.: General Services Administration, 1956.
NYHT	*New York Herald Tribune.*
NYPLSC	Schomburg Collection of Negro Literature and History. New York Public Library. New York, New York.
NYT	*The New York Times.*
NYWT	*New York World-Telegram.*

PNG   Newspaper Guild of Greater Philadelphia
                       papers. Philadelphia. Pennsylvania.

SHSW   State Historical Society of Wisconsin. Madi-
                       son, Wisconsin.

TCNG   Newspaper Guild of the Twin Cities of
                       Minneapolis and St. Paul papers. Minne-
                       apolis, Minnesota.

notes

INTRODUCTION: NEWSPAPERMEN AND WHITE COLLAR WORKERS

1. Gompers quoted in Mills, *White Collar*, p. 301; Kassalow, "United States," in *White Collar Trade Unions*, ed. by Sturmthal, pp. 317-27. There is a paucity of up-to-date monographic material on white collar unions but for musicians, see Leiter, *Musicians and Petrillo*, pp. 13-25; for actors, see Harding, *Revolt of the Actors;* for postal workers, see Baarslag, *Post Office Clerks*, and Spero, *Labor Movement*, pp. 57-305, *passim;* for teachers, see Commission on Educational Reconstruction, *Teaching Profession*, pp. 19-51.

2. Bernstein, *Lean Years*, p. 55; Macdonald, *Labor Problems*, p. 194; Kassalow, "Unionization of White Collar Workers," in *Labor in a Changing America*, ed. by Haber, pp. 159-60.

3. Kassalow, "United States," p. 305.

4. Galenson, *CIO Challenge*, p. 565. Similar sentiments are expressed in Minton and Stuart, *Men Who Lead Labor*, pp. 133-34; Macdonald, *Labor Problems*, p. 199; and Kassalow, "United States," p. 329.

5. Kramer, *Heywood Broun*.

6. Stolberg, for example, attacks what he calls the leadership's "Stalinist ideology" in *Story of the CIO*, p. 251; Harris, *American Labor*, pp. 175-91, is friendlier but has an anti-AFL slant; the very pro-CIO Levinson in *Labor on the March* confuses (pp. 246-48) names, dates, and facts; and so it goes in many of the works written during this period.

7. Taft, in his massive, detailed study, *The AFL*, does not deem it necessary to mention the ANG's affiliation with the AFL. Galenson, *CIO Challenge*, deals well with the ANG after 1936 but skips quickly over the earlier history (pp. 348-65).

8. Perhaps the best contemporary account is Lee, *Daily Newspaper*, pp. 678-97.

9. The late dean of journalism historians, Frank Mott, in the 3d edition of *American Journalism* spent but four paragraphs on the

ANG's early years (pp. 676-77); Emery's *Press and America* devotes a little more space to that time (pp. 589-96).

10. It has become more difficult to charge Communist influence, for the courts have held such charges without adequate proof to be libelous and defamatory (Phelps and Hamilton, *Libel*, p. 305).

CHAPTER 1: BEFORE THE BLUE EAGLE

1. Macey, "Journalism," in *Civilization in the United States*, ed. by Stearns, p. 36.

2. Evans, "Justice for the Reporter," *The American Press*, LII (Nov., 1933), 3; U.S., Personnel Classification Board, *Routine Clerical Work*, pp. 5-7, 9.

3. E&P, Apr. 28, 1934, p. 54; Gleason, "The Editorial Management of the Small City Newspaper," p. 59; E. Rogers, *Peachtree Parade*, p. 28; Crowell, "The Press Gets a Code," *New Republic*, LXXVI (Dec. 29, 1933), 164,

4. Markham, *Bovard*, p. 71; Ferdinand Lundberg to Oliver Pilat, Oct. 23, 1963, in author's possession; Rosenberger, "Personnel Problems in the Larger Newspaper Editorial Offices," p. 17; Lord, *The Young Man and Journalism*, p. 146.

5. International Labour Office (hereafter, ILO), *Conditions of Life and Work*, p. 158.

6. American Society of Newspaper Editors, *Problems of Journalism* (1927), p. 10; ILO, *Conditions of Life and Work*, p. 159; Slosson, *Great Crusade*, p. 170.

7. U.S., Industrial Commission on the Relations and Conditions of Capital and Labor Employed in Manufacture and General Business, *Report*, VII, 275; Walker, *City Editor*, pp. 4-5.

8. Williams, *Newspaperman*, p. 164; ILO, *Conditions of Life and Work*, pp. 11-12.

9. Crowell, "Press Gets a Code," p. 165; MacNeil, *Without Fear or Favor*, p. 290; Rascoe, *Before I Forget*, p. 238.

10. R. S. Mann, "Turnover in Newspaper Editorial Staffs," p. 30; "Reporters' Unions," *The American Press*, LI (Aug., 1933), 4.

11. Quoted in Rosenberger, "Personnel Problems," p. 22; Tunney, "A Man Must Fight," *Colliers*, IC (Mar. 5, 1932), 14; Sinclair, *Brass Check*, p. 427. In the 1930s especially there was much dissatisfaction with the venality of the American press, and a number of studies were made. An interesting and caustic one is Seldes' *Freedom of the Press*.

12. Crist, "Gentlemen and Scholars of the Press," *Columbia University Forum,* II (Winter, 1959), 41; the whole "game" idea, as well as a profile of American newspapering at the time, is set forth splendidly in the first and last installments of a six-part series, "The Newspaper Game," *The Saturday Evening Post,* CLXXXIV (Apr. 6-May 11, 1912), 3-5, 56-58/ 16-17; Harris, *American Labor,* p. 174.

13. Lee, *Daily Newspaper,* p. 603; Clarke, *Man of the World,* p. 114; Lord, *Young Man and Journalism,* pp. 152-53, 158; Evans, "Justice for the Reporter," p. 3; for a survey of the changing concept of the journalist, see Leab, "The 'Image' of the Journalist, 1864-1964," *Columbia Journalism Review,* III (Spring, 1964), 38-43.

14. Emery, *Press and America,* pp. 735-38; O'Dell, *Journalism Education,* passim; Pulitzer quoted in Baker, *Graduate School of Journalism,* p. 50.

15. U.S., National Labor Relations Board (1935-), Division of Economic Research, *Collective Bargaining,* p. 104; Moskin, "Origins of the American Newspaper Guild," p. 4; according to Heywood Broun, one of the prime movers in the creation of the ANG, it was "built upon the earlier experiences of such cooperative movements. . . ." (Broun, "Hands and Brain," *Nation,* CXL [Mar. 6, 1935], 279).

16. *Reach's Official American Association Baseball Guide,* pp. 34-35; Seymour, *Baseball,* pp. 34-35. There are active in journalism today a number of associations, including such well-established ones as the National Press Photographers Association.

17. Lee, *Daily Newspaper,* pp. 666-69.

18. *First Annual Address to the Reporters' Club of Philadelphia, 1886.* pp. 3-4.

19. NLRB, *Collective Bargaining,* p. 105.

20. Tracy, *Typographical Union,* p. 452; Lee, *Daily Newspapers,* pp. 667-68.

21. Tracy, *Typographical Union,* pp. 480, 538.

22. A complete tabular breakdown of the ITU locals, including charter-granting and suspension dates, is in NLRB, *Collective Bargaining,* p. 108. For capsule histories of some of the ITU locals, see Loftus, "Scranton and Its Press," pp. 57-69.

23. O'Sullivan quoted in Tracy, *Typhographical Union,* pp. 587, 671-72; Winnick, "The American Newspaper Guid," p. 26; Loftus, "Scranton and Its Press," p. 61.

24. Bracken quoted in Tracy, *Typographical Union,* p. 761; Underwood and newspapermen quoted in Loftus, "Scranton and Its Press," p. 65; Tom V. Nealon to Heywood Broun, Dec. 11, 1933, ANG.

25. O'Sullivan quoted in Tracy, *Typographical Union*, p. 630; Lee, *Daily Newspaper*, p. 67.

26. NLRB, *Collective Bargaining*, pp. 106-8.

27. Douglas, *Real Wages*, p. 57.

28. Emery, *Press and America*, p. 521; E&P, Sept. 4, 1919, p. 10.

29. "News Writers Union Local No. 1," *New Republic*, XX (Aug. 6, 1919), 8-9; NYT, July 4, 1919, p. 9, July 6, p. 7, July 7, p. 13, July 23, p. 3.

30. E&P, Aug. 28, 1919, p. 12, Sept. 4, p. 10; *Newsdom*, Mar. 5, 1932, p. 4; Quinn, *San Francisco-Oakland Newspaper Guild*, p. 102; "News Writers Local No. 1," p. 8.

31. E&P, Aug. 28, 1919, p. 12; Ferguson quoted in Loftus, "Scranton and Its Press," p. 68.

32. NYT, July 24, 1920, p. 20, Aug. 12, p. 6; "Proceedings of the 65th Session of the International Typographical Union," pp. 43-44, Supplement to *Typographical Journal*, LVII (Sept., 1920); NLRB, *Collective Bargaining*, p. 110; *Epochal History of the ITU*.

33. Lee, *Daily Newspaper*, p. 673; publisher quoted in Gauvreau, *My Last Million Readers*, p. 89; Bryant quoted in E&P, Sept. 4, 1919, p. 10.

34. Bleyer quoted in E&P, June 5, 1919, p. 20; Sinclair, *Brass Check*, pp. 421, 423.

35. E&P, Sept. 18, 1919, p. 74, Sept. 25, p. 16. The attitude behind the formation of this group can best be understood by reading its constitution, to be found in *Ibid.*, pp. 11-12, 40.

36. It was also by far the smaller. The other organization, the National Union of Journalists, a much more militant group with close trade-union ties, in the 1930s had over 2½ times the membership of the Institute. (Murasken, "Newswriters Unions in English-Speaking Countries," pp. 2-4.)

37. E&P, Oct. 16, 1919, p. 8; Lee, *Daily Newspaper*, p. 677; ILO, *Conditions of Life and Work*, p. 45.

38. NLRB, *Collective Bargaining*, p. 112; Loftus, "Scranton and Its Press," pp. 60, 63-64.

39. NLRB, *Collective Bargaining*, p. 111; letter from Gannett, Jan. 5, 1965; statement by Gannett in Lewis et al., *Heywood Broun*, pp. 33-34. At the time, nothing resulted from independent movements or from the AFL locals, but later their members often served as nuclei for ANG chapters; in 1936 those of the AFL locals which remained in existence joined the ANG upon its affiliation with the AFL.

40. Another ITU-established newswriters' local chartered in 1899

in Milwaukee survived into the 1930s, but throughout most of its existence it had a very small membership, limited mostly to the Socialist labor daily (Loftus, "Scranton and Its Press," pp. 57-58).

41. Brislin, "Scranton Reporters' Union Unique Among U.S. Newspaper Groups," E&P, Oct. 25, 1930, p. 50; Loftus, "Union for the City Room?" *The Quill,* XX (Nov., 1932), 2-3; comments by John Mead, Jr., of the *Erie Times,* in American Society of Newspaper Editors, *Problems of Journalism* (1934), p. 161; interview with Phillips Butler, past president of ANG Local 177 (Scranton), Mar. 18, 1965; GR, Dec. 15, 1943, p. 12.

42. Weisberger, *American Newspaperman,* p. 154; Mott, *American Journalism,* pp. 647-50.

43. See tables in Ernst, *First Freedom,* pp. 279-81.

44. Lee, *Daily Newspaper,* pp. 168-69.

45. Nelson, "The Newspaper Industry," Nov. 11, 1933, p. 23, in NRA Document Series; Ray, "Economic Factors as Forces in Daily Newspaper Concentration," *Journalism Quarterly,* XXIX (Winter, 1952), 37-38.

46. Lee, "Recent Developments in the Newspaper Industry," *Public Opinion Quarterly,* II (Jan., 1938), 128; Willey and Rice, *Communications Agencies,* p. 124; Nelson, "The Newspaper Industry," p. 9; Bleyer, "Freedom of the Press," *Journalism Quarterly,* XI (Spring, 1934), 29; Moskin, "Origin of the American Newspaper Guild," p. 16.

47. Walker, *City Editor,* p. 65; Swanberg, *Citizen Hearst,* p. 363; Bent, *Ballyhoo,* p. 251; Willey and Rice, *Communications Agencies,* p. 174; Luce, "The Press Is Peculiar," *Saturday Review of Literature,* VII (Mar. 7, 1931), 246.

48. Johnson and Robb, *The South and Its Newspapers,* p. 137; Willey and Rice, *Communications Agencies,* pp. 165, 174.

49. Pew, "Professional vs. Trades Union News Departments," p. 5; Lee, *Daily Newspaper,* pp. 202-3.

50. Boylan, "The Daily Newspaper Business in the National Recovery Administration," pp. 4-5, 127-28; Case, "A History of the Code of Fair Competition for the Daily Newspaper Publishing Business," Dec. 27, 1935, p. 4, in NRA Document Series; Hyde, "United States Journalism in 1931," *Journalism Quarterly,* VIII (Dec., 1931), 819; "Newspaper Publishing," *The Index,* XIV (Oct., 1934), 209; Lee Drake papers, Box Two, Income and Expense Folder; Ray, "Concentration and Ownership and Control in the American Daily Newspaper Industry," pp. 312, 341.

51. E&P, Apr. 25, 1936, p. 12; Lee, *Daily Newspaper,* p. 369; Emery,

ANPA, p. 200; Hurd, "American Press Adopts 'Air Brakes,'" *Christian Science Monitor Weekly,* Apr. 25, 1934, p. 4.

52. Adams, "Freedom of the Press," *New Republic,* IVC (Feb. 9, 1938), 15.

53. *Newsdom,* Sept. 26, 1931, p. 1; Johnson and Robb, *The South and Its Newspapers,* p. 152; "Salaries and Working Conditions of Newspaper Editorial Employees," *Monthly Labor Review,* XL (May, 1935), 1138.

54. "Salaries and Working Conditions of Newspaper Editorial Employees," 1138; Quinn, *San Francisco-Oakland Newspaper Guild,* pp. 19-20; Henry Doorly, president of the Omaha *World-Herald,* to S. M. Williams, manager of the Code Authority for the Daily Newspaper Publishing Business, NRA, Box 1936; White, "Genesis of the Guild," *The Quill,* XXI (Dec., 1933), 5; Walker, *City Editor,* p. 43; Pew, "Shop Talk at Thirty," E&P, Feb. 11, 1933, p. 32, Apr. 8, p. 14.

55. E&P, Aug. 13, 1932, p. 11; *Newsdom,* Mar. 19, 1932, p. 1; Quinn, *San Francisco-Oakland Newspaper Guild,* p. 20; Brandenburg, "Staff Morale Tested by Depression," E&P, Mar. 4, 1933, p. 10; "This Matter of Morale," *The Quill,* XII (Apr., 1933), 14.

56. Gilmount, "The Low Pay of Reporters," *The American Press,* LI (Aug., 1933), 22; E&P, Dec. 31, 1932, p. 20.

CHAPTER 2: THE BEGINNINGS

1. Stewart, *News Is What We Make It,* p. 133.

2. Quoted in *Handbook of NRA Laws,* p. 1.

3. *Ibid.,* p. 9.

4. Schlesinger, Jr., *Coming of the New Deal,* pp. 98-102.

5. Lyon et al., *National Recovery Administration,* p. 52.

6. Johnson quoted in *Handbook of NRA Laws,* p. 276; Leuchtenburg, *Roosevelt and the New Deal,* p. 65.

7. Boylan, "Daily Newspaper Business," p. 6; "Publishers Activities," ANPA *Bulletin,* XLVII (June 15, 1933), 372.

8. Emery, *ANPA,* p. 224; "Newspapers and the N.R.A.," Chapter 2, *passim;* Burns, "Daily Newspapers," in *How Collective Bargaining Works,* p. 43.

9. E&P, June 24, 1933, p. 26, July 15, p. 5; Johnson, *Blue Eagle,* p. 310.

10. "Federal Laws," ANPA *Bulletin,* XLVII (July 21, 1933), 419; Boylan, "Daily Newspaper Business," p. 12.

11. Quoted in E&P, July 29, 1933, p. 6; *Ibid.,* p. 20; Lee Drake to

Fred Lamplin, Aug. 1, 1933, Lee Drake Papers, Box Two, Income and Expense Folder.

12. Later, Charles R. Butler was added to the subcommittee. He was the publisher of the Mankato, Minn., *Free Press* and president of the Inland Daily Press Association, the oldest and largest of the regional publishers associations.

13. Boylan, "Daily Newspaper Business," p. 12; "Newspapers and the NRA," Chapter 4, pp. 1-4; "Tribute to Elisha Hanson," ANPA *Bulletin*, LXXVII (May 9, 1962), 65; "Legal Ajax," *Literary Digest*, CXXI (Apr. 18, 1936), 45.

14. Manning, "Johnson Says Labor Contracts Stand," E&P, Aug. 5, 1933, p. 7; Johnson, *Blue Eagle*, p. 213; NYT, Sept. 2, 1933, p. 2; Johnson quoted by Richberg in E&P, Nov. 18, 1933, p. 14; "National Industrial Recovery Act," ANPA *Bulletin*, XLVII (Aug. 10, 1933), 449-50.

15. "Newspapers and the N.R.A.," Chapter 4, p. 8. Indicative of many publishers' attitudes is the reply to Johnson's outburst by Bryan, who asserted that conditions in the newspaper business were so different from those in manufacturing and commercial that the press required exceptional treatment. *(Ibid.)*

16. Case, "History of the Code," pp. 4-8.

17. Perry, "Codes for Dailies Filed at Washington," E&P, Aug. 12, 1933, p. 3; NYT, Aug. 9, 1933, p. 2; "Newspapers and the N.R.A.," Chapter 6, p. 8; Boylan, "Daily Newspaper Business," p. 20; Anderson, "Johnson and the Freedom of the Press," *Nation*, CXXXVII (Aug. 30, 1933), 235; "The Newspaper Code," ANPA *Bulletin*, XLVII (Aug. 16, 1933), 461; *Handbook of NRA Laws*, p. 326.

18. NYT, July 29, 1933, p. 1, Aug. 1, p. 10, Aug. 2, p. 10, Aug. 4, p. 9.

19. NYHT, Aug. 9, 1933, p. 17; Richard Cornish to Hugh Johnson, Aug. 8, 1933, A. F. Finestone to Johnson, July 26, 1933, NRA, Box 1931; Johnson, *Blue Eagle*, p. 308.

20. U.S., Congress, House of Representatives, Committee on Labor, *Hearings on 30-Hour Week Bill*, pp. 203, 699; Moskin, "Origins of the American Newspaper Guild," pp. 23, 27.

21. Moskin, "Origins of the American Newspaper Guild," p. 48.

22. Marshall, "Columnists on Parade VII: Heywood Broun," *Nation*, CXLVII (May 21, 1937), 580; Kramer, *Heywood Broun*, passim; Woollcott quoted in Reynolds, *By Quentin Reynolds*, p. 34; Ashcraft, "25th Anniversary Notes."

23. NYWT, Aug. 7, 1933, p. 21.

24. *Newsdom*, Jan. 9, 1932, p. 4, Feb. 6, p. 4. *Newsdom*, "edited and published by and for newspaper workers," began publishing on a

weekly basis August 23, 1931, staffed mostly by former members of the New York *World* who helped to make it a trade weekly describing personal events in the business. For a while in 1931-32 it became a very strident recorder of the hard times New York newspapermen experienced, and attempted to defend their interests. Never financially secure, the newspaper by 1933 had come to depend heavily on the support of public utilities operator H. L. Doherty, who changed the staff and the format, and soon turned *Newsdom* into a more conservative, less comprehensive version of *Editor & Publisher*. The weekly survived Doherty's death in December, 1939, by less than a month.

25. Interview with Wishengrad, May 2, 1965. *Newsdom's* very limited circulation made it doubtful that Broun saw it, yet it is hard to believe that nobody called his attention to this appeal. Moreover, at ANG headquarters in Washington, on the last page of a scrapbook of clippings by and about Broun, there is a copy of the *Newsdom* open letter. Alexander Crosby, who went through this and other Broun scrapbooks to cull the columns and stories that made up the Broun compilation published in 1935, doubts that Broun personally kept any scrapbook, though he knew about them. (Interview with Crosby, Oct. 12, 1965.) The person most likely to have kept the scrapbook, Luella Henkel, had no recollection of the *Newsdom* open letter. (Interview with Miss Henkel, Oct. 12, 1965.)

26. Interviews with Watson, Oct. 12, 1965, Miss Henkel, Oct. 12, 1965, Miss Fleeson, Aug. 2, 1965, Ernst, Oct. 8, 1965, and Britt, July 12, 1965.

27. H. B. Slocum to Heywood Broun, Aug. 9, 1933, ANG.

28. Lee, *Daily Newspaper*, p. 678; E&P, Aug. 12, 1933, p. 4.

29. E&P, Aug. 19, 1933, p. 6, Sept. 23, p. 37, Dec. 9, p. 16; Stern, *Memoirs*, p. 285; printed open letter to Johnson, dated Aug. 14, 1933, ANG; Moskin, "Origins of the American Newspaper Guild," p. 48; Andrew Parker to Heywood Broun, Aug. 17, 1933, ANG.

30. Interview with Bordner, June 14, 1965.

31. Interviews with Ashcraft, Oct. 20, 1965, White, Oct. 27, 1965, and Bordner, Oct. 28, 1965; Stolberg, *Story of the C.I.O.*, p. 246; Ashcraft, "Guild's First Chapter Takes a Bow," GR, Dec. 15, 1934, p. 10; "It Got Hot in '33," *Cleveland Newspaper Guild Page One Ball Yearbook*, 1953, p. 9; Goski, "First Member of First Guild Unit Tells How and Why It Started," GR, Feb. 15, 1944, p. 7. Ashcraft—who says, contrary to what has been written in many articles and books, that none of these organization meetings took place in his home—also believes that many writers have given too much emphasis to the

location of the speakeasy discussions (Ashcraft interview, Oct. 20, 1965).

32. I. L. Kenen, a founder of the CNG, to Clyde Beals, editor of GR, Aug. 21, 1938, p. 1 of a 16-page letter outlining the Guild's origins in Cleveland and elsewhere (hereafter referred to as Kenen to Beals), Kenen papers.

33. *Ibid.*, p. 2; letter from Lloyd White, July 18, 1966; Ashcraft, "Guild's First Chapter Takes a Bow," p. 10; interview with White, Oct. 27, 1965; E&P, Aug. 26, 1933, p. 6.

34. Bordner, "Another Footnote to Guild History," GR, Jan. 1, 1944, p. 5; interviews with White, Oct. 27, 1965, Bordner, Oct. 28, 1965, and Ashcraft, Oct. 20, 1965; Stolberg, *Story of the C.I.O.*, p. 246.

35. E&P, Aug. 26, 1933, p. 6; Kenen to Beals, pp. 3-5.

36. Thomas Lempertz to Heywood Broun, Oct. 9, 1933, A. L. Roberts to Broun, Aug. 20, 1933, ANG; interview with Kenen, Aug. 15, 1965.

37. Both quoted in full in E&P, Sept. 2, 1933, p. 9.

38. The differences, in fact, have never been completely resolved, and they remain a problem for the Newspaper Guild to this day even though after long and hard-fought debate its membership voted in 1937 to extend jurisdiction to include the business, advertising, and circulation departments as well as most other kinds of non-mechanical, non-editorial newspaper employees. An interesting exposition of these divergences of opinion appearing 25 years after they were voted on and supposedly settled is Bracker, "Dilemma of a Guild Reporter," *The Reporter*, XXVIII (Jan. 17, 1963), 31-34.

39. Porter, "Cleveland Newspapermen Split," *The American Press*, LII (Oct., 1933), 3; interviews with Bordner, June 14, 1965, and White, Oct. 27, 1965; Kenen to Beals, p. 11; Ashcraft, "Guild's First Chapter Takes a Bow," p. 10; Bordner, "Why We Organized," *The Quill*, XXI (Oct., 1933), 6.

40. Kenen to Beals, pp. 8-11; E&P, Sept. 7, 1933, p. 17, Sept. 16, p. 10; interviews with White, Oct. 27, 1965, Kenen, Aug. 15, 1965, and Bordner, Oct. 28, 1965; letter from Garland Ashcraft, Dec. 27, 1965.

41. Kenen to Beals, pp. 7-8; E&P, Aug. 26, 1933, p. 6.

42. E&P, Oct. 21, 1933, p. 18; interviews with White, May 24, 1966, and William Davy, first executive secretary of the CNG, May 29, 1966; "It Got Hot in '33," p. 10.

43. American Society of Newspaper Editors, *Problems of Journalism* (1929), p. 110.

44. Letter from Jonathan Edwards, *Newsdom*, Jan. 16, 1933, p. 5.

45. E&P, Aug. 12, 1933, p. 4.

46. No answer as to why Broun chose October 1 came from the people interviewed. An unsigned obituary in the ANG newspaper concluded that "whatever the reason Broun had . . . , it is at present blurred." (GR, Jan. 1, 1940, p. 2.)

47. Interview with Leon Svirsky, Nov. 14, 1965.

48. E&P, Sept. 16, 1933, p. 42; interviews with Britt, Nov. 14, 1965, and Ernst, Oct. 8, 1965; A. L. Roberts to Heywood Broun, Aug. 20. 1933, ANG. Miss Henkel, who wrote and signed almost all of Broun's correspondence at this time, used a shorthand system of her own invention. She does not remember the meanings of all the symbols she used, and her transcription of the jottings reads: "We are having a meeting Wednesday night and will endeavor at that time to get up (?) some temporary New York organization. I am (all, also?) for such a movement." (Miss Henkel to author, Oct. 10, 1965.)

49. Bade quoted in Kramer, *Heywood Broun*, p. 145; Randau, "It Happened One Day in September 14 Years Ago," *Frontpage*, Sept.-Oct., 1947, p. 6.

50. Fleeson, "Our Guild," *The Matrix*, XIX (Apr., 1934), 5; interviews with Britt, July 12, 1965, Svirsky, Nov. 14, 1965, and Jonathan Eddy, first ANG Executive Secretary, Aug. 15, 1965; Gannett, "1933—When the Guild Was Very Young," GR, Dec. 26, 1958, p. M-4; Randau, "It Happened One Day"; letters from Morris Watson, Dec. 2, 1965, Lewis Gannett, May 24, 1965, and Lloyd White, July 20, 1966; Kramer, *Heywood Broun*, p. 245.

51. Perry, "New York News Writers Organize," E&P, Sept. 23, 1933, p. 7; Watson, "History Is Now Being Written Behind Nation's Front Pages," GR, Nov. 23, 1933, p. 1; Section 14 quoted in E&P, Aug. 19, 1933, p. 7.

52. E&P, Sept. 16, 1933, p. 42.

53. Perry, "New York News Writers Organize," 7; NYT, Sept. 18, 1933, p. 4.

54. Stewart, *News*, p. 132; Perry, "New York Writers Organize," 7, 42; Watson, "History," p. 1.

55. Quoted anonymously in Pew, "Shop Talk at Thirty," E&P, Sept. 23, 1933, p. 44.

56. New York *Daily News*, Sept. 19, 1933, p. 23. Captain Joseph Patterson had instituted the five-day, forty-hour week on his *Daily News* in 1932. Doris Fleeson, then a correspondent on that newspaper, believes that Patterson, whose sensational tabloid was constantly being attacked as scandalous by other newspapers, supported the editorial workers not only because he felt they deserved support but

also because he enjoyed exposing the hypocrisy of the publishers who had been baiting him (interview with Miss Fleeson, Aug. 2, 1965).

57. E&P, Aug. 26, 1933, p. 30, Sept. 23, p. 24; Stockbridge, "A Question of Leadership," *The American Press*, LI (Sept., 1933), 1; "Editorial Union Evils," *Newsdom*, Sept. 9, 1933, p. 4.

58. E&P, Sept. 23, 1933, pp. 6, 37; E. N. Pomeroy to Broun, Sept. 21, 1933, Herman G. Nelson, secretary of the Rockford Editorial Employees Association, to Newspaper Guild of New York, Dec. 4, 1933, ANG; Stockbridge, "Professional Association or Trade Union," *The American Press*, LI (Sept., 1933), 1-2.

CHAPTER 3: ORGANIZATION

1. Eddy, "Gentlemen of the Press in Revolt," *Today*, II (Aug. 11, 1934), 2.

2. Case, "History of the Code," p. 8; E&P, Sept. 2, 1933, p. 35.

3. Robb, "Unions Call A.N.P.A. Code 'Inadequate to Effect NRA Purposes,' " E&P, Sept. 30, 1933, p. 5.

4. *Hearings on Code of Fair Practices and Competition Presented by Newspaper Publishing Industry*, NRA Series 44, Box 7175, pp. 1208-9, 1223.

5. *Ibid.*, pp. 1229-30.

6. Although they sent no representative, the Cleveland Plain Dealer Editorial Employees Association submitted a brief. It differed from the position taken by the other editorial employees' spokesmen mainly in that while asking for a forty-hour week, it left up to the individual publisher whether this would be a five- or six-day week. ("Petition from Plain Dealer Editorial Employees Association," NRA, Box 1934.)

7. Case, "History of the Code," pp. 11-12; *Hearings on Code*, pp. 1361-62, 1382-83. In his testimony Morrison referred (p. 1453) to an AFL local in Seattle, but that reference was probably an error. No mention at this time of these locals is to be found in either the AFL convention proceedings or Executive Council reports. Five years later Morrison provided a group putting together a historical survey of editorial workers unions with a complete list of AFL newswriters locals (including charter members, dates, and locations), and no mention was made of Seattle (NLRB, *Collective Bargaining*, p. 112). The The Secretary-Treasurer's office of the AFL-CIO searched its records and made inquiries among former union officials, but found no record of a Seattle newswriters' local extant in 1933 (letters from

Wesley Reedy, Mar. 4, 14, 23, 1966). For detail about the AFL locals, see p. 22 in Chapter 1. Harrison's career is reviewed in the Cleveland *Plain Dealer*, Apr. 3, 1938, p. A22.

8. NYT, Sept. 20, 1933, p. 8; interviews with White, Jan. 8, 1966, and L. Rogers, Sept. 14, 1965; Rogers to James Boylan, Jan. 25, 1960, Rogers papers.

9. *Hearings on Code*, pp. 1361-64.

10. *Ibid.*, pp. 1373-74; interview with L. Rogers, Sept. 14, 1965.

11. *Hearings on Code*, p. 1374.

12. *Ibid.*, pp. 1366-67.

13. *Ibid.*, pp. 1378-82.

14. *Ibid.*, pp. 1382-1414.

15. Moskin, "Origins of the American Newspaper Guild," p. 64.

16. *Hearings on Code*, p. 1389.

17. *Ibid.*, pp. 1424-27.

18. *Ibid.*, p. 1417.

19. *Ibid.*, pp. 1444-50.

20. *Ibid.*, pp. 1451-53.

21. Moskin, "Origins of the American Newspaper Guild," p. 57; Lindsay Rogers to James Boylan, Jan. 25, 1960, Rogers papers; Broun, "N.R.A. Set Up a Spring Board and It Worked," GR, Nov. 23, 1933, pp. 1-2; Dave Abramson to Heywood Broun, Sept. 22, 1933, ANG.

22. NYHT, Sept. 24, 1933, p. 2.

23. E&P, Aug. 26, 1933, pp. 3-4, Sept. 2, p. 16; Irwin Taubkin to Jonathan Eddy, Oct. 29, 1933, ANG; statement by Morris Ernst, transcript of conferences on the code, Oct. 31 and Nov. 1, 1933, New York, Boylan papers, p. 103; Evans, "Justice for the Reporter," p. 3; "Special NRA Bulletin from Pennsylvania Newspaper Publishers Association," Aug. 23, 1933 (in author's possession); "NRA Inquiries," Folders 2-11, 2-12, File 91-14, Hanson papers.

24. Against a background of Nazi suppression of the German press these fears may be more understandable, but too many of the publishers' spokesmen carried their defense to ridiculous extremes and thus weakened their position. Marlen Pew told a convention of the journalism fraternity Sigma Delta Chi, Oct. 14, 1933, that "newspapermen would be fools to sign away their rights. Why trifle with the eternal virtues?" (typescript of Pew speech, Pew folder, E&P library, New York), and Col. Robert McCormick, chairman of the ANPA Freedom of the Press Committee, told the New York State Chamber of Commerce, Nov. 16, 1933, that "the freedom of the press is the freedom of the American people. Circumstances have imposed upon

the publishers of America the holy duty to preserve that freedom and hand it down to posterity." (*The Case for the Freedom of the Press*, p. 2.)

25. Lee, *Daily Newspaper*, p. 249; Lippmann, *Interpretations*, p. 100. This column appeared Nov. 15, 1933; E&P, Oct. 7, 1933, p. 4, Oct. 14, p. 6, Nov. 4, p. 5, Nov. 15, p. 4, Nov. 25, p. 6; interview with L. Rogers, Sept 14, 1965; transcript of conferences on the code, Oct. 31 and Nov. 1, 1933, pp. 97-103; Emery, *ANPA*, p. 219; Bleyer, "Freedom of the Press," p. 22; Boylan, "Daily Newspaper Business," pp. 29-33; Ernest Gross, COHC, 293, 298.

26. Lee, *Daily Newspaper*, pp. 242-43; GR, Nov. 23, 1933, p. 1; E&P, Dec. 23, 1933, p. 34; Manning, "Provisions for Small Dailies in Code," E&P, Feb. 23, 1934, p. 9.

27. Unsigned memorandum of the meeting, Dec. 1, 1933, NRA, Box 1943; Hanson outlined in detail the publishers' position as well as some of the steps leading up to this meeting in testimony before the first NLRB (C-193 NLRB, NRC, pp. 18-22, 58-60, 135-44).

28. Howard Davis to NRA, Dec. 11, 1933, in NRA Document Series; Johnson quoted in NYT, Dec. 13, 1933, p. 2; Case, "History of the Code," pp. 13-14; NYHT, Dec. 24, 1933, p. 16.

29. NYT, Dec. 23, 1933, p. 6, E&P, Dec. 2, 1933, p. 4, Dec. 9, p. 12, Dec. 23, pp. 4, 34.

30. Jonathan Eddy to Hugh Johnson, Dec. 9, 1933, NRA, Box 1934; text of proposed newspaper code, E&P, Dec. 23, 1933, pp. 4, 34.

31. Memorandum on the code, OF466, NRA Codes, N, 1933-35, FDRL. Although undated and unsigned it is possible from the text to be certain that the writer was a newsman and that the analysis was written about the middle of December.

32. Text of proposed newspaper code, E&P, Dec. 23, 1933; Case, "History of the Code," p. 2; "Newspapers and the N.R.A.," Chapter 17, p. 8.

33. Eddy, "City Guilds Unite in National Body Dec. 15 at Capital," GR, Nov. 23, 1933, p. 1; E&P, Dec. 9, 1933, p. 32.

34. Gilfillan, "The ANG—An Idea That Worked," GR, Jan. 9, 1959, p. 5; letter from A. L. Roberts, *Newsdom*, Sept. 23, 1933, p. 4; Marshall and Willy, "History and Organization and Chronology of Adoption of Policies of Detroit Newspaper Industrial Credit Union," p. 5; interview with Ralph Novak, a former ANG and Detroit Newspaper Guild officer, June 12, 1965; Russ Wilson to Newspaper Guild of New York, Dec. 4, 1933, ANG; McConnell, "Buffalo Press Club's Obituary with Notes on Its Guild Successor," GR, Apr., 1934, p. 6.

35. Committee, Twin Cities Guild of Newspaper Workers to Heywood Broun, Sept. 24, 1933, ANG.

36. Newspaper Guild of Cincinnati to Jonathan Eddy, Oct. 31, 1933, Nathan Goldberg to Eddy, Nov. 19, Rupert Fuller to Eddy, Dec. 13, ANG; E&P, Oct. 24, 1933, p. 14, Dec. 16, p. 6, Dec. 23, p. 28; Baxter, "Newspaper Women and the Guild," *The Matrix*, XIX (Feb. 1934), 3.

37. By contrast, after long years of successful unionism the mechanical workers' unions in all the paper, printing, publishing, and allied industries had organized only about 30.8 percent of that work force by 1933. (Wolman, *Trade Unionism*, p. 226.)

38. Ernest L. Meyer quoted in E&P, Aug. 12, 1933, p. 36; Ashley Greene to Jonathan Eddy, Dec. 4, 1933; Bruce Grant and Francis Healy to Eddy, Dec. 8, 1933, Irwin S. Taubkin to Eddy, Oct. 29, 1933, ANG.

39. Ashcraft, "Dues and Professionalism Were Early Guild Issues," GR, Dec. 25, 1953, p. 4; Donald Willard quoted in Lovell, Jr., "Historical Study of the American Newspaper Guild Particularly as Exemplified in Boston," p. 68; Harry A. Visel to NRA complaint committee, Newark, N.J., Oct. 17, 1933 (copy), ANG; interview with Miss Fleeson, Aug. 2, 1965; E&P, Nov. 4, 1933, p. 20.

40. E&P, Dec. 9, 1933, p. 32; Cole, "Guild Idea Praised by Blumenfeld," E&P, LXVI (Dec. 17, 1933), 5; *Ibid.*, p. 34; "The Newspaper Guilds," *The American Press*, LII (Nov., 1933), 4; "Reporters and Labor Unions," *Publishers Service Magazine*, IV (Oct. 19, 1933), 1-2; Robins letter headed "Opposes Union Idea" appeared in E&P, Oct. 7, 1933, p. 38.

41. Harris, "U.S. Press Facing Its Greatest Crisis," E&P, Oct. 21, 1933, p. 9; Harvey J. Kelly to Elisha Hanson, Nov. 21, 1933, "Code Authority," Folder 2-22, File 91-27, Hanson papers.

42. E&P, Oct. 7, 1933, p. 38.

43. Heywood Broun to Robert Bordner, Oct. 14, 1933, letter in Bordner's possession.

44. "Editorial Men Form Guild in Duluth," E&P, Nov. 18, 1933, p. 8.

45. Interviews with Britt, July 12, 1965, Eddy, Aug. 15, 1965, Ernst, May 18, 1966, Watson, May 17, 1966; former NYT reporter Louis Gnaedinger, Dec. 12, 1965, and one-time International News Service correspondent and New York Guild executive committee member Luther Huston, May, 17, 1966, also contributed information about the early New York Guild. For details of the Cleveland split, see pp. 53-55 in Chapter 2.

46. E&P, Sept. 30, 1933, p. 8, Oct. 7, p. 10, Oct. 21, p. 14; Jonathan

Eddy to John Keefe, temporary secretary of the Editorial Workers' Guild of Duluth, Oct. 12, 1933, ANG; "The Newspaper Guild of New York, What It Is . . . Why It Is and Other Salient Facts," (pamphlet issued in Apr., 1954, in author's possession), pp. 3-4.

47. Articles II and IV of the constitution of the Newspaper Guild of New York, quoted in "How the N.Y. Guild Drafted and Adopted Its Constitution," GR, Nov. 23, 1933, pp. 1-2.

48. Heywood Broun to Robert Bordner, Oct. 15, 1933, letter in Bordner's possession; the anonymous author of "How the New York Guild Drafted and Adopted Its Constitution."

49. E&P, Nov. 18, 1933, p. 13.

50. Interviews with Eddy, Aug. 15, 1965, Huston, May 17, 1966, and Gnaedinger, Dec. 12, 1965; "Code Dispute," *Newsweek*, III (June 23, 1934), 34; Eddy to G. B. Wollan, Oct. 12, 1933, ANG; Gilfillan, "The ANG."

51. Robert Bordner to Heywood Broun, Oct. 12, 1933; Edward Burks to Broun, Sept. 19, 1933, ANG.

52. "Statement by the Guild of New York Newspaper Men and Women," Sept. 20, 1933, NRA, Box 1934; Jonathan Eddy to Edward Burks, Oct. 17, 1933, ANG.

53. Jonathan Eddy to Robert Bordner, Oct. 15, 1933, ANG.

54. Minutes of the meeting, Oct. 17, 1933, minutes of the executive committee, Oct. 20, 1933, CNG; Carl Costello to Jonathan Eddy, Oct. 23, 1933, ANG.

55. Jonathan Eddy to Nathan Goldberg, Oct. 25, 1933, ANG.

56. Interview with Lindsay Rogers, Sept. 14, 1965; Jonathan Eddy to A. L. Roberts, Oct. 26, 1933, Eddy to Frank Rising, Oct. 26, 1933, ANG.

57. E&P, Nov. 4, 1933, p. 7; Jonathan Eddy to Louis Stark, Nov. 7, 1933, ANG; Eddy, "City Guilds Unite in National Body Dec. 15 at Capital."

58. Eddy, "Guild Idea Spreads as Delegates Face Toward Washington," GR, Dec. 8, 1933, p. 1; "In the New York Guild," *Ibid.*, p. 2.

59. Jonathan Eddy to John J. Givney, Nov. 24, 1933, William J. Kirby to Newspaper Guild of New York, Dec. 6, 1933, ANG.

60. Letter from Emmet Crozier on the 1933 meeting, Sept. 13, 1965, p. 2 (hereafter referred to as Crozier, 9/13/65), letter from Jonathan Eddy to H. B. Slocum, Dec. 12, 1933, ANG.

61. George W. Lofton to Robert Bordner, Dec. 12, 1933, H. Richmond Campbell, chairman of Yonkers Guild, to Jonathan Eddy, Dec. 14, 1933, W. E. Keys, *Express*, Cliff Potter, *San Antonio Light*, and

Ben Baines, *News,* to Eddy, Dec. 14, 1933, ANG; Eddy, "Gentlemen of the Press in Revolt."

62. "Proposed Constitution for the American Newspaper Guild," Article 10, Section I, draft of proposed set-up for a national organization, submitted by the Newspaper Guild of New York, Kenen papers; Huston, " 'Professional' Idea Lost in Guild," E&P, Jan. 3, 1959, p. 10; Crozier, 9/13/65, pp. 3-4; Kenen to Beals, pp. 15-16; ANG Proceedings, 1933, p. 1; interview with Gilfillan, May 18, 1966; R. Mann, "National Guild Asks Five-Day Week"; text of constitution is in E&P, Dec. 23, 1933, pp. 6, 77.

63. After a long interval of silence, events had moved rapidly. On Dec. 7 Eddy had wired a select few: "ROOSEVELT IS RECEIVING A FEW NEWSPAPERMEN TO DISCUSS NEWSPAPER PROBLEMS . . . CAN YOU ARRANGE TO STAND BY AND GET LEAVE TO GO TO WASHINGTON ON VERY BRIEF NOTICE. . . . (Eddy to Andrew Parker, Dec. 7, 1933, ANG.) The next day Eddy wired: "PRESIDENT WANTS TO SEE YOU FIVE FIFTEEN P.M. MONDAY. . . . (Eddy to Parker, Dec. 8, 1933, ANG.)

64. Ernest Lindley to Heywood Broun, Oct. 16, 1933, ANG; Memo: Jonathan Eddy to Lindsay Rogers, Dec. 13 or 14, 1933, Rogers papers; NYT, Dec. 12, 1933, p. 2; White, "What the Guild Told Roosevelt at a Tea Party," GR, Jan. 12, 1934, pp. 1, 3; "Report of the Delegates to ANG Meeting," Dec. 15, 1933, TCNG.

65. Interview with Bordner, June 14, 1965; "Report of the Delegates to ANG Meeting," TCNG; Johnson quoted in NYT, Dec. 16, 1933, p. 15.

66. ANG Proceedings, 1933, p. 1. That same day Roosevelt had suggested to Johnson that the press associations might voluntarily agree to conform to a code. Johnson believed they should, but his reaction to Watson's proposal was that the law did not provide for employees submitting a code. (E&P, Dec. 23, 1933, p. 28.)

67. Crozier, 9/13/65, p. 4; R. Mann, "National Guild Asks Five-Day Week"; ANG Proceedings, 1933, pp. 1-2.

68. Interviews with Eddy, Aug. 15, 1965, Gilfillan, May 18, 1966, and White, Oct. 27, 1965; Crozier, 9/13/65, p. 5.

69. This account is based on interviews with Eddy, Aug. 15, 1965, Gilfillan, May 18, 1966, Kenen, Aug. 15, 1965, L. Rogers, Sept. 14, 1965, and Watson, May 17, 1966; Crozier, 9/13/65, pp. 5-6; Kenen to Beals, p. 16; Heywood Broun to Hugh Johnson, Jan. 5, 1934, ANG.

70. Memorandum from Lindsay Rogers to Hugh Johnson, Dec. 14, 1933, Rogers papers.

71. Lloyd White to Heywood Broun, Dec. 31, 1933, ANG, attempts to recount verbatim a three-way conversation of White, Ernst, and Rogers wherein the last expressed forcefully and in detail his views that affiliation "would be a great mistake, a calamity which would kill off the organization, so it would never amount to anything."

72. Lindsay Rogers to Raymond Moley, Jan. 19, 1934, Rogers papers; Jonathan Eddy to Rogers, Dec. 13 or 14, 1933, Rogers papers; interview with Rogers, Sept. 14, 1965.

73. Crozier, 9/13/65, p. 6; ANG Proceedings, 1933, p. 2; Heywood Broun to Hugh Johnson, Jan. 5, 1934, ANG; letter from Morris Watson, Dec. 2, 1965.

74. Strouse, "25th Anniversary Notes"; Crozier, 9/13/65, p. 7; Fleeson, "Our Guild," p. 15; ANG Proceedings, 1933, p. 2.

CHAPTER 4: FROM MEETING TO CONVENTION: THE FIRST SEVEN MONTHS

1. E&P, Dec. 23, 1933, p. 22.

2. The text of the constitution is in E&P, Dec. 23, 1933, pp. 6, 26.

3. Burns, "Daily Newspapers," p. 110; Broun quoted in R. Mann, "National Guild Asks Five-Day Week," p. 7.

4. Quoted in Lissner, "National Convention at St. Paul June 5 to Plan Bargaining," GR, May, 1934, p. 1.

5. In his column on the ANG's founding meeting Broun wrote: "At the present time a very large majority of the Guild membership is against any sort of affiliation." (NYWT, Dec. 19, 1933, p. 21.)

6. Minutes of the Executive Committee Meeting, Dec. 15, 1933, ANG; Crozier, 9/13/65, pp. 9-11; Broun quoted in R. Mann, "National Guild Asks Five-Day Week," p. 7.

7. Resolutions quoted in R. Mann, "National Guild Asks Five-Day Week," p. 28; interview with Bordner, Sept. 15, 1965, who had brought the Akron group's application to the Washington meeting; Crozier, 9/13/65, p. 9.

8. Letter from Morris Watson, Dec. 2, 1965.

9. Curtis R. West to Jonathan Eddy, Jan. 8, 1934, ANG.

10. Memorandum on the meeting of the Finance and Organization Committees, Dec. 15, 1933, G. B. Wollan to Heywood Broun, Mar. 26, 1934, ANG.

11. Jonathan Eddy to Andrew Parker, Dec. 22, 1933, Eddy to Lloyd White, Dec. 21 and 26, 1933, Emmet Crozier to William F. Gould,

secretary of the St. Louis Guild, Mar. 21, 1934, Morris Watson to Eddy, Mar. 15, 1934, ANG.

12. According to a report by the New York Guild's treasurer, receipts for Nov.-Dec., 1933 (including a loan of $100 from Broun) were $1,833.00 and disbursements were $1,615.57. (Treasurer's Report to the Members of the Newspaper Guild of New York, Jan. 31, 1934, ANG.)

13. E&P, Dec. 30, 1933, p. 6; Jonathan Eddy to R. S. Gilfillan, Jan. 15, 1934, Eddy to G. B. Wollan, Jan. 11, 1934, ANG.

14. R. W. Howard and E. B. Winterstein to Jonathan Eddy, Dec. 19, 1933; Eddy to H. E. Lichsholm and Eric Tyler, Dec. 21, Eddy to Charles Willoughby of the Albany *Times-Union,* Dec. 26, Eddy to W. J. Monahan of Troy, N.Y., Jan. 8, 1934, ANG; GR, Feb. 17, 1934, p. 2.

15. Robert L. Perry to Jonathan Eddy, Jan. 1, 1934, ANG.

16. Jonathan Eddy to North Carolina Newspapermen (mimeo. statement), c. April, 1934, ANG. Often such statements sent to one city (e.g., Des Moines) giving step-by-step procedure would be used again: an Elizabeth, N.J., newsman received a letter saying that the Des Moines statement also covered the situation in Elizabeth (Eddy to Des Moines Newspapermen, Feb. 5, 1934, Eddy to J. W. Adams, Mar. 9, ANG).

17. Jonathan Eddy to J. W. Adams, Mar. 9, 1934, Eddy to R. S. Gilfillan, Feb. 5, 1934, ANG.

18. Emmet Crozier to Guild Officers, Mar. 3, 1934, ANG; E&P, Dec. 23, 1933, p. 8, Jan. 27, 1934, p. 4, Feb. 3, p. 41, Feb. 10, p. 12, Feb. 17, p. 27, Feb. 24, p. 12.

19. Donald Pond to Heywood Broun, Jan. 22, 1934, Thomas R. Nevitt to Emmet Crozier, Jan. 16, 1934, ANG.

20. NYT, Dec. 24, 1933, p. 16; E&P, Jan. 6, 1934, Jan. 13, p. 6, Feb. 17, p. 6; Doris Fleeson to Jonathan Eddy, Jan. 28, 1934, ANG.

21. Jonathan Eddy to Lloyd White, Jan. 16, 1934, Paul C. French, president of the Newspaper Guild of Philadelphia and Camden, to Eddy, Jan. 20, 1934, ANG; E&P, Jan. 13, 1934, p. 14, Feb. 3, p. 10.

22. Alfred Segal to Jonathan Eddy, Jan. 5, 1934, R. S. Gilfillan to Eddy, Jan. 31, 1934, ANG.

23. The stubborn Johnson, after learning of the New York Guild's resolutions, promoted Pulitzer to divisional administrator. He had known almost nothing about Pulitzer before appointing him, but he would not immediately accept his resignation, for the General resented interference with his plans. Pulitzer refused to change his

mind. (Boylan, "Daily Newspaper Business," pp. 48-49; NYT, Feb. 3, 1934, p. 4, Feb. 4, p. 32.)

24. E&P, Jan. 20, 1934, p. 4, Feb. 3, p. 10; Eddy, "Unity Awakens Stouter Spirit in Journalists," GR, Feb. 23, 1934, pp. 1, 7; mimeo. statement by Heywood Broun, Jan. 23, 1934, Eddy to Newspaper Guilds and Executive Committees, Jan. 30, 1934, Edward Burks to Eddy, Feb. 5, 1934, Doris Fleeson to Eddy, Jan. 28, 1934, Eddy to R. S. Gilfillan, Feb. 3, 1934, ANG.

25. Executive Order, and Franklin D. Roosevelt to Hugh Johnson, Feb. 17, 1934, in "Code of Fair Competition for the Daily Newspaper Publishing Business," pp. 69-71, Exhibit O in Case, "History of the Code"; Perry, "Five-Day Week O.K. Publishers Say," E&P, Feb. 24, 1934, p. 8; Manning, "President's Approval of Dailies' Code Raises New Questions for Publishers," *Ibid.*, p. 3.

26. GR, Feb. 23, 1934, pp. 1, 3; E&P, Mar. 10, 1934, pp. 12, 35; Jonathan Eddy to D. A. de Souza, president of the Washington Newspaper Guild, Feb. 20, 1934, Thomas R. Nevitt to Eddy, Feb. 24, 1934, Eddy to Fellow Guild Officers, Local and National, Feb. 28, 1934, ANG.

27. D. A. de Souza to Jonathan Eddy, Mar. 9, 1934, Eddy to Lloyd White, Mar. 1, 1934, Eddy to Guild Officers, Mar. 12, 1934, Eddy to A. Judson Evans, Mar. 27, 1934, Eddy to J. W. Haas, secretary of the CNG, Mar. 28, 1934, ANG.

28. Broun, "Jonathan Eddy's Credentials," GR, May, 1934, pp. 1, 7; interview with Eddy, Aug. 15, 1965.

29. Stern claims as apocryphal the story current at the time that Parker, chairman of the guild negotiating committee, and he played a game of chess to decide whether a vacation clause would be included in the contract. (Stern, *Memoirs*, p. 186.)

30. French, "Guild Negotiates Initial Contract," GR, May, 1934, pp. 1, 9; Parker, "Philadelphia Record Signs Agreement with Newspaper Guild Unit," E&P, Apr. 14, 1934, pp. 5, 46; Wharton, "J. David Stern," *Scribner's*, C (Dec., 1936), 44-49; J. David Stern, COHC, 63; Lee, *Daily Newspaper*, p. 682. The text of the *Record* contract is in E&P, Apr. 14, 1934, pp. 20, 24.

31. Andrew M. Parker to Jonathan Eddy, Mar. 19, 1934, ANG.

32. Eddy quoted in French, "Guild Negotiates Initial Contract," p. 9.

33. Anderson, "Mr. Anderson in a Tender Mood," *Nation*, CXXXVIII (Apr. 18, 1934), 443; Paul Frederickson, secretary of the New York Guild, to Franklin D. Roosevelt, Apr. 10, 1934, OF466,

NRA Codes, N, 1933-35, FDRL; Bulletin Board Statement (copy), Mar. 22, 1934, ANG.

34. F. von Falkenberg to Franklin D. Roosevelt, Nov. 18, 1934, J. F. Rottermel to Hugh Johnson, Apr. 4, 1934, NRA, Box 1937.

35. Robert L. Huston to Murray Neal, Mar. 26, 1934, NRA, Series 25, Box 1936. Insensitivity marks some of these bureaucrats. A bitter letter from B. F. James to the President, Nov. 10, 1934, about the inadequacies of the code and the ignominy of being supported by his wife has a note attached: "Shall I tell him he's lucky to have a wife to support him. . . ." (NRA, Box 1937.)

36. Perry, "Dailies Come Under Blue Eagle Aegis as President Clarifies Freedom Stand," E&P, Mar. 3, 1934, pp. 4-5; "Amendments to Codes of Fair Competition for the Graphic Arts Industry and the Daily Newspaper Publishing Business," p. 2, Exhibit IV in Case, "History of the Code"; Ernest Lindley to Stephen Early, the President's press secretary, Apr. 19, 1934, OF466, NRA Codes, N, 1933-35, FDRL.

37. E&P, May 5, 1934, pp. 10-11, 37-38; "Statement Submitted at the Newspaper Code Authority Hearing, Apr. 30, at the Waldorf-Astoria, New York City, by Jonathan Eddy, Executive Secretary of the American Newspaper Guild," ANG.

38. Both ANPA surveys covered more than 15,000 employees; the less than comprehensive ANG data which the NRA's research division collated covered about 2,500; the BLS samplings covered only about 1,500. (David J. Brown, "Wages and Hours of Editorial Employees," comparison of surveys for the NRA, Jan. 15, 1935, NRA, Box 1937.)

39. Solomon Barkin to Robert Buck, May 1, 1934, NRA, Box 1936; Case, "History of the Code," pp. 32-33; NYT, May 19, 1934, p. 4; Mac Dougall, *Newsroom Problems*, pp. 573-74.

40. "Jurisdiction in Labor Cases," ANPA *Bulletin*, XLVIII (Apr. 12, 1934), 171; Boylan, "Daily Newspaper Business," p. 68; Judge Robert Nevin quoted in "Newspaper Industrial Board, March 5, 1935," NRA, Box 1937; "The Publishers Crack Down," *New Republic*, LXXXI (Feb. 6, 1935), 248; Jonathan Eddy to Guild Officers, May 1, 1934, ANG.

41. Eddy quoted in Scribner, "Newswriters Versus the NRA," *New Republic*, LXXIX (July 4, 1934), 201; there is a lengthy account of the negotiations to put an ANG representative on the NIB in the ascerbic report Buck presented to the June convention: Buck, "Report to the Convention of the American Newspaper Guild," GR, June 15, 1934,

pp. 5-6; Jonathan Eddy to Heywood Broun, Apr. 13, 1934, ANG; Hugh Johnson to Franklin D. Roosevelt, Apr. 20, 1934, and George Buckley to Donald Richberg, May 5, 1934, NRA, Box 1937; Boylan, "Daily Newspaper Business," p. 74; Elisha Hanson letter, "Correspondence," *New Republic*, LXXX (Sept. 26, 1934), 185-86 (answering the Scribner article); Hanson to Cranston Williams, July 6, 1934, Folder 2-24, File 91-30, "Code Authority," Hanson papers; "Newspapers and the N.R.A.," Chapter 15, pp. 2-5; E&P, May 5, 1934, p. 38, June 16, p. 6; Eddy to Hugh Johnson, NRA, Box 1937; NLRB, *Collective Bargaining*, p. 147.

42. Crozier, "Notes on the Early History of the American Newspaper Guild for Daniel J. Leab," p. 6.

43. Hugh Johnson to Franklin D. Roosevelt, Feb. 16, 1934, in "Code of Fair Competition for the Daily Newspaper Publishing Business," p. 76, Exhibit O in Case, "History of the Code." Although written earlier, the letter was released when the code was promulgated and was dated accordingly.

44. E&P, Apr. 14, 1934, p. 14, May 19, p. 6; Harvey J. Kelly, chairman of the committee, to the Publisher Addressed (copy), May 15, 1934, ANG.

45. E&P, Jan. 27, 1934, p. 4, Feb. 10, p. 26; Jonathan Eddy to Jean Whitaker, secretary of the Dayton Guild, Mar. 21, 1934, ANG.

46. "Remembrances of Francis Jamieson," COHC, p. 70; Quinn, *San Francisco-Oakland Newspaper Guild*, pp. 26, 30.

47. Quinn, *San Francisco-Oakland Newspaper Guild*, pp. 26, 30; E&P, Mar. 31, 1934, p. 9; "Only Journalism School of Its Kind," *Publishers Auxiliary*, LXIX (Dec. 29, 1934), 1; Lee, *Daily Newspaper*, p. 683; letter from Lloyd White, July 20, 1966; Boylan, "The Daily Newspaper Business," p. 72; GR, June 15, 1934, pp. 1, 7.

48. Girardin, "Little Hope for Guild, Detroit 25 Years Ago," in *Detroit Page One Ball Annual Yearbook*, 1959, p. 10; GR, May 1934, p. 2; John Janett to Jonathan Eddy, May 27, 1934, Gerard B. Dobbon, secretary-treasurer of the Muskegon Guild, to Eddy, May 21, 1934, ANG.

49. Lewis, "To the Left? Or Right?" GR, May, 1934, p. 5.

50. Jonathan Eddy to Heywood Broun, May 12, 1934, ANG; GR, June, 1934, pp. 1, 11.

51. Garland Ashcraft to Jonathan Eddy, July 11, 1934, Union Audit Bureau to the American Newspaper Guild, Sept. 25, 1934, Emmet Crozier to Andrew M. Parker, May 24, 1934, ANG; Financial statements in ANG files.

52. Morris Watson to Emmet Crozier, May 4, 1934, Watson to Crozier, May 7, 1934, promissory note signed by Allen Raymond and Watson, May 7, 1934, ANG; interviews with Watson, July 6, 1966, and Crozier, July 12, 1966.

53. For the convention, see NYHT, June 6, 1934, p. 15, June 7, p. 6, June 8, p. 7; Brandenburg, "Guild Starts Drive to Oust Buckley, E&P, June 9, 1934, pp. 7, 41; GR, June 15, 1934; ANG Proceedings, 1934; interviews with Crozier, Gilfillan, Watson, and White, Aug. 14, 1966; Draft Report of the Executive Secretary to the 1935 ANG Convention (hereafter referred to as Draft Report), Report of Convention Delegate to Current and Eligible Members of Des Moines Newspaper Guild, June 30, 1935, ANG.

54. Session of June 7, 4:15 p.m., p. 4, ANG Proceedings, 1934; Lee, *Daily Newspaper*, p. 687.

55. The text of the constitution is in E&P, June 16, 1934, p. 42.

56. Article IX in *Ibid*.

57. Quoted in GR, June 15, 1934, p. 1.

58. *Ibid*.

59. Crozier, "Notes on Early History," p. 1.

60. Session of June 7, 4:15 p.m., p. 6, ANG Proceedings, 1934.

61. Draft Report.

62. Session of June 5, morning, pp. 10-11, ANG Proceedings, 1934; Burgess quoted in Brandenburg, "Guild Starts Drive to Oust Buckley," p. 14; "Newspaper Guild," *Newsweek*, III (June 16, 1934), 29.

63. Session of June 5, afternoon, p. 2, ANG Proceedings, 1934. Burgess also had received job offers from the Federal Government and from Minnesota's Governor, Floyd Olson, who had welcomed the ANG to St. Paul with radical rhetoric. Burgess chose to accept a position with the Federal Government.

64. The bill proposed by Ernest Lundeen (D-Minn.) would have paid unemployed workers their full wages as long as they were out of work. The Federal funds necessary for this would come supposedly from sums appropriated for defense purposes and from taxation on all incomes over $2,500.00.

65. Minutes of the General Membership Meeting, June 19, 1934, CNG.

CHAPTER 5: TOWARD THE PICKET LINE . . .

1. Jonathan Eddy to Garland Ashcraft, July 9, 1934, Emmet Crozier to W. Allen, president of the Grand Forks, N.D., Newspaper

Guild, June 15, 1934, statement of June-July Dues Payments by Local Guilds as of July 31, 1934, ANG; Draft Report, p. 6. Dues payments to the ANG for June and July eventually totaled $2,315.00 when a number of local groups overcame difficulties in making collections and forwarded their payments for those months in August and later.

2. Jonathan Eddy to Ralph Holmes, president of the Detroit Guild, Aug. 31, 1934, ANG; minutes of the CNG Executive Committee, July 29, 1934, CNG.

3. In the case of the Mooney resolution, for example, Eddy found it necessary to reassure them that "perhaps we were wrong in proclaiming our feelings. . . ." (Eddy to Winston Phelps, June 15, 1934, ANG.)

4. E. C. Eyler to Eddy, Oct. 2, 1934, Prescott to Paul C. French, Region III vice president, July 18, 1934, ANG; for strikes against Newhouse, see below, pp. 137-42, 144-47.

5. Miller quoted in E&P, June 23, 1934, p. 5; Walter Lyon, editor of the Binghamton, N.Y., *Sun*, quoted in S. M. Cavanaugh, president of the Binghamton Guild, to Jonathan Eddy, Aug. 25, 1934, Brooks Hays to Eddy, Aug. 30, 1934, ANG. The editor of the *Arkansas Gazette* wrote Eddy that "I told our city editor we should prefer that our men should not enter the Guild." The editor said that he did not consider this theatening or intimidating. (J. N. Heiskell to Eddy, Aug. 8, 1934, ANG.)

6. Pew firmly believed that if the ANG adopted Broun's policies, "the Jeffersonian tradition in American newspaper life would die." (O'Dell, "Fighting Editor," p. 157.)

7. Financial data in author's possession; Jonathan Eddy to Garland Ashcraft, July 9, 1934, Ashcraft to Eddy, Sept. 3, 1934, Eddy to Local Guild Officers (mimeo.), Sept. 8, 1934, Eddy to William Davy, executive secretary of the CNG, July 16, 1934, Eddy to G. B. Wollan, TCNG secretary-treasurer, Sept. 13, 1934, ANG.

8. E&P, July 14, 1934, p. 8.

9. "The Inside Story," *The Guild Journal*, July 16, 1934, p. 1; interviews with Samuel H. Friedman, one-time Socialist candidate for Vice President of the United States, who worked for the *Press* in 1933, July 20, 1967, and with Hochstein, July 20, 1967.

10. E&P, July 21, 1934, pp. 5, 30; interviews with Hochstein, July 20, 1967, and Knowles, July 19, 1967; Newspaper Guild of New York to Members of the Newspaper Guild of New York (mimeo.), July 10, 1934, ANG.

11. Hochstein quoted in *The Guild Journal*, July 16, 1934, p. 1; interviews with Hochstein, July 20, 1967, and Knowles, July 19, 1967.

12. *The Guild Journal*, July 16, 1934, p. 1; Randau quoted in E&P, July 14, 1934, p. 8; Jonathan Eddy to William Davy, July 16, 1934, ANG.

13. NYT, July 13, 1934, p. 11; guild newspaper quoted in E&P, July 21, 1934, p. 30; Hochstein quoted in ANPA *Bulletin*, July 27, 1934, p. 442.

14. Interviews with Knowles, July 19, 1967, and Widick, Aug. 1, 1965; Garland Ashcraft to Jonathan Eddy, Sept. 8, 1934, Philip Hochstein to Heywood Broun, Aug. 10, 1934, ANG; NYHT, July 13, 1934, p. 4.

15. NYT, July 14, 1934, p. 11, July 15, p. 2; the agreement is in NYHT, July 15, 1934, p. 9; letter from Clayton Knowles, Feb. 13, 1968.

16. NYHT, July 15, 1934, p. 9; NYT, July 21, 1934, p. 11; E&P, July 28, 1934, p. 9; interview with Knowles, July 19, 1967; Jonathan Eddy to William Davy, July 16, 1934, ANG; Walker, *City Editor*, p. 16.

17. E&P, July 14, 1934, p. 8, July 28, p. 9; Aug. 4, p. 10, Sept. 1, p. 39, Sept. 15, p. 11; GR, Sept., 1934, pp. 1-3; E. W. Preston, general manager of the *Herald* and the *Traveler*, to David Frederick, president of the Boston Guild, Aug. 14, 1934, Jonathan Eddy to Garland Ashcraft, Sept. 14, 1934, ANG.

18. NYT, Aug. 30, 1934, p. 19, Dec. 22, 1935, p. 5; E&P, Sept. 1, 1934, pp. 5, 39, Jan. 19, 1935, p. 12; interview with Iueshewitz, Sept. 29, 1967; GR, Sept., 1934, pp. 1-2, Feb. 1, 1935, pp. 1, 7. The text of the first agreement is in E&P, Sept. 8, 1934, p. 9.

19. "The Advance Strike," in "Guild Strikes—1934-1951," (typewritten history of ANG strikes), ANG.

20. Material supplied by Crosby to Greenbaum, Wolff, and Ernst so that the firm might draw up a statement for presentation to the NIB, Crosby v. *Staten Island Advance*: complaint folder, and Norman Newhouse to Paul Fredericksen, secretary of the New York Newspaper Guild, Aug. 10, 1934, Crosby v. *Staten Island Advance*: evidence folder, Ernst papers; Carl Randau quoted in E&P, July 21, 1934, p. 30; Crosby quoted by Heywood Broun, "An Army with Banners," *Nation*, CXL (Feb. 2, 1935), 184; interview with Alexander Crosby, July 30, 1964.

21. E&P, Aug. 18, 1934, p. 4; GR, Aug., 1934, p. 1, Sept., p. 5; *Staten Island Advance*, Aug. 16, 1934, p. 1.

22. Joseph, "The Strange Case of Alexander Crosby"; *Staten Island Advance*, Aug. 25, 1934, p. 2.

23. NYT, Aug. 28, 1934, p. 3; E&P, Nov. 3, 1934, p. 16, Dec. 22, p. 12; Crosby material in Ernst papers; GR, Oct. 1, 1934, p. 8, Nov. 15, p. 3, Feb. 1, 1935, p. 3.

24. Letter from Alexander Crosby, Oct. 11, 1965; Eddy quoted in Seldes, *Freedom of the Press*, p. 325; William Green to William Mahoney (copy), Aug. 25, 1935, ANG; NYT, Sept. 6, 1934, p. 2, Sept. 15, p. 8.

25. E&P, Sept. 15, 1934, p. 24; Draft Report, p. 6.

26. Jonathan Eddy to Garland Ashcraft, Sept. 18, 1934, ANG.

27. Jonathan Eddy to G. B. Wollan, Sept. 13, 1934, Eddy to David Fredericks, Sept. 28, 1934, Eddy to National Executive Committee, Oct., 1934, Eddy to Julius M. Klein, Nov. 7, 1934, Paul C. French to Erle Homan, president of the Bucks County Newspaper Guild, Nov. 26, 1934, ANG.

28. Hyde, "Company Unionism," GR, Sept., 1934, pp. 6-7; Jonathan Eddy to Louis Greene, TCNG contracts committee secretary, July 29, 1934, ANG.

29. Daniel Latus to Jonathan Eddy, Oct. 4, 1934, Harold Taylor, secretary of the Akron Guild, to Heywood Broun, Oct. 26, 1934, Brevard Stephenson to Eddy, Nov. 6, 1934, ANG; Quinn, *San Francisco-Oakland Newspaper Guild*, p. 25.

30. Jonathan Eddy to W. D. Wolfe, Oct. 23, 1934, ANG; Draft Report, pp. 11-12.

31. E&P, Sept. 22, 1934, p. 10; GR, Oct. 1, 1934, p. 3; K. R. Kennedy to Jonathan Eddy, Oct. 18, 1934, Eddy to Daniel Mich, Oct. 16, 1934, H. D. Linton to Eddy, Nov. 7, 1934, ANG.

32. GR, Oct., 1934, pp. 1, 3; the results of the poll and comments by the participants are contained in *Ibid.*, Nov. 1, 1934, pp. 1, 3; letter from H. T. Meek, *Post-Dispatch* chapter, *Ibid.*, p. 5; E&P, Oct. 6, 1934, p. 24; Curtis D. MacDougall, secretary-treasurer of the St. Louis Newspaper Guild, to Jonathan Eddy, Oct. 6, 1934, Wayne Parker to Eddy, Sept. 25, 1934, Eddy to Curtis D. MacDougall, Oct. 9, 1934, ANG.

33. Letters from Don Stevens and Robert Buck, GR, Nov. 1, 1934, p. 5; Executive Committee to GR Editor, Apr. 3, 1935, ANG.

34. Broun, "Too Much Is Enough, Says Broun," GR, Nov. 15, 1934, p. 3; E&P, Oct. 20, 1934, p. 44. The death of his first wife a month earlier may have influenced his decision; although divorced, they had remained close, and her death greatly saddened him (Kramer, *Heywood Broun*, pp. 258-59).

35. GR, Nov. 15, 1934, pp. 1, 3; E&P, Oct. 20, 1934, p. 22, Nov. 3,

p. 16; interview with Ernst, Oct. 8, 1965; Roger Butterfield to Heywood Broun, Oct. 21, 1934, ANG.

36. Elisha Hanson to J. R. Knowland, Dec. 6, 1934, Folder 2-28, File 91-36, Harvey Kelly to Hanson, Oct. 20, 1934, *Ibid.*, Hanson papers; Kelly quoted in Emery, *ANPA*, p. 187.

37. NLRB, *Collective Bargaining*, p. 120; Draft Report, p. 7.

38. A story, possibly apocryphal, has him returning from vacation, drawing an imaginary line down the middle of the city room, and firing everybody on one side. (GR, Dec. 15, 1934, p. 3.)

39. GR, Dec. 1, 1934, p. 2; interview with Berlinrut, former Newark Guild executive committee member, Aug. 21, 1967; E&P, Nov. 24, 1934, p. 44. A guildsman estimated that Russell had fired sixteen managing editors, society editors, and hundreds of reporters in the preceding dozen years (GR, Dec. 15, 1934, p. 3).

40. GR, Nov. 15, 1934, p. 6.

41. Lee, *Daily Newspaper*, p. 688; copy of Russell statements of Nov. 1 and 10, 1934, ANG.

42. Crozier says Eddy and others from the New York Guild insisted for tactical reasons that the initial statement announcing the reasons for the strike declare all eight were dismissed for guild activities. He recalls that at least two of the fired joined the guild that afternoon (letter from Crozier, Oct. 10, 1967).

43. E&P, Nov. 17, 1934, p. 6; GR, Dec. 1, 1934, pp. 1-3; Pasche, "Strength of Guild and Its Right to Bargain Tested Successfully," GR, Apr. 15, 1935, pp. 1-2.

44. Crozier, "Notes on the Newark Ledger Strike for Daniel J. Leab," pp. 2-3.

45. Interview with Berlinrut, Aug. 21, 1967; letter from Berlinrut, Oct. 30, 1967; Broun quoted in Crozier, "Notes on Newark Ledger Strike," p. 3.

46. E&P, Nov. 24, 1934, p. 7.

47. "The Newark Ledger Has Nothing to 'Mediate' with the Guild at This Late Date," advertisement signed by L. T. Russell, Dec., 1934, C-971, NLRB-NRC; Crozier, "Notes on Newark Ledger Strike," pp. 4-7.

48. Crozier, "Notes on Newark Ledger Strike," pp. 7-9; NYT, Nov. 18, 1934, p. 32; GR, Dec. 1, 1934, pp. 1, 3; "Newark Fights Guild Cause in Crucial Strike," *Twin Cities Guild Reporter*, Dec., 1934, pp. 1-2.

49. NYT, Nov. 21, 1934, p. 3; GR, Dec. 15, 1934, p. 2; copy of L. T. Russell Statement to Negotiations Committee of Newark Newspaper Guild, Nov. 26, 1934, ANG; E&P, Dec. 22, 1934, p. 16; Ring, "Newark

Guild Found Organized Labor Strong Ally During Strike," GR, Apr. 15, 1935, p. 2.

50. NYT, Nov. 21, 1934, p. 3, Nov. 22, p. 3; E&P, Dec. 8, 1934, p. 6; interview with Crozier, July 6, 1967; GR, Dec. 1, 1934, p. 1; letter from Crozier, Oct. 10, 1967.

51. "Ledger Strike Bulletins," Nov. 22, 1934—Mar. 28, 1935, ANG. Usually a single mimeo. legal-size page, these bulletins were sent out daily by the strikers to report to the guilds on what was happening; GR, July 1, 1935, p. 8.

52. Copies of Russell's advertisements in author's possession. The ANPA *Labor Bulletin* (Dec. 1, 1934), pp. 694-95, reprinted some of Russell's statements to cite the "strikers' preposterous control demands."

53. GR, Mar. 1, 1934, p. 1; interviews with Crozier, July 6, 1967, and Berlinrut, Aug. 21, 1967.

54. NYT, Jan. 24, 1935, p. 24; E&P, Jan. 26, 1935, pp. 1, 3; interview with Crozier, July 6, 1967; Crozier, "More Notes on Newark Ledger Strike," Oct. 10, 1967.

55. GR, Feb. 15, 1935, pp. 1-2; E&P, Feb. 23, 1935, p. 14; Russell to Harvey Kelly, Feb. 16, 1935, Folder 2-28, File 91-39, Hanson papers; "Ledger Strike Bulletin," Feb. 20, 1935, ANG.

56. "Ledger Strike Bulletin," Feb. 28, Mar. 5, 1935, ANG.

57. L. T. Russell to Harvey Kelly, Folder 2-28, File 91-34, Hanson papers; GR, Mar. 15, 1935, pp. 1, 3. The complete order is in NYHT, Mar. 8, 1935, p. 11.

58. The trade press called the order, as did E&P, an assault on the First Amendment; many newspapers editorialized against the order in the same vein as did the NYHT, which called it unsound and bad law. ("Clippings—New Jersey, Newspaper Guild Strike," Reel 122, Vol. 821, ACLU.)

59. NYHT, Mar. 11, 1935, p. 10; NYT, Mar. 27, 1935, p. 16; interview with Isserman, July 10, 1967.

60. Interview with Hochstein, July 21, 1967; NYT, Mar. 29, 1935, p. 11; the complete agreement is in E&P, Mar. 30, 1935, p. 12.

61. By March no striker received more than $18.50, and 72 percent of those receiving benefits got less than $15.00 (financial data in author's possession).

62. Interview with Berlinrut, Aug. 21, 1967; Bronson Conway to Frank McGaughan, Mar. 22, 1935, ANG; Lee, *Daily Newspaper*, p. 68.

63. "Ledger Strike Bulletin," Mar. 28, 1935, ANG; GR, May 15,

1935, pp. 1, 8, Dec. 15, p. 3, Apr. 1, 1936, p. 8; NYT, Feb. 19, 1936, p. 2, Mar. 18, p. 3.

64. Interviews with Kaufman, Aug. 30, 1967, and Crozier, July 6, 1967; E&P, Dec. 29, 1934, p. 33; "Ledger Strike Bulletin," Jan. 3, 1935, and Nov. 28, 1934, ANG.

65. Emmet Crozier to Guild Members (mimeo.), Dec. 12, 1934, Hugh Holahan to Veterans of the Staten Island and Long Island Campaigns (mimeo.), Jan. 7, 1935, ANG.

66. Broun had married again on Jan. 9, 1935. Kramer, *Heywood Broun*, p. 360; Lewis et al., *Heywood Broun*, p. 44-45; Jean McCafferty, striker, to Broun, Dec. 31, 1934, ANG; "Strike," *Newsweek*, V (Mar. 23, 1935), 23; Broun, "White Collar into Plume," *Nation*, CXL (Apr. 11, 1935), 420.

67. Minutes of the General Meeting, Dec. 2, 1934, TCNG; Draft Report, p. 2.

68. Interview with Richard Rohman, one-time labor correspondent for Fairchild publications and an Emergency Fund Committee member, Sept. 18, 1967; Jonathan Eddy to National Executive Committee, Jan. 11, 1935, ANG; Crozier, "Notes on Dubinsky Offer of Financial Aid to the ANG," Mar. 13, 1967.

69. An audit estimated total disbursements between Nov. 17, 1934, and May 18, 1935, at $26,492.76. (Draft Report, p. 9.)

70. Carl Johnson, secretary-treasurer of the Duluth Guild, to Jonathan Eddy, Mar. 4, 1935; Eddy to Johnson, Mar. 6, 1935, ANG; financial data in author's possession.

71. E&P, Dec. 22, 1934, p. 16; "Ledger Strike Bulletin," Dec. 11, 1934, ANG; Minutes (Mar. 11, 1935), ACLU; I. D. Robbins, secretary of the League, to Roger Baldwin, Aug. 15, 1935, "Newark Injunction," Reel 125, Vol. 486, ACLU. The ACLU lent $250 and later waived repayment; it also agreed to participate in an *amicus curiae* role in any court action and to assist the League in raising funds.

72. Green quoted in NYT, Dec. 2, 1934, p. 16; Goldberg, Pasche, and Ring, "Labor Lesson Taught at Newark," GR, Apr. 15, 1935, p. 5; ANG Proceedings, 1935, pp. 333-34; E&P, May 5, 1935, p. 37.

73. "Report on the Contract Between the Publisher of the Cleveland News and the Cleveland Newspaper Guild and How It Was Negotiated," (mimeo.), Jan., 1935, CNG, p. 3.

74. From the *News*: Elmer Fehlhaber, I. L. Kenen, A. L. Roberts, and as alternate, Jack Clawser; from the *Press*: Lloyd White and Garland Ashcraft. The CNG's executive secretary, William Davy, originally had been on the committee, but Hanna insisted that his

employees must have a majority and, even though this went against the ANG's recommended bargaining procedure, Davy withdrew (*Ibid.,* p. 2).

75. *Ibid.,* pp. 4-6; CNG to Daniel Hanna, Apr. 4, 1934, CNG; William Davy to Hanna (copy), May 15, 1934, ANG.

76. "Report on the Contract," p. 7; Garland Ashcraft to Jonathan Eddy, Aug. 14, 1934, ANG.

77. "Report on the Contract," p. 7.

78. E&P, Sept. 15, 1934, p. 11, Sept. 22, p. 14; Roberts, "Cleveland News Signs Contract," GR, Jan. 1, 1935, p. 1, 3.

79. Jonathan Eddy to Garland Ashcraft, Sept. 14, 1934, ANG; A. L. Roberts to Eddy, Nov. 29, 1934, ANG; "Report on the Contract," pp. 7-8.

80. E&P, Dec. 22, 1934, p. 10; NYT, Dec. 22, 1934, p. 13; GR, Jan. 1, 1935, p. 3; William Davy to Jonathan Eddy, Mar. 21, 1935, ANG.

81. "Report on the Contract," p. 8.

82. *Ibid.,* p. 10; Garland Ashcraft to Jonathan Eddy, Oct. 3, 1934, ANG.

83. Winthrop, "A Newspaper Game," *Controversy,* I (Nov. 23, 1934), 65-66; Knowland to Hanson, Nov. 30, 1934, Folder 2-28, File 91-39, Hanson papers; GR. Dec. 1, 1934, pp. 1, 6; E&P, Dec. 1, 1934, p. 16; clippings from California labor and weekly newspapers, Jennings scrapbook; Jonathan Eddy to National Executive Committee, Jan. 10, 1935, ANG.

84. E&P, Dec. 8, 1934, p. 10; Laurence Brown, "The Press Faces a Union," *New Republic,* LXXXI (Jan. 23, 1935), 24.

85. E&P, Jan. 12, 1935, p. 8; Quinn, *San Francisco-Oakland Newspaper Guild,* p. 49; GR, Feb. 1, 1935, p. 8.

86. GR, Apr. 1, 1934, p. 3, Apr. 15, p. 8.

87. Quinn, *San Francisco-Oakland Newspaper Guild,* pp. 34-38.

CHAPTER 6: . . . AND AWAY FROM THE GOVERNMENT

1. GR, Feb. 1, 1935, p. 7.

2. Garland Ashcraft to Jonathan Eddy, Aug. 21, 1934, David Frederick to Eddy, Aug. 29, 1934, Eddy to Ashcraft, July 9, 1934, ANG.

3. GR, Nov. 15, 1934, pp. 1, 6; E&P, Nov. 10, 1934, p. 6; NYT, Nov. 6, 1934, p. 23. The New York slant to the delegation resulted from the less than 48 hours' notice Kieran received of the meeting. But it is doubtful whether Eddy's plans for a broad-based delegation would have worked had there been more notice, for the ANG had

no funds to pay expenses (Eddy to Wayne Parker, Sept. 17, 1934, ANG; GR, Nov. 15, 1934, p. 6).

4. Harvey Kelly to H. J. Auth, general manager of the Newark *Star-Eagle,* Oct. 25, 1934, Folder 2-28, File 91-39, Hanson papers; E&P, Oct. 20, 1934, p. 44, Oct. 27, p. 5, Nov. 3, p. 10, Dec. 1, pp. 10, 33, Mar. 2, 1935, p. 6; Broun letter to the editor, *Ibid.,* Oct. 27, 1934, p. 5; GR, Apr. 15, 1935, p. 8.

5. Harry Saylor, editor in chief of the Stern newspapers, to Paul C. French, Oct. 27, 1934, read by French to the Philadelphia Guild's executive council, Nov. 11, 1934, Minutes, executive council, PNG; E&P, Feb. 16, 1935, p. 5, Feb. 23, p. 24, Apr. 13, p. 18, Apr. 27, p. 30; GR, Mar. 1, 1935, p. 2, May 1, pp. 1-2, May 15, p. 1.

6. Jonathan Eddy to Harold J. Taylor, president of the Akron Guild, May 13, 1935, ANG; Draft Report, p. 6.

7. Prentiss Bailey to Elisha Hanson, Nov. 28, 1934, Folder 2-28, File 91-34, Hanson papers; Henry Doorly, president of the *Omaha World Herald,* to S. M. Williams, manager of the Code Authority, Dec. 1, 1934, NRA, Box 1936.

8. Payson Irwin to David Frederick, Aug. 20, 1934, ANG; Leuchtenburg, *Roosevelt and the New Deal,* pp. 68-69, 107-8; Schlesinger, Jr., *Coming of the New Deal,* pp. 145-46, 396.

9. Lorwin and Wubnig, *Labor Relations Boards,* Chapter 4, *passim;* John F. Neylan to California Regional Labor Board, May 31, 1934, quoted in full in E&P, June 9, 1934, p. 8.

10. Schlesinger, Jr., *Coming of the New Deal,* pp. 397-99; Lorwin and Wubnig, *Labor Relations Boards,* pp. 291-97. This board usually is called the first NLRB to differentiate it from the board established by the Wagner Act in 1935.

11. E&P, Nov. 24, 1934, p. 8; "Supplement to Petition of R. L. Burgess for Review of Decision," C-85, NLRB-NRC; Garrison to Paul Frederickson, New York Guild secretary, Aug. 16, 1934, ANG.

12. Digest of Minutes of NIB, OF716, NLRB, Jan.-Dec., 1935, Box 2, FDRL; Boylan, "Daily Newspaper Business," pp. 75-79; GR, Oct. 1, 1934, p. 5.

13. Clippings, Jennings Scrapbook; "Unnecessary Torture," *Time,* XXIV (Dec. 24, 1934), 14; Quinn, *San Francisco-Oakland Newspaper Guild,* pp. 28-30; transcript of hearing, C-92, NLB-NRC, pp. 6-14. Jennings' testimony is summarized in E&P, Oct. 20, 1934, p. 13; U.S., National Labor Relations Board, *Decisions of the National Labor Relations Board,* II, 6; Jennings to James Boylan, July 14, 1959, Boylan papers; E&P, June 30, 1934, p. 10.

14. NLB to San Francisco Regional Labor Board, June 9, 1934, and June 18, 1934, C-92, NLB-NRC.

15. Grove J. Fink to Albert A. Rosenshine, chairman of the Regional Labor Board, text, E&P, Oct. 20, 1934, p. 49.

16. NLRB to Henry Robinson, Oct. 26, 1934, Jennings scrapbook; Boylan, "Daily Newspaper Business," p. 89.

17. "Stenographic Transcript of Hearing in the Matter of the San Francisco Call-Bulletin, et al.," Nov. 13, 1934, C-185, NLRB-NRC, pp. 2-61.

18. *Ibid.,* p. 40.

19. *Ibid.,* p. 61.

20. *Ibid.,* p. 65.

21. NYT, Nov. 14, 1934, p. 7.

22. "Stenographic Transcript of Hearing," C-185, NLRB-NRC, pp. 70-78, 85-86; NYHT, Nov. 14, 1934, p. 9.

23. Biddle, *In Brief Authority,* p. 33.

24. U.S., NLRB, *Decisions,* II, 1-7.

25. NYHT, Dec. 5, 1934, p. 7; NYT, Dec. 5, 1934, pp. 4, 22; Biddle, *In Brief Authority,* p. 33.

26. Broun, "A 'Gentlemen's Agreement' Bobs Up," GR, Dec. 15, 1934, p. 6.

27. GR, Dec. 15, 1934, p. 5; full text of the NLRB release is in NYHT, Dec. 5, 1934, p. 7.

28. Broun's statement is in GR, Dec. 15, 1934, p. 5; Butler, "Guild Walks Out of Hearing," E&P, Dec. 8, 1934, p. 5.

29. Biddle, *In Brief Authority,* p. 34; "Stenographic Transcript of Hearing," Dec. 7, 1934, C-195, NLRB-NRC, pp. 9-20; U.S., NLRB, *Decisions,* II, 11.

30. *The New York Times*'s astute labor correspondent, Louis Stark, shortly after the reaffirmation of the ruling said that "a critical situation appeared to be developing . . . . this case has now reached the stage where lines are being drawn tightly" (NYT, Dec. 14, 1934, p. 3).

31. Richberg to Marvin McIntyre, Assistant Secretary to the President, Dec. 6, 1934; Richberg to Louis Howe, Secretary to the President, Dec. 18, 1934, OF466, NRA Codes, N, 1933-35.

32. "Unnecessary Torture."

33. NYWT, Dec. 5, 1934, p. 27, Dec. 21, p. 21. Paul C. French reported to his fellow Philadelphia guild leaders that Broun had told him the decision to reinstate Jennings would not be enforced (Minutes, executive council, Dec. 20, 1934, PNG).

34. Broun, Buck, Eddy, and Watson to Richberg, Dec. 12, 13, 15, 1934, all in GR, Jan. 1, 1935, p. 7.

35. ANPA *Bulletin,* Dec. 14, 1934, p. 585; Davis to Harvey Kelly, Dec. 12, 1934, Folder 2-28, File 91-39, Hanson papers; Campbell, "Riding the Fire Engine," *American Spectator,* III (Dec., 1934), 7-8.

36. Text of the letter is in ANPA *Bulletin,* Dec. 29, 1934, pp. 593-96; E&P, Dec. 23, 1934, p. 10; Boylan, "Daily Newspaper Business," pp. 96-97.

37. Clippings in Jennings scrapbook; E&P, Dec. 29, 1934, p. 35; NYT, Dec. 28, 1934, p. 1.

38. NRA release, Dec. 28, 1934, C-92, NLB-NRC; NYT, Dec. 29, 1934, p. 3; E&P, Jan. 5, 1935, p. 5. His biographer says that Howe had been under some publisher pressure all along on this case (Rollins, Jr., *Roosevelt and Howe,* p. 396).

39. GR, Jan. 15, 1935, pp. 1-2; E&P, Jan. 12, 1935, p. 4; Eddy to W. M. O'Brien, secretary-treasurer of the Sheet Metal Workers' International Association, Jan. 7, 12, 1935, ANG.

40. Biddle, *In Brief Authority,* p. 36.

41. E&P, Jan. 26, 1935, p. II.

42. E&P, Jan. 19, 1935, p. 9; NIB Proceedings, p. 39, Folder 2-28, File 91-39, Hanson papers; "Digest of Minutes, Newspaper Industrial Board," OF716, NLRB, Jan.-Dec., 1935, Box 2, FDRL, p. 22; GR, Feb. 1, 1935, p. 1; Draft Report, pp. 4, 8.

43. "Digest of Minutes, Newspaper Industrial Board," OF716, NLRB, Jan.-Dec., 1935, Box 2, FDRL, pp. 25-26.

44. E&P, Jan. 26, 1935, p. II; "Memorandum of Services of Elisha Hanson for the Code Authority, Jan. 1 to 31, 1935," Folder 2-28, File 91-39, Hanson papers, pp. 2, 3; "President and Publisher," *Time,* XXV (Feb. 4, 1935), 49.

45. Boylan, "Daily Newspaper Business," p. 100; "Proceedings of the Conference Called by Labor Members of the NIB," Jan. 18, 1935, NRA, Box 1927; GR, Feb. 1, 1935, p. 2; NYT, Jan. 19, 1935, p. 3.

46. Roosevelt's letter is in NYT, Jan. 23, 1935, p. 1; Biddle, *In Brief Authority,* pp. 36-37; Lorwin and Wubnig, *Labor Relations Boards,* p. 303; E&P, Jan. 26, 1935, p. II.

47. Biddle, *In Brief Authority,* p. 39; Boylan, "Daily Newspaper Business," p. 100-1; Fine, *The Automobile,* pp. 320-22. One can discount Paul Ward's explanation, which attributed the President's decision to the fact that Roosevelt's press secretary had mistakenly informed his boss that no guildsmen covered the White House. ("Roosevelt Keeps His Vow," *Nation,* CXLI [Sept. 25, 1935] 349.)

48. E&P, Jan. 26, 1935, p. II; NYT, Jan. 23, 1935, p. 1. The publishers had a victory they would allow nothing to tarnish. When Roosevelt at his press conference said he thought the Code Authority's inability to deal with the case had resulted in the NLRB stepping in, Davis immediately wrote the White House a detailed letter pointing out that the NIB existed before the NLRB (Davis to Marvin McIntyre, Jan. 23, 1935, PPF1433, Amon Carter, 1933-35, FDRL).

49. Nathan Witt to NLRB, Dec. 11, 1934, C-85, NLRB-NRC; Francis Biddle to Henry Robinson, Feb. 20, 1935, ANG.

50. Interview with Jennings, Nov. 16, 1967. In March, 1951, the *Call-Bulletin* hired him to do a column, but in a final irony fired him again in October because of pressure from an advertiser (letter from Jennings, July 8, 1967).

51. E&P, Jan. 26, 1935, p. II; NYT, Jan. 23, 1935, p. 1; GR, Feb. 15, 1935, p. 1; Wayne Parker to Eddy, Jan. 23, 1935, ANG.

52. "Press Conferences," Vol. 5, Jan. 23, 1935, FDRL, p. 66; NYT, Jan. 24, 1935, p. 9; GR, Feb. 1, 1935, p. 1, Feb. 15, pp. 1, 6; E&P, Feb. 2, 1935, p. 4; "Report of Industrial Board Members," *Ibid.,* Apr. 27, 1935, p. 98.

53. Jonathan Eddy to Garland Ashcraft, Feb. 1, 1935, ANG.

54. Lorwin and Wubnig, *Labor Relations Boards,* p. 460; Francis Biddle to Franklin Roosevelt, Mar. 15, 1935, OF716, NLRB, Jan.-Dec., 1935, Box 2, FDRL; E&P, Feb. 16, 1935, p. 6; the Harriman and Kelly letters are in *Ibid.,* Mar. 16, p. 16, and Mar. 30, p. 8; Boylan, "Daily Newspaper Business," p. 81.

55. Draft Report, pp. 6-8.

56. GR, Feb. 15, 1935, p. 3.

57. See pp. 123-24 in Chapter 4.

58. Johnson, secretary-treasurer of the Duluth Guild, to Eddy, Nov. 2, 1934, Eddy to Broun, July 5, 1934, ANG; Buck, "Hearing on Pay Set in December," GR, Nov. 1, 1934, pp. 1, 2; NRA notice of Hearing 98B, Exhibit IX in Case, "History of the Code."

59. Julius Klein, chairman of the St. Louis Guild code committee, to Jonathan Eddy, Nov. 7, 1934, ANG; Minutes of Executive Board Meeting, Nov. 25, 1934, TCNG; Carl Randau to Members of the Newspaper Guild of New York, Dec. 7, 1934, copy in author's possession; K. G. Bellairs, acting secretary of the St. Louis Guild, to Eddy, Dec. 10, 1934, Association of the Rockford Newspaper Guild to Eddy, Dec. 8, 1934, ANG.

60. Buck to Broun, Dec. 12, 1934, ANG; Tate to Jonathan Eddy,

Dec. 20, 1934, NRA, Box 1935; GR. Jan. 1, 1935, pp. 1, 7, Jan. 15, p. 6; E&P, Oct. 6, 1934, p. 6.

61. ANPA had informed members of the survey and advised them that "it is optional . . . to either supply or refuse to supply . . . information, in other words . . . [newspapers] are under no obligation to do so." ANPA *Bulletin,* July 13, 1934, pp. 431-32, Sept. 28, p. 527.

62. Text of ANG amendment is in E&P, Jan. 19, 1935, p. 12; Case, "History of the Code," pp. 35-36; GR, Feb. 1, 1935, pp. 1, 2, 6.

63. Boylan, "Daily Newspaper Business," p. 62; Mills to Tate, Mar. 2, 1935, Reed to Tate and Peck, Mar. 20, 1935, Mills to Tate, Apr. 9, 1935, NRA Document Series; S. M. Williams to Tate, Apr. 15, 1935, Mills to Tate, Apr. 27, 1935, NRA, Box 1936.

64. GR, Apr. 15, 1935, p. 1; Watson, "Report of National Press Association Committee," drawn up at end of May, 1935, for presentation to the convention, ANG.

65. E&P, June 1, 1935, pp. 1, 2; ANPA *Bulletin,* May 29, 1935, pp. 393-96, contains committee and Davis statements; Boylan, "Daily Newspaper Business," p. 107; Schlesinger, Jr., *Politics of Upheaval,* p. 280.

66. U.S., Congress, Senate, Committee on Education and Labor, *Hearing on National Labor Relations Board,* 74th Congress, 1st session, 1935, p. 725; GR, July 1, 1935, p. 4.

67. Eddy to Davy, Apr. 20, 1935, CNG; interviews with Davy, Jan. 25, 1968, Kenen, Aug. 15, 1965, and Robbins, Feb. 1, 1968; GR, May 1, 1935, pp. 1, 7.

68. Kaufman, "Organization Report," Apr. 22, 1935, Gunnar Mickelsen, Milwaukee *Journal* reporter, to Heywood Broun, Jan. 1, 1935, Jonathan Eddy to H. R. Palmer, Lansing Newspaper Guild secretary, Jan. 16, 1935, ANG.

69. Interview with Davy, Jan. 25, 1968; Buck quoted in GR, July 1, 1935, p. 4.

70. Eddy, "Guild, Government, Future," GR, Feb. 15, 1935, p. 3; Broun quoted in *Ibid.,* Feb. 1, p. 4.

CHAPTER 7: DISSENSION

1. ANG Proceedings, 1935, p. 3; GR, July 1, 1935, p. 7; in addition to the other sources cited for the 1935 convention, I benefited from a talk with I. D. Robbins, one of the New York Guild delegates, Feb. 1, 1968.

2. GR, July 1, 1935, p. 7; Jonathan Eddy to Russell Gideon, a Tulsa newsman, Apr. 16, 1935, ANG.

3. "Report of Delegates to 1935 ANG Convention," pp. 1-3, TCNG; interviews with Crozier, Feb. 1, 1968, and Isserman, Aug. 10, 1967; Broun, "Openly Arrived At," *Nation*, CXL (June 19, 1935), 712.

4. They estimated that of the total possible maximum vote of 136 (and because of the coming and going of delegates that total was rarely reached at the convention) the New York bloc had 52 votes and the National bloc had 51. The New York, Hudson County, Newark, and Westchester delegates formed the core of one bloc; their allies included the El Paso, Milwaukee, Omaha, Northern California, Springfield (Ohio), and Youngstown guilds as well as half the Cleveland delegation. At the core of the other bloc were the Duluth, Philadelphia, St. Louis, Southern Minnesota, and Twin Cities guilds, whose allies included the delegates from the Battle Creek, Buffalo, Detroit, Durham, Greensboro, Lansing, Lehigh Valley, Salt Lake City, Tri-City (Albany-Schenectady-Troy), and Winston-Salem guilds as well as half the Cleveland delegation. The 33 generally uncommitted votes belonged to the delegates from the Baltimore, Harrisburg, Madison, Pittsburgh, Reading, Richmond, Rochester, Rockford, Toledo, Washington, and Wilmington guilds. ("Report of Delegates to 1935 ANG Convention," pp. 2-4, TCNG.)

5. Jonathan Eddy to Fred L. Strong, chairman of the TCNG special committee on affiliation, Dec. 15, 1934, ANG; minutes of the general membership meeting, Dec. 2, 1934, TCNG; Broun, "The Question of Affiliation," *Nation*, CXL (Apr. 24, 1935), 484.

6. "Pro-Affiliation Report of Committee on AFL Affiliation," Apr. 23, 1935, *The Michigan Guild Reporter*, May 15, 1935, pp. 2-3, ANG; *The Bronx Angle* (shop paper of the Home News chapter of the New York Guild), May 6, 1935; p. 1; *The Bulletin of the City News Unit*. May 9, 1935, p. 2, in author's possession.

7. GR, May 15, 1935, p. 6, June 1, pp. 1, 3.

8. Jonathan Eddy to Fred L. Strong, Dec. 15, 1934, Eddy to Gunnar Mickelsen, Apr. 18, 1935, ANG.

9. ANG Proceedings, 1935, pp. 41, 43-44.

10. "Report of the Sub-Committee on Labor Relations in Favor of Affiliation of the American Newspaper Guild with the American Federation of Labor," ANG; Bassett, "Guild Members to Act on Affiliation," E&P, June 8, 1935, p. 5.

11. "Report of Delegates to 1935 ANG Convention," pp. 4-5, TCNG; NYT, June 7, 1935, p. 3.

12. ANG Proceedings, 1935, pp. 348-76.

13. *Ibid.*, pp. 376-409; E&P, June 15, 1935, p. 20.

14. "Report of Delegates to 1935 ANG Convention," p. 5, TCNG. In addition to those sources cited re adoption of the constitution, I benefited from interviews with Crozier, Feb. 4, 1968, Gilfillan, Feb. 5, 1968, Isserman, Feb. 6, 1968, and Kenen, Jan. 30, 1968.

15. Kenen, "Guild Locals Are Studying Constitution," GR, July 15, 1935, p. 7; letter from R. S. Gilfillan, Sept. 26, 1967; "Report of Delegates to 1935 ANG Convention," pp. 3, 8, TCNG; "Preliminary Report of the Constitution Committee," Kenen papers.

16. ANG Proceedings, 1935, pp. 175-217 (the quotation is from a speech by David Kessler of the Rochester Guild, a regional vice president, p. 213).

17. *Ibid.*, pp. 244-65 (Broun's statement is on p. 259).

18. *Ibid.*, pp. 265-91 (Isserman's statement is on pp. 266-70); NYT, June 6, 1935, p. 19.

19. "Report of the Constitution Committee," ANG; ANG Proceedings, 1935, pp. 206, 425-571; E&P, June 15, 1935, p. 20. The new constitution was published in GR, July 15, 1935, pp. 5-7. In it the term "unit" replaced "chapter."

20. Financial information in author's possession.

21. "Report of Delegates to 1935 ANG Convention," p. 1, TCNG.

22. ANG Proceedings, 1935, pp. 618-25, 640-53; interviews with Kenen, Jan. 30, 1968, and Gilfillan, Feb. 5, 1968.

23. Interview with Gilfillan, Feb. 5, 1966.

24. ANG Proceedings, 1935, pp. 624-40; NYT, June 8, 1935, p. 19; NYHT, June 8, p. 5; E&P, June 15, 1935, p. 30; interviews with Crozier, Feb. 4, 1968, Davy, Jan. 24, 1968, Gilfillan, Feb. 5, 1968, and Nelson, Feb. 11, 1968.

25. Lorain Strike Edition of *The Michigan Guild Reporter,* June 24, 1935, Garland Ashcraft to the NEB, July 14, 1935, Eddy, "Report to the NEB on Lorain," Aug. 12, 1935, p. 1, ANG; E&P, Aug. 15, 1935, p. 6.

26. The next day ITU international headquarters, citing the union's ban on sympathy strikes, ordered the *Journal* printers to cross the picket line or hand in their membership cards (E&P, June 22, 1935, p. 6).

27. [Lorain] *Guild Reporter,* June 22, 1935, Kenen papers; E&P, June 22, 1935, p. 6; GR, July 15, 1935, pp. 1, 3; William Davy to Jonathan Eddy, July 15, 1935, ANG.

28. Garland Ashcraft to NEB, July 14, 1935, Eddy, "Report to the

NEB on Lorain," Aug. 12, 1935, pp. 2-4, ANG; E&P, July 20, 1935, p. 29.

29. "The Lorain Lockout," in "Guild Strikes—1934-1951" (typewritten), ANG.

30. "NEB Report to 1936 Convention," GR, May 15, 1936, p. 9.

31. Draft Report, p. 12; GR, June 15, 1936, p. 6. Eddy obviously had boosted the membership figure for public consumption; just a few weeks before the convention he had informed a Lansing Guild officer that "speaking organizationally we have about 4,000 reliable dues-paying members" (Eddy to J. H. Creighton, Apr. 3, 1935, ANG).

32. Financial data in author's possession.

33. Garland Ashcraft to Fellow Guild officers (mimeo.), Sept. 22, 1935, ANG; GR, July 15, 1935, p. 1.

34. Robert Buck to NEB, June 23, 1935, ANG.

35. GR, July 15, 1935, pp. 1, 8; Garland Ashcraft to Fellow Guild Officers, Sept. 22, 1935, ANG.

36. Julius Klyman to NEB, July 7, 1935, ANG; GR, Aug. 1, 1935, pp. 1-2; Robert Buck to NEB, July 3, 1935, Buck papers.

37. Robert Buck to NEB, July 16, Aug. 1, 1935, Garland Ashcraft to NEB, Aug. 22, 1935, Jonathan Eddy to Don Stevens, Oct. 1, 1935, ANG.

38. John B. Rand, ANG, to Edward Carr, USIS, n.d., Ideology-Communism, ANG; letter from Ferdinand Lundberg, July 7, 1967; interview with Stevens, Feb. 28, 1968; Jonathan Eddy to Stevens, Oct. 1, 1935, Garland Ashcraft to NEB, Aug. 22, 1935, ANG; Voros, *American Commissar,* p. 256.

39. Harvey Kelly to All Former NIB Members, July 12, 1935 (copy), Edward J. Volz of the Photo-Engravers Union to All NIB Employee Members, July 17, 1935 (copy), Jonathan Eddy to NEB, July 18, 1935, Garland Ashcraft to NEB, July 22, 1935, Robert Buck to NEB, July 24, 1935, Carl Johnson to NEB, July 26, 1935, Johnson to NEB, July 30, 1935, Buck to NEB, Aug. 19, 1935, Eddy to NEB, Aug. 21, 1935, Heywood Broun to NEB, Aug. 19, 1935, ANG.

40. Jonathan Eddy to NEB, Aug. 21, 1935, Garland Ashcraft to NEB, Aug. 23, 1935, ANG; GR, Sept. 1, 1935, pp. 1-2.

41. Garland Ashcraft's draft statement, n.d., Jonathan Eddy to Don Stevens, Oct. 1, 1935, Robert Buck to Eddy, Aug. 22, 1935, Morris Watson to NEB, Aug. 23, 1935, Buck to *Guild Reporter,* Sept. 9, 1935, Buck to NEB, Sept. 12, 1935, Ashcraft to Fellow Guild Officers (mimeo.), Sept. 22, 1935, Ashcraft to NEB, Sept. 14, 1935, Eddy to NEB, Sept. 30, 1935, ANG; GR, Sept. 1, 1935, pp. 1, 6, Nov. 15, p. 5.

42. Washington Guild letter is in GR, Oct. 1, 1935, p. 2; *Ibid.,* p. 1;

financial data in author's possession; Jonathan Eddy to NEB, Sept. 30, 1935, ANG.

43. GR, Sept. 1, 1935, p. 3, Oct. 1, p. 1.

44. A debate on the "pros and cons of affiliation" in *The American Press*, LIII (Sept., 1935), 3, for instance, was nothing more than a rehash of the arguments made at Cleveland.

45. Elmer Fehlhaber to Jonathan Eddy, July 9, 1935, Eddy to Fehlhaber, July 10, ANG; text of the statement is in GR, Sept. 1, 1935, p. 7.

46. Jonathan Eddy to NEB, Oct. 2, 1935, ANG; E&P, Oct. 20, 1935, p. 40. According to GR (Nov. 1, 1935, p. 3), the official tally of the vote on affiliation was as follows:

Guild	Yes	No	Guild	Yes	No
Akron	17	27	Rochester	37	27
Baltimore	22	22	Rockford	8	6
Buffalo	29	44	St. Louis	36	133
Cleveland	132	102	Salt Lake City	20	17
Columbus	14	7	San Antonio	9	0
Detroit	29	7	San Francisco	101	16
Duluth	25	7	South. Minnesota	12	5
Durham	9	1	Spokane	3	0
Greensboro	8	7	Springfield, Mass.	13	9
Hudson County	27	3	Springfield, Ohio	14	11
Lansing	5	19	Tri-City	14	18
Milwaukee	38	15	Twin Cities	114	38
Muskegon	8	1	Washington, D.C.	52	25
Newark	83	15	Westchester County	15	3
New York	730	180	Wilmington	11	18
Philadelphia	92	162	Youngstown	17	9
Pittsburgh	62	15	Members at large	18	3
Reading	17	0			

Total   Yes: *1,841*   No: *973*

Votes disqualified:
1. because they certified after September 5:

Brockton	13	1	Toledo	51	28
Cincinnati	41	8	Valley	0	2
Kansas City	8	4	Winston-Salem	0	14

2. because of lack of an official return:
   El Paso
   Lehigh Valley

3. because ballots sent but no certification:

Des Moines   5   3

4. because of failure to pay dues up to August 31, 1935:

Boston   25   8

Total disqualified   *Yes: 153*   *No: 74*

47. Buck's letter is in GR, Nov. 1, 1935, p. 2.

48. NEB Proceedings, Oct. 19-20, 1935, passim, ANG; GR, Nov. 1, 1935, pp. 1-2; interview with Stevens, Feb. 28, 1968.

49. NEB Proceedings, Oct. 20, 1935, pp. 35-40, ANG; GR, Feb. 15, 1936, p. 3.

50. Interviews with Eddy, Aug. 15, 1965, and Watson, Mar. 7, 1968.

51. Interviews with Buck, Aug. 5, 1965, and Homan, July 29, 1968; Jonathan Eddy to NEB, Nov. 13, 1935, William D. Wolfe to Morris Watson, Nov. 25, 1935, Wolfe to Garland Ashcraft, Nov. 25, 1935, Eddy to NEB, Nov. 26, 1935, Heywood Broun to NEB, Dec. 13, 1935, ANG; GR, Nov. 15, 1935, p. 8, Jan. 1, 1936, p. 1, Feb. 1, p. 1.

52. Garland Ashcraft, William Davy, and Jonathan Eddy to NEB, Nov. 25, 1935, ANG; interview with Stevens, Mar. 8, 1968.

53. Financial data in author's possession; Garland Ashcraft to All Guilds (mimeo.), Oct. 28, 1935, Jonathan Eddy to NEB, Nov. 12, 1935, Ashcraft to NEB, Nov. 16, 1935, Eddy to William Davy, Dec. 18, 1935, ANG; GR, Nov. 1, 1935, p. 2, Dec. 15, p. 3.

54. Interview with Eddy, Aug. 15, 1965; GR, Dec. 1, 1935, p. 2, Feb. 1, 1936, p. 3; Galenson, *CIO Challenge*, pp. 3-6; a condensed text of Lewis's speech is in GR, Jan. 1, 1936, p. 4; Eddy to William Davy, Dec. 18, 1935, ANG.

55. Ashcraft, "A Report on Cleveland Press Negotiations," July 20, 1935, Kenen papers; GR, Aug. 1, 1935, p. 8, Nov. 1, p. 3, Jan. 1, 1936, p. 8; E&P, Mar. 7, 1936, p. 14.

56. GR, Jan. 15, 1936, p. 4, Oct. 15, 1935, p. 1, Nov. 15, pp. 1-2, 7, Dec. 1, p. 7; E&P, Oct. 26, 1935, p. 34.

57. E&P, June 15, 1935, p. 6, June 22, p. 22, June 29, p. 10; GR, July 1, 1935, p. 2, July 15, p. 3, Aug. 15, p. 3; Garland Ashcraft to NEB, July 3, 1935, ANG; Lee, *Daily Newspaper*, p. 691.

58. "Gift on a Platter," *Business Week*, Aug. 3, 1935, p. 22; NYT, July 27, 1935, p. 11; Milton Kaufman to Jonathan Eddy, June 19, 1935, July 2, July 26, ANG; GR, Aug. 1, 1935, pp. 1, 7.

59. Myrdal, *American Dilemma*, p. 921; "Financial Status of the Negro Press," one of the working papers for the project "Negroes of New York," NYPLSC; GR, Oct. 15, 1935, p. 7; interview with Theo-

dore R. Poston, former chairman o fthe *Amsterdam News* unit, Mar. 19, 1968.

60. Milton Kaufman to Jonathan Eddy, Aug. 29, 1935, Oct. 10, ANG; GR, Oct. 15, 1935, pp. 1, 7.

61. Franklin, *Negro Labor Unionist,* pp. 180, 210-11; interview with Poston, Mar. 19, 1968.

62. GR, Jan. 1, 1936, p. 2; *Negro in New York,* ed. by Ottly and Weatherby, pp. 284-85; North, *No Men Are Strangers,* pp. 116-17; NYT, Oct. 19, 1935, p. 15; *New York Amsterdam News,* Oct. 26, 1935, p. 10; "Amsterdam News Strike Bulletin," Dec. 16, 1935, ANG.

63. E&P, Oct. 12, 1935, p. 48, Oct. 19, p. 6; NYT, Oct. 7, 1935, p. 10; "Amsterdam News Strike Bulletin," Nov. 8, 1935, ANG.

64. GR, Dec. 15, 1935, pp. 1, 7, Jan. 1, 1936, p. 14; *Amsterdam News* contract (copy), "Negroes of New York," NYPLSC; NYT, Dec. 23, 1935, p. 14; *New York Amsterdam News,* Jan. 11, 1936, p. 1.

65. At the end of three months the new owners fired Poston and Henry Lee Moon, the prime movers of the unit. The impartial chairman of the adjustment committee accepted these discharges. The ANG, deeply involved in another strike, found it politic to accept the chairman's decision and arranged other jobs for Moon and Poston. (NLRB, *Collective Bargaining,* p. 132; interview with Poston, Mar. 19, 1968.)

66. *Nation,* CXLII (Jan. 8, 1936), 30; membership figures based on initiation fees paid to the ANG, which came from financial data in author's possession; GR, Nov. 1, 1935, p. 7, Dec. 1, p. 3.

CHAPTER 8: THE GUILD BECOMES A UNION

1. Interview with Stevens, Mar. 8, 1968; Edward P. Doyle, president of the Newspaper Guild of Rochester, to Jonathan Eddy, Oct. 30, 1935, Eddy to Doyle, Nov. 4, 1935, ANG.

2. Ashcraft, "A Report of the Application of Article VIII of the Constitution of the ANG in Regard to Collective Bargaining and Strikes," n.d., ANG.

3. Seldes, "Roy Howard and His Newspapers," *New Republic,* XCV (July 27, 1938), 323; interviews with Catton, Apr. 19, 1968, and Eddy, Aug. 15, 1965; quotation from Kramer, *Heywood Broun,* p. 193.

4. GR, Sept., 1934, p. 3.

5. NLRB, *Collective Bargaining,* pp. 124-25; E&P, Jan. 11, 1936, p.

30, Feb. 15, p. 32; GR, Jan. 15, 1936, p. 2; Howard quoted in Liebling, "Publisher," *New Yorker*, XVII (Aug. 23, 1941), 26.

6. GR, Mar. 1, 1936, pp. 1, 5; E&P, Feb. 29, 1936, p. 9; interview with Catton, Apr. 19, 1968.

7. The complete text of the *Press* contract is in E&P, Feb. 29, 1936, pp. 9, 45.

8. NEB to All Local Guilds (mimeo.), Mar. 16, 1936, NEB Minutes, Mar. 6-7, 1936, pp. 5-6, ANG; Lee, *Daily Newspaper*, p. 691.

9. Interviews with Catton, Apr. 19, 1968, and Stevens, Aug. 8, 1968.

10. Lundberg, *Imperial Hearst*, p. 311; Swanberg, *Citizen Hearst*, pp. 474, 476; Swing, *Forerunners of American Fascism*, pp. 149-50; "Hearst," *Fortune*, XII (Oct., 1935), 113. The *Fortune* article, which Hearst apparently saw and revised before publication, shed much light on his newspaper holdings, whose exact extent he had kept obscure over the years for a variety of reasons. Unhappily, especially in view of what shortly would happen to these holdings, the article also gave a very erroneous impression of the financial soundness of Hearst and his newspaper properties.

11. GR, Jan. 15, 1936, p. 2; Lundberg, *Imperial Hearst*, p. 197; Jonathan Eddy to Julius Klyman, July 13, 1935, ANG.

12. Gunnar Mickelsen to Jonathan Eddy, Jan. 2, 1936, ANG.

13. Gunnar Mickelsen to Jonathan Eddy, Oct. 31, Nov. 10, 1935, Carl Johnson to NEB, Nov. 5, 1935, ANG; interview with Miss Van Vuren (Mrs. Colin Welles), Aug. 11, 1968. In addition to the sources cited for the Wisconsin News strike, I benefited greatly from talks with Gunnar Mickelsen, Aug. 14, 25, 1968.

14. *Milwaukee Guild News*, Jan. 10, 1936, pp. 1, 5, ANG; GR, Jan. 15, 1936, p. 2.

15. Interviews with Miss Van Vuren, Aug. 11, 1968, and former *News* employees Miss Dessel (Mrs. Peter Bellamy), Aug. 11, 1968, and Hymie Polinsky (Hy Paul), Aug. 14, 1968; *Milwaukee Guild News*, Feb. 10, 1936, pp. 1, 6, ANG; GR, Feb. 15, 1936, p. 2.

16. *Milwaukee Leader*, Feb. 3, 1936, p. 2, Feb. 11, p. 2; Gunnar Mickelsen to Jonathan Eddy, Feb. 8, 1936, ANG; Black quoted in GR, Mar. 1, 1936, p. 2.

17. Interviews with Davy, Aug. 14, 1968, and Paul, Aug. 14, 1968; G. Mann, "A Bit of Guild History," *The Press Cocktail*, June, 1941, pp. 5-6.

18. Interviews with Miss Van Vuren, Aug. 4, 1968, Miss Dessel, Aug. 11, 1968, and Leland Benfer, then a *News* photographer, Aug.

12, 1968; *Milwaukee Leader,* Feb. 17, 1936, p. 1; G. Mann, "Scab Rumors about Strike Collapse on Investigation," GR, Mar. 15, 1936, p. 7; *Guild Striker,* July 1, 1936, p. 1, SHSW.

19. Minutes of the Executive Board, Federated Trades Council of Milwaukee, Feb. 5, 1936, p. 2, SHSW; GR, Feb. 15, 1936, p. 2.

20. Gunnar Mickelsen to Jonathan Eddy, Jan. 12, Feb. 8, 1936, Stevens to Carl Johnson, Nov. 7, 1935, ANG.

21. Interviews with Davy, Aug. 14, 1968, Stevens, Aug. 14, 1968, and Miss Van Vuren, Aug. 11, 1968; Kerstein, *Milwaukee's All-American Mayor,* pp. 117-77, passim; Gavett, *Labor Movement in Milwaukee,* p. 157. The text of the Boncel Ordinance is in Hoan, *City Government,* pp. 352-56.

22. *Milwaukee Leader,* Feb. 19, 1936, p. 2, Feb. 21, p. 2, Feb. 25, p. 1, Feb. 28, p. 2, Apr. 22, p. 2, May 21, p. 7; E&P, Feb. 29, 1936, p. 16; Minutes of the Executive Board, Federated Trades Council of Milwaukee, Feb. 19, 1936, p. 2, SHSW; William Davy to Jonathan Eddy, June 25, 1936, ANG; text of Green telegram is in GR, Mar. 1, 1936, p. 4.

23. E&P, Mar. 14, 1936, p. 8, Mar. 21, p. 8, Apr. 4, p. 16, Apr. 11, p. 40; *Milwaukee Leader,* Mar. 9, 1936, p. 4, Black quoted in Apr. 4, p. 2; GR, Apr. 15, 1936, p. 2, Sept. 15, p. 2, Bitner quoted in Mar. 15, p. 2; memorandum by Kaufman, Mar. 27, 1936; ANG; "Broun's Page," *Nation,* CXLIII (Aug. 29, 1936), 243.

24. In working on this they learned to their surprise that neither the *News* nor the *Sentinel* contracted with the printing trades unions. For corporate and tax reasons Hearst used the Milwaukee Publishing Co. to publish both newspapers. This twist posed one more obstacle to the strikers (*Guild Striker,* July 1, 1936, p. 3, SHSW).

25. Interviews with Miss Dessel, Aug. 11, 1968, Paul, Aug. 14, 1968, and Miss Van Vuren, Aug. 11, 1968; *Milwaukee Leader,* Feb. 17, 1936, p. 1, Feb. 18, p. 2; GR, Mar. 1, 1936, p. 5; E&P, Sept. 5, 1936, p. 5; ANG Proceedings, 1936, p. 102; Jonathan Eddy to NEB, Feb. 20, 1936, Kaufman to NEB, Mar. 27, 1936, ANG; *Guild Striker,* May 13, 1936, pp. 1, 3, SHSW; *Milwaukee Newspaper Guild News,* Sept. 10, 1936, p. 1, in author's possession.

26. *Milwaukee Leader,* Mar. 7, 1936, p. 2; E&P, Feb. 29, 1936, p. 16, Mar. 7, p. 14, Mar. 14, p. 8, Apr. 4, p. 16; ANG Proceedings, 1936, p. 287; *Guild Striker,* July 1, 1936, pp. 1, 3, SHSW; "Strike Flash," June 22, 1936, p. 2, ANG.

27. Broun compliments Milwaukee for handling its prosecutions "with so much politeness." (NYWT, Apr. 15, 1936, p. 19.)

28. E&P, Mar. 21, 1936, p. 8, Mar. 28, p. 10, Apr. 18, p. 82, May 16, p. 48, June 1, p. 36; *Milwaukee Leader,* Mar. 21, 1936, p. 2, Apr. 17, p. 8, May 6, p. 1; GR, Apr. 1, 1936, p. 2, May 1, p. 2; ANG Proceedings, 1936, p. 276; NYT, Mar. 22, 1936, p. 5, Apr. 17, p. 16; "Strike Bulletin," May 29, 1936, ANG.

29. GR, Mar. 1, 1936, p. 4, Mar. 15, p. 7; Minutes of the Executive Board, Feb. 17, 1936, TCNG; "Treasurers' Reports 1936-1940," Series I, Box 4, DNG; Frank Pritchard, secretary of the Lansing Guild, to the ANG, Mar. 4, 1936, J. Nash McCrea to Jonathan Eddy, May 16, 1936, ANG; financial data in author's possession.

30. GR, Apr. 1, 1936, p. 1, May 15, p. 1, July 1, p. 2; Don Stevens to Jonathan Eddy, Mar. 23, 1936; Eddy to George Mann, president of the Milwaukee Guild, Apr. 29, 1936, ANG; NLRB, *Collective Bargaining,* pp. 46-47.

31. NYT, Apr. 26, 1936, p. 18; Milton Kaufman to Jonathan Eddy, Apr. 14, 1936, William Davy to Eddy, June 25, 1936, Eddy to Davy, June 26, 1936, Davy to Eddy, July 14, 1936, ANG; *Milwaukee Leader,* July 13, 1936, p. 1; interviews with Bellamy, Aug. 11, 1968, and Miss Dessel, Aug. 10, 1968; GR, July 1, 1936, p. 2.

32. GR, Sept. 1, 1936, p. 7, Sept. 15, p. 2; E&P, Aug. 22, 1936, p. 6, Sept. 5, pp. 5, 14; Minutes of the Executive Board, Federated Trades Council, Aug. 12, 1936, SHSW; *Milwaukee Leader,* Aug. 19, 1936, p. 2, Sept. 2, p. 9; *Milwaukee Guild News,* Sept. 10, 1936, p. 3, ANG.

33. GR, Sept. 15, 1936, p. 2; E&P, Sept. 5, 1936, pp. 5-6, 14; interviews with Miss Dessel, Aug. 14, 1968, and Benfer, Aug. 12, 1968; Morgan Hull to Jonathan Eddy, Sept. 2, 1936, J. Nash McCrea to Eddy, Oct. 7, 1936, ANG; *Milwaukee Leader,* Sept. 2, 1936, pp. 1, 9.

34. Mann and Black quoted in E&P, Sept. 5, 1936, p. 14; Bitner quoted in NYT, Sept. 2, 1936, p. 23; Broun quoted in GR, Sept. 15, 1936, p. 2; "Victory on Points," *Time,* XXVIII (Sept. 14, 1936), 34.

35. GR, Dec. 15, 1935, pp. 1-2, Apr. 15, 1936, p. 1, June 15, p. 4; Jonathan Eddy to Local Guild Secretaries (mimeo.), July 8, 1935, ANG; Don Stevens to Morgan Hull (copy), Apr. 6, 1936, Pettus papers.

36. The *Times* fired Kelley again a month later probably because of his militant guild stance, but this time it managed to avoid the issue by successfully but wrongly charging him with having compromised his usefulness to the newspaper by having served as a "stool pigeon" for a fanatically prohibitionist local district attorney. Kelley never returned to newspaper work; he feels he was blacklisted. (Terrence Pettus, president of the Tacoma Guild, to Jonathan

Eddy, June 25, 1936, Pettus papers; interview with Kelley, Sept. 2, 1968.)

37. Morgan Hull to Jonathan Eddy, May 5, 1936, May 8, May 13, ANG; E&P, May 30, 1936, p. 45; GR, June 1, 1936, pp. 1, 5; *The Daily Worker,* Nov. 30, 1946, p. 3.

38. GR, Mar. 15, 1936, pp. 1, 12, May 15, p. 9; E&P, Mar. 7, 1936, p. 11; interview with Homan, July 29, 1968.

39. *The Post Guildsman,* May 2, 1936, ANG; E&P, Apr. 26, 1936, p. 62; GR, May 1, 1936, pp. 1, 5.

40. GR, Mar. 1, 1936, pp. 4, 8, Apr. 1, p. 5, May 15, p. 3; ANG Proceedings, 1936, p. 471; Harold T. Meek to Jonathan Eddy, Jan. 31, 1936, ANG.

41. GR, Apr. 1, 1936, p. 3, May 15, p. 9; Model Contract (mimeo.), ANG.

42. NEB Minutes, March 6-7, 1936, passim, Jonathan Eddy to J. Nash McCrea, Apr. 29, 1936, ANG; GR, Mar. 15, 1936, pp. 8, 9; financial data in author's possession.

43. Eddy's and Stevens' reports are in GR, May 15, 1936, pp. 8-12; W. Earle Homan to Jonathan Eddy, Apr. 28, 1936, Eddy to William Davy, May 12, 1936, ANG.

44. GR, June 1, 1936, pp. 1, 3; E&P, Mar. 28, 1936, p. 38; minutes of the executive committee, May 3, 1936, DNG.

45. NYT, May 30, 1936, p. 9; Treasurer's Office to Local Guilds (mimeo.), May 16, 1936, ANG; GR, June 15, 1936, p. 6; ANG Proceedings, 1936, pp. 610, 710; interviews with Catton, Apr. 19, 1968, Schick, Sept. 10, 1968, and Stevens, Mar. 8, 1968.

46. "Newshawks Union," *Time,* XXVIII (June 8, 1936), 39; GR, June 15, 1936, p. 6; E&P, June 6, 1936, p. 36; financial data in author's possession. The Cleveland, Philadelphia, and Washington guilds each had 5 votes; Twin Cities and St. Louis had 4; the Boston, Newark, Northern California, Pittsburgh, and Tri-Cities each had 3; the Akron, Baltimore, Buffalo, Chicago, Cincinnati, El Paso, Hudson County, Milwaukee, Rochester, and Toledo guilds each had 2; all the rest (15 guilds) had 1.

47. Ferdinand Lundberg to Robert Buck, Sept. 10, 1940, Buck papers; U.S., Congress, House of Representatives, Committee on Education and Labor, *Hearings on Amendments to the National Labor Relations Act,* 80th Congress, 2d session, 1947, p. 3739 (testimony by Milton Murray, the anti-Communist Detroit guildsman who won the ANG presidency in 1941); letter from Earl Browder, May 11, 1966; U.S., Congress, Senate, Subcommittee of the Committee on the Ju-

diciary, *Hearings on the Strategy and Tactics of World Communism,* 84th Congress, 2d session, 1956, p. 1572; Broun, "We Still Want the United Front," *Nation,* CXL (Jan. 1, 1936), 20; Thomas quoted in NYT, Feb. 19, 1939, p. 4; interview with Catton, Apr. 19, 1968.

48. NYHT, May 31, 1936, p. 25; GR, June 15, 1935, pp. 1, 2; ANG Proceedings, 1936, pp. 61-62, 160-91, 211-16 (Levinson comments, pp. 162-63; Broun statement, p. 175).

49. Robert Buck to Fellow Guildsmen, preface to his *Constitution and Bylaws* (in author's possession); ANG Proceedings, 1936, p. 269; interview with Buck, Aug. 15, 1965.

50. GR, June 1, 1936, p. 7; Robert Buck to Edward Hunter, Victor Riesel, Oliver Pilat, and Norman McKenna, Feb. 25, 1941, Buck papers.

51. NYHT, June 1, 1936, p. 16, June 2, p. 67; Bassett, "Guild Votes to Become Labor Union," E&P, June 6, 1936, pp. 7-8, 36; ANG Proceedings, 1936, pp. 397-434, 581-632, 635-83, 722-64 (David Schick's remarks on Broun, p. 407; Kaufman's remark, p. 401; Ashcraft exchange, pp. 425-28; Catton remarks on "punch drunk," p. 679).

52. GR, July 1, 1936, pp. 1, 6; Nicolet, "The Newspaper Guild," *The American Mercury,* XXXIX (Oct., 1936), 192; American Newspaper Guild, *Manual 1936-37,* passim.

53. ANG Proceedings, 1936, pp. 561-71; GR, July 1, 1936, pp. 1, 3; Galenson, *CIO Challenge,* p. 552.

54. GR, June 15, 1936, pp. 1, 4; ANG Proceedings, 1936, pp. 587-95, 670-75, 685-92.

55. Text of most of the resolutions passed is in GR, June 15, 1936, pp. 7-8, July 1, pp. 5-6; Pringle, "The Newspaper Guild," *Scribner's,* CV (Jan., 1939), 44; ANG Proceedings, 1936, 430-34, 698-714 (Broun's comment, pp. 438-39).

56. ANG Proceedings, 1936, p. 709; interview with Dinsmore, June 29, 1965; minutes of the executive council, July 12, 1936, PNG; Broun quoted in Bassett, "Guild Votes to Become Labor Union," p. 8.

57. Sulzberger quoted in E&P, Aug. 8, 1936, p. 6; that journal's judgment is in *Ibid.,* June 6, p. 24; ANPA, *Labor Bulletin,* Aug. 15, 1936, p. 697; copies of the *World-Telegram* statement and reply to it are in GR, Aug. 15, 1936, pp. 1, 4-5.

58. GR, Aug. 1, 1936, pp. 1, 6; *Twin Cities Guild Reporter,* Sept., 1936, pp. 1-2, in author's possession; Emery, *ANPA,* pp. 236-39; Lee, *Daily Newspaper,* pp. 693-94. There is a full discussion of the Watson case in Cortner, *Wagner Act Cases,* pp. 55-56, 126-33, 138-39, 158-60, 168, 172-73, 179-80.

59. Klyman reported to the delegates that in a telephone conversation with Green the AFL president had expressed pleasure over the vote on affiliation and had said that he had no doubt that the ANG would enter the AFL very shortly (GR, June 15, 1936, p. 3).

60. GR, June 15, 1936, p. 3, July 1, p. 1; Jonathan Eddy to William Davy and Morgan Hull, June 26, 1936, ANG; interview with Eddy, Feb. 27, 1966.

61. Interviews with Catton, Apr. 19, 1968, Eddy, Feb. 27, 1966, and Stevens, Mar. 8, 1968; Galenson, *CIO Challenge,* pp. 9-16.

62. Jonathan Eddy to Elmer Fehlhaber, June 25, 1936, Eddy to William Davy and Morgan Hull, June 30, 1936, Eddy to John L. Lewis, June 30, 1936, Eddy to Hull, July 6, 1936, ANG; E&P, Aug. 1, 1936, p. 14.

63. Galenson, *CIO Challenge,* pp. 17-18; GR, July 15, 1936, pp. 1, 3; letter from Wesley Reedy, assistant to the secretary-treasurer of the AFL-CIO, Mar. 3, 1967; NYT, July 9, 1936.

64. GR, Aug. 1, 1936, pp. 1, 3; Green's letter is in *Ibid.,* pp. 1-2; NYHT, July 23, 1936, p. 9.

65. GR, Aug. 1, 1936, p. 3; Jonathan Eddy to Clyde Beals et al. (telegram), July 15, 1936, Eddy to William Davy, July 20, 1936, ANG; interview with Stevens, Mar. 8, 1968; Mayer, "The Guild Invades Chicago," *Nation,* CXLIV (Jan. 16, 1937), 68-69.

66. Quotations from Broun, Green, and Lewis are in NYHT, Aug. 8, 1936, p. 5, and GR, Aug. 15, 1936, pp. 1, 3; Broun, "Shoot the Works," *New Republic,* CXLIII (Jan. 12,1938), 280; NYWT, Aug. 11, 1936, p. 23; Galenson, *CIO Challenge,* pp. 20-21; GR, Sept. 1, 1936, pp. 1, 6; Oct. 1, p. 6.

bibliography

A. MANUSCRIPT COLLECTIONS

American Civil Liberties Union papers. Microfilm copy. New York Public Library. New York, New York.

American Newspaper Guild papers. As of this writing the ANG's records for its early years, with few exceptions, are scattered about its Washington, D.C., offices and storerooms. The ANG plans to deposit its papers with a library.

James Boylan papers. In his possession. New York, New York.

Robert Buck papers. At the time I used these, they were in his possession. Since his death in 1968 they apparently have been scattered.

Cleveland Newspaper Guild papers. In possession of that guild. Cleveland, Ohio.

C. I. O. papers. Catholic University of America. Washington, D.C.

Columbia University Oral History Collection. Columbia University. New York, New York. Recollections of Ernest Gross, Francis Jamieson, and J. David Stern.

Detroit Newspaper Guild Collection. Labor History Archives of Wayne State University. Detroit, Michigan.

Lee Drake papers. University of Oregon. Eugene, Oregon.

Morris Ernst papers. The vast bulk of his papers are at the University of Texas in Austin, Texas. The files I used (Early Cases of Newspaper Guild) are still in his possession.

Federated Trades Council of Milwaukee. State Historical Society of Wisconsin. Madison, Wisconsin.

Elisha Hanson papers. In possession of the law firm of Hanson, O'Brien, Cobb, and Tucker. Washington, D.C.

Dean Jennings scrapbook. A miscellaneous collection of correspondence and clippings in possession of Mr. Jennings. Tiburon, California.

I. L. Kenen papers. In his possession. Washington, D.C.

National Labor Board case files. C-92. Washington National Records Center. Washington, D.C.

National Labor Relations Board (1934-35) case files. C-85, 185, 193, 971. Washington National Records Center. Washington, D.C .

National Labor Relations Board (1935-) case files. C-84. National Labor Relations Board. Washington, D.C.

National Recovery Administration. Record Group 9. Files on the Daily Newspaper Publishing Business. Consolidated files on industries governed by Approved Codes. National Archives. Washington, D.C.

Newspaper Guild of Greater Philadelphia papers. In possession of that guild. Philadelphia, Pennsylvania.

Newspaper Guild of the Twin Cities of Minneapolis and St. Paul papers. In possession of that guild. Minneapolis, Minnesota.

Terrence Pettus papers. University of Washington. Seattle, Washington.

Lindsay Rogers papers. In his possession. New York, New York.

Franklin D. Roosevelt papers. Franklin D. Roosevelt Memorial Library. Hyde Park, New York.

U.S. Conciliation Service. Dispute Case File 176. National Archives. Washington, D.C.

B. UNPUBLISHED MATERIAL

1. Theses and dissertations

Boylan, James R. "The Daily Newspaper Business in The National Recovery Administration." Unpublished Master's essay, Faculty of Political Science, Columbia University, 1960.

Gleason, Nell K. "The Editorial Management of the Small City Newspaper." Unpublished Master's essay, School of Journalism, Columbia University, 1930.

Loftus, Joseph. "Scranton and Its Press: A Study of Trade Unionism in Journalism." Unpublished Master's essay, School of Journalism, Columbia University, 1931.

Lovell, Joseph, Jr. "A Historical Study of the American Newspaper Guild Particularly as Exemplified in Boston." Unpublished Master's essay, School of Public Relations, Boston University, 1949.

Mann, Robert S. "Turnover in Newspaper Editorial Staffs." Unpublished Master's essay, Columbia University, 1927.

Moskin, John R. "Origins of the American Newspaper Guild: A Genetic Study in American History." Unpublished Master's essay, Faculty of Political Science, Columbia University, 1947.

Ray, Royal. "Concentration and Ownership and Control in the American Daily Newspaper Industry." Unpublished Ph.D. dissertation, Faculty of Political Science, Columbia University, 1950.

Rosenberger, Graham. "Personnel Problems in the Larger Newspaper Editorial Offices." Unpublished Master's essay, School of Journalism, Columbia University, 1932.

Winnick, Louis. "The American Newspaper Guild." Unpublished Master's essay, Faculty of Political Science, Columbia University, 1947.

2. *Other*

Ashcraft, Garland. "25th Anniversary Notes." Unpublished notes on the history of the ANG written sometime in 1958 and filed February 5, 1960. Guild: Early History folder. American Newspaper Guild. Washington, D.C.

Crozier, Emmet. "More Notes on the Newark Ledger Strike." October 10, 1967.

——. "Notes on Dubinsky Offer of Financial Aid to the ANG." March 13, 1967.

——. "Notes on the Early History of the American Newspaper Guild for Daniel J. Leab." August 4, 1966.

——. "Notes on the Newark Ledger Strike for Daniel J. Leab." August 18, 1966.

"Draft Report of the Executive Secretary to the 1935 ANG Convention." Mimeographed. American Newspaper Guild. Washington, D.C.

"Guild Strikes: 1934-1951." Typewritten history of ANG strikes. American Newspaper Guild. Washington, D.C.

Joseph, Richard. "The Strange Case of Alexander Crosby." Typescript. In author's possession.

Marshall, R. C., and Dan Willy. "History and Organization and Chronology of Adoption of Policies of Detroit Newspaper Industrial Credit Union." c. 1961. Unpublished manuscript in files of Detroit Newspaper Industrial Credit Union. Detroit, Michigan.

Murasken, Estelle. "Newswriters Unions in English-Speaking Countries." Mimeographed report prepared for the Works' Progress Administration. 1937. Journalism Library, Columbia University. New York, New York.

"Newspapers and the N.R.A.: The Battle To Maintain a Free Press in America, 1933-35." Compiled for the American Newspaper Publishers Association by S. M. Williams. No date. Typescript in the ANPA library. New York, New York.

O'Dell, De Forest. "Fighting Editor." Unpublished manuscript apparently completed within a few years after Marlen Pew's death. Library, *Editor & Publisher.* New York, New York.

Pew, Marlen. Speech to Sigma Delta Chi convention, October 14, 1933. Pew folder. Library, *Editor & Publisher.* New York, New York.

"Report on the Contract Between the Publisher of the Cleveland News and the Cleveland Newspaper Guild and How It Was Negotiated." January, 1935. Mimeographed. Cleveland Newspaper Guild. Cleveland, Ohio.

"Special NRA Bulletin from Pennsylvania Newspaper Publishers Association." August 23, 1933. In author's possession.

Strouse, Don. "25th Anniversary Notes." Unpublished notes on the history of the ANG written sometime in 1958. Guild: Early History folder. American Newspaper Guild. Washington, D.C.

C. PUBLIC DOCUMENTS

U.S. Bureau of the Census. *Historical Statistics of the United States: Colonial Times to 1957.* Washington, D.C.: Government Printing Office, 1960.

U.S. House of Representatives. Committee on Education and Labor. *Hearings on Amendments to the National Labor Relations Act.* 80th Congress, 2nd session, 1947.

———. Committee on Labor. *Hearings on 30-Hour Week Bill.* 73rd Congress, 1st session, 1933.

U.S. Industrial Commission on the Relations and Conditions of Capital and Labor Employed in Manufacture and General Business. *Report.* Vol. 7. Washington, D.C.: Government Printing Office, 1901.

U.S. National Archives and Record Service. *Document Series of the National Recovery Administration 1933-36.* National Archives Microfilm Publication: Microcopy No. 213, Roll 44. Washington, D.C.: General Services Administration, 1956.

U.S. National Labor Relations Board (1934-35). *Decisions of the National Labor Relations Board.* Washington, D.C.: Government Printing Office, 1935.

U.S. National Labor Relations Board (1935-). Division of Economic Research. *Collective Bargaining in the Newspaper Industry.* Washington, D.C.: Government Printing Office, 1939.

U.S. Personnel Classification Board. *Salaries for Routine Clerical*

Work in Private Industry, 1929. Washington, D.C.: Government Printing Office, 1931.

U.S. Senate. Committee on Education and Labor. *Hearings on National Labor Relations Boards*. 74th Congress, 1st session, 1935.

——. Subcommittee of the Committee on the Judiciary. *Hearings on the Strategy and Tactics of World Communism*. 84th Congress, 2nd session, 1956.

D. *INTERVIEWS*

(A number of these interviews were conducted by telephone.)

Garland Ashcraft. October 20, 1965.

Joseph Barnes. January 5, 1965.

Richard Bellamy. August 11, 1968.

Leland Benfer. August 12, 1968.

E. B. Berlinrut. August 21, 1967.

Robert Bordner. June 14, October 28, 1965.

George Britt. July 12, November 14, 1965.

Robert Buck. August 15, 1965.

Phillips Butler. March 18, 1965.

Bruce Catton. April 19, 1968.

Alexander Crosby. October 12, 1965; July 30, 1966.

Emmet Crozier. July 12, August 14, 1966; July 6, 1967; February 1, 4, 1968.

William Davy. May 29, 1966; January 25, August 14, 1968.

Jean Dessel (Mrs. Peter Bellamy). August 11, 1968.

Herman Dinsmore. June 29, 1965.

Jonathan Eddy. August 15, 1965; February 27, 1966.

Morris Ernst. October 8, 1965; May 18, 1966.

Doris Fleeson. August 2, 1965.

Samuel Friedman. July 20, 1967.

R. S. Gilfillan. May 18, August 14, 1966; February 5, 1968.

Louis Gnaedinger. December 12, 1965.

Luella Henkel. October 12, 1965.

Philip Hochstein. July 20, 1967.

W. Earle Homan. July 29, 1968.

Luther Huston. May 17, 1966.

A. J. Isserman. July 10, August 10, 1967; February 6, 1968.

Morris Iueshewitz. September 29, 1967.

Dean Jennings. November 16, 1967.

Milton Kaufman. August 30, 1967.

Rex Kelley. September 2, 1968.

I. L. Kenen. August 15, 1965; January 30, 1968.

Clayton Knowles. July 19, 1967.

Gunnar Mickelsen. August 14, 25, 1968.

Herman Nelson. February 11, 1968.

Ralph Novak. June 12, 1965.

Hymie Polinsky (Hy Paul). August 14, 1968.

Theodore Poston. March 19, 1968.

I. D. Robbins. February 1, 1968.

Lindsay Rogers. September 14, 1965.

Richard Rohman. September 18, 1967.

David Schick. September 10, 1968.

Don Stevens. February 28, March 8, August 8, 1968.

Leon Svirsky. November 14, 1965.

Mary Van Vuren (Mrs. Colin Welles). August 4, 11, 1968.

Morris Watson. May 17, August 14, 1966; July 6, 1967; March 7, 1968.

Lloyd White. October 27, 1965; May 24, August 14, 1966.

B. J. Widick. August 1, 1965.

Hyman Wishengrad. May 2, 1965.

E. LETTERS

Garland Ashcraft. December 27, 1965.

E. B. Berlinrut. October 30, 1967.

Earl Browder. May 11, 1966.

Alexander Crosby. October 11, 1965.

Emmet Crozier. September 13, 1965; October 10, 1967.

Lewis Gannett. January 5, 1965; May 24, 1965.

R. S. Gilfillan. September 26, 1967.

Luella Henkel. October 10, 1965.

Dean Jennings. July 8, 1967.

Clayton Knowles. February 13, 1968.

Ferdinand Lundburg. July 7, 1967.

Wesley Reedy. March 4, 14, 23, 1966; March 3, 1967.

Morris Watson. December 2, 1965.

Lloyd White. July 18, 20, 1966.

F. BOOKS

Baarslag, Karl. *History of the National Federation of Post Office Clerks.* Washington, D.C.: National Federation of Post Office Clerks, 1945.

Baker, Richard T. *A History of the Graduate School of Journalism, Columbia University.* New York: Columbia University Press, 1954.

Bent, Silas. *Ballyhoo.* New York: Boni and Liveright, 1927.

Bernstein, Irving. *The Lean Years.* Boston: Houghton Mifflin Company, 1960.

——. *The New Deal Collective Bargaining Policy.* Berkeley: University of California Press, 1950.

Biddle, Francis. *In Brief Authority.* New York: Doubleday, 1962.

Clarke, Donald H. *Man of the World.* New York: Vanguard Press, 1951.

Commission on Educational Reconstruction. *Organizing the Teaching Profession.* Glencoe: The Free Press, 1955.

Cortner, Richard. *The Wagner Act Cases.* Knoxville: University of Tennessee Press, 1964.

Douglas, Paul. *Real Wages in the United States.* Boston: Houghton Mifflin Company, 1930.

Emery, Edwin. *History of the American Newspaper Publishers Association.* Minneapolis: University of Minnesota Press, 1950.

——. *The Press and America.* 2nd ed. Englewood Cliffs: Prentice-Hall, 1962.

Epochal History of the ITU. Compiled under the supervision and direction of James Lynch. Indianapolis: no publisher, 1925.

Ernst, Morris. *The First Freedom.* New York: The Macmillan Company, 1946.

Fine, Sidney. *The Automobile Under The Blue Eagle.* Ann Arbor: University of Michigan Press, 1963.

Franklin, Charles L. *The Negro Labor Unionist of New York.* New York: Columbia University Press, 1936.

Galenson, Walter. *The CIO Challenge to the AFL.* Cambridge: Harvard University Press, 1960.

Gauvreau, Emil. *My Last Million Readers.* New York: E. P. Dutton and Company, 1941.

Gavett, Thomas. *Development of the Labor Movement in Milwaukee.* Madison: University of Wisconsin Press, 1965.

A Handbook of NRA Laws, Regulations, Codes. Washington, D.C.: Federal Codes, Inc., 1933.

Harding, Alfred. *The Revolt of the Actors.* New York: William Morrow and Company, 1929.

Harris, Herbert. *American Labor.* New Haven: Yale University Press, 1938.

Hoan, Daniel. *City Government.* New York: Harcourt, Brace, and Company, 1936.

Johnson, Hugh S. *The Blue Eagle from Egg to Earth.* New York: Doubleday, Doran, and Company, 1935.

Johnson, Walter, and Arthur Robb. *The South and Its Newspapers 1903-1953.* Chattanooga: Southern Newspaper Publishers Association, 1954.

Kerstein, Edward S. *Milwaukee's All American Mayor: Portrait of Daniel Webster Hoan.* Englewood Cliffs: Prentice-Hall, 1966.

Kramer, Dale. *Heywood Broun.* New York: A. A. Wynn, 1946.

Lee, Alfred M. *The Daily Newspaper in America.* New York: The Macmillan Company, 1937.

Leiter, Robert. *The Musicians and Petrillo.* New York: Bookman Associates, 1953.

Lent, John A. *Newhouse, Newspapers, Nuisances.* New York: Exposition Press, 1966.

Leuchtenburg, William E. *Franklin D. Roosevelt and The New Deal.* New York: Harper and Row, 1963.

Levinson, Edward. *Labor on the March.* New York: Harper and Brothers, 1938.

Lewis, John L., and others. *Heywood Broun as He Seemed to Us.* New York: published for the Newspaper Guild of New York by Random House, 1940.

Link, Arthur. *American Epoch.* New York: Alfred A. Knopf, 1955.

Lippmann, Walter. *Interpretations 1932-35.* Selected and edited by Allan Nevins. New York: The Macmillan Company, 1936.

Lord, Chester. *The Young Man and Journalism.* New York: The Macmillan Company, 1922.

Lorwin, Lewis, and Arthur Wubnig. *Labor Relations Boards.* Washington, D.C.: The Brookings Institution, 1935.

Lundberg, Ferdinand. *Imperial Hearst.* New York: Equinox Cooperative Press, 1936.

Lyon, Leverett S., and others. *The National Recovery Administration.* Washington: The Brookings Institution, 1935.

Macdonald, Lois. *Labor Problems and the American Scene.* New York: Harper and Brothers, 1938.

MacDougall, Curtis D. *Newsroom Problems and Policies.* New York: The Macmillan Company, 1941.

MacNeil, Neil. *Without Fear or Favor.* New York: Harcourt, Brace, and Company, 1940.

Markham, James. *Bovard of the Post-Dispatch.* Baton Rouge: Louisiana State University Press, 1954.

Mills, C. Wright. *White Collar.* New York: Oxford University Press, 1947.

Minton, Bruce, and John Stuart. *Men Who Lead Labor.* New York: Modern Age Books, 1937.

Mott, Frank. *American Journalism.* 3rd. ed. New York: The Macmillan Company, 1962.

Myrdal, Gunnar. *An American Dilemma.* New York: Harper and Brothers, 1944.

The Negro in New York: An Informal Social History. Edited by Roi Ottly and W. J. Weatherby. New York: New York Public Library, 1967.

The Newspaper as an Advertising Medium. New York: Bureau of Advertising, American Newspaper Publishers Association, 1940.

North, Joseph. *No Men Are Strangers.* New York: International Publishers, 1958.

O'Dell, DeForest. *The History of Journalism Education in the United States.* New York: Bureau of Publications, Teachers College, Columbia University, 1935.

Phelps, Robert, and E. Douglas Hamilton. *Libel.* New York: The Macmillan Company, 1966.

Quinn, Russell. *History of the San Francisco-Oakland Newspaper Guild.* Vol. III of "The History of San Francisco Journalism." Compiled under the auspices of the Works Progress Administration. 4 vols. San Francisco: Works Progress Administration, 1940.

Rascoe, Burton. *Before I Forget.* New York: Doubleday, Doran, and Company, 1937.

Reynolds, Quentin. *By Quentin Reynolds.* New York: McGraw-Hill Book Company, 1963.

Rogers, Ernest. *Peachtree Parade.* Atlanta: Tupper and Love, 1956.

Rollins, Alfred B., Jr. *Roosevelt and Howe.* New York: Alfred A. Knopf, 1962.

Schlesinger, Arthur, Jr. *The Coming of The New Deal.* Boston: Houghton Mifflin Company, 1959.

——. *The Politics of Upheaval.* Boston: Houghton Mifflin Company, 1960.

Seldes, George. *Freedom of the Press.* Indianapolis: Bobbs-Merrill Company, 1935.

Seymour, Harold. *Baseball: The Early Years.* New York: Oxford University Press, 1961.

Sinclair, Upton. *The Brass Check.* Rev. ed. with index. New York: Albert and Charles Boni, 1936.

Slosson, Preston. *The Great Crusade and After: 1914-1928.* New York: The Macmillan Company, 1930.

Spero, Sterling. *The Labor Movement in a Government Industry.* New York: George Doran Company, 1924.

Stern, J. David. *Memoirs of a Maverick Publisher.* New York: Simon and Schuster, 1962.

Stewart, Kenneth. *News Is What We Make It.* Boston: Houghton Mifflin Company, 1943.

Stolberg, Benjamin. *The Story of the CIO.* New York: Viking Press, 1938.

Swanberg, W. R. *Citizen Hearst.* New York: Charles Scribner's Sons, 1961.

Swing, Raymond G. *Forerunners of American Fascism.* New York: Julian Messner, 1935.

Taft, Philip. *The AFL from the Death of Gompers to the Merger.* New York: Harper and Brothers, 1959.

Tracy, George. *History of the Typographical Union.* Indianapolis: International Typographical Union, 1913.

Voros, Sandor. *American Commissar.* New York: Chilton Company, 1961.

Walker, Stanley. *City Editor.* New York: Frederick Stokes and Company, 1934.

Weisberger, Bernard. *The American Newspaperman.* Chicago: University of Chicago Press, 1961.

Williams, Talcott. *The Newspaperman.* New York: Charles Scribner's Sons, 1922.

Willey, Malcolm, and Stuart Rice. *Communications Agencies and Social Life.* New York: McGraw-Hill Book Company, 1933.

Wolman, Leo. *Ebb and Flow in Trade Unionism.* New York: National Bureau of Economic Research. 1936.

G. ARTICLES

(In order to avoid a hopelessly long listing of articles, I have followed the practice of listing signed articles only from *Editor & Publisher* and *The Guild Reporter.*)

Adams, Franklin P. "Freedom of the Press." *New Republic,* XCIV (February 9, 1938), 15.

Anderson, Paul Y. "Johnson and the Freedom of the Press." *Nation,* CXXXVII (August 30, 1933), 235-36.

——. "Mr. Anderson in a Tender Mood." *Nation,* CXXXVIII (April 18, 1934), 443.

Ashcraft, Garland. "Dues and Professionalism Were Early Guild Issues." *The Guild Reporter* (December 25, 1953), p. 4.

——. "Guild's First Chapter Takes a Bow." *The Guild Reporter* (December 15, 1934), p. 10.

Bassett, Warren L. "Guild Members To Act on Affiliation." *Editor & Publisher,* LXVIII (June 8, 1935), 5.

——. "Guild Votes to Become Labor Union." *Editor & Publisher,* LXVIII (June 6, 1936), 7-8, 36.

Baxter, Ouida. "Newspaper Women and the Guild." *The Matrix,* XIX (February, 1934), 3.

Bleyer, Willard G. "Freedom of the Press." *Journalism Quarterly,* XI (Spring, 1934), 29-36.

Bordner, Robert. "Another Footnote to Guild History." *The Guild Reporter* (January 1, 1944), p. 5.

——. "Why We Organized." *The Quill,* XXI (October, 1933), 6.

Bracker, Milton. "Dilemma of a Guild Reporter." *The Reporter,* XXVII (January 17, 1963), 31-34.

Brandenburg, George A. "Guild Starts Drive to Oust Buckley." *Editor & Publisher,* LXVII (June 9, 1934), 7, 41.

——. "Staff Morale Tested by Depression." *Editor & Publisher,* LXV (March 4, 1933), 10.

Brislin, Tom. "Scranton Reporters' Union Unique Among U.S. Newspaper Groups." *Editor & Publisher,* LXIII (October 25, 1930), 50.

Broun, Heywood. "An Army with Banners." *Nation,* CXL (February 2, 1935), 184.

——. "A 'Gentlemen's Agreement' Bobs Up." *The Guild Reporter* (December 15, 1934), p. 6.

——. "Jonathan Eddy's Credentials." *The Guild Reporter* (May, 1934), pp. 1, 7.

——. "Hands and Brain." *Nation,* CXL (March 6, 1935), 279.

——. "N.R.A. Set Up a Spring Board and It Worked." *The Guild Reporter* (November 23, 1933), pp. 1-2.

——. "Openly Arrived At." *Nation,* CXL (June 19, 1935), 712.

——. "The Question of Affiliation." *Nation,* CXL (April 24, 1935), 484.

——. "Shoot The Works." *New Republic,* XCIII (January 12, 1938), 280.

———. "Too Much Is Enough, Says Broun." *The Guild Reporter* (November 15, 1934), p. 3.

———. "We Still Want the United Front." *Nation*, CXL (January 1, 1936), 20.

———. "White Collar into Plume." *Nation*, CXL (April 11, 1935), 420.

"Broun's Page." *Nation*, CXLIII (August 29, 1936), 243.

Brown, Laurence. "The Press Faces a Union." *New Republic*, LXXXI (January 23, 1935), 24-25.

Buck, Robert. "Hearing on Pay Set in December." *The Guild Reporter* (November 1, 1934), pp. 1-2.

———. "Report to the Convention of the American Newspaper Guild." *The Guild Reporter* (June 15, 1934), pp. 5-6.

Burns, Robert. "Daily Newspapers." *How Collective Bargaining Works*. New York: The Twentieth Century Fund, 1942.

Butler, James. "Guild Walks Out of Hearing." *Editor & Publisher*, LXVII (December 8, 1934), 5.

Campbell, Kenneth. "Riding the Fire Engine." *American Spectator*, III (December, 1934), 7-8.

"Code Dispute." *Newsweek*, III (June 23, 1934), 34.

Cole, Percy T. "Guild Idea Praised by Blumenfeld." *Editor & Publisher*, LXVI (December 17, 1935), 5.

Crist, Judith. "Gentlemen and Scholars of the Press." *Columbia University Forum*, II (Winter, 1959), 40-42.

Crowell, Chester T. "The Press Gets a Code." *New Republic*, LXXVI (December 20, 1933), 164-65.

Eddy, Jonathan. "City Guilds Unite in National Body Dec. 15 at Capital." *The Guild Reporter* (November 23, 1933), p. 1.

———. "Gentlemen of the Press in Revolt." *Today*, II (August 11, 1934), 2.

———. "Guild, Government, Future." *The Guild Reporter* (February 15, 1935), p. 3.

———. "Guild Idea Spreads as Delegates Face Toward Washington." *The Guild Reporter* (December 8, 1933), p. 2.

———. "Sigma Delta Chi and the Guild." *The Quill*, XXII (January, 1934), 6.

———. "Unity Awakens Stouter Spirit in Journalists." *The Guild Reporter* (February 23, 1934), pp. 1, 7.

"Editorial Union Evils." *Newsdom* (September 9, 1933), p. 4.

Evans, Rockwell. "Justice for the Reporter." *The American Press*, LII (November, 1933), 3.

Fischler, Stan. "The Newsmen: Where Do They Go From Here?" *The Village Voice* (May 19, 1966), pp. 14-16.

Fleeson, Doris. "Our Guild." *The Matrix,* XIX (April, 1934), 5.

French, Paul C. "Guild Negotiates Initial Contract." *The Guild Reporter* (May, 1934), pp. 1, 9.

Gannett, Lewis. "1933—When the Guild Was Very Young." *The Guild Reporter* (December 26, 1958), M-4.

"Gift on a Platter." *Business Week* (August 3, 1935), p. 22.

Gilfillan, R. S. "The ANG—An Idea That Worked." *The Guild Reporter* (January 9, 1959), p. 5.

Gilmount, Arvid. "The Low Pay of Reporters." *The American Press,* LI (August, 1933), 22.

Girardin, Ray. "Little Hope for Guild, Detroit 25 Years Ago." *Detroit Page One Ball Annual Yearbook* (1959).

Goldberg, Nathan, Victor Pasche, and Robert Ring. "Labor Lesson Taught at Newark." *The Guild Reporter* (April 15, 1935), p. 5.

Goski, John. "First Member of First Guild Unit Tells How and Why It Started." *The Guild Reporter* (February 15, 1944), p. 7.

Hanson, Elisha. "The Publisher, the Code, and the Government." *Bulletin of the Inland Daily Press Association* (March 15, 1935), pp. 27-29.

Harris, E. H. "U.S. Press Facing Its Greatest Crisis." *Editor & Publisher,* LXVI (October 21, 1933), 9.

"Hearst." *Fortune,* XII (October, 1935), 40-48, 110-16.

Hurd, Volney D. "American Press Adopts 'Air Brakes.'" *Christian Science Monitor Weekly* (April 25, 1934), p. 4.

Huston, Luther. "'Professional' Idea Lost in Guild." *Editor & Publisher,* XCII (January 3, 1959), 10.

Hyde, Grant. "United States Journalism in 1931." *Journalism Quarterly,* VIII (December, 1931), 816-27.

Hyde, Richard. "Company Unionism." *The Guild Reporter* (September, 1934), pp. 6-7.

"The Inside Story." *The Guild Journal* (July 16, 1934), p. 1.

"It Got Hot in '33." *Cleveland Newspaper Guild Page One Ball Yearbook* (1953), p. 9.

Kassalow, Everett. "Unionization of White Collar Workers," *Labor in a Changing America,* ed. by William Haber. New York: Basic Books, 1966.

——. "United States," *White Collar Trade Unions,* ed. by Adolf Sturmthal. Urbana: University of Illinois Press, 1967.

Kenen, I. L. "Guild Locals Are Studying Constitution." *The Guild Reporter* (July 15, 1935), p. 7.

Leab, Daniel J. "The 'Image' of the Journalist, 1864-1964." *Columbia Journalism Review,* III (Spring, 1964), 38-43.

Lee, Alfred M. "Recent Developments in the Newspaper Industry." *Public Opinion Quarterly,* II (January, 1938), 128-41.

"Legal Ajax." *Literary Digest,* CXXI (April 18, 1936), 45.

Lewis, Thomas E. "To the Left? Or Right?" *The Guild Reporter* (May, 1934), p. 5.

Liebling, A. J. "Publisher." *New Yorker,* XVII (August 23, 1941), 19-32.

Lissner, Will. "National Convention at St. Paul June 5 to Plan Bargaining." *The Guild Reporter* (May, 1934), p. 1.

Loftus, Joseph. "Union for the City Room?" *The Quill,* XX (November, 1932), 2-3.

Luce, Henry. "The Press Is Peculiar." *Saturday Review of Literature,* VII (March 7, 1931), 246.

McConnell, Oviatt. "Buffalo Press Club's Obituary with Notes on Its Guild Successor." *The Guild Reporter* (April, 1934), p. 6.

Macey, John. "Journalism," *Civilization in the United States,* ed. by Harold Stearns. New York: Harcourt, Brace, and Company, 1922.

Mann, George. "A Bit of Guild History." *The Press Cocktail* (June, 1941), pp. 5-6.

——. "Scab Rumors About Strike Collapse on Investigation." *The Guild Reporter* (March 15, 1936), p. 7.

Mann, Robert. "National Guild Asks Five-Day Week." *Editor & Publisher,* LXVI (December 23, 1933), 7.

Manning, George H. "Johnson Says Labor Contracts Stand." *Editor & Publisher,* LXVI (August 5, 1933), 7.

——. "President's Approval of Dailies' Code Raises New Questions for Publishers." *Editor & Publisher,* LXVI (February 24, 1934), 3.

——. "Provisions for Small Dailies in Code." *Editor & Publisher,* LXVI (February 24, 1934), 9.

Marshall, Margaret. "Columnists on Parade VII: Heywood Broun." *Nation,* CXLVII (May 21, 1937), 580-82.

Mayer, Milton. "The Guild Invades Chicago." *Nation,* CXLIV (January 16, 1937), 68-69.

"Newark Fights Guild Cause in Crucial Strike." *Twin Cities Guild Reporter* (December, 1934), pp. 1-2.

"Newshawks Union." *Time,* XXVIII (June 8, 1936), 39.

"The Newspaper Game." *The Saturday Evening Post,* CXCIV (April 6, May 11, 1912), 3-5, 56-58; 16-17.

"Newspaper Guild." *Newsweek*, III (June 16, 1934), 29.

"The Newspaper Guilds." *The American Press*, LII (November, 1933), 4.

"Newspaper Publishing." *The Index*, XIV (October, 1934), 209.

"New Writers Union Local No. 1." *New Republic*, XX (August 6, 1919), 8-9.

Nicolet, C. C. "The Newspaper Guild." *The American Mercury*, XXXIX (October, 1936), 189-94.

"Only Journalism School of Its Kind." *Publisher's Auxiliary*, LXIX (December 29, 1934), 1.

Parker, Andrew M. "Philadelphia Record Signs Agreement with Newspaper Guild Unit." *Editor & Publisher*, LXVI (April 14, 1934), 5, 46.

Pasche, Victor. "Strength of Guild and Its Right to Bargain Tested Successfully." *The Guild Reporter* (April 15, 1935), pp. 1-2.

Perry, John W. "Code for Dailies Filed at Washington: Many Publishers Endorse Regulations." *Editor & Publisher*, LXVI (August 12, 1933), 3.

——. "Dailies Come Under Blue Eagle Aegis as President Clarifies Freedom Stand." *Editor & Publisher*, LXVI (March 3, 1934), 4-5.

——. "Five-Day Week O.K. Publishers Say." *Editor & Publisher*, LXVI (February 24, 1934), 8.

——. "New York News Writers Organize." *Editor & Publisher*, LXVI (September 23, 1933), 7, 42.

Pew, Marlen. "Shop Talk at Thirty." *Editor & Publisher*, LXV (February 11, 1933), 32.

——. "Shop Talk at Thirty." *Editor & Publisher*, LXVI (September 23, 1933), 44.

Porter, Philip. "Cleveland Newspapermen Split." *The American Press*, LII (October, 1933), 3.

"President and Publisher." *Time*, XXV (February 4, 1935), 49.

Pringle, Henry. "The Newspaper Guild." *Scribner's*, V (January, 1939), 41-47.

"The Publishers Crack Down." *New Republic*, LXXXI (February 6, 1935), 348.

Randau, Carl. "It Happened One Day in September 14 Years Ago. *Frontpage* (September-October, 1947), p. 6.

Ray, Royal. "Economic Factors as Forces in Daily Newspaper Concentration." *Journalism Quarterly*, XXIX (Winter, 1952), 32-45.

"Report of Industrial Board Members." *Editor & Publisher*, LXVIII (April 27, 1935), 98.

"Reporters and Labor Unions." *Publishers Service Magazine*, IV (October 19, 1933), 1-2.

"Reporters Unions." *The American Press*, LI (August, 1933), 4.

Ring, Robert. "Newark Guild Found Organized Labor Strong Ally During Strike." *The Guild Reporter* (April 15, 1935), p. 2.

Robb, Arthur. "Unions Call A.N.P.A. Code 'Inadequate to Effect NRA Purposes.' " *Editor & Publisher*, LXVI (September 30, 1933), 5.

Roberts, A. L. "Cleveland News Signs Contract." *The Guild Reporter* (January 1, 1935), pp. 1, 3.

"Salaries and Working Conditions of Newspaper Editorial Employees." *Monthly Labor Review*, XL (May, 1935), 1134-39.

Scribner, John. "Newswriters Versus the NRA." *New Republic*, LXXIX (July 4, 1934), 201-3.

Seldes, George. "Roy Howard and His Newspapers." *New Republic*, VC (July 27, 1938), 323-24.

Stockbridge, Frank P. "Professional Association or Trade Union." *The American Press*, LI (September, 1933), 1-2.

——. "A Question of Leadership." *The American Press*, LI (September, 1933), 1.

"Strike." *Newsweek*, V (March 23, 1935), 23.

"This Matter of Morale." *The Quill*, XXI (April, 1933), 14.

Tunney, James J. ("Gene"). "A Man Must Fight." *Colliers*, LXXXIX (March 5, 1932), 13-14, 48-49.

"Unnecessary Torture." *Time*, XXIV (December 24, 1934), 14.

"Victory on Points." *Time*, XXVIII (September 14, 1936), 34.

Ward, Paul. "Roosevelt Keeps His Vow." *Nation*, CXLI (September 25, 1935), 349.

Watson, Morris. "History Is Now Being Written Behind Nation's Front Pages." *The Guild Reporter* (November 23, 1933), p. 1.

Wharton, Don. "J. David Stern." *Scribner's*, C (December, 1936), 44-49.

White, Lloyd. "Genesis of the Guild." *The Quill*, XXI (December, 1933), 5-6.

——. "What the Guild Told Roosevelt at a Tea Party." *The Guild Reporter* (January 12, 1934), pp. 1, 3.

Winthrop, Jean. "A Newspaper Game." *Controversy*, I (November 23, 1934), 65-66.

H. NEWSPAPERS

Cleveland *Plain Dealer*, 1933-37.

The Daily Worker, 1933-37.

The Guild Reporter, 1933-39.

Milwaukee Journal, 1933-37.

Milwaukee Leader, 1936.

Newsdom, 1931-39.

New York Amsterdam News, 1935-36.

New York Daily News, 1933-37.

New York Herald Tribune, 1933-37.

The New York Times, 1930-39.

New York World-Telegram, 1931-39.

Staten Island Advance, 1934.

I. PERIODICALS

American Press, 1930-39.

Bulletin of the American Newspaper Publishers Association, 1933-37.

Labor Bulletin of the Special Standing Committee of the American Newspaper Publishers Association, 1933-37.

Nation, 1933-37.

New Republic, 1933-37.

The Quill, 1933-37.

Time, 1933-37.

J. OTHER SOURCES (Pamphlets, reports, strike bulletins, speeches, and letters).

American Newspaper Guild. Manual, 1936-37. New York: ANG, 1936.
——. "Proceedings of the Founding Meeting and of the Annual Conventions." 1933-36. Microfilm copy. University of California. Berkeley, California.

American Society of Newspaper Editors. Problems of Journalism: Proceedings of the Annual Meeting. Washington, D.C.: American Society of Newspaper Editors, 1927, 1929, 1934.

"Amsterdam News Strike Bulletin." American Newspaper Guild. Washington, D.C.

Case, Daryl J. "A History of the Code of Fair Competition for the Daily Newspaper Publishing Business." December 27, 1935. U.S. National Archives and Record Service. Document Series of the National Recovery Administration 1933-36. National Archives Microfilm Publications: Microcopy No. 213, Roll 44. Washington, D.C.: General Services Administration, 1956.

First Annual Address to the Reporters' Club of Philadelphia, 1886. Pamphlet. Journalism Library, Columbia University. New York, New York.

The Guild Striker. May-June, 1936 (scattered). State Historical Society of Wisconsin. Madison, Wisconsin.

International Labour Office. Conditions of Life and Work of Journal-

ists. "Studies and Reports," Series L, No. 2. Geneva: no publisher, 1928.

International Typographical Union. "Proceedings of the 65th Session." Supplement to the *Typographical Journal*, LXII (September, 1920).

Kenen, I. L., to Clyde Beals. August 21, 1938. Carbon. Kenen papers.

"Ledger Strike Bulletins." November 22, 1934-March 28, 1935. American Newspaper Guild. Washington, D.C.

Lundberg, Ferdinand, to Oliver Pilat. October 23, 1963. In author's possession.

McCormick, Robert R. *The Case for the Freedom of the Press.* 1933. Pamphlet. Journalism Library, Columbia University. New York, New York.

Nelson, Saul. "The Newspaper Industry." November, 1933. U.S. National Archives and Record Service. *Document Series of the National Recovery Administration 1933-36.* National Archives Microfilm Publication: Microcopy No. 213, Roll 44. Washington, D.C.: General Services Administration, 1956.

"The Newspaper Guild of New York, What It Is . . . Why It Is and Other Salient Facts." April, 1954. Pamphlet. In author's possession.

Pew, Marlen. "Professional vs. Trades Union News Departments." Address before 16th Annual Convention of the University Press Club of Michigan, Ann Arbor, Michigan, November 8, 1934. Privately printed. Journalism Library, Columbia University. New York, New York.

Reach's Official American Association Baseball Guide. Philadelphia: A. J. Reach Company, 1889.

index

Advertising revenue, newspaper, 25-27, 28, 180, 233

Akron, O.: editorial employees, 56, 68, 94; Newspaper Circulation Guild, 106, 326n46, 332n46

Akron *Times-Press*, 149, 179

Albany, N. Y.: editorial employees, 92, 109-10; *see also* Tri-City Guild

American Federation of Labor: 1923-1933 attempts to unionize newspapermen, 22; strike support, 146, 168, 248, 250, 258; support of ANG, 173-74, 191, 193, 235; financial assistance to ANG, 277-78

    ANG affiliation with, 100, 126-27, 131, 133, 135, 168, 175, 204, 206-8, 227-28; at 1935 convention, 208-10, 326n46; referendum on, 225-26, 230; at 1936 convention, 264, 268-69; final vote, 257, 258, 269; Charter granted, 277-81

American Journalists Association (AJA), 21-22

American Newspaper Guild (ANG): question of radical leadership, 135, 153, 159, 206; concept of ANG as trade union, 137, 142, 146, 151, 166, 175, 187, 190, 208, 209; ties with labor unions, 146, 191, 193, 230, 235, 262; Communist influences, 152, 159, 222, 228-29, 235, 267-68, 282; split between "New York and national" blocs, 206, 210, 215, 255-56, 260-61, 265-66, 274-75, 323n4; friction in leadership, 221-22, 224-25, 227, 228-29, 237-38; summary of growth and development, 281-83

    activities: relations with Newspaper Industrial Board, 75, 120-21, 146, 182, 184, 188, 191-92, 195, 196-97, 203; assistance from New York Guild, 108-9, 112-13, 128; informational, 109-10; organizational, 111-12, 130, 202-3, 261, 279 (*see also* Davy, William; Eddy, Jonathan; Hull, Morgan; Stevens, Don); representation on Newspaper Industrial Board, 121-22, 182, 195, 197, 203; Code of Ethics, 125; 1934 (first) convention, 128-33; relations with NRA, 176, 187-88; 1935 convention, 205-15; 1936 convention, 265-75

    administration: National Executive Committee actions, 105-7, 113, 116, 129, 130-31, 134, 137, 147, 148, 149-50, 166, 202, 208, 211; Executive Secretary, 107-8 (*see also* Eddy, Jonathan); members, number of, 111, 128, 130, 136, 219, 325n31; revised constitution and bylaws (1934), 129-30; regional vice presidential system, 129-30, 149-50; employment of organizers, 202-3, 261-62, 279; 1935 constitution and bylaws, 210-11, 212-13; district regional councils, 211, 213; National Council, 213; National Executive Board (NEB), actions, 213, 214, 219-20, 221, 223-25, 227-28, 242, 255, 263, 265; 1936 constitution and bylaws, 269-73; International Executive Board (IEB), 272

    affiliation with AFL, 100, 126-27, 131, 133, 135, 168, 175, 204, 206-8, 227-28; 1935 convention consideration, 208-10, 326n46; referendum on, 225-26, 230; final vote, 257, 258, 269; 1936 convention,

affiliation with AFL (Continued)
264, 268-69; Charter granted,
277-81; areas of jurisdiction
with printing trades unions defined, 278-79
contracts, 117-18, 123-24, 129, 141,
142, 143, 148, 150, 171-72, 178-79,
230-35, 251, 259, 262-63, 276;
emphasis on collective bargaining, 98, 102, 118, 124, 126, 127,
128-29, 132-33, 175, 177, 181, 212,
213, 272, 273; negotiating procedure, 148-49, 178-79, 264; opposition of publishers to collective
bargaining, 177-78; "bulletin-
board" contracts and lack of
written agreements, 178-79, 231-
32, 276; limited benefits in, 179-
80; model, 263; ANG Dismissal
Bonus Rate, 264; chains, coordi-
nated bargaining councils, 273;
see also Hours of work; Wages
establishment, 2-3, 42-44, 92-102;
not originally a labor union, 2,
42; as white collar union, 2-3;
predecessors, 49-63; Washington meeting, 90, 92-102; New
York meeting, 90-91; New York
Guild activities, 90-92, 96; first
constitution and bylaws, 93, 96,
98-99, 103-4, 205; delegates, 94-
95 (table); stated purpose, 98;
officers, 99-101, 104, 129; National Executive Committee,
101, 104
finances: dues, 104, 127-28, 130,
134, 147, 212, 219-20, 222, 229,
261, 264-65, 270, 271, 311n1; financial crises, 107-8, 127-28,
130-31, 136-37, 147, 219-20, 222-
25, 229-30, 261, 277-78; Emergency Defense Fund, 166-67,
2:3, 217; proposal for centralization of funds, 212; strike assessments, 213, 217, 219, 255-56,
264, 266; assessments, 219-20,
222, 223, 224, 225, 227; defense
certificates, 227, 264
local guilds and chapters: Number 1, Cleveland, 48, 112; in first
constitution, 103; relations with
national organization defined,
103-4, 134-35, 150-51, 211-13, 270-
73; number, 111, 136, 237, 265;
organization of, 111-12, 130; op-

position to final NRA code, 115-
16; opposition to centralized
(New York) authority, 150-52,
204, 206, 215, 260-61; guilds represented at 1935 convention,
205, 323n4; guilds at 1936 convention, 265, 332n46; see also
place and newspaper names
strikes, 143, 144, 153-68, 248-61;
picketing, 139-40, 145-46, 157,
161, 163, 165, 216-17, 248, 253,
258; labor union support, 146,
167-68, 173-74, 248, 250, 256, 258,
264; calls for, 212, 270, 271; see
also Lockouts
American Newspaper Publishers
Association (ANPA), 35-36, 276;
National Arbitration Agreement
(with ITU), 16; NRA newspaper
draft code, 35-42, 74; Daily
Newspaper Code Committee,
38; Special Standing Committee
on labor questions, 123, 153;
see also Newspaper Industrial
Board; Publishers
American Press, The, 64, 72; quoted,
4, 8, 63, 82
Anderson, Paul Y., 40-41, 61, 68, 70
Angly, Edward, 59, 60, 61, 62, 67, 69
Ardmore, Pa., Main Line Daily
Times, 262
Ashcraft, Garland, 48-49, 50-51, 54,
55, 80, 110, 127, 170, 273, 316n74;
ANG Treasurer, 214, 217, 223,
224, 229, 264, 267
Associated Press, 124, 231; Watson
case, 273, 276-77
Atlantic City, N. J.; editorial em-
ployees, 95
Austin, Tex.: newsmen, 79; editorial
employees, 95

Ballantine, Betty, 274
Baltimore, Md.: editorial employees,
94; guild, 228, 269, 323n4, 326n46,
332n46
Barkin, Solomon, 120
Baseball Reporters Association of
America, 11
Battle Creek, Mich., guild, 323n4
Bay City, Mich., editorial employees,
95
Beals, Clyde, 206, 220
Bellamy, Paul, 55-56
Bellamy, Richard, 257

Biddle, Francis, 186, 191
Birmingham, Ala., editorial employees, 77, 95
Bitner, H. L., 250-51, 259
Black, John H., 245, 246-48, 250-51, 259
Blankenhorn, Heber, 121
Bleyer, Willard G., quoted, 20-21
Block, Paul, 24, 113, 240, 244
Bordner, Robert, 48, 50, 54, 94, 96, 98
Boston, Mass.: 1918-1919 unionization efforts in, 17; AFL local, 22, 68; Headline Club, 68; editorial employees, 77, 81, 95; guild, 142, 176, 327n46, 332n46
Brandt, Raymond P., 97
Bridgeport, Conn., guild, 265
Bridgeport *Standard-Telegram,* 18
Brisbane, Arthur, 5
Britt, George, 45, 58, 59
Brooklyn *Eagle,* 26, 263
Brooks, Ned, 95
Broun, Heywood: role in establishment of ANG, 2-3, 43-45, 91, 92, 93, 94, 98; syndicated columnist, 5, 43-44, 240; President of Presswriters Union, 23, 44; journalistic background, 43-44; criticism of NRA code, 44, 46, 58, 68; call for "union of reporters" and reaction, 44-45, 52, 57, 65; organization of Guild of New York Newspaper Men and Women, 57-61; and organization movement, 81, 83; at NRA code hearings, 67, 68, 69, 71; organization of New York Guild, 84-86; Vice President of New York Guild 86-87; final NRA code, 96, 97; champion of AFL affiliation, 99-100
President of ANG, 2, 99-101, 102, 105-7, 108, 113, 115, 116, 123, 131, 140, 152-53, 177, 187; in *Long Island Daily Press* boycott, 138-39, 140-41, 142; actions in crises, 140-41, 145, 147; in *Newark Ledger* strike, 155-56, 165; and jurisdictional problems, 187, 193, 195; reelection, 214; in Lorain lockout, 217, 218; in Amsterdam News lockout, 235; in Milwaukee strike, 254, 256, 260; reelection, 273
Browder, Earl, 267

Brown, Emily, 138, 140, 141
Bryan, John Stewart, 38, 295n15
Buck, Robert, 120, 121, 152, 193, 198, 203, 208, 214, 221, 224, 226, 269; resignation, 226-27
Buckley, George, 119, 132
Buffalo, N. Y.: editorial employees, 63-64, 68, 77, 90, 91; guild, 78-79, 94, 127, 323n4, 326n46, 332n46
Burgess, Louis, 124, 131, 181-82, 244, 310n63
Burks, Edward D., 88, 95, 101
Butler, Charles R., 67, 295n12

Camden, N. J.: editorial employees, 47, 68; see *also* Newspaper Guild of Philadelphia and Camden
Carter, Amon G., 38
Cassidy, Edward F., 41
Cates, Dudley, 38
Catton, Bruce, 132, 241, 243, 268
Champaign-Urbana (Ill.) Newspaper Guild, 265
Chicago, Ill.: AFL local, 22, 68; editorial employees, 77; newsmen, 80; guild, 265, 332n46
Christian Science Monitor, 37
Cincinnati, O.: editorial employees, 77; guild, 79, 94, 13, 237, 326n46, 332n46
Clarke, Donald Henderson, quoted, 9
Cleveland, O., editorial workers, 30
Cleveland Editorial Employees Association: establishment and activities, 49-56, 63, 77, 78; representation at NRA code hearings, 68, 69-70; change of name to Cleveland Newspaper Guild, 89
Cleveland *News,* 49, 50, 53, 54, 56, 142, 168-72, 178, 230, 262
Cleveland Newspaper Guild, 89, 90, 91, 92, 93, 100, 111, 124, 127, 136, 142, 149, 168-72, 176, 178, 202, 205, 215-18, 241-43, 323n4, 326n46, 332n46
Cleveland *Plain-Dealer,* 49, 50, 52, 53-55; Editorial Employee Association, 54, 55, 299n6
Cleveland *Press,* 50, 51, 53, 56, 169, 230, 241-43; staff protest against NRA code, 48-49
Cohn, Morris, 159-60
Columbia (S. C.) *State,* editorial staff, 79, 95

Columbia University School of Journalism, 10
Columbus, O.: editorial employees, 56; guild, 94, 326n46
Committee for Industrial Organization (CIO): relations with and financial assistance to ANG, 230, 277-78, 280-81
Connery, William P., Jr., quoted, 41-42
Cornish, Richard, quoted, 41
Council Bluffs, Ia., editorial employees, 95
Crist, Judith, quoted, 9
Crosby, Alexander, 144-46
Crozier, Emmet, 94, 100-1, 154, 156-57, 159-60, 168, 210; ANG Treasurer, 101, 106, 108, 113, 123, 131, 134

Dallas, Tex., newsmen, 80, 93, 95
Davis, Howard, ANPA President, 36, 37-38, 39, 186, 189, 190, 192, 194, 201
Davis, Mrs. Sadie Warren, 234-36
Davy, William, 202, 214, 215, 217, 220, 247, 250, 252, 257, 279, 316n74
Del-Mar-Va Association, 67
Denver, Colo.: ITU newswriters local, 15; guild, 265
Depression, The Great, 1; effect on newspaper industry, 28-32
Des Moines, Ia., guild, 327n46
Des Moines Tribune, 78, 95
de Souza, D. A., 95, 116, 164; excellence awards, 264
Detroit, Mich.: editorial employees, 77; guild, 78, 110, 126, 256, 265, 323n4, 326n46
Detroit Mirror, 31
Detroit Times, 78
Dinsmore, Herman, 275
Doherty, H. L., 296n24
Donaldson, Ralph J., 50, 55
Drake, Lee, 37
Duluth, Minn.: editorial employees, 77; guild, 84, 89, 95, 323n4, 326n46
Durham, N. C., guild, 323n4, 326n46

Eddy, Jonathan, 59, 75-76, 97; secretary of New York Guild, 86, 109; establishment of ANG, 87-91, 92, 94, 99-100; Secretary of ANG, 101, 105, 107, 116; Executive Secretary, 107-8, 116-17, 118, 122-23, 124, 131, 134, 136-37, 138-40, 147, 150, 151, 153, 155, 166, 176, 177, 179, 184, 195, 198, 202, 206, 219, 224, 228, 249, 252, 255, 261, 277; reelection, 214-15, 274; appointment to Newspaper Industrial Board, 122
Editor & Publisher, 46, 63, 75, 80, 111, 124; quoted, 16, 32, 36, 78, 81, 103, 136, 146-47, 151
Editorial employees: job stability, 7-8; local press clubs and groups, 11-12; effect of Depression on, 29-32; NRA assistance to, 33; see also Hours of work; Newspapermen; Wages
National Recovery Administration codes: designation as professionals not subject to maximum-hour regulations, 39, 40-41; draft code, 40-42; attitude toward temporary code, 42, 46-47, 50, 61-62, 64-65, 66; Philadelphia Code (counterproposal), 47-48, 56; hearings, 56, 61-62, 64, 66, 67-71; final code, 73, 75, 97; objections to final code provisions, 75-76, 104-5; New York meeting, 90, 91; White House talks with editorial workers, 96-97; Newspaper Code Authority, 100
unionization: establishment of ANG, 3-4, 42-44, 92-102; ITU attempts to organize, 12-16, 18-20, 22, 23-24; 1919 activities, 16-19, 32; early attitudes toward, 20-21; post-World War I, 20-24, 32; AFL attempts (1923-1933), 22; independent groups (1920s), 22-23, 32; opinion on need for organization, 40-43, 64; Cleveland Association, 49-56, 63; Guild of New York Newspaper Men and Women, 57-63; organization movement, post-NRA code, 77-87; disinterest of publishers, 80-81; failures, 80-81; reaction of trade press, 81-82; concern re dangers of union control, 82-83; goal of affiliation

with labor unions, 83, 305n71; eligibility for membership, 83-84; Newspaper Guild of New York, 84-87; interest in national organization, 88-92; *see also* names of cities and newspapers

El Paso, Tex.: editorial employees, 95; guild, 124, 323n4, 326n46, 332n46

Emery, Francis, 62

Ernst, Morris, 45, 58, 62, 73, 85, 152, 199

Evans, A. Judson, 95, 101

Fehlhaber, Elmer, 50, 226

Fleeson, Doris, 45, 59, 60, 62, 67, 81, 94, 101, 112

Fort Wayne, Ind., editorial employees, 95

Fort Worth, Tex., guild, 127

Frederick, J. F., 250, 258

Freedom of the press: NRA licensing regulation, 35, 36-37; guarantee of in NRA draft code, 29-40; in final NRA code, 73-74, 76-77, 119

French, Paul C., 95, 210, 270

Gannett, Lewis, 59, 60; quoted, 23

Gannett newspapers, 24, 39, 239

Garrison, Lloyd, 181, 185

Gary, Ind., editorial employees, 95

Gilfillan, R. S., 93, 94, 99; ANG Vice President, 101, 214

Goldberg, Nathan J., 79, 93, 94, 268

Goski, John, 49, 50

Grand Forks, N. D., guild, 135

Great Falls, Mont., guild, 265

Green, William, 146, 168, 227, 250, 277, 278, 280

Greensboro, N. C., guild, 323n4, 326n46

Gross, Ernest, 73

Guild of New York Newspaper Men and Women: organization, 46, 57-63; representation at NRA code hearings, 67-68, 69, 85; renamed, 84 (*see* Newspaper Guild of New York)

Guild Reporter, The: established by New York Guild, 91-92; ANG publication, 108, 110, 136, 147, 151-52, 220, 223, 224; quoted, 115, 126, 129, 151, 197, 199

Haas, John, 50, 51-52

Hackensack, N. J., editorial employees, 94, 124

Hanna, Dan R., Jr., 169-71

Hanson, Elisha, ANPA counsel, 38, 39, 66, 67, 72, 73, 74, 191, 192, 194; and ANG, 38, 177, 184, 185

Harriman, W. Averill, 195, 196

Harrisburg, Pa.: editorial employees, 94; guild, 115, 323n4

Harrison, Marvin C., 68, 69-70

Hearst, William Randolph, 24, 26, 35, 39; opposition to guilds, 131-32, 250-51

Hearst newspapers, 124, 131-32, 243-44, 256, 260-61, 275-76

Heath, Louis, 228

Henkel, Luella, 45, 58, 87

Hoan, Daniel, 248-49, 255

Hochstein, Philip, 137-39

Holmes, Ralph, 78, 207

Homan, W. Earle, 228, 262, 264, 268, 273

Honolulu, Hawaii, editorial employees, 77

Horvitz, Samuel, 215-16, 218

Hostetler, Joseph, 169-70

Hours of work of newspapermen, 6-7, 23, 31-32; in NRA draft codes, 34, 37, 40-41, 42, 67, 69, 72; in early contracts, 47; in final NRA code, 75-76, 112, 114-15, 118-20, 124; in ANG contracts, 117, 148, 150, 171, 178, 179, 231, 232, 233, 241, 242, 245-46, 251, 259, 263; NRA code amendments, 187, 197-201

Howard, Roy, 230, 240, 275

Howe, Louis, 190, 191

Howey, Walter, 7

Hudson County, N. J., guild, 323n4, 326n46, 332n46

Hudson Dispatch, 263

Hull, Morgan, 261-62, 279

Huston, Luther, 93, 94, 96, 98

Indianapolis, Ind., guild, 265

Inland Daily Press Association, 28, 67, 82

International Labour Office, quoted, 5-6

International League of Press Clubs, 12

International Typographical Union (ITU), 208; attempts to unionize newspapermen, 12-16, 18-20; relinquishment of jurisdiction over newspapermen, 22, 279; Newswriters Union, 68, 245, 292n40; New York local, 146
Isserman, A. J., 161, 162, 212, 263

Jennings, Dean, 125; case, 182-88, 190, 191-92, 194-95
Jersey City, N. J., Hudson County Guild, 111, 323n4
Jersey Journal, 263
Jewish Daily Bulletin (N.Y.C.), strike, 143-44
Johnson, Carl, 197, 214, 221, 245, 248, 264
Johnson, Hugh S., 35-36, 38, 39, 75, 97, 98, 114, 119, 121-22, 180

Kansas City, Mo.: AFL local, 22, 68; guild, 326n46
Kaufman, Milton, 157, 202, 232, 253, 257, 271
Kelley, Rex, 261-62, 331n36
Kelly, Harvey J., 82-83, 153, 196, 223, 251
Kenen, I. L., 49-50, 52, 55, 93, 94, 96, 210
Kieffer, Evelyn B., 216
Kieran, James, 59, 62, 67, 96-97, 99, 177
Klyman, Julius, 221, 223, 268, 274
Knowland, Joseph R., 172-73
Knowles, Clayton, 138
Knoxville, Tenn., guild, 265

Labor unions: support of ANG strikes and boycotts, 146, 167-68, 173-74, 248, 250, 256, 258, 264; cooperation with ANG, 191, 193, 230, 235, 262
La Guardia, Fiorello, 141, 236
Landau, Jacob, 143
Langendorff, Herbert, 252
Lansing, Mich., guild, 95, 256, 323n4, 326n46
Larke, Alfred, 268
Lehigh Valley Guild, 111, 323n4, 326n46
Leider, Ben, 140
Levinson, Edward, 268, 269
Lewis, John L., 230, 277, 280

Lewis, Thomas A., 95, 126
Lilly, Joseph, 59, 61, 62
Lindey, Alexander, 67, 69, 184
Lindley, Ernest K., 96, 97
Lippmann, Walter, 73
Little Rock, Ark., editorial employees, 136
Lockouts: Lorain Journal, 215-18; New York Amsterdam News, 233-37
Long Island Daily Press, boycott by ANG chapter, 137-42
Lorain (O.) Journal, lockout, 215-18
Los Angeles, Calif., editorial employees, 77
Los Angeles Examiner, 118, 124
Louisville (Ky.) Courier-Journal and Times, unionization effort, 17
Lundberg, Ferdinand, 5

McCarter, George W. C., 160-61
McConnell, Oviatt, 79
McCormick, Robert, 300n24
McCrea, J. Nash, 252, 254, 255, 257, 259
McKenney, Ruth, 101
Madison, Wis.: newsmen, 80; guild, 150-51, 178, 276, 323n4
Main Line Daily Times (Ardmore, Pa.), 262
Mann, George, 260, 268
Mason, Redfern, 173
Meek, Harold T., 208, 210, 214
Mich, Daniel, 150
Mickelsen, Gunnar, 245, 246, 248, 255, 257, 274
Millis, Harry, 184, 185
Mills, Clyde, 200
Milwaukee, Wis.: ITU Newswriters Union, 68, 245, 292n40; guild, 243, 244-61, 323n4, 326n46, 332n-46; see also Wisconsin News
Milwaukee Journal, 37, 244, 246, 252, 260
Milwaukee Leader, 245
Milwaukee Sentinel, 244, 246, 252, 260
Minneapolis, Minn., see Twin Cities Newspaper Guild
Minneapolis Journal, 276
Minneapolis Tribune, 263
Missoulian, The (Mont.), ITU union, 18-19
Mobile, Ala., newsmen, 125-26

Monroe, La., newsmen, 93, 94, 127
Moon, Henry Lee, 328n65
Morrison, Frank W., 68, 70, 94
Morse, Mrs. Odessa, 236
Muskegon, Mich., guild, 126, 326n46

National Editorial Association (NEA), 35; and NRA codes, 72, 74
National Labor Board (NLB), disputes involving NRA codes, 181-82, 183, 188
National Labor Relations Board (NLRB): disputes involving ANG, 40, 183; and NRA code, 75, 120; establishment, 181; Jennings case, 184-86, 193, 194; Watson case, 276-77
National Press Club, 97
National Recovery Administration (NRA), 33-41; industry code program, 34; President's Re-Employment Agreement (PRA), 34, 36, 37, 39, 72, 181; guarantee of collective bargaining (Section 7a), 37, 73, 76, 177, 180, 184, 185, 186, 193, 201; Blue Eagle campaign, 34-35, 37; newspaper code, 34-77 *passim* (*see also* Newspaper industry, *subhead* NRA codes); and ANPA, 35-42; unconstitutionality of, Supreme Court decision, 77, 177, 201-2; attitudes in labor disputes, 180-81, 188-89
National Union of Journalists, 82, 292n36
Nelson, Herman, 215
Newark, N. J., guild, 63, 68, 79, 90, 91, 94, 111, 113, 152, 154-68, 228, 231, 272, 323n4, 326n46, 332n46
Newark Ledger, strike, 153-68, 231
New England Daily Newspaper Association, 67
New Haven, Conn.: 1919 strike, 20; editorial employees, 95
Newhouse, Norman, 144
Newhouse, Samuel I., 135, 137-41, 144-46, 163, 231, 272
New Jersey Press Association, 28, 77
Newsboys (delivery), 253; in NRA codes, 39, 75, 112
Newsdom, 29-30, 63, 295n24; open letter to Broun, 44-45, 57, 296n25

Newspaper Guild of New York, 84-87; predecessor (Guild), 46, 57-63, 67-68, 69; constitution and bylaws, 84-86, 96; form of organization, 85; purpose, 85-86; officers, 86-87; activities toward establishment of ANG, 90-92, 93, 94, 96, 100; assistance to ANG, 108-9, 112-13, 128; contracts, 143, 177-78, 232-37; in *Newark Ledger* strike, 157, 164, 165; size and voting strength at 1935 convention, 205, 206, 323n4, 326n46; leadership split with national bloc, 206, 210, 215, 255-56, 260-61; size and voting strength at 1936 convention, 266-68, 274-75
Newspaper Guild of Philadelphia and Camden, 79-80, 90, 91, 93, 95, 112, 117-18, 125, 127, 142, 149, 178-79, 205, 231, 262, 265, 323n4, 326n46, 332n46
Newspaper Industrial Board (NIB), 75-76, 120-21, 181, 188, 189-90, 194, 195, 196-97, 223; cases, 121, 146, 182, 183, 184, 191-92, 195-96; ANG representative on, 122, 182, 195, 223
Newspaper industry: mergers, 16, 26-27; chains, 24; economic changes in, 24-28; changes in 1900-1932, 24-32; mortality of newspapers, 25-26; competition of radio, 28; effect of Depression on, 28-32; *see also* Advertising; Publishers
NRA code: draft, 34, 35-42; temporary, 46, 47, 56, 60, 64-65; Cleveland Editorial Employees Association opposition to, 48-49, 69-70; New York Guild opposition, 58, 60, 61-62
NRA final code, 66-67; hearings, 56, 61-62, 64, 66-71; preparation of terms, 72-75; reaction to, 75-77; voluntary nature of, 77; presidential approval, 112, 114-15, 123; ANG opposition to Pulitzer as Administrator, 113-14, 124; ANG opposition, 115, 118-20, 123; Newspaper Code Authority, 120, 195; amendments on hours and wages, 187,

NRA final code *(Continued)*
197-201; ANG walkout on hearings, 187, 198
Newspapermen: status and working conditions, 4-11, 30-31; "romance of newspapering," 8-11, 32, 125; education, 10-11, 125; job insecurity, 7-8, 31; local press clubs and groups, 11-12; effect of Depression on, 28-32; as professionals in NRA draft codes, 39, 40-41; *see also* Editorial workers; Reporters
Newspapers, small-town, 29; provisions of NRA codes, 72, 74; *see also* National Editorial Association
New York Amsterdam News, lockout and boycott, 233-37
New York City guilds, see Guild of New York Newspaper Men and Women; Newspaper Guild of New York
New York City Presswriters Union, 23, 43, 44
New York *Daily News,* 62-63, 232
New York *Evening Mail,* 25
New York Post, 232, 263, 276
New York Press Club, 82
New York Telegram, 18
New York Times, 27, 75; quoted, 19, 68
New York *World-Telegram,* 62, 178, 240
Neylan, John F., 184, 186
Norfolk, Va., editorial employees, 94
Northern California Newspaper Guild, 261, 323n4, 332n46

Oakland (Calif.) *Tribune,* ANG boycott, 172-73
Ohl, Henry, Jr., 248, 251, 258
Oklahoma City, guild, 142
Omaha, Neb., 30; guild, 111, 323n4
Omaha Bee, 18
Open shop, in NRA codes, 39, 73, 76
Orange, N. J., Hudson County Guild, 111, 326n46

Pacific Northwest Association, 67
Parker, Andrew M., 68, 70, 93, 95, 97; quoted, 47-48, 116; ANG Vice President, 101, 107

Pasche, Victor, 226, 263
Passaic, N. J., editorial employees, 95
Paterson, N. J., *Press-Guardian,* 20, 94
Patterson, Joseph, 232
Peck, Gustav, 199
Pennsylvania Newspaper Publishers Association, 72
Perkins, Frances, 112, 191, 192
Pew, Marlen, 136; quoted, 27-28, 30, 62
Philadelphia, Pa.: editorial employees, 56, 77; counterproposals to NRA code, 47-48, 56, 68, 70; guild, see Newspaper Guild of Philadelphia and Camden
Philadelphia *Evening Bulletin,* 48, 70
Philadelphia *Evening Ledger,* 142
Philadelphia *Inquirer,* 70, 231
Philadelphia *North American,* 25
Philadelphia *Record,* 37, 47, 117-18, 178-79, 262-63
Pittsburgh, Pa.: ITU editorial workers local, 13; guild, 323n4, 326n-46, 332n46
Pittsburgh Post-Gazette, 149
Pope, Aiken, 236
Pope, Generoso, 192
Poston, Theodore, 235, 328n65
Powell, C. B., 237
Press associations: employees, lack of code for, 98, 115, 177; ANG bargaining with, 104
Printers: hours of work, 6-7; wages, 27, 72; effect of Depression on, 29, 30; commercial department of newspapers, 72, 74; areas of jurisdiction with ANG, 279; *see also* International Typographical Union
Progresso, Il, 192
Publishers: attitude toward early employee unionization attempts, 15, 17-18, 22, 63, 64-65; effects of corporate ownership on, 24; effects of Depression, 29-32; and President's Re-Employment Agreement, 34, 36, 37; and NRA, 35-42, 189-90; and temporary NRA code, 62-63, 64-65, 66-67; at NRA code hearings, 66-67; reaction to establishment of

N.Y.C. Guild, 62-63; and final NRA code, 73-74, 76-77, 119; indifference to unionization, 80-81; concern re dangers of union control, 82-83; relations with guilds, 112-13; first ANG contract with, 116-17; hostility to ANG, 124-26, 135-36, 153; opposition to collective bargaining, 177-78, 180; and NLRB ruling on jurisdiction of newspaper cases, 189, 193-94; dissatisfaction with NRA code, 190-91, 194; attitude toward ANG as labor union, 275-76; see also American Newspaper Publishers Association; Newspaper Industrial Board

Publishers Service Magazine, quoted, 82

Pulitzer, Ralph, 113-14, 124

Quill, The, quoted, 31

Randau, Carl, 59, 138, 139, 177
Raymond, Allen, 59, 84-85; President of New York Guild, 86, 91, 97, 112
Reading, Pa.: editorial employees, 95, 149; guild, 124, 178, 228, 231, 323n4, 326n46
Reading *Times*, 149, 178
Reporters: hours of work, 7; salaries, 4-5, 6; unionization attempts in 1918-1919, 18
Richberg, Donald, 40, 74, 180, 187, 188-89, 191
Richmond, Va.: editorial employees, 95; guild, 108, 323n4
Ring, Robert, 154, 156
Roberts, A. L., 50, 52, 170-71
Robins, Nelson, quoted, 82, 83
Rochester, N. Y.: editorial employees, 92; guild, 323n4, 326n46, 332n46
Rockford, Ill.: editorial employees, 46, 56; Editorial Employees Association, 64, 68, 78, 94; guild, 105, 198, 215, 323n4, 326n46
Rogers, Lindsay, 66, 68, 71, 73, 90, 97, 98, 99-100, 101, 113
Roosevelt, Franklin D., 33, 34, 74-75, 96-97, 99-100, 177, 193-94
Russell, Lucius T., 153-68

Saginaw, Mich., editorial employees, 95
St. Louis, Mo.: association of journalists, 21-22; editorial employees, 77, 95; guild, 151, 164, 198, 205, 256, 269, 323n4, 326n46, 332n46
St. Louis *Post-Dispatch*, 5, 151-52, 263
St. Paul, Minn., *Daily News*, 206; see also Twin Cities Newspaper Guild
Salaries of newspapermen, see Wages and salaries
Salt Lake City, Utah, guild, 126, 323n4, 326n46
San Antonio, Tex.: editorial employees, 93, 95; guild, 326n46
San Antonio *Express*, 5
San Francisco, Calif.: unionization attempts, 18; editorial employees, 30, 77; guild, 149, 172-74, 326n46
San Francisco *Call-Bulletin*, 125, 182-86
San Francisco *Examiner*, 124, 173, 181
Santa Monica, Calif., guild, 265
Savory, P. M. H., 237
Schenectady, N. Y., editorial employees, 109-10; see also Tri-City Guild
Scranton, Pa.: Newswriters Union, 15, 23-24, 61, 68; guild, 24
Scripps-Howard newspapers, 24, 39, 48, 56, 113, 199, 230, 240-41, 242, 262
Seattle, Wash., guild, 261, 265
Seattle *Post-Intelligencer*, strike, 257, 258-59, 260
Seide, Herman, 250, 251, 258
Seltzer, Louis, 50-51, 230
Sherman, Thomas, 214, 224, 274
Sinclair, Upton, quoted, 8, 21
Sioux Falls, S. D., newsmen, 79
Slocum, H. B., 46, 92
Smith, Blackwell, 187
Smith, Edwin, 184-85
Smith, H. Bowen, 228
Southern Newspaper Publishers Association, 67
Spokane, Wash., guild, 326n46
Springfield, Mass., guild, 326n46
Springfield, O., guild, 323n4, 326n46

Staten Island *Advance*, 144-46
Stern, J. David, 47, 117-18, 172, 178, 232-33
Stevens, Don, 149, 214, 223, 248, 261; Treasurer, 274, organizer, 279
Stewart, Kenneth, quoted, 33, 61
Stockbridge, Frank Parker, 63
Strikes: ITU (1890s), 12; N. Y. C. Jewish dailies (1912), 14, 16; *Omaha Bee* (1919), 18; New Haven, Conn. (1919), 20; ANG, *see under* American Newspaper Guild
Strouse, Don, 93, 94
Sulzberger, Arthur Hays, 275
Svirsky, Leon, 58
Syracuse (N. Y.) *Herald*, 28

Tacoma, Wash., guild, 237, 262
Tacoma *Times*, 262
Tate, Jack, 199, 200
Teaneck, N. J., editorial employees, 95
Texarkana (Ark.) News Craft, 46-47
Toledo, O.: newsmen, 56; guild, 111, 123, 125, 323n4, 326n46, 332n46
Tri-City (Albany-Schenectady-Troy) Guild, 109-10, 323n4, 326n46, 332n46
Troy, N. Y., editorial employees, 92, 95, 109-10; *see also* Tri-City Guild
Tulsa, Okla.: editorial employees, 77; Oklahoma Newspaper Guild of, 84, 95, 114
Tulsa Daily World, 28, 88
Twin Cities (Minneapolis and St. Paul, Minn.) Newspaper Guild, 78, 90, 94, 98, 113, 123, 165-66, 198, 205, 206, 210, 256, 274, 323n4, 326n46, 332n46

Unionization: white collar workers, 1-2; *see also subhead* "Unionization" *under* Editorial workers
University of Missouri Graduate School of Journalism, 10

Van Vuren, Mary, 245, 247, 248

Wages and salaries of newspapermen, 4-6, 17, 21, 23, 27-28, 233; effect of Depression on, 30-31; in NRA draft codes, 37, 40-41, 42, 69, 70, 72; in early contracts, 47; in final NRA code, 73, 75-76, 112, 114-15, 120, 124; in ANG contracts, 117, 142, 143, 148, 150, 171, 178, 179, 232, 241, 242, 245-46, 251, 259, 263, 276; dismissal or severance pay, 117, 264; NRA code amendments, 187, 197-201
Washington, D. C.: editorial employees, 95; guild, 111, 115, 116, 120, 142, 193, 225, 241, 274, 323n4, 326n46, 332n46
Washington *Daily News*, 241
Washington *Star*, 142
Watson, Morris, 45, 59, 62, 68, 91, 92, 94, 98, 100-1, 177, 201, 206, 214, 219, 224, 231; AP discharge case and hearings, 273, 276-77
Westchester County (N. Y.) Guild, 323n4, 326n46
Westchester County Publications, 35, 77
Wheeling, W. Va., ITU editorial workers local, 13-14
White, Lloyd, 48, 50, 51, 54, 55, 60, 68, 70, 93, 94, 96, 97, 99, 316n74; ANG Vice President, 101, 107, 110
Williams, Talcott, quoted, 6
Wilmington, Del., guild, 323n4, 326n46
Winston-Salem, N. C., guild, 323n4, 326n46
Wisconsin News (Milwaukee), strike, 243, 244-61
Wishengrad, Hyman, 45
Wollan, G. B., 95, 107

Yonkers, N. Y., editorial employees, 91, 93, 95
Youngstown, O.: editorial employees, 56, 68; guild, 95, 323n4, 326n46